MODERN ITALIAN POETS

Translators of the Impossible

JACOB S.D. BLAKESLEY

Modern Italian Poets

Translators of the Impossible

UNIVERSITY OF TORONTO PRESS
Toronto Buffalo London

Toronto Buffalo London
www.utppublishing.com

ISBN 978-1-4426-4642-1

Toronto Italian Studies

Library and Archives Canada Cataloguing in Publication

Blakesley, Jacob S. D., 1978-, author
Modern Italian poets : translators of the impossible / Jacob S. D. Blakesley.

(Toronto Italian studies)
Includes bibliographical references and index.
ISBN 978-1-4426-4642-1 (bound)

1. Poetry – Translations into Italian – History and criticism. 2. Poetry – Translating – Italy – History – 20th century. 3. Poets, Italian – 20th century – History and criticism. 4. Translators – Italy – History – 20th century. 5. Translating and interpreting – Italy – History and criticism. 6. Montale, Eugenio, 1896–1981 – Knowledge – Language and languages. 7. Caproni, Giorgio – Knowledge – Language and languages. 8. Giudici, Giovanni, 1924–2011 – Knowledge – Language and languages. 9. Sanguineti, Edoardo – Knowledge – Language and languages. 10. Buffoni, Franco – Knowledge – Language and languages. I. Title. II. Series: Toronto Italian studies

PN1059.T7B63 2014 418'.041 C2013-905578-9

University of Toronto Press acknowledges the financial assistance to its publishing program of the Canada Council for the Arts and the Ontario Arts Council.

University of Toronto Press acknowledges the financial support of the Government of Canada through the Canada Book Fund for its publishing activities.

To the memory of my grandmother
Marcia Schreiber Deutsch
1922–2012

To Chiara:
L'amor che move il sole e l'altre stelle

To Nanni and Lucy:
May your lives and dreams be filled with poetry

To my parents and Ana:
for all your love and support

In memory of Edoardo Sanguineti and Giovanni Giudici:
incidetele a lettere di scatola, miei lettori testamentari
[…]
me la sono goduta, io, la mia vita:

Contents

Tables

Acknowledgments

First of all, I would like to thank Rebecca West, who patiently and generously followed this book from the very beginning. Her precious guidance and mentorship has been fundamental ever since my first days in Chicago over a decade ago.

Then I would like to thank my dissertation committee members Paul Friedrich, Armando Maggi, Jennifer Scappettone, and Elissa Weaver, who, along with Rebecca, provided me with extensive comments and helpful suggestions on the precursor to this book.

I would additionally like to thank Laura Barile, Fabio Pedone, and John Welle, who significantly aided me through their incisive observations and critiques on a number of chapters.

I would also like to thank the following people who helped me at various stages of this project: Stefano Adami, Massimo Bacigalupo, Francesca Billiani, Francesco Bruni, Joseph A. Buttigieg, Irena Cajkova, Theodore Cachey Jr., Joel Calahan, Gianni Celati, Paolo Chirumbolo, Federico M. Federici, Giulio Ferroni, James Fortney, Maggie Fritz-Morkin, David Gasperetti, Lorenzo Geri, Roberto Gigliucci, Robert Kendrick, Sergey Levchin, Ernesto Livorni, Niva Lorenzini, Boris Maslov, Guido Mazzoni, Pier Vincenzo Mengaldo, Jeremy Munday, John Picchione, Jennifer Scappettone, Gianluigi Simonetti, Marco Sonzogni, Maria Luisa Spaziani, Justin Steinberg, Enrico Testa, Sergey Tyulenev, Lawrence Venuti, Robert von Hallberg, Henry Weinfield, and the members of the University of Chicago Poetry and Poetics workshop.

Special thanks are due to Franco Buffoni, who generously responded to all of my persistent questioning; Rodolfo Zucco, who provided me with private documents relating to Giovanni Giudici's final *quaderno di traduzioni*; and Attilio Mauro Caproni, who guided me through the labyrinth of his father's archives and gave me permission to cite from them.

Thank you to my parents and Ana, for their encouragement and their constant rereading and proofreading of chapter after chapter.

Thank you to my *suoceri*, Carlo and Patrizia, who enabled me to find time to write much of this book.

Thanks to the late, lamented Ron Schoeffel for his editorial support; the two anonymous Toronto readers for their invaluable comments; and Beth McAuley and her assistant Avery Peters for their meticulous copy-editing.

And one last thanks to Chiara, who immeasurably improved this book.

MODERN ITALIAN POETS

Translators of the Impossible

Introduction

The Impact of Foreign Literature on Italian Literature

Italian literature has always been written and cultivated in a larger historical, linguistic, and cultural milieu. The first movement of Italian poetry, *La scuola siciliana* (The Sicilian school), which grew up around the emperor (and poet) Frederick II in the first half of the 1200s, was born from troubadour verse. In fact, one of Giacomo da Lentini's first *canzoni* is partly a translation of a poem by Folquet de Marselha, as has been well established.[1] As Michelangelo Picone writes, "It is therefore within the depths of linguistic translation that the origin of the dawning [Italian] literary tradition is hidden."[2] If Italian poetry, thanks to the vast influence of Petrarch's *Canzoniere,* provided a model for much of European lyric verse, and if Italian literature dominated Europe with Machiavelli, Ariosto, and Tasso in the Renaissance, things were no longer the same in the eighteenth century. As Pascale Casanova argues in *La république mondiale des lettres* (The world republic of letters), France became the centre of the literary republic of letters during the reign of Louis XIV: French was now considered the "Latin of the moderns."[3] Italian novels owed their birth in the eighteenth century to translations and adaptations of Richardson and other English novelists, often through intermediary French translations.[4] Likewise, in the twentieth century both Italian poetry and prose drew on foreign models.

Italian Poet-Translators

The category of poet-translator was not unknown to Italy before our era. I have already mentioned Giacomo da Lentini, whom Gianfranco

Folena aptly calls "the first poet-translator of Italian literature."[5] Yet something new occurred in the twentieth century: poets began translating to earn a living. Indeed, all of the five poets concentrated on in this study – Eugenio Montale, Giorgio Caproni, Giovanni Giudici, Edoardo Sanguineti, and Franco Buffoni – were professional translators for a period, and they weren't the only Italian poets who relied on such income. But in a broader sense, these figures turned abroad and to other languages, because Italian literature had definitively lost its international dominance: it had become "peripheral" to the European system of literature. The overwhelming importance of French (and German) symbolist poetry was crucial for the development of modern Italian poetry. In short, Italian poets developed an additional vocation: translator. Along with translation, however, Italian poets generally incorporated another aspect into their careers: they were often the foremost literary critics of their era. One thinks naturally of figures such as Eugenio Montale, Andrea Zanzotto, Pier Paolo Pasolini, and Franco Fortini. Thus, Pier Vincenzo Mengaldo observes, "An aspect that distinguishes twentieth-century Italy from other countries, on the whole or on average, is not so much the frequency of poet-translators … as much as the fact that these figures are placed at the center of the triangle poet-critic-translator."[6] A poet-critic like Piero Bigongiari went so far as to say that "translation was a 'primordial act of criticism.'"[7] It is this threefold combination of poet, critic, and translator, which developed in the twentieth century that was the catalyst for the birth of *quaderni di traduzioni* (notebooks of translations). Translation, considered the most profound way to read a text and "una superiore filologia"[8] (a superior philology) as one of Italy's most distinguished poet-translators commented, became the preferred occupation for generations of Italian poets. Through translation, Italian poets honed their poetic techniques, experimented with new poetic metres, and theorized new poetics; indeed, they often published more translations than original work. As the critic Oreste Macrì pointed out,

> Between poetry and criticism, a broad, dense, and continuous activity of translation by poet-translators and translator-poets was situated, such that *translation* was strictly specified as a veritable autonomous literary genre: an initiative specific to a sort of *animus traduttorio*, as poetry and criticism were strictly understood. The three genres converged into the metagenre of the anthology.[9]

This metagenre found its apex in the *quaderno di traduzioni* (notebook of translations). With this new genre, the land of Petrarch gave rise to a quintessentially modern volume: an anthology of foreign verse drawn from different languages and different cultures, structured according to definite criteria, translated by one poet. Yet for poetic versions to acquire such importance, translations needed to be distinguished from mere *volgarizzamenti* (vernacularisations), a process first described by Gianfranco Folena in his *Volgarizzare e tradurre* (Vernacularising and translating),[10] and then Alison Cornish in her *Vernacular Translation in Dante's Italy: Illiterate Literature.*[11] From Annibal Caro's 1581 translation of Virgil onwards, translations into Italian began to be regarded as original works in their own right. But Caro's *Eneide* revealed another prejudice still at play: namely, the superiority of epic (and drama) over lyric poetry.[12] As Gérard Genette makes clear, lyric poetry struggled hard over the centuries to attain an equal footing with the other two genres, due to the "massive silence"[13] about it in Aristotle's *Poetics*. Only during the nineteenth century did lyric poetry finally attain the same theoretical status as the other two poetic genres, thanks to its reconceptualization by Friedrich Schlegel, August Wilhelm Schlegel, and Friedrich Schelling. This in turn would lay the ground for the custom of poets collecting their translations of lyric poetry.

Bibliography on Italian Poet-Translators

Scholarship on modern Italian poetry has long been disfigured by the sins of omission and neglect with regard to poet-translators. While Folena's classic study examined the role of translation in the Italian Middle Ages, scholars have been slow to recognize the overwhelming importance of translation for twentieth- and twenty-first-century Italian poetry. The relative absence of translation studies in Italy is due to the fact that tradition (*la tradizione*) has always been overvalued at the expense of translation (*la traduzione*).[14] Most major studies of modern Italian poetry ignore or downplay the importance of translation: one will look in vain for chapters dealing exclusively with this theme in histories of twentieth-century Italian poetry like Gianni Pozzi's *La poesia italiana del novecento* (Twentieth-century Italian poetry),[15] Silvio Ramat's *Storia della poesia del novecento* (History of twentieth-century [Italian] poetry),[16] and Frederic Jones's *The Modern Italian Lyric.*[17] The same absence is seen in multi-volume histories of Italian literature, such as the *Storia della letteratura italiana* (History of Italian literature)[18] published by Salerno and the *Storia letteraria d'Italia* (Literary history of Italy)[19] published by Vallardi. If we turn to academic journals, the case is quite similar. Over a 113-year period, the *Giornale storico della letteratura italiana* published only thirty-nine articles dealing with translation, about one every three years.[20] And, to take another type of example, the prestigious journal *Studi novecenteschi* has devoted, on average, less than one article a year to translation studies of any sort. The foregoing should not be considered remarkable if anthologies such as *Poesia del Novecento* (Twentieth-century poetry)[21] are published, which take for granted that the title refers explicitly to *Italian* poetry. This type of parochialism is shared by all literary cultures. Yet this myopic view of Italian literary history overlooks the vitally important role of translation.

Turning to poet-translators, there have been very few books dedicated to individual modern Italian poets *qua* translators.[22] Most often, monographs about Italian poet-translators give short shrift to their translation activity, often not even including it in their bibliography. *Quaderni di traduzioni* themselves are treated summarily, if not ignored. Then again, in most languages, poetic anthologies have been little studied. Anthologies of translations have been justly described as forming part of a "shadow culture"[23] by literary scholar Armin Paul Frank. This is definitely the case with anthologies of poetry in Italian.

Despite this overwhelming critical neglect, there have been exceptions. The Italian critic who has drawn the most attention to poetic translations in modern Italy has been Pier Vincenzo Mengaldo, with a series of incisive articles and introductions dating back to his editorship of the anthology *Poeti italiani del Novecento* (Italian twentieth-century poets), where he championed Italian poet-translators.[24] Just recently, Antonio Prete published a volume dealing with poetic translation in modern Italy,[25] and other critics, like Laura Barile,[26] Daniela La Penna,[27] and Francesca Billiani,[28] have published important articles surveying and analysing poet-translators. One shouldn't forget the articles written by poet-translators themselves, such as Franco Fortini[29] and Franco Buffoni, who have abundantly reflected on the process of translation.[30] Likewise, valuable essay collections such as *Traduzione e poesia nell'Europa del Novecento* (Translation and poetry in twentieth-century Europe) demonstrate the growth of interest in the figure of poet-translator. Three studies in particular stand out for their treatment of translation in modern Italy, although their focus is not on poetry translation, and all deal with the first half of the twentieth century: Francesca Billiani's *Culture nazionali e narrazioni straniere: Italia, 1903–1943* (National cultures and foreign fiction: Italy, 1903–1943),[31] Christopher Rundle's *Publishing Translations in Fascist Italy*,[32] and Valerio Ferme's *Tradurre è tradire: la traduzione come sovversione culturale sotto il Fascismo* (To translate is to betray: Translation as cultural subversion under Fascism).[33]

My book has two goals: to write a history of the new genre of the *quaderno di traduzioni*, and to demonstrate how translation constellates the poetic careers of five of the most important modern Italian poets. Drawing on translation theory, I will examine the ideologies and methods underlying the translation activities of Eugenio Montale, Giorgio Caproni, Giovanni Giudici, Edoardo Sanguineti, and Franco Buffoni.

Translation in Modern Italian Poetic Culture

The following brief summary is not meant to be comprehensive but simply suggestive of certain key phases in modern Italian literary culture. This book, after all, is not a history of poetry translation in modern Italian culture; there remains so much work to be done, which exceeds the competence and time of the present writer. The following remarks, then, are meant to simply offer some context for the five case studies in chapters two through six, from Montale to Buffoni. I will draw mainly on Franco Fortini's posthumous lectures (*Lezioni sulla traduzione* [Lectures on translation]), and articles by Francesca Billiani, Anna Dolfi, Nicola Gardini, Daniela La Penna, Pier Vincenzo Mengaldo, and Antonio Prete.

Normally poets translate from literatures (and languages) considered prestigious, which for Italian poets, until the twentieth century, meant Latin and Greek. For instance, the most translated poets in the nineteenth century, as evidenced by CLIO,[34] were Virgil, Horace, and Homer, with the moderns significantly lagging behind. Yet the twentieth century witnesses a huge change, which is registered in the burgeoning genre of *quaderni di traduzioni*, always featuring more modern than ancient writers. If, for instance, the volumes of translations by Carducci and Pascoli were oriented towards the past, with little room given to modern poets, the *quaderni* of Anedda, Bertolucci, Caproni, Dal Fabbro, Erba, Fortini, Luzi, Montale, Raboni, Risi, Sereni, and Solmi, for example, don't include any Greek or Latin poetry. As Nicola Gardini summed up,

> In the most recent history of Italian literature the dearth of classical translations by poets becomes downright embarrassing ... among collections of

translations by the leading Italian poets (Montale, Luzi, Sereni, Fortini, Giudici, and others) not one, *not a single one* of the great ancients can be found in translation.[35]

From what languages did modern Italian poetry draw inspiration in the twentieth century, then, if not Greek and Latin? French and English, above all, as well as German, Spanish, and Russian. Modern Italian poets of all stripes translated both prose and verse. About 60 per cent of twentieth- and twenty-first-century poets translated at least one volume.[36] Yet there was a clear break between eras. The generation of Italian Futurist and *vociani* poets generally didn't translate poetry or they translated it into prose.[37] The new period came into being, however, with the publication of the literary journal *La Ronda*, which opposed the avant-gardes.[38] Through *La Ronda*'s repudiation of the "dissolution of genres and poetic meters" practised by the Futurists, the magazine ushered in "a revival of poetic translation."[39] While one of its first fruits was Mario Praz's anthology of nineteenth-century English poetry,[40] the new wave of poetry translation really began in earnest, as Mengaldo notes, between the end of the 1920s and the beginning of the 1930s: in short, "between the affirmation of the 'new poets' (*lirici nuovi*) and the take-off and consolidation of hermeticism."[41] The prime motor of this was the poet-translator Giuseppe Ungaretti, who, according to Franco Fortini, "open[ed] a new epoch for translation," with his influential versions of Shakespeare, Góngora, and others.[42] At this time, Italian poets "made the recognition of a great European tradition an indispensable element in the formation of their poetics."

In Fortini's opinion, poets in the 1930s translated foreign and remote texts in which they recognized themselves: "the poetry of the French Pléiade, the latter half of the Spanish sixteenth century, the English metaphysical poets, and then the nineteenth century, beginning with Hölderlin, Novalis, and Nerval, and the twentieth century with the first movement of symbolism and then the later one, up to some surrealist offshoots."[43] In other words, the Italian hermetic poets did not tackle poetry that was foreign to their own aesthetic preferences: the complete opening up to the rest of the world would only happen after the end of the Second World War.

Nonetheless, poetic translations weren't carried out solely by recognized poets. Professional translators, critics, and professors contributed as well. As Luzi writes, "the translators (Leone Traverso, Sergio Baldi, Renato Poggioli, Carlo Bo, Vittorio Bodini, and Vittorio Pagano) gave a valuable contribution, who put into circulation poetic ideas and images, with input from other countries."[44] The category of translator-poets flourished.

Of course, the 1930s would also be known for prose translations: this decade, famously called the "decennio delle traduzioni" (decade of translations)[45] by Cesare Pavese, whose translations (along with those by other authors like Elio Vittorini) from writers such as Melville, Joyce, Faulkner, Dos Passos, Anderson, and Stein marked an era. Italian prose would come to terms with this infusion of foreign narrative with the rise of neorealism.

In the 1920s, 1930s, and 1940s, the overwhelming number of translations, above all of Stéphane Mallarmé, along with Paul Valéry, while to a lesser extent Charles Baudelaire and Arthur Rimbaud, attest to the poetic masters and the poetic language Italian poets were looking to. Mallarmé, specifically, was the key poet for the Hermetic poets, like Mario Luzi, Alessandro Parronchi, and Piero Bigongiari, all of whom produced translations of "L'après-midi d'un faune" (The afternoon of a faun).[46] The utopia of a perfect poetic language unsullied by the tribe was part and parcel of these poets' ideology and faith, though their utopia was at times religious, at times aesthetic.

Yet American and British poetry attracted Italian poets as well: notably William Shakespeare, Ezra Pound, T.S. Eliot, and W.B. Yeats. Yet, while modern American narrative was in vogue in the 1930s during Fascism's heyday, due to its anti-Fascist political connotations, both modern American and British poetry was much less translated.

German-language poetry was occasionally translated by Italian poets during this period, yet the influence of Johann Wolfgang von Goethe, Friedrich Hölderlin, Rainer Maria Rilke, and other German-language poets was seen more in translations in magazines than in separate volumes until the late 1930s and early 1940s, when Leone Traverso,[47] Gianfranco Contini,[48] and Giaime Pintor[49] came out with their volumes of translations of Hölderlin and Rilke. Their renderings inspired more than one generation of poets, and they inspired the most important translations by Franco Fortini.

Modern Spanish poetry owed a great deal to its spread in Italy to translations by translators Oreste Macrì,[50] Carlo Bo,[51] Vittorio Bodini,[52] and Dario Puccini,[53] in particular. Poets like Piero Bigongiari, Mario Luzi, and Eugenio Montale translated poems by Jorge Guillén.

Readers of Russian poetry were well served by translations by Renato Poggioli,[54] Tommaso Landolfi,[55] and Angelo Maria Ripellino,[56] who became the pre-eminent post-war translators of Russian literature. Russian literature was widely read and was always considered important because of the strong current of Communism among Italian intellectuals. Giudici made an impact here, too, with his later translation of *Eugene Onegin*; one might also remember that Ungaretti also translated some poems from Russian.

The canonization of translated poems in modern Italy progressed slowly. Luciano Anceschi's 1943 anthology, *Lirici nuovi: antologia di poesia contemporanea* (New lyric poets: Anthology of contemporary poetry),[57] provided the first, most significant inclusion of modern poetic translations into Italian within an Italian poetic anthology, so that along with original compositions by Italian poets were their translations of foreign poetry. This was complemented by Anceschi's second anthology, completely dedicated to translations, the 1945 *Poeti antichi e moderni tradotti dai lirici nuovi* (Ancient and modern poets translated by the new poets).[58] Anceschi later recounted that this volume, co-edited by Domenico Porzio, "was born from the realization any poetry reader could have: all of our most representative poets dedicated themselves to translation."[59] According to Anceschi, this was a historical novelty, since "previously it rarely happened."[60] This anthology featured translations by ten poets: Attilio Bertolucci, Piero Bigongiari, Beniamino Dal Fabbro, Mario Luzi, Eugenio Montale, Salvatore Quasimodo, Camillo Sbarbaro, Sergio Solmi, Giuseppe Ungaretti, and Giorgio Vigolo, and would constitute a precedent for many other anthologies to come.

The post–Second World War period signalled a change in translation practice. There was a significant increase in published translations,[61] and an even greater opening up to poetry from all across the world. Anthologies of foreign poetry thrived: as Leonardo Manigrasso writes, "The 1950s are a decade packed with anthologies of foreign poetry."[62] In line with this, translations often were "traduzioni di servizio" (service translations): much, if not a majority of this translation work was not carried out by poets but by professional translators. Moreover, Italian poetics had changed: *ermetismo* (hermeticism) was no longer at the forefront of poetic discourse. Francesca Billiani revealingly quotes a 1949 letter from the publisher Giulio Einaudi to Francesco Tentori Montalto, a translator aiming to publish with him: "Your volume on Spanish poetry ... is not totally satisfactory either in its historical perspective or its hermeticist [*ermetizzante*] tone."[63]

In 1956, the small press Scheiwiller published the important volume, *Poeti stranieri del '900 tradotti da poeti italiani*. Here, thirty-eight translators were included (some of whom no longer form part of the recognized canon of modern Italian poets): Luigi Bartolini, Giorgio Bassani, Attilio Bertolucci, Carlo Betocchi, Piero Bigongiari, Vittorio Bodini, Luciano Budigna, Giorgio Caproni, Raffaele Carrieri, Emilio Cecchi, Beniamino Dal Fabbro, Luciano Erba, Luigi Fallacara, Franco Fortini, Giovanni Giudici, Vittoria Guerrini, Margherita Guidacci, Piero Jahier, Libero de Libero, Mario Luzi, Curzio Malaparte, Eugenio Montale, Alessandro Parronchi, Corrado Pavolini, Giaime Pintor, Renato Poggioli, Giacomo Prampolini, Salvatore Quasimodo, Roberto Rebora, Nelo Risi, Camillo Sbarbaro, Vittorio Sereni, Leonardo Sinisgalli, Maria Luisa Spaziani, Francesco Tentori, Leone Traverso, Giuseppe Ungaretti, and Diego Valeri. Scheiwiller would go on to publish a handful of mini anthologies of foreign poets translated by prominent Italian poets: Eugenio Montale's 1958 translations of T.S. Eliot and Jorge Guillén, Giuseppe Ungaretti's 1961 versions of Murilo Mendes, Mario Luzi's 1961 renderings of Jorge Guillén, and Nelo Risi and Edith Bruck's co-translated 1966 volume of Gyula Illyés's poetry.[64] In 1963, Scheiwiller published a bona fide *quaderno di traduzioni*, Sergio Solmi's *Versioni poetiche da contemporanei*,[65] and the following year, the Milanese publisher came out with an especially interesting anthology of André Frénaud, translated by fifteen Italian authors, nearly all poets.[66]

In 1958, Garzanti published *Poesia straniera del Novecento* (Foreign twentieth-century poetry), edited by poet-translator Attilio Bertolucci, who was editor of the most important series of foreign poetry in post-war Italy, namely, Guanda's "La Fenice." This landmark volume stood out for its heft (875 pages) and its comprehensiveness: poetry from Czech, Danish, English, French, German, Hungarian, Modern Greek, Polish, Russian, and Spanish. The translators were some of the most respected poets: Attilio Bertolucci, Carlo Betocchi, Piero Bigongiari, Cristina Campo, Giorgio Caproni, Margherita Guidacci, Mario Luzi, Eugenio Montale, Alessandro Parronchi, Pier Paolo Pasolini, Salvatore Quasimodo, Vittorio Sereni, and Giuseppe Ungaretti.

The year 1959, as Beatrice Sica reminds us, "is an important date in the Italian editorial panorama of anthologies: the publisher Garzanti, in fact, publishes within a few months *L'idea simbolista* [The symbolist idea], edited by Mario Luzi and *Il movimento surrealista* [The surrealist movement], edited by Franco Fortini."[67]

The 1960s would see, as Riccardo Capoferro writes, "the proliferation of 'academic' anthologies, exclusively based on a historical-cultural criterion."[68] The 1960s were also the decade of *Il gruppo 63*, the Italian neo-avant-garde. This generation of poets would be less interested, as Fortini noted, in translation than the "third-generation" poets. Yet some of the neo-avant-garde – exemplified in poets like Sanguineti (whom we will discuss in chapter 5) and Antonio Porta, Adriano Spatola and Giulia Niccolai – would actually translate considerably, but more often non-poetic texts.

The most forthright justification for including poetic translations in the Italian poetic canon came from Pier Vincenzo Mengaldo, in his 1978 *Poeti italiani del Novecento* (Italian twentieth-century poets).[69] Mengaldo not only strongly defended the inclusion of translations but also included an exemplary translator, Giaime Pintor, who was not a poet. In the critic's words, "The study of poetic translations, a fundamental chapter of this century's Italian literary culture, has been more wished for than truly begun, up until now …" But a reversion to old prejudice can be seen in the most important recent anthology of twentieth-century Italian poetry, *Antologia della poesia italiana: Novecento*, edited by Cesare Segre and Carlo Ossola,[70] which excludes translations and translators like Pintor. In addition, with the general consolidation of the Italian publishing industry, the opportunities to publish foreign poetry have decreased. Thus, the series of *Quaderni di traduzioni*, formerly published by Einaudi, can be seen as a swan song for a certain vision of international culture and poetics.

Quaderni di Traduzioni

Anthologies of foreign poetry translated by one writer published before the twentieth century were different in nature from *quaderni di traduzioni*. These precursors to twentieth- and twenty-first-century *quaderni di traduzioni*, most of which come from the nineteenth century, bore different titles, were rarely translated by canonical poets, and contained translations from predominantly classical languages. Such collections were variously entitled *un saggio* (a specimen), *una raccolta* (a collection), and *fiori* (flowers) of *traduzioni* (translations), or *versioni poetiche* (poetic versions). Notably missing is the twentieth-century term *quaderno* (notebook). The translators of these pre-twentieth-century volumes were above all intellectuals and writers, but not famous poets. These anthologies generally abounded in translations from Greek and Latin. Often these books were divided into two sections: one with translations and one with poems by the (poet-)translator.

If we consider the collections of translations published by important nineteenth-century poets like Vincenzo Monti, Giosué Carducci, and Giovanni Pascoli, one thing immediately stands out: they are all posthumous. None of the poets organized their anthologies of foreign poetry in any way. There was no intention, therefore, on the part of these poets, to publish a *quaderno di traduzioni*.

For example, Carducci edited the posthumous volume, *Versioni poetiche di Vincenzo Monti: Persio, Voltaire, Omero, Pyrker, Lemercier, Ec.: con giunta di cose rare o inedite* (Poetic translations by Vincenzo Monti: Persius, Voltaire, Homer, Pyrker, Lemercier, etc.: with the addition of rare and unpublished material).[71] He chose to begin it with Monti's translation of Persius, followed by portions from three disparate works, namely, *The Iliad*, Voltaire's *La Pulcelle d'Orléans* (The maid of Orleans), and János László Pyrker's *Tunisias*, then a section of "little versions" (*piccole versioni*), ending with a selection of rare and unpublished original poems by Monti.

Though Carducci edited Monti's collection of foreign poetry, he did not do the same for his own translations, which were collected by later editors. Carducci's posthumous *Versioni da antichi e da moderni* (Versions from ancients and from moderns), published more than thirty years after his death, is arranged haphazardly, with a section of Greek verse, then Latin poetry, followed by a mixture of essays on Greek and Latin literature, and an all-purpose section of modern language verse.[72] The confusing mixture of versions and essays doesn't form a unified whole.

Likewise, Pascoli's posthumous *Traduzioni e riduzioni* (Translations and adaptations), edited by his sister Maria shortly after his death, is a hodgepodge of translations separated by various headings: *Dall'Iliade* (From the *Iliad*), *Dall'Odissea* (From the *Odyssey*), *Miscellanea* (Miscellany), *Da Catullo* (From Catullus), *Da Orazio* (From Horace), *Da Virgilio* (From Virgil), *Favole* (Fables), and *Poesia popolare eroica civile* (Popular heroic civic poetry).[73] The sections *Miscellanea*, *Favole*, and *Poesia popolare eroica civile* have no chronological, linguistic, or alphabetical order.

We could additionally single out two examples of volumes of translations published by forgotten nineteenth-century writers, which similarly lack a fixed structure. The first book, Michele de Bellis's 1894 *Traduzioni poetiche* (Poetic translations), mixes translations in seven languages (Ancient Greek, Latin, French, German, Spanish, English, and Modern Greek) without any order. The volume opens with versions of Tibullus and Heine and ends with translations of Horace and Musaeus, without any linguistic or chronological separation. The second collection, Luigi di Treville's[74] 1883 *Saggio di traduzioni poetiche* (Specimen of poetic translations), includes both translations and original poetry. The first part is dominated by versions of Heine (62 poems), followed by two translations from Romanian, nineteen versions "from the German of diverse [poets]," ten from English (predominantly P.B. Shelley and Thomas Moore), two from French, ten of Anacreon (and followers of Anacreon), one ode of Horace's, and a handful of adaptations; the second part, *Originals*, contains some poems written in German as well as Italian, followed by thirty-one "epigrams, little stories and riddles." The order is again pell-mell (German, Romanian, German again, English, French, Greek, and Latin), and the inclusion of original compositions varying in language and genre makes it a miscellany without a clear structure.

In short, the collections of poetic translations published by pre-twentieth-century Italian poets like Vincenzo Monti, Giosué Carducci, and Giovanni Pascoli as well as lesser-known writers do not constitute authorial, cohesive volumes of translations. The essential requisite for making such specific translation anthologies was missing, namely, the prestige of translation. Translation was still generally regarded as inferior to the composition of original verse. The chaotic structure of their translations reveals a lack of interest among both poet-translators and Italian literary culture for an organized volume showcasing comparative poetic encounters. Italian poets were still, to a great degree, imprisoned within their national literary tradition, or else they were focused on retranslating their Latin predecessors. The poetic rush towards the modern and the foreign, which would begin at the opening of the twentieth century, was still in the future.

The Birth of *Quaderni di Traduzioni*

The first appearance of a *quaderno di traduzioni* is Giuseppe Ungaretti's 1936 volume, *Traduzioni: St.-J. Perse, William Blake, Góngora, Essenin, Jean Paulhan, Affrica* (Translations: St.-J. Perse, William Blake, Góngora, Esenin, Jean Paulhan, Africa). It has already been mentioned that Ungaretti played a fundamental role, "beginning … the practice of translating the great, foreign classics"[75] such as Góngora, Mallarmé, Racine, and Shakespeare. His eclectic collection of poetic versions[76] was the first volume of pure translations – unmixed with original poetry

– published by a famous Italian poet during his lifetime. While there is little coherence to the volume, either in terms of language, structure, or intertextuality, the central theme is defined by the poet-translator himself as "nostalgia." Ungaretti would later intend to publish a more cohesive volume of translations, but this plan never materialized.[77] In any case, while Ungaretti's collection was widely read, it nonetheless did not cement the new literary genre.

Meanwhile, another anthology of foreign poetry that was published several years later provided additional impetus for the development of the *quaderno di traduzioni*. It was Leone Traverso's 1942 *Poesia moderna straniera* (Modern foreign poetry)[78] that had a mixture of predominantly German, Greek, English, and French poetry.[79] Traverso, a gifted translator but not a recognized writer of verse, was an influential mentor for many Italian poets of the "third generation," thanks to the "extraordinary richness of his skills, and his literary and linguistic passions."[80] His important volume would be a model for the following *quaderni di traduzioni* due to the immense respect in which he was held as translator (he was nicknamed "the Khan"). Yet his title indicates more than a personal, subjective anthology; rather, a canon, "modern foreign poetry" *tout court*.[81] This differentiates his collection from a *quaderno di traduzioni*. Moreover, Traverso was a translator and a professor, not a canonized poet.

Beniamino dal Fabbro was one of the up and coming Italian poets anthologized by Anceschi; he would later become a music critic. His collection, *La sera armoniosa* (The harmonious evening), published by a small press during the Second World War as well, was enlarged and published by Rizzoli in 1966. Dal Fabbro had a precise goal in mind: with his volume, consisting mostly, but not entirely, of French verse, he wanted to "make accessible to a public, in Italian verses, a poetry whose works were becoming unobtainable." Unobtainable, he said, because in 1940, Italy was obviously at war with France, and censorship of foreign literature was becoming heavier and heavier.[82] Dal Fabbro's volume is not to be regarded as a *quaderno* precisely because it is a systematic collection, an anthology of predominantly (French) symbolist poetry. As he writes, his book gives a representation of symbolist poetry "a certainly incomplete map, but sketched out in its principal regions."[83]

In 1948, Eugenio Montale would publish his *Quaderno di traduzioni* (analysed in chapter 2), and from this point the genre was definitively born. Let us go over the characteristics of this genre.

Quaderni di Traduzioni

Quaderni di traduzioni belong to the literary genre of anthologies, but their novelty resides in the particular nature of the anthologist: a poet-translator. Teresa Spignoli defines the relationship between "translation and poetic elaboration" as "the particular characteristic of *quaderni di traduzioni.*"[84]

As personalized, authorial collection of translations, these volumes have six primary and defining attributes, dealing with authorship, content, and paratextual information.

(1) *Quaderni di traduzioni* are translated by one poet. This distinguishes them from multi-translator anthologies. In addition, the poet-translator-anthologist structures the *quaderno* as he wishes. The authorial, personal nature of the collection is evident from this very fact.

(2) The volume is composed entirely of translations and not original compositions. This trait distances *quaderni* from mixed volumes of translations and original work, often composed in the nineteenth and twentieth centuries.[85]

(3) The collection predominantly consists of poetry. Occasionally, *quaderni* include excerpts from theatrical works or prose pieces, but the main content of the *quaderno di traduzioni* is always verse.

(4) The poetry is generally translated from more than one language. There are exceptions – and I have cited Luzi's *Francamente: versi dal francese*, for example – but the majority of *quaderni* draw on a multilingual corpus of texts.

(5) The aim and the title of the collection – often, but not necessarily entitled *Quaderno di traduzioni* – makes no reference to canonicity or comprehensiveness (e.g., modern foreign poetry, Greek poetry, etc.). This is perhaps the most knotty issue in differentiating *quaderni* from other types of anthologies. Therefore, anthologies by two poet-translators, Salvatore Quasimodo's justifiably famous *Lirici greci* (Greek lyric poets) and Diego Valeri's *Lirici francesi*[86] (French lyric poets) and *Lirici tedeschi* (German lyric poets) are not to be regarded as *quaderni.*

We can cite Luzi again for his comment on another of his *quaderni di traduzioni*, namely, *La cordigliera delle Ande*,

> This is definitely not my ideal book [*libro ideale*] of French poetry, but simply the graph of certain points of spontaneous or provoked ignition ... this is truly a *quaderno*, a faithful and project-less register [*registro fedele*].[87]

Luzi demonstrates the difference, here, between a normal anthology and this new series of *quaderni di traduzioni*. These latter are not *libri ideali* (ideal books) but more modest *registri fedeli* (faithful registers). Likewise, Sergio Solmi indicates that "the poems gathered here [in his 1969 *Quaderno di traduzioni*] do not at all represent ... a critical selection."[88] On the other hand, the anthology of foreign poetry, as published in post-war Italy, represents this very "critical selection" spoken of by Solmi. Such an anthology, in contrast to a *quaderno di traduzioni*, "has to be a coherent and a carefully configured assortment of examples from the historical point of view. These examples have to reflect textual and extratextual elements alike."[89]

(6) There is introductory material that speaks to the poet-translator's project of collecting his or her verse. This serves to reinforce the personal nature of the *quaderno*, separating it from more objective and academic collections.

The term *quaderno* itself simply means "a notebook," and is a rather modest word (like *registro fedele*), rarely used by twentieth-century Italian poets. Its lack of prestige is thus inherent in its name. *Quaderno* implies an association with school and scholastic exercises, like translations from classical languages, which were, until recently, a fundamental part of the Italian school system. Indeed, this scholastic reference undoubtedly inspired the title of poet-translator Nelo Risi's volume of translations, *Compito di francese e d'altre lingue* (Homework from French and other languages).[90] Yet rather than constituting volumes of classical translations, *quaderni* are generally constituted by versions from modern vernaculars. The word *quaderno* humbly describes its content; whatever is in a *quaderno* does assuredly not deserve to be considered on the same level as a *canzoniere*, for example, or even on the same level as an "anthology of foreign poetry." While a *canzoniere* immediately recalls Petrarch, the *quaderno* could refer to any anonymous notebook kept in a long-forgotten desk drawer. The *quaderno di traduzioni* has even been minimized as a *Quadernetto di traduzioni* (little notebook of translations), in Luciano Erba's anthology of poetic versions.[91]

Despite these humble associations, the *quaderno di traduzioni* has become surprisingly prestigious. This can be traced to two factors: the prominence of the most famous author of a *quaderno* – Montale – and the consequent imitation by other poets; and the initiative of the publisher Giulio Einaudi, the most prestigious Italian publishing house, which published a series of such books, which I will shortly describe.

It was Montale, indeed, whose title *Quaderno di traduzioni* gave the name to this new genre,[92] and the same title was used not only by other poet-translators but also by editors of posthumous volumes. Thus, the volumes of translations of the nineteenth-century writer Ippolito Nievo and the twentieth-century poet Margherita Guidacci and novelist Beppe Fenoglio were all collected in *quaderni di traduzioni.*[93] A canonizing editorial strategy appeared in 1980, when the poet-translator Franco Fortini and the critic Pier Vincenzo Mengaldo independently suggested to Einaudi that the publishing house start a series of *Quaderni di traduzioni.* These books wouldn't necessarily contain the same title, but they would be conceived along the lines of Montale's volume.[94] In the words of Mengaldo,

> In the very beginning of the 80s, Franco Fortini and the undersigned had, with singular and significant independence, the idea of proposing to Giulio Einaudi a series of self-anthologies of the greatest Italian poet-translators ... The editor welcomed the proposal with the culturally and editorially acute enthusiasm that make him unique. Thus were published in turn personal choices of poetic versions of Sereni (*Il musicante di Saint-Merry*), of the same Fortini (*Il ladro di ciliege*), of Giudici (*Addio, proibito piangere*), [and] of Luzi (*La cordigliera delle Ande*); then the series was blocked, by reasons, let us say, of *force majeure* [unforeseeable circumstances].[95]

In Fortini's account of the birth of this genre, contained in his review of Vittorio Sereni's 1981 *quaderno di traduzioni,* he unjustifiably leaves out the name of Mengaldo:

> In order to be clear: this most beautiful book of Sereni's is placed at the beginning of a series[96] of the Einaudi publishing house. The series intends to include books that the poet can consider as his own, although composed of translations; a series that I myself proposed, and which one hopes will welcome works of Luzi, Giudici, Caproni, [and Andrea] Zanzotto.[97]

That Mengaldo was crucial in the formulation of this project is, however, clear both by his own writing as quoted above and in a letter to this author, as well as by the fact that his name appears in the Einaudi archives in Turin as an "inventor" of the series.[98]

The third source of our information about the birth of this project comes from a private letter from Giulio Einaudi to Giorgio Caproni (written on 14 January 1981), inviting him to participate:[99]

> Dear Caproni,
> It is our aim to give life to a series of volumes in which some of our greatest poets – and very often of our publishing house – present a selection of their poetry translations, at times very numerous but also very scattered. They are usually most precious (and not marginal) pages, from which emerge splendid models of work and style of the word, verse, and sounds of poetic language.
> I would be very grateful to be able to also have yours among these "quaderni di traduzioni" next to those of Luzi, Sereni, [and] Zanzotto.[100]

The Einaudi series built on the previously published *quaderni* of Ippolito Nievo (1964), and Sergio Solmi (1969 and 1977),[101] and would go on to include the *quaderni* of six poets: Vittorio Sereni, Franco Fortini, Giovanni Giudici, Mario Luzi, Giorgio Caproni, and Edoardo Sanguineti.[102] These works – Sereni's *Il musicante di Saint-Merry* (The Musician of Saint-Merry, 1982),[103] Fortini's *Il ladro di ciliege e altre versioni di poesia* (The thief of cherries and other poetic versions, 1982),[104] Giudici's *Addio, proibito piangere e altri versi tradotti* (Farewell, forbidden mourning and other translated poems, 1982),[105] Luzi's *Il cordigliera delle Ande* (The Cordillera of the Andes, 1983),[106] Caproni's *Quaderno di traduzioni* (1998),[107] and Sanguineti's *Quaderno di traduzioni* (2006)[108] – sum up a crucial period of translations.[109]

Einaudi wasn't the sole editor of *quaderni di traduzioni*, and we can find numerous such collections published by other publishing houses both before the official Einaudi series and afterwards. To cite some of the most prominent: Tolmino Baldassari's *Quaderno di traduzioni*;[110] Attilio Bertolucci's *Imitazioni* (Imitations); Piero Bigongiari's *Il vento d'ottobre: da Alcmane a Dylan Thomas* (The October wind: From Alcman to Dylan Thomas); Giovanni Bonalumi's *La traversata del Gottardo: quaderno di traduzioni (1948–1998)* (The crossing of the Gotthard Pass: notebook of translations, 1948–1998) and *Album inglese: quaderno di traduzioni (1948–1998)* (English album: notebook of translations, 1948–1998);[111] Franco Buffoni's *Songs of Spring* and *Una piccola tabaccheria* (A small tobacco shop), both of which we will discuss in chapter 6; Gianni D'Elia's *Taccuino francese* (French notepad);[112] Luciano Erba's *Dei cristalli naturali e altri versi tradotti (1950–1990)*[113] (Some natural crystals and other translated poems, 1950–1990) and *Il tranviere metafisico, seguito da Quadernetto di traduzioni* (The metaphysical streetcar operator, followed by a little notebook of translations);[114] Tomaso Kemeny's *Notturno* (Nocturne);[115] Attilio Lolini's *Imitazioni* (Imitations);[116] Gilda Musa's

Incontri con T. S. Eliot, K. Mansfield, R. Bridges, R. Kipling, T. Hardy, W. Blunt, G. Hopkins, F. Thompson, M. Arnold, S. Coleridge, H. Longfellow (Meetings with T.S. Eliot, K. Mansfield, R. Bridges, R. Kipling, T. Hardy, W. Blunt, G. Hopkins, F. Thompson, M. Arnold, S. Coleridge, H. Longfellow);[117] Alessandro Parronchi's *Quaderno francese*[118] (French notebook); and Giovanni Raboni's *Ventagli e altre imitazioni* (Fans and other imitations).

The Structures of *Quaderni di Traduzioni*

Modern *quaderni di traduzioni* are normally arranged with particular care, and I will discuss several criteria (although more exist): title, arrangement, chronological order, theme, and intertextuality. Note that these are not exclusive, so more than one of these elements can be at play in a *quaderno di traduzioni*.

Poets frequently entitle their collections after a poem of a translated author who dominates the *quaderno* in terms of quantity of translations, or spirit, or literary influence. Here are some examples: Franco Buffoni's *Songs of Spring* comes from Keats and *Una piccola tabaccheria* (A small tobacco shop) from Pound; Franco Fortini's *Il ladro di ciliege* (The cherry thief) is a title of Brecht's; Vittorio Sereni's *Il musicante di Saint-Merry* comes from a poem by his cherished Apollinaire; and Attilio Bertolucci's *Imitazioni*[119] derives from Robert Lowell's eponymous volume of translations. Gérard Genette has spoken of the significance of titles and demonstrated their various typologies: titles are highly significant since they reveal the poet's conception of his own work.[120]

Besides the structure given by a title, there is often the structure provided by the arrangement of the translations. Poems chosen to begin or end the volume, or poems that are at the centre of the work, provide a framework through which to read the *quaderno*. By placing Ronsard's poem at the front of his volume, Mario Luzi emphasizes how lyric poetry in the European tradition is tied to the Petrarchan loss of the beloved. Franco Fortini, consciously situating the poem by Brecht at the centre, reflects his own indebtedness to the German poet in his work; and he ends with a metapoetic poem by Raymond Queneau, "La spiegazione delle metafore" (The explanation of metaphors). Other poets conclude their volumes with their original poems, creating a link between them and the poets they translate: Piero Bigongiari ends his *quaderno di traduzioni* with a poem of his own written in French, "Pour ce rêve" (For this dream); and Montale concludes his own *Quaderno di traduzioni* with his poem "La bufera" (The storm), translated into Latin (by poet-translator Fernando Bandini). Giovanni Giudici's *Addio proibito piangere* incorporates both structuring elements by borrowing his title from a poem by Donne and beginning and ending the volume with poets significant to the translator:

> Curious destiny, how this book is made, respectfully ordered by chronology: it begins with a metaphysical (the type of poet that, for the sheer suggestiveness of the epithet, I would have liked to have been then) and ends with a romantic (the type of poet which, at this point without any more suggestions, I will regret not having been able to become).[121]

In this case, the opening and closing poets are bookends that exhibit the predilections of Giudici, and orient the reader towards his personal affinities.

An additional criterion of arrangement is chronological, as in Attilio Bertolucci's and Edoardo Sanguineti's. Other poets use such an approach, but arrange their translations not by the year of birth of the chosen authors but by the year of translation, such as Giudici's *Addio, proibito piangere.*

Another principle underlying some *quaderni* is thematic cohesion. For instance, Sanguineti's volume, with translations from three poets (Lucretius, Shakespeare, and Goethe), revolves around the theme of erotic desire and fervour. Ungaretti proclaims that his *Traduzioni* rotates around a core of "nostalgia." Generally, however, this criterion functions only in volumes with few texts or authors.

One additional type of structure can be seen at the micro-level of words, when there is a notable amount of intertextuality linking poetic translations within the collection. As Silvia Zoico notes, Vittorio Sereni's *quaderno di traduzioni* "quickly reveals itself as a 'canzoniere,' with a dense and continuous intertextual web … Sereni's book of translations is chosen and calibrated like one of his own books."[122] We can additionally think of the intertextual links within Eugenio Montale's and Franco Buffoni's *quaderni di traduzioni,* which connect up with certain lexical ties throughout their own poetic works, as will be shown later. This sort of dense continuity is, however, not very common.

An anthology implies, by nature, a canon; likewise, it would be difficult to argue that Solmi's *quaderni* are anything more than personal canons in miniature. These poetic canons (in Italian translation) are not necessarily the same as the officially received ones. As Mengaldo remarks, "As is normal, the transmission of foreign literary experiences doesn't always occur through main streets and the lesson of the greatest [*maggiori*]."[123] For instance: Fortini translates the Hungarian poet Attila József, Caproni translates Manuel Machado (instead of his better-known brother, for instance), Sereni translates poets belonging to the *Négritude* movement, Luzi translates the critic Sainte-Beuve, Giudici translates Hart Crane, Montale translates the Catalan poet Joan Maragall, Solmi translates the Scottish translator and poet Edwin Muir, Bigongiari translates Maurice Scève (instead of Ronsard), Dal Fabbro translates Ivan Goll, Sanguineti translates Lucretius, Ungaretti translates Jean Paulhan (instead of Claudel), and Buffoni translates Stephen Spender. None of these poets were frequently translated in the Italian literary system.

Nonetheless, the poems selected by the poet-translators often belong to different periods and/or styles of the respective poets' careers. For instance, Montale, Ungaretti, Sanguineti, Giudici, and Buffoni all translated Shakespeare's sonnets, and yet there is little overlap between them. Montale selected poems that recalled his beloved and muse, Irma Brandeis; Ungaretti preferred sonnets about time's ravages through history; Sanguineti chose sonnets about desire; Giudici translated metapoetic poems; Buffoni picked poems dealing with old age. Each translator fashioned a particular image of a foreign author through his selections and omissions. Through these five translators, Shakespeare emerges as a kaleidoscopic poet, changing colour and figure according to translation. The figure of the English writer, like that of other translated poets, offers a mirror within which the diverse translators are reflected.

Structure of the Present Book

This book is organized into six chapters. The first chapter provides a rapid panorama of translation theory relevant to the study of poetic translation. Here, I introduce the themes of foreignization, compensation, and poetics, which will subsequently be used as interpretative guides in the following chapters.

In chapters 2 through 6, I examine the *quaderno* (or *quaderni*) *di traduzioni* of Eugenio Montale, Giorgio Caproni, Giovanni Giudici,

Edoardo Sanguineti, and Franco Buffoni. Naturally, this involves a consideration of their poetic and translation careers, as well as an examination of how their translations fit into the larger Italian literary context. These five poet-translators are chosen for several reasons. First, they belong to several generations that had different literary expectations and different poetic styles. Montale was born in the last decade of the nineteenth century and poetically made his first appearance after the First World War; Caproni was born before the First World War, and he began publishing only immediately before the Second World War; Giudici and Sanguineti were born during the rise of Fascism, and they started their careers in the post–Second World War period; and Buffoni was born after the Second World War, and he initiated his career in the 1970s. Second, each poet-translator has a distinctive profile in terms of the languages and poets he preferred translating. Montale was an Anglophile, not only the first true Anglophile poet of modern Italy but the greatest Anglophile poet in all of Italian literature. Caproni belonged to the dominant trend of Francophile poets which numbered a majority of Italian twentieth-century poets, from Giuseppe Ungaretti to hermetic poets like Mario Luzi and down to the present day. Giudici, meanwhile, was a particular case, because he translated abundantly not only from English, with more volumes of Anglo-American poetry than any of his contemporaries, but also from little-translated languages like Russian and Czech. He put *Eugene Onegin,* which he retranslated several times, back on the Italian map, so to speak. Edoardo Sanguineti had an even more idiosyncratic translation profile, since he translated more classical drama than any other modern Italian poet. In turn, Buffoni, who has translated poetry from English and nine other languages, is the most important translation theorist in Italy and the editor of the most important journal of translation studies in Italy, *Testo a fronte* (Parallel text).

The second chapter studies Montale's *Quaderno di traduzioni* within a career in which he was often forced to translate for economic reasons. Montale's own translation philosophy was based on Benedetto Croce's: namely, faithful poetic translation is impossible. Montale's translation approach was founded on domesticating the source text and translating it according to his own poetic style. This meant that he would rarely translate into rhyme and canonical poetic form. His *quaderno* would be recognized as the canonical exemplar of the newborn genre of the *quaderno di traduzioni.*

The third chapter investigates the translation activity of Giorgio Caproni, which culminated in his posthumous *Quaderno di traduzioni*. Through an examination of Caproni's translation ideology, modelled, like Montale's, on Croce, we will see how he pursues the goal of creating similar *vibrazioni* (vibrations) to the original poem, through the use of equivalent metres. Yet he is more concerned than Montale with the question of "fidelity," as will be apparent with his versions of Char and Frénaud. What is lost, inevitably in translation, can be somewhat recovered through a process of compensation by increasing assonance and alliteration, as Franco Fortini suggested with his idea of "compensi" (compensation).

The fourth chapter analyses the *quaderni* of Giovanni Giudici: *Addio, proibito piangere e altri versi tradotti (1955–1980), A una casa non sua: nuovi versi tradotti (1955–1995)*, and *Vaga lingua strana: dai versi tradotti*. His translation philosophy precisely corresponds to his poetic theory, influenced by Yury Tynjanov: poetry is *una lingua strana* (a strange language), and the poet's job is to alienate the reader through a mixture of languages, registers, and tones. The poet-translator, then, utilizes the same techniques, choosing a specific "constructive principle" (metre, rhyme scheme, diction, etc.), which creates what translation theorist Lawrence Venuti has called a "foreignizing translation."

The fifth chapter examines Sanguineti and his *Quaderno di traduzioni*. For Sanguineti, there is no relationship between the source text and the target text: there is no difference between translation and pseudotranslation. Translators are our "contemporaries," because they are the true authors of translations. We will see how his conception of translation both draws on Bertolt Brecht's idea of theatrical alienation and appropriates Walter Benjamin's notion of interlinear translation. Sanguineti's "foreignizing" translation method is aimed at reproducing certain features of the source text, especially through syntactical and lexical calquing.

The sixth chapter studies Buffoni and his two *quaderni di traduzioni*, *Songs of Spring*, and *Una piccola tabaccheria* (A small tobacco shop). Rather than viewing translation as a zero-sum process, Buffoni considers it a supremely creative activity. Translations are the result of what he calls "poietic encounters" (*incontri poietici*) between the poetics of the translator and the original author. Buffoni's translations will be examined through the same framework that he has developed for examining the translations of others, namely, the avant-text, the movement of language through time, rhythm, intertextuality, and poetics.

Appendix

Following the six chapters is an appendix that contains a catalogue of published translations by 251 modern Italian poets. This appendix is the first comprehensive bibliography of translations by modern Italian poets, and it is only the beginning of what, I hope, will be an increase in studies devoted to this topic.

1 A Brief Tour of Western Translation Theory

In translation, as I.A. Richards famously asserted, "we have here indeed what may very probably be the most complex type of event yet produced in the evolution of the cosmos."[1] His claim about translation is hardly an exaggeration. Two thousand years of translation theory, running from Marcus Tullius Cicero to Lawrence Venuti, have not settled the issues at stake. In this chapter, I will offer a brief summary of Western translation theory relevant to the following chapters on poet-translators, dealing with some crucial philosophers and theorists, writers and poets. I will not trace this history in depth, but rather focus on four underlying concepts: untranslatability, compensation, foreignization, and poetics.

The notion of untranslatability, widespread from German romanticism onwards, thanks to the notion of linguistic and cultural differences, became less dominant with the rise of polysystem theory and Descriptive Translation Studies in the 1970s and 1980s. The methodological impasse of untranslatability was overcome through a shift of focus from the source text and culture to the target text and culture operated by these systems theories. In addition, the notion of "compensation," which makes up for what is lost through substitution; the concept of "foreignization," which bypasses the emphasis on equivalence, and the phenomenological approach to translation based on the poetic (or "poietic") encounter, offer alternative models to untranslatability.

Untranslatability

There is perhaps no other concept like untranslatability that has so exercised modern theorists of translation. This notion is, as Andrew

Chesterman called it, one of the "memes" (or "supermemes") of translation studies.[2] The concept of "meme" (on analogy to gene), was originated by the scientist Richard Dawkins, in *The Selfish Gene*, who describes it as

> a unit of cultural transmission, or a unit of *imitation* … Examples of memes are tunes, ideas, catch-phrases, clothes fashions, ways of making pots or building arches. Just as genes propagate themselves in the gene pool by leaping from body to body via sperm or eggs, so memes propagate themselves in the meme pool by leaping from brain to brain via a process which, in the broad sense, can be called imitation.[3]

The concept of untranslatability, for our purposes, dates back to the German romantics. From the Romans until the late eighteenth century, writers on translation generally spoke of methods of translation. The major question was not whether a text is by nature translatable, considering the source and target languages and cultures, but how best to render the source text in the target language. The basic dichotomy – word for word and sense for sense – had initially been expressed by Cicero, who prescribed translating freely, "as an orator" (*ut orator*), not word-for-word, "like an interpreter"[4] (*ut interpres*). For St. Jerome, too, literary texts should be translated "sense for sense" (*nec verbum de verbo, sed sensum exprimere de sensu*); only when translating the Bible should word-for-word translation be practised, since "the very order of the words is a mystery."[5] The dichotomy – word for word, sense for sense – would be opened up by John Dryden's formulation of three types of translation: "metaphrase," namely, "turning an Author word by word, and Line by Line, from one Language into another"; "paraphrase," or "translation with latitude, where the author is kept in view by the translator, so as never to be lost, but his words are not so strictly followed as his sense"; and "imitation, where the translator (if now he has not lost that name) assumes the liberty, not only to vary from the words and sense, but to forsake them both as he sees occasion; and taking only some general hints from the original, to run division on the groundwork, as he pleases."[6]

In general, language was not assumed to be an irrevocable stumbling block: cultural differences, which would lead scholars like Eugene Nida to defend translating "lamb of god" as "seal of God" for cultures without experience with sheep, were not yet on the horizon. It is true there were exceptions, like the thirteenth-century philosopher

Roger Bacon who argued that "it is impossible that the peculiar quality of one language should be preserved in another."[7] But this was a decidedly minority viewpoint: when pressed, writers might speak of the differences in languages, but not in such a pessimistic manner. For example, Joachim du Bellay, in his 1549 *La deffence, et illustration de la langue françoyse* (The defence and illustration of the French language) writes "it is impossible to translate [the text] with the same grace used by the author, since each language has something intangible [je ne sais quoi] specific only to itself."[8] But this doesn't get at the heart of the problem: we are still dealing with a framework in which language is conceived of as a mirror of thought. As Theo Hermans notes, "Renaissance and Enlightenment ideas" conceive of the "differences of languages" as "surface phenomena compared with the universal nature of all human speech and thought."[9] But for the Romantics, for whom "theories of translation stress the bond between language and thought, and language and nation,"[10] the question of translatability came to the fore.

The dominant viewpoint of German romantics, as well as others following them in the twentieth century, held that individual languages, and therefore texts, are unable to be perfectly translated. A major exponent of this thought was Wilhelm von Humboldt, whose words in a 1796 letter to A.W. Schlegel eloquently state this new view:

> All translation seems to me simply an attempt to solve an impossible task. Every translator is doomed to be done in by one of two stumbling blocks: he will either stay too close to the original, at the cost of taste and the language of his nation, or he will adhere too closely to the characteristics peculiar to his nation, at the cost of the original. The medium between the two is not only difficult, but downright impossible.[11]

What differentiates Humboldt's thought from his predecessors is that translation is judged to be "impossible." The question no longer is about the translator's method (word for word, sense for sense, or imitation). No correct translation is possible. Moreover, as Humboldt says in his preface to his translation of Aeschylus's *Agamemnon*,

> It has often been said, and confirmed by both experience and research, that, if one excepts those expressions which designate purely physical objects, no word in one language is completely equivalent to a word in another. Different languages are, in this respect, but collections of synonyms.[12]

This notion – that there are no real equivalent words between languages – would later be expounded on by Roman Jakobson. And yet, as Peter Newmark notes, "A translation is always closer to the original than any intralingual rendering or paraphrase."[13] To support Newmark's claim, one can think of scientific discourse, for instance a sentence drawn from a recent issue of *Nature* magazine: "In mice, transfer between fertilized eggs (zygotes) is effective in preventing the transmission of pathogenic mtDNA7 and in rhesus monkeys, genome exchange between unfertilized oocytes gave rise to live births."[14] How could we rephrase that, translate it "intralingually" in Roman Jakobson's terminology? Perhaps, "in rodents, exchange among inseminated ova is useful in hindering the spread of infectious maternal genetic material and in Macaca mulattas, DNA transfer among non-inseminated immature ova generated non-dead parturitions." Surely an Italian interlingual translation, however, would be closer than the English intralingual translation: "Nei topi, il transferimento fra le uova fecondate (zigoti) è efficace nel prevenire la trasmissione di patogeni mtDNA7 e lo scambio di genoma tra ovociti non fecondati nelle scimmie rhesus ha originato nascite." Using synonyms forces an unhelpful and inexact generalization of terms – rodents, genetic material – that are unnecessary in the Italian, first because Italian favours "borrowing" from English in scientific areas, and second, because *mice* and *topi* refer to the same denotational referent. The translation is surely more semantically accurate than the English paraphrase.

Humboldt's original assertion, meanwhile, occurs in the preface to his own translation of a drama he labels "untranslatable." Untranslatable, yes, but, as Humboldt goes on, "this should not deter us from translating. On the contrary, translation, and especially the translation of poets, is one of the most necessary tasks in a literature."[15] The contradiction – poetry is "untranslatable," and yet "one of the most necessary tasks" – is readily apparent.

The linguistic arguments for untranslatability found currency in the twentieth century as well, but even more so when applied to cultural differences. Émile Benveniste, a noted French linguist, in his essay entitled "Catégories de pensée et catégories de langue" (Categories of thought and categories of language) claimed that the Greeks developed such an elaborate metaphysics on account of the nature of their language, specifically the verbal intricacies of "εἰμί" (to be): "the linguistic structure of Greek predisposed the concept of 'being' for a philosophical vocation."[16] In a language such as Ewe, spoken in Ghana and Togo,

> One has practically speaking five distinct verbs which correspond approximatively to the functions of our verb "to be" ... We would not be able to say what place "being" holds in Ewe metaphysics, but *a priori* the concept must be articulated completely differently.[17]

The more general notion of this is found in the Sapir-Whorf Hypothesis, which exists in a "strong" version and a "weak" version. The "strong" version, or theory of linguistic determinism, alleges that "not only does our perception of the world influence our language, but that the language we use profoundly affects how we think. Language can be said to provide a framework for our thoughts."[18] This is the underlying concept behind Benveniste's argument. The "weak" version, or the theory of linguistic relativity, states that "different cultures interpret the world in different ways, and that languages encode these differences. Some cultures will perceive all water as being the same, while others will see important differences between different kinds of water."[19]

Against these claims Roman Jakobson responds by positing that everything expressible in one text can be expressed in another even if exact synonyms do not exist: "all cognitive experience and its classification is conveyable in any existing language."[20] David Bellos, professor of comparative literature at Princeton and practising translator, goes so far as to affirm in his engaging book *Is That a Fish in Your Ear? Translation and the Meaning of Everything*, that "translation presupposes not the loss of the ineffable in any given act of interlingual mediation such as the translation of poetry but the irrelevance of the ineffable to acts of communication."[21] Drawing on the American philosopher Jerrold Katz's notion of effability, Bellos writes,

> Any thought a person can have ... can be expressed by some sentence in any natural language; and anything can be expressed in one language can also be expressed in another. What cannot be expressed in any human language (opinions vary as to whether such things are delusional or foundational) lies outside the boundaries of translation and, for Katz, outside the field of language, too. This is his *axiom of effability*. One of the truths of translation – one of the truths that translation teaches – is that everything is effable.[22]

This is certainly one way of turning the argument for untranslatability on its head.

Douglas Robinson has elegantly stated the differences in translation theory by framing the argument around the translation of a single sentence: "A mí me no gustan moles."[23] Robinson chose this sentence because it contains a culturally specific food: *mole* is a Mexican spicy chocolate-based sauce.[24] The following are the thirteen possible translations he provides, which increasingly bring the text towards the reader:

1. For me, me not please moles.
2. Me, me not please moles.
3. Me, I not like moles.
4. Me, I don't like moles.
5. Me, I don't like mole.
6. Me, I don't like mole dishes.
7. Me, I don't like *mole* dishes.
8. I don't like *mole* dishes.
9. I personally don't like *mole* dishes.
10. I personally don't like curry dishes.
11. I personally don't like Mexican curry dishes.
12. I personally don't like Mexican chocolate curry dishes.
13. I personally don't like Mexican chocolate candy dishes.

As Robinson notes,

> In order to define or "place" the limits of translation (the absolute borderline between "translation" and "non-translation") in any kind of fixed or essentializing way – the central project of traditional translation theory – we must select a single gap in the sorites series and draw the dividing line there: say, between [9] and [10], or perhaps between [12] and [13].[25]

Where does one draw the line? Certainly some of these translations are what Venuti would describe as "foreignizing": where the source text leeches into the target text, through calqued syntax ("me, I don't like") or *moles*, remaining invariant. Other versions are more examples of "domesticated" translations, such as "I personally don't like Mexican chocolate curry dishes," where the source-specific *moles* has disappeared, along with the particular Spanish syntax. If this ambiguity exists in a translation of a single sentence, it would be best to acknowledge, along with Lawrence Venuti, that "the same source-language poem can support multiple translations which are extremely different yet equally acceptable as poems or translations."[26] It is this fact, continues Venuti, which suggests that "no invariant exists."[27] Therefore, "the practice of translation is fundamentally variation."[28]

While many have agreed with the Spanish philosopher José Ortega y Gasset (himself influenced by the German romantics), who suggested that translation is "a utopian operation and an impossible proposition," it is hard to discount the reality noted by George Steiner, namely, "we *do* speak of the world and to one another. We *do* translate intra- and interlingually and have done so since the beginning of human history. The defense of translation has the immense advantage of abundant, vulgar fact." As the poet-translator W.S. Merwin said, "They say translation is impossible; sure it is. We do it because it's necessary, not because it's possible."[29]

Yet another sustained argument for untranslatability, however, comes from the twentieth-century American analytic philosopher Willard Quine, in his indeterminacy theory, which is among the most contentious and provocative theories of modern linguistic thought. Translation studies, on the whole, haven't much dealt with it,[30] at times preferring to ignore the problem at stake.[31] In an influential symposium, which would result in the 1964 collection *Craft and Context of Translation*, the editors, William Arrowsmith and Roger Shattuck, both eminent translators, prefaced the volume by stating that "for the sake of good conversation and self-confidence, we deliberately excluded from the panel all machine-translators, logicians, metalinguists, and literal minded scholars. Our conference was a closed shop, or nearly so."[32] Naturally, Quine wasn't invited. While this conference took place before the formalization of the Translation Studies discipline, it is still quite indicative of a mentality that has changed comparatively little.

Quine describes his argument as follows: "the thesis is then this: manuals for translating one language into another can be set up in divergent ways, all compatible with the totality of speech dispositions, yet incompatible with one another." Quine asks us to imagine a case of "radical translation": a "jungle linguist" goes out to do field work in a community of unknown speakers. In the presence of a native speaker, he sees a rabbit run by and the native says "gavagai." How does the linguist know that "gavagai" means rabbit(s)? For Quine, it could equally mean "rabbits, stages of rabbits, integral parts of rabbits, the rabbit fusion, and rabbithood."[33] There is no exact translation possible, so

> The infinite totality of sentences of any given speaker's language can be so permuted, or mapped onto itself, that (a) the totality of the speaker's dispositions to verbal behavior remains invariant, and yet (b) the mapping is no mere correlation of sentences with *equivalent* sentences ...[34]

Many philosophers have weighed in on this argument, from Richard Rorty to Donald Davidson,[35] but perhaps the most effective rebuttal is provided by P.M.S. Hacker, who writes:

> From the point of view of a normative conception of meaning such as Wittgenstein defends, a behavioristic conception like Quine's is simply no conception of meaning at all, not even an ersatz one. Indeed it is no conception of language, for a language stripped of normativity is no more language than chess stripped of its rules is a game.[36]

Yet, if we move from the viewpoint of an analytic philosopher to hermeneutics and deconstructionism – as evident in the writings of Paul de Man and Jacques Derrida – we come to a series of intractable conclusions (nicely encapsulated by S.C. Chau): "There is no truly 'objective' understanding"; "There is no final or definitive reading"; "The translator cannot but change the meaning of the source text"; and "no translation can represent its source text fully."[37] Agreeing with the above four statements does not imply, however, "untranslatability." It simply means that no perfect equivalence exists between two different texts. Let us call again on George Steiner, who recapitulated the arguments of philosophers against translation:

> No two speakers mean exactly the same thing when they use the same terms; or if they do, there is no conceivable way of demonstrating perfect homology. No complete, verifiable act of communication is, therefore, possible. All discourse is fundamentally monadic or idiolectic.[38]

Steiner is correct that these statements on the untranslatability of language have not been "formally refuted." But the fact remains, as he states, that these statements would themselves be meaningless "if speech did not have a relationship of content to the real world (however oblique the relationship may be)."[39] The French linguist Jean-René Ladmiral calls the whole question of untranslatability "the problem of the preliminary objection," writing as follows:

> Can one imagine another human activity, comparable in importance, extent and continuity, see its existence denied in law, despite the facts observable daily? Will it be demonstrated that it is impossible for us to walk?[40]

In the 1970s, a new stage of translation theory developed: rather than dealing head-on with the intractable problem of untranslatability, translation scholars began focusing on translation from the perspective of the target text and culture and the communicative process as a whole.[41] As the translation studies scholar Jeremy Munday synthesizes the contributions of two of the main contributors, Itamar Even-Zohar and Gideon Toury,

> Even-Zohar's polysystem theory moves the study of translations out of a purely linguistic analysis of shifts and a one-to-one notion of equivalence to an investigation of the position of translated literature as a whole in the historical and literary systems of the target culture. Toury then focuses attention on finding a methodology for descriptive translation studies.[42]

Israeli theorist Itamar Even-Zohar, influenced by Russian formalists (such as Yury Tynjanov, whom we will discuss in chapter 4), developed a theory of translation based on a conception of literature as a system. He showed how translations can occupy a primary or a secondary position in the literary system. Working with Even-Zohar, and then systematizing and going beyond his theory, was Gideon Toury, whose 1980 book, *In Search of a Translation Theory*, promoted Descriptive Translation Studies (DTS). This new approach "embod[ied] the aim of establishing translation research as an empirical and historically oriented scholarly discipline."[43] Toury argued that "translational phenomena could ultimately be explained by their systemic position and role in the target culture."[44] As Theo Hermans, another one of its leading practitioners states, this method is based on "an interest in translation as it actually occurs, now and in the past, as part of cultural history."[45] The idea of untranslatability has been put aside and shelved.

The Presumed Untranslatability of Poetry

Three proponents of the view that poetry is untranslatable are the linguist Roman Jakobson, poets such as Dante, and the Italian philosopher Benedetto Croce. Both Dante and Croce are frequently called upon by modern Italian poet-translators. Croce, in particular, will feature explicitly in chapters 2 and 3: Montale and Caproni draw on his claims that one cannot faithfully translate poetry, and that the best aim of poetic translation is to create an independent work of art that contains vibrations of the original. But let us begin with Jakobson, whose argument for the untranslatability of poetry remains one of the most cited, even today.

Jakobson considers prose translatable, but claims that poetry "by definition is untranslatable." His argument is as follows:

> In poetry, verbal equations become a constructive principle of the text. Syntactic and morphological categories, roots, and affixes, phonemes and their components (distinctive features) – in short, any constituents of the verbal code – are confronted, juxtaposed, brought into contiguous relation according to the principle of similarity and contrast and carry their own autonomous signification. Phonemic similarity is sensed as semantic relationship. The pun, or to use a more erudite, and perhaps more precise term – paronomasia, reigns over poetic art, and whether its rule is absolute or limited, poetry by definition is untranslatable. Only creative transposition is possible.[46]

Jakobson goes on to define "creative transposition" as either "intralingual transposition," "interlingual transposition," or "intersemiotic transposition,"[47] without explaining the nature of "transposition."

The argument for poetic untranslatability has been a favourite among poets themselves, such as Dante, who maintained that poetic translation was impossible, since he wrote, "may everyone know that nothing harmonized according to the rules of poetry can be translated from its language into another without destroying all its sweetness and harmony" (*E però sappia ciascuno che nulla cosa per legame musaico armonizzata si può de la sua loquela in altra transmutare sanza rompere tutta sua dolcezza e armonia*).[48]

In addition, philosophers like Benedetto Croce argued for the impossibility of poetic translation (although, like Jakobson, he held that "prose can be translated"). Since Croce was such a dominant figure for twentieth-century Italian cultural life and the poets in our study, I will now consider him more in depth. As Federico M. Federici notes, Croce "persisted in the Dantean tradition of asserting that translation is an illogical task."[49] If Croce's arguments for the untranslatability of poetry were different from that of the medieval Italian poet, they nonetheless remained unchanging throughout his career,[50] beginning in the *Tesi fondamentali di un'Estetica come scienza dell'espressione e linguistica generale* (Fundamental theses of an aesthetic as a science of expression and general linguistics, 1900),[51] then the *Estetica come scienza dell'espressione e linguistica generale* (The aesthetic as science of expression and general linguistics, 1902),[52] and continuing through *La poesia: introduzione alla critica e storia della poesia e della letteratura* (Poetry: Introduction to the criticism and history of poetry and literature, 1936).[53] His rationale for untranslatability is based on the nature of language itself. For Croce, "Every word [*parola*] that we hear is a new and foreign language [*lingua*], because it was never said before."[54] The Saussurian distinction between *langue* and *parole* doesn't exist for the Italian philosopher, since each word is a monad and unconnected to every other one. Therefore, "the impossibility of translation is the very reality [*realtà*] of poetry in its creation and its re-creation."[55] Every expression is unique and individual, owing both to its form and its content: "each content is different from any other, because nothing is repeated in life and the irreducible variety of expressive facts, aesthetic synthesis of impressions follows the various continuation of content."[56] Thus, as Norbert Matyus writes, for Croce, translation is impossible "because two works will never be equivalent."[57]

While Croce gradually came to value unaesthetic translations (*traduzioni inestetiche*), for their help in understanding the originals, he remained solid in his conviction that faithful translations of poetry are impossible. As the Italian philosopher writes, literal translations, *brutte fedeli* (ugly faithful [translations]), whether *ad verbum* or interlinear, are not true translations, but rather "simple commentaries on the originals." Not works of art, they are instead "instruments for learning about the original works."

Croce's favoured metaphor for speaking of the impossibility of translation is the image of a *vaso* (vase), insofar as

> translations claim to effect the transfer [*travasamento*] from one expression into another, like a liquid from a vase into another of a different form. One can logically elaborate what was first elaborated in aesthetic form, but not reduce what has already had its aesthetic form to another form also aesthetic.[58]

Since every expression is irremediably unique, "every translation, in fact, either diminishes and spoils, or else creates a new expression, placing the first again into the crucible and mixing it with the personal impressions of the person called a translator." In other words, the translator infuses the translation with his own personal impressions and forms a new work of art. The most he can do, to try to reproduce the original text's content and style, is to attempt to imitate its expressions:

> In such similarities the relative possibility of translations is founded; not as reproductions [*riproduzioni*] (which it would be vain to attempt) of the same original expressions, but productions of similar expressions and more or less near to those. The translation, which is called good, is an approximation [*approssimazione*], which has original value [*valore originale*] of a work of art and can exist by itself.[59]

The key word here is *approssimazione.* Translations of poetic texts cannot be *riproduzioni,* but *approssimazion(i)* that are true separate works of art. The original text is inevitably altered by the personal attributes of the translator. As Croce says,

> Poetic translations ... moving from the re-creation of original poetry, accompany it with other feelings that are in the person who receives it, who, because of a different historical condition [*diversa condizionalità storica*] and different individual personality [*diversa personalità individuale*], is different from the author; and on this new sentimental situation rises that so-called translating, which is writing poetry from an ancient [*antica*] into a new soul [*nuova anima*].[60]

Besides the linguistic elements that defy perfect translations (the individuality of each word and expression), the different historical circumstances (the *diversa condizionalità storica,* the *diversa personalità individuale)* of the translator irrevocably change the substance of the original. Thus, poetic translations are transformed in the voyage from the *antica* (the original poet) to the *nuova anima.*

Croce's hegemony in Italian cultural life[61] meant that generations of Italian writers were influenced by his pronouncements. As Giulio Lepschy notes, "The reflection on translation was dominated in Italy, in our [twentieth] century, by the judgment of Benedetto Croce on the 'impossibility of translations.'"[62] We will see more of this in the following chapters.

I will now discuss two currents of thought – Marxist and phenomenological in origin – which reacted against Croce, namely, the theories of the Marxist philosopher Galvano della Volpe (1895–1968) and the phenomenological literary scholars Luciano Anceschi (1911–95) and Emilio Mattioli (1933–2007).

Galvano della Volpe's major work is *Critica del gusto* (Critique of taste). Here he expounds a theory based on the polysemic nature of poetry, and strenuously argues for the translatability of poetry. Indeed, for della Volpe, "poetry worthy of the name is always translatable" (*poesia degna del nome è sempre traducibile*).[63] This is in contrast with the symbolist and modern notion that poetry is worthy of its name precisely because it is untranslatable.[64] According to della Volpe, the "euphony" (*eufonia*)[65] of the poem (viz., its "external-instrumental elements")[66] cannot be translated, but that is not the essential characteristic of the poem. Rather, a poem's fundamental quality is "its polysemic (*polisenso*) nature."[67] Translation is "facilitated in the final analysis by the *arbitrariousness* [arbitrarietà] and therefore *indifference* of the linguistic sign in respect of the signified."[68] What della Volpe recommends then is a prose translation based on the "criterion of *literal fidelity*, which is simultaneously *fidelity to the spirit* of the original text."[69]

Another anti-Crocean position was held by Luciano Anceschi and Emilio Mattioli. Anceschi, who studied under the noted phenomenological philosopher Antonio Banfi, was the *maestro* of both Mattioli and Franco Buffoni. Anceschi was a philosopher of aesthetics at the University of Bologna, and he spearheaded key anthologies in twentieth-century Italian literary history as we have seen, and he promoted the neo-avant-garde (he was instrumental in having Edoardo Sanguineti's first book published). He also famously introduced Quasimodo's controversial translation of the *Lirici greci.* According to Anceschi, "infinite ways of translation"[70] are possible. Yet he didn't concentrate on theorizing the process of translation. Mattioli took this up: he writes, "Following Anceschi's method, I tried to resolve the knotty problem of poetic translation."[71] As Mattioli indicated, "[Italian] idealistic philosophy [e.g., Croce], with a firm gesture, established the impossibility of translating poetry at the beginning of the [twentieth] century and by many, still today [1965], translation is considered an activity founded on a misunderstanding." As he then suggested,

> To the traditional question: "can one translate" we propose to substitute other questions: "How does one translate" and "What meaning does translating have"? Again, we propose to substitute a phenomenological question for a metaphysical question. This way we will avoid all of the aporias by responding to the latter question.[72]

Mattioli thus sidesteps the issue of translatability, just like translation theorists like Itamar Even-Zohar and Gideon Toury. What becomes of prime importance then is examining the process of translation by those translators who, in our case, are bona fide poets.

Only Poets Can Translate Poetry

Poets from John Dryden onwards upheld that a poet must translate a poet: "No man is capable of translating poetry who besides a genius to that art, is not a master both of his author's language, and of his own."[73] In brief, "to be a thorough translator, he must be a thorough poet."[74] Likewise, Giacomo Leopardi maintained, with experience backed up by translating, that "having found out by trial, I can tell you that without being a poet one cannot translate a true poet."[75] This theory depends on the cultural norms of what signifies a good translation: certainly, poetry translations done by writers into English are differently received, for instance, than poetry translations into other languages that place more prestige on the poetic genre. But a prescriptive rule such as Dryden's does not necessarily apply, since, for example, verse translations are acclaimed in various languages even if the translator is not a poet; in the Italian context, one might think of Leone Traverso's translations as a symptomatic case. Even today Traverso is revered for his versions of German, French, and English poems, though he was by no means a canonical poet.[76] Luciano Anceschi, in fact, wrote that "it's not the case that a poet necessarily translates better than a scholar."[77] And Emilio Mattioli avers that "a priori rules" about whether a poet must translate a poet "cannot be established," but rather how the "variety of relationships" between author and translator can be distinguished.[78] This frame of thought is repeated by Fortini as well, who decidedly turned against translations by poet-translators in the last period of his life. As he wrote,

> above all as regards the so-called classics, I militate for scientific and non-subjective translations as much as possible, to be conducted with verifiable, explicit and systematic criteria, while the versions that I publish here [in his *quaderno di traduzioni*] are my writings, constructed according to an entirely other method, or, better, with no method.[79]

In any case, our study doesn't have to deal with this particular issue, since all five of our translators are widely anthologized and critically recognized poets.

Treatises on Poetry Translation

In the scholarly history of poetry translation, there have been rather few theoretical texts.[80] In this section, I will summarize the methods of four recent and not-so-recent books that deal with this subject: Robert de Beaugrande's *Factors in a Theory of Poetic Translation* (1978), Cees Koster's *From World to World: An Armamentarium for the Study of Poetic Discourse in Translation* (2000), Francis Jones's *Poetry Translating as Expert Action* (2011), and Barbara Folkart's *Second Finding: A Poetics of Translation* (2007).

The first two, Robert de Beaugrande's *Factors in a Theory of Poetic Translation*[81] and Cees Koster's *From World to World*,[82] approach the analysis of poetry translation from restricted points of view. De Beaugrande co-wrote a textbook on text linguistics[83] and his approach to translation is largely indebted to it.[84] My own methodology does not make use of this approach. Meanwhile, Koster analyses translations through textual shifts, drawing especially on the work of Kitty van Leuven-Zwart,[85] simplifying the latter's elaborate model, and aiming at the "text world" of the author. Koster contends that he has drawn a line between Gideon Toury's "lack of instruction … for target text-source text comparison" and the "abundance of instruction to be found in van Leuven-Zwart's method."[86] Koster's work can certainly be illuminating, and his case study of deictics in Celan's translation of Shakespeare is penetrating. Yet a hole lies at the centre of Koster's "positivistic"[87] study (as well as de Beaugrande's volume), as Dirk Delabastita makes clear in a very balanced review of *From world to world*: "Interpretation is basically construed as something which occurs between original and translation – at the object-level – but which the competent researcher – operating at the meta-level – should know how to handle." In other words, Koster leaves "unexplored: the potentially endless semantic productivity of intertextuality … the impact of ideology … the role of psycho-analytically based projections, and so on."[88] In brief, Koster's volume ends on a coda of (and these are his very words) "theoretical and methodological desperation," which can only be "overcome" by "sheer pragmatism."[89] Moreover, the notion of the "invariant," an "unchanging essence inherent in or produced by the source text and freely acceptable to the translator, regardless of the time and place in which the translating occurs," is certainly suspect.[90] While de Beaugrande's volume was written, as Francis Jones remarked, before "the late-1980s shift in translation studies towards viewing translation as not just a textual act, but also a psychological and a social one,"[91] Koster's later monograph ignores any new cross-disciplinary interests, which would go on to pollinate translation studies.

Jones's recent book, however, *Poetry Translating as Expert Action,* fills this important gap in studies on poetry translation. He bases his method on "sociological and social-network models of human agency and interaction": "a 'cognitive processing' framework"; "a cognitive pragmatics approach"; and "post-structuralist terms."[92] Yet I have not followed his methodology because my orientation throughout has been to study the poet-translator as a translating poet, as someone individually working on a translation (or, at most, with an informant). The role of poetics in translation has formed a basis for my analyses. And it is this notion that is given short shrift in Jones's otherwise admirable volume.

Barbara Folkart's book, *Second Finding: A Poetics of Translation,* stems from her engagement as a poet and a translator, and from a theoretical background deeply steeped in French theory of translation (e.g., Henri Meschonnic and Antoine Berman). While definitely not systematic in any sense of the word, her method of translation aims to produce "esthetically reliable" poems in translation, and what she calls synonymously "writerly translations" and "derived poems." She attacks the notion of a "foreignized" or "resistant" translation, considering it a sort of "translationese." While this criticism can at times be valid,[93] her overgeneralization hurts her study as a whole. Certainly, an approach recognizing the value of the concept of "foreignization" is essential in a study of translation. I will now talk briefly about this very concept, which I repeatedly use in subsequent chapters.

Foreignization

Replacing the binary opposition of literal and free, or word-for-word and sense-for-sense, a new dichotomy appeared in recent years in Translation Studies: namely, the mutual concepts of foreignization and domestication. These can be traced back to Friedrich Schleiermacher's 1813 essay: "Either the translator leaves the writer in peace as much as possible and moves the reader towards him; or he leaves the reader in peace, as much as possible and moves the writer towards him."[94] In the late twentieth century, this method was first taken up by Philip E. Lewis, formerly professor of French at Cornell University, in his notion of "abusive fidelity."[95] Lewis derives his notion from Derrida's claim that "a good translation must always commit abuses." For Lewis, "weak, servile" translations are those that are dominated by "the message, context, or concept over language texture."[96] This critic desires a "strong, forceful translation that values experimentation, tampers with usage, seeks to match the polyvalencies or plurivocities or expressive stresses of the original by producing its own." Lewis wants to replicate the "abuse that occurs in the original" by "displac[ing], remobiliz[ing], and extend[ing] this abuse in another milieu."[97]

It was Lawrence Venuti, "one of the leading and most eloquent voices in modern translation studies,"[98] who fashioned together an innovative approach, drawing together this concept of "abusive translation," along with Antoine Berman's studies of German romantics,[99] and his own wide-ranging study of translation theory and practice. Venuti's approach runs counter to descriptive translation studies, as Edwin Gentzler favourably remarks: "[Venuti's] method provides a refreshing alternative to the quasi-scientific, empirical case studies favored by the translation studies scholars in Belgium and Holland or polysystem theory used by Israeli scholars."[100] As Venuti writes in *The Translator's Invisibility,*

> A translator can not only choose a foreign text that is marginal in the target-language culture, but translate it with a canonical discourse (e.g. transparency). Or a translator can choose a foreign text that is canonical in the target-language culture, but translate it with a marginal discourse (e.g. archaism). In this foreignizing practice of translation, the value of a foreign text or a discursive strategy is contingent on the cultural situation in which the translation is made.[101]

In sum, foreignization refers both to the text selected as well as the approach. This is why the criticism levelled at Venuti's approach, especially by Folkart,[102] is not well-aimed. Folkart is reacting against the notion of a foreignized translation ("grainy," in her formulation) by dint of its "marginal discourse." What is undoubtedly true is that the border separating a "foreignized translation" that is successful from a poem in "translationese" (e.g., a "servile translation" in Lewis's words) is not fixed in stone. The belief that poetry is by nature "inherently alien" and therefore the translation does not need to "foreignize it" can be valid in certain cases – and this is precisely, as we will see, Giovanni Giudici's conception of the poem. Folkart's prescriptive and rigid approach cannot account for poetics alien to her own: what she claims is "translationese" could equally be claimed by Venuti as a resistant translation. Chapters 4 and 5 will heavily draw on the concept of "foreignization."

Translation Ideologies

The concept of "foreignization" leads us naturally to the more general concept of ideology. The term "ideology" originally came from the French word *ideologie*. It was coined at the end of the eighteenth century by the French philosopher Destutt de Tracy, referring to the "science of ideas," which "was broadly that of Locke and the empiricist tradition."[103]

There are three core meanings at the root of the term, as the critic Raymond Williams has indicated:

1. a system of beliefs characteristic of a particular class or group;
2. a system of illusory beliefs – false ideas or false consciousness – which can be contrasted with true or scientific knowledge;
3. the general process of the production of meanings and ideas.[104]

The first and third meanings are expressed by Marx in his preface to *A Contribution to the Critique of Political Economy*:

> The distinction should always be made between the material transformation of the economic conditions of production ... and the legal, political, religious, aesthetic or philosophic – in short, ideological – forms in which men become conscious of this conflict and fight it out.[105]

The negative sense is clearly expressed by Engels in his 1893 *Letter to Mehring*:

> Ideology is a process accomplished by the so-called thinker consciously indeed but with a false consciousness. The real motives impelling him remain unknown to him, otherwise it would not be an ideological process at all. Hence he imagines false or apparent motives. Because it is a process of thought he derives both its form and its content from pure thought, either his own or his predecessors'.[106]

Certainly, one of the key problems in determining the ideology of a translator is, as Peter Fawcett and Jeremy Munday ask, "[W]hen is something 'ideology' rather than just 'culture,' and what is the difference between the two?"[107] A potential response comes from Christina Schäffner:

> Ideological aspect can ... be determined within a text itself, both at the lexical level (reflected, for example, in the deliberate choice or avoidance

> of a particular word ...) and the grammatical level (for example, use of passive structures to avoid an expression of agency). Ideological aspects can be more or less obvious in texts, depending on the topic of a text, its genre and communicative purposes.[108]

It should be noted that often ideology can be read in assumptions, and is often only implicit in statements by poet-translators. On the other hand, sometimes it is quite evident, as in Sanguineti's Marxist writings, or the metapoetic essays of Buffoni and Giudici. Yet Montale's and Caproni's ideologies are less easy to work out and more hidden within the depths of their poetics.

Compensation

One of the cardinal notions on which translation – and the translation of poetry – relies upon is compensation. As the scholar Keith Harvey rightly notes,

> Explicit references to compensation are scattered throughout the literature on translation studies. These references often represent piecemeal, non-formalized uses of the term. Particularly in texts dating from before the mid-1980s, words such as compensation, compensatory and compensate for are usually employed in a loose, common sense way. Close examination of examples reveals that practically anything that did not involve straightforward formal correspondence was subsumed under this label.[109]

The idea of "compensation" finds its first modern expression in Jean-Paul Vinay and Jean Darbelnet's 1958 book, *Stylistique comparée du français et de l'anglais: méthode de traduction* (Comparative stylistics of French and English: A methodology for translation).[110] For these French linguists, compensation is essential to regain what is lost in translation. As they state,

> [O]ne of the major concerns of translators is to ensure that the translation preserves the content of the original without losses; any loss, regardless of whether it is of meaning or tone should be recovered by the procedures of compensation.[111]

They define compensation as a "gain" in contrast to the loss ("entropy") inherent in translation. It is, in short, "the stylistic translation technique by which a nuance that cannot be put in the same place as in the original is put at another point of the phrase, thereby keeping the overall tone." Yet Vinay and Darbelnet do not include it among their seven procedures of translation. Likewise, it is hardly mentioned by the influential translation theorist Eugene Nida, who mentions in passing that compensation of idioms for non-idioms is acceptable in order not to weaken the "figurative force of the translation."[112]

With the publication of George Steiner's 1975 *After Babel*, compensation takes a truly leading role. For Steiner, translation is a four-part process beginning with trust, passing through the second and third stages of aggression and incorporation, and ending with the final phase of "compensation." As he says,

> The final stage or moment in the process of translation is that which I have called "compensation" or "restitution." The translation restores the equilibrium between itself and the original, between source-language and receptor-language which had been disrupted by the translator's interpretative attack and appropriation. The paradigm of translation stays incomplete until reciprocity has been achieved, until the original has regained as much as it has lost.
>
> Translation fails where it does not compensate, where there is no restoration of radical equity. The translator has grasped and/or appropriated less than is there. He traduces through diminution. Or he has chosen to embody and restate fully only one or another aspect of the original, fragmenting, distorting its vital coherence according to his own needs or myopia.[113]

For all their differences,[114] Peter Newmark follows Steiner in suggesting that "compensation is the procedure which in the last resort ensures that translation is possible."[115]

Yet compensation is defined more in detail by successive scholars. In their pedagogical volume, *Thinking French Translation*,[116] Sándor Hervey and Ian Higgins define four types of compensation: compensation in kind ("making up for one type of textual effect in the ST by another type in the TT"); compensation in place (such as "using different sounds in different places [in the text]"), compensation by merging (e.g., translating two French terms by one combined English term), and compensation by splitting (e.g., translating one French word by two English words).[117]

Keith Harvey, whose 1995 article in *The Translator* still remains the most up-to-date description of this procedure, critiques Hervey and Higgins's distribution of compensation into four types, arguing that the latter two (compensation by merging and by splitting) really relate only to systemic differences between languages. Harvey insists, instead, that compensation is "a technique for making up the loss of a source text effect by recreating a similar effect in the target text through means that are specific to the target language and/or the target text."[118]

In Italy, the notion of compensation was promoted by Franco Fortini, first in a 1988 speech at the important conference in Bergamo, Italy, *La traduzione del testo poetico,* organized by Franco Buffoni. In Fortini's words, *i compensi* (compensation) and *le supplenze* refer to the fact that

> an increase, for example, of the density of assonance, alliteration [and] homophony compensates for the decrease in rhymes; an increase in types of discourse tends to augment the density of the text and therefore to diminish the dimension of communicative directness, combating the amount of paraphrase, and restituting, in the target text, the status of separateness and of "literariness" which is possessed by the source text.[119]

I will return to the notion of compensation most explicitly in chapter 3, when dealing with Giorgio Caproni's translations.

Categories of Poetic Translation

Two of the most helpful categorizations of poetry translation have been offered by the translation scholars André Lefevere[120] and James Holmes.[121] For convenience's sake, I will merge the two classifications together and discuss six categories of poetic translation.[122] The first two types are translations in formal verse: "mimetic translation,"[123] and "analogical translation." The third category is "organic translation"; the fourth is "prose translation"; the fifth is "phonemic translation"; and the sixth is "imitation."[124]

Mimetic translation – a translation written in the same or formally similar metre as the original – is fundamentally "optimistic" as regards cross-cultural transfer, as Holmes notes. The translator has faith that the reproduction of the original form is possible and meaningful within a different language and culture. It is described by Lefevere as "a very rigorous straitjacket imposed on the target text."[125] While I don't promote the Dutch translation scholar's prescriptivism, I do agree that such an approach is indeed very challenging. This does not always lead to disastrous results, however, as we will see with Giudici's creative version of Pushkin's *Eugene Onegin* in *novenari* that attempts to replicate the

Russian iambic tetrameter. One cannot deny, though, that such a method can end up badly: Giovanni Pascoli's decision to attempt to translate Homer's quantitative poetry into syllabic verse ("barbaric meters") was heavily criticized,[126] for example, by no less than Benedetto Croce.

The second category of translation is the analogical translation: in short, the translator attempts to find functionally equivalent or equally prestigious metres in the target language (e.g., iambic pentameter for dactylic hexameter; hendecasyllable for Pushkin's iambic tetrameter). The strength of this approach lies in the prominence of the adopted form, which corresponds to target language readers' expectations. One can think of such translations that have achieved canonical status in English and Italian: for example, Alexander Pope's *Iliad*, rendered in heroic couplets (rhyming iambic pentameter couplets) and Vincenzo Monti's version of the *Iliad*, translated into unrhymed hendecasyllables. On the other hand, the original rhythm is completely lost – especially flagrantly in the case of translating from non-cognate versification systems.[127] Catullus, translated from Latin quantitative non-rhyming verse into accentual-syllabic English-rhyming verse, becomes, in Lefevere's words, "a clumsy poetaster ... the rhymer has merely succeeded in transmitting a caricature."[128]

The third category, "organic form," is a "content-derivative" approach in which "the semantic material ... take[s] on its own unique poetic shape as the translation develops."[129] There is no relationship between the *form* of the source text and the target text. So Ungaretti's translation of Frénaud's poem is fifteen verses, not thirteen; Buffoni's translation of Shakespeare's sonnets is not in an equivalent metre to the English iambic pentameter or in a regular poetic metre in Italian.

The fourth category, poetry translated in prose, is notable, as Lefevere comments, for being more "accurate" than verse translations, and for "avoiding most of the distortions ... one finds in such translations." If Lefevere speaks from the point of view of dynamic equivalence (and "communicative value"), which has come to be seen as a vague concept, it remains true that poetry translated into prose often more effectively reproduces the denotative meaning of the source text (although other connotative meanings are lost, not to mention formal aspects such as metre and rhyme). But the eighteenth-century Scottish translation theorist Alexander Tytler had already inveighed against this method, in his *Essay on the Principles of Translation*: "to attempt ... a translation of a lyric poem into prose, is the most absurd of all undertakings, for the characters of the original which are essential to it, and which constitute its highest beauties, if transferred to a prose translation, become unpardonable blemishes."[130] Indeed, even Lefevere speaks of an "uneasy hybrid structure, forever groping towards a precarious equilibrium between verse and prose and never really achieving it."[131] Yet proponents of this approach include such important writers as Galvano della Volpe (as above), Vladimir Nabokov (whose translation ideology I will discuss in the fourth chapter), and Robert Browning. Browning advocated that one should "be literal at every cost save that of absolute violence to our language."[132] On the whole, modern Italian poets mostly eschew this approach, because of the normalcy in Italian of rendering verse into verse (with exceptions as noted by Fortini); there is no modern equivalent to the Anglo-American translations of the Greek and Latin epic poems into prose.

The fifth type, phonemic (or homophonic) translation, which is notably the path chosen by Louis and Celia Zukofsky in their translation of Catullus, is certainly the least likely to get across the semantic meaning of the poem. As Lefevere says,

> [A]ll too often the much-sought equilibrium between dominance of sound and undercurrent of meaning is shattered. What remains are few blessed oases of plain sense, devoid of successful sound-imitation, between vast bewildering stretches of moderately successful sound-imitation either altogether devoid of immediate sense or running contrary to the sense of the source text.[133]

Yet Lawrence Venuti has written strongly in favour of such a method, describing Zukofsky's "remarkable" rendition, whose

> discursive heterogeneity ... mixes the archaic and the current, the literary and the technical, the elite and the popular, the professional and the working-class, the school and the street. In the recovery of marginal discourses, this translation crosses numerous linguistic and cultural boundaries ...[134]

None of our five Italian poet-translators practised such a form of translation; and among Italian poet-translators, Franco Fortini might be the sole one who carried out such a method in a poem.[135] Yet Edoardo Sanguineti, with his interlinear approach, and his calques, does at time seemingly "transliterate" between languages for brief stretches of time.

Another category is "imitation," which, according to Lefevere, no longer belongs to the realm of translation proper. John Dryden was the first in English to speak of imitation within the framework of translation theory, scornfully writing, as we have already seen, of "the translator [who] ... run[s] division on the groundwork as he pleases." In France, no one in the seventeenth century was as famous for his imitations as the translator Nicolas Perrot D'Ablancourt. He wrote, "I do not always bind myself either to the words or the reasoning of this author [Lucian]; and I adjust things to our manner and style with his goal in mind. Different times demand different reasoning as well as different words ... Nonetheless, that is not translation; yet it is worth more than translation."[136] It was in reference to D'Ablancourt's free translations of the classics that the term "les belles infidèles" (beautiful and unfaithful [translations]) was coined by Gilles Ménage.

Certainly, some translations done in such a manner can have (as Lefevere disparagingly notes) "only title and point of departure, if those, in common with the source text."[137] However, one must bear in mind that the notion of translation depends on the target culture and target poetics. In addition, the methods of translation grouped under "imitation" are astonishingly numerous, depending on which aspects of the source text are changed or eliminated, and/or whether additional material is added.

In Italy, the notion that a translation of poetry should be an imitation is widely held. Translation is often conceived as a way of composing original works. The term "imitazione" enjoys wide usage in modern Italy, thanks to the prestige of Leopardi's own "imitazione"[138] of Antoine-Vincent Arnault's poem "La feuille" (The leaf). Many of the poet-translators discussed in my study, from Bertolucci,[139] Buffoni,[140] and Caproni[141] to Fortini,[142] Raboni,[143] and Sanguineti,[144] entitle some of their translations "imitations."[145]

There is one additional category I will speak of now, which isn't specifically addressed by either Lefevere or Holmes, but is widely practised. This is the method of choosing one specific "constructive principle" and translating accordingly. This approach derives from Yury Tynjanov's idea of literature as a system, although the Russian formalist did not apply this specifically to translation. In the Italian scene, two poet-translators have selected this method: Giovanni Giudici and Franco Buffoni. It has additionally been argued by Pier Vincenzo Mengaldo that this is the most successful method of translation:

> As is known, the Russian formalists asserted that in every literary text there is a dominant that regulates the remaining components ... for translations of poetry I think this is *literally* true. The translator of poetry cannot be "faithful" to all the components of the original text, but only, fundamentally, to one, to whom he subordinates the others: faithful to one, unfaithful to the others, to paraphrase one of [Karl] Kraus's witticisms about women.[146]

Yet for Lefevere, any translation method emphasizing "one aspect of the source text," is naturally a "distorting" translation.[147] However, in response to Lefevere, we might add that every translation is "distorting." Following a "constructive principle" allows the translator to maintain a coherent strategy when tackling a text. It should be obvious that many poet-translators follow such a method, even if they don't cite Tynjanov. For example, Raboni speaks of "developing a system of 'programmed' moments of unfaithfulness," just as Valerio Magrelli writes that "we must decide to which of the finite, but very numerous functions of the text, we want to be faithful ... fidelity is always fidelity to one function."[148]

Translation Theories among Italian Poet-Translators

Among poet-translators, Franco Fortini and Franco Buffoni have dedicated the most time and writing to theoretical elaboration on translation, although others, such as Caproni, Dal Fabbro, Giudici, and Sanguineti, have written illuminating essays. We have already mentioned Fortini several times, but it's necessary to underline the time and attention he paid to reflecting on translation. His history of twentieth-century Italian poetry, *I poeti del Novecento* (Twentieth-century poets), was described by Mengaldo as "the first book about twentieth-century [Italian] poetry in which a section, dense with facts and reflections, is dedicated to the problem of poetry translations."[149] We might note that Fortini's conception of *quaderni di traduzioni*, authorial books of translation, explicitly contradicted, as he himself noted, his newer scientific theory of translation.[150] Likewise, Franco Buffoni's reflections on translation have accompanied his poetic and academic career that was first influenced by Anceschi and Mattioli, and then evolved independently. For Buffoni, as we will see, "there are two great diseases always necessary to try to eradicate [*debellare*]: the idea that the translation can be the reproduction of a text, and the idea that it is a re-creation [*ricreazione*]." Buffoni will instead turn to the notion of poetics and the *poietic* encounter (*incontro poietico*) in his theorization of poetic translation.

At the opposite pole there are many Italian poets who translated without leaving critical reflections about the process, or who lamented their own critical incapacities as theorists of translation.[151] For instance, Mario Luzi says that he "never thought to be able to theorize an object as empirical" as translation. Giovanni Raboni doesn't consider himself a translation theorist (*traduttologo*). Luciano Erba allows himself "the luxury of a complete indifference regarding eventual scientific itches and an equal absolute deafness regarding possible methodological temptations."[152] Vittorio Sereni matter-of-factly states that "the 'problem' of literary translation – literal or 'artistic,' whether *bella infedele* [beautiful and unfaithful] o *brutta fedele* [ugly and faithful] – has no interest for me."[153] Alessandro Parronchi prefaces his *Quaderno francese* (French notebook) by stating that it would be "excessive [*eccessivo*] if I attempted to prefix theoretical notions to the collection of almost all that I have translated."[154] And Eugenio Montale, despite many reviews of translations, never wrote a real essay about translation, to the "shock" of at least one critic.[155]

I have already spoken of the crushing influence of Croce on Italian poets. His tenet of the untranslatability of poetry is, in fact, supported by many: from Ungaretti and Montale, to Caproni, Sanguineti, and Zanzotto. Ungaretti claims, "Poetry is individual and inimitable to such a degree that it is untranslatable."[156] Montale frequently describes writers as "untranslatable," such as Apollinaire, Joyce, Proust, and Yeats.[157] Caproni states that translators "pay a very large (and often ruinous) discount rate [*tasso di sconto*]."[158] Sanguineti goes so far as to state "there is no difference between a translation and a pseudo-translation,"[159] since nothing from the original remains in the translation. Zanzotto affirms that "translation, 'the transfer' of poetry in a complete sense, we know is impossible."[160]

A common trend among Italian poets is to equate translating with composing original verse. Dal Fabbro writes, "Translating poetry ... cannot be distinguished from originally composing it." Diego Valeri suggests that "the activity of translating poetry is, at bottom, the activity of poetry."[161] In the same vein, Margherita Guidacci affirms that "there is not a substantial difference between translating ... and creating original poetry,"[162] and Montale proposes that "a good [*buona*] translation is that which doesn't seem [a translation]; that which presents a text which one would call original [*originale*]."[163]

Some translators, like Fortini and Montale, believe that the precise knowledge of the source language is necessary, even when they themselves do not possess that knowledge.[164] Others, like Giudici and dal Fabbro, don't think this is a requisite. This obviously leads to diverse conclusions; a theory that requires philological mastery does not generally demand poetic imitations. A theory that does away with language mastery does not generally expect interlinear translations, for instance. In this latter theory, domestication is preferred: translations aim to be invisible, and the poems to read as though they were written in the target language, Italian. So, for instance, Beniamino dal Fabbro freely adapts, translating from translations, just as Ungaretti translates Esenin from French and not Russian, and Sergio Solmi translates Omar Khayyam from Edward FitzGerald's English translation.

Poet-translators often translate poets whose poetry resembles their own. This ties into the concept that Venuti calls "simpatico":[165] the supposedly natural affinity between translators and the poems they translate. Translators like Sergio Solmi and Diego Valeri translated in this mode. As Solmi writes, he finds necessary "that participation, that complicity with the author, which to me seems indispensable for poetic translation."[166] This links to Solmi's belief that a translator should be a contemporary of the translated author; in contrast, Giudici thinks that it is precisely distance in time, space and language that allows for the deepest connection between the translator and the original text. Sanguineti, on the other hand, has insisted that it is not original authors we encounter and read in translations, but rather the translators themselves. So Homer and Virgil are not our contemporaries, their translators are.

Yet many poets decide to translate poets whom they *least* resemble. As Vittorio Sereni writes,

> One also translates, if not just for opposition, also for comparison. In translation, one doesn't appropriate for oneself so much, nor make another's text one's own, as much as it is the other's text that absorbs a zone up until now uncertain in our sensibility and illuminates it – and one learns more from someone who doesn't resemble us.[167]

Indeed, an important consideration for Italian poets is how translation enriches the translator. As Caproni writes, difficulty in translating dissimilar authors allows the poet-translator to experience an "enlargement in the field of one's own experience and consciousness, of one's existence or being."[168] Sereni notes that with some texts "the only way to read them, or to read them most deeply, is to translate them."[169] This is not only the view of Sereni and Caproni, but that of Luzi as well as most of the other Hermetic poets associated with Florence, whose translations of Mallarmé were intimately connected with their literary criticism. This ties in to the confluence of poet-translator-critic, mentioned earlier, which is indicative of modern Italian culture. Almost all of the poet-translators mentioned in my study, from Montale and Ungaretti, to Luzi, Sereni, Caproni, Fortini, Giudici, Sanguineti, and Buffoni, produced volumes of criticism.[170]

Conclusion

In conclusion, this chapter aimed at presenting the intractable problem of untranslatability and demonstrating different methods of resolving this issue, or simply sidestepping it. Approaches based on systems theories and concepts such as foreignization, compensation, and poetics allow us to reconfigure the notion of poetic translation. The translated poem is no longer a site for an inert theoretical dichotomy (faithful or unfaithful?). The interrelations between the author, translator, source text/culture and target text/culture acquire visibility and importance. In the following examination of the five poet-translators, certain theoretical models will be favoured, most of which I have already presented: Croce's *poetic recreation* (chapters 2 and 3), Fortini's *compensi* (chapter 3), Venuti's *foreignization* (chapters 4 and 5), Tynjanov's *constructive principle* (chapters 4 and 6), Walter Benjamin's *interlinear translation* (which will be introduced in chapter 5), and Anceschi's and Mattioli's *poietic encounter* (chapter 6).

2 Eugenio Montale: Translation, *Ricreazioni*, and *Il Quaderno di Traduzioni*

I also consider some translations as my critical works [*opere critiche*]: *Hamlet*, Marlowe's *Faust*, Melville's *Billy Budd*, the *Quaderno di traduzioni* which I published with Meridiana and some *Entremeses* of Cervantes, very much praised by Croce, etc. Other translations instead were the result of economic necessity.[1]

–Eugenio Montale

This chapter has three goals. First, to describe and provide a brief history of Eugenio Montale's translations, which have often been studied but never entirely accurately appraised because of Montale's tendency to use "ghost-translators" (Lucia Rodocanachi and Maria Luisa Spaziani) to provide him with literal versions or complete translations. Second, to analyse Montale's philosophy of translation, which has long and unjustly remained at the margins of the critical discourse about his poetics. We will see how Montale's translation ideology was shaped by two beliefs of Benedetto Croce: that poetry is impossible to translate, and consequently that poetic translations should ideally constitute original works of art, or poetic *ricreazioni* (recreations). Finally, I will take a fresh look at Montale's *Quaderno di traduzioni*, while contextualizing the translations within Montale's poetics and poetic career.

This chapter is thus structured in several parts. I begin with an introduction to the poetry and poetics of Montale; I offer a panorama of Montale's translations and his own views on translation with an analysis of two ignored texts (his French translation of his poem "Ripenso il tuo sorriso" [I think again of your smile] and his 1955 interview on translation); third, I examine his *Quaderno di traduzioni*; next, I compare

Montale's and Ungaretti's translations of Shakespeare Sonnet 33; after this, I give an appraisal of Montale's translation techniques, followed by a general conclusion.

Poetic Career

Eugenio Montale (Genoa, 1896–Milan, 1981) is the most famous Italian poet of the twentieth century. Both drawing on and transforming the poetic language handed down by the two most important turn-of-the-century Italian poets, Giovanni Pascoli and Gabriele D'Annunzio, Montale constructed a multi-faceted *Opera in versi* (Poetic works).[2] His main muses, who both shape and are reshaped in his own poetry, are four: Anna d'Uberti (*Arletta/Annetta*), Irma Brandeis (*Clizia* [Clytia]), Maria Luisa Spaziani (*la Volpe* [the Fox]), and Drusilla Tanzi (*la Mosca* [the Fly]). Montale's poetic career is generally divided into two periods, authorized by the poet himself who speaks of them metaphorically as his *recto* (front [page]) and *verso* (back [page]). The first period consists of three volumes: *Ossi di seppia* (Cuttlefish bones, 1925),[3] *Le occasioni* (The occasions, 1939),[4] and *La bufera e altro* (The storm and other things, 1956).[5] After a hiatus of fifteen years, Montale then came out with a series of four works over the next ten years: *Satura* (Satura, 1971),[6] *Diario del '71 e '72* (Diary of '71 and '72, 1973),[7] *Quaderno di quattro anni* (Notebook of four years, 1977),[8] and *Altri versi e poesie disperse* (Other verses and unpublished poems, 1981).[9]

Montale's first collection, *Ossi di seppia,* sprang forth in part from a desire to make music in words: "I obeyed a need of musical expression [*Ubbidii a un bisogno di espressione musicale*]."[10] Yet this musical and linguistic necessity inhabited a poet who thought he lived

> under a glass bell jar, and yet I felt near to something essential. A subtle veil, barely a thread separated me from that definitive *quid.* Absolute expression would have been the ripping of that veil, that thread: an explosion, the end of the deception of the world as representation. But this was an unreachable limit. And my desire for adherence remained musical, instinctive, not programmatic. I wanted to twist the neck of the eloquence of our old courtly language, perhaps at the risk of a counter-eloquence.[11]

The "counter-eloquence" (*controeloquenza*) did not run contrary to the musical impulse motivating his pen; it is the rebellion against "courtly language" (*lingua aulica*), or the overcoming of the linguistic hegemony of Pascoli and D'Annunzio. Montale described the specific content of these poems to Piero Gadda Conti (using the important musical term, *motivi* [motifs]):

> My motifs are simple and are: the landscape (sometimes hallucinated, but often naturalistic: our Ligurian landscape, which is very universal); love, under the form of ghosts who *haunt* [*frequentano*] the various poems and provoke the usual "intermittencies of the heart, ..." and evasion, the flight from the iron chain of necessity, the secular miracle, let us say (search for the broken stitch, etc.). Sometimes the motifs can merge together, sometimes they are isolated. Nothing is simpler; if there is some obscurity, it is certainly not intentionally desired, nor loved by me.[12]

That he didn't, at this stage, insist on obscurity is important. Montale's successive volume, *Le occasioni*, is certainly obscure. There, Montale deliberately hid the original motivations of his poems and therefore the analogies he uses are difficult to follow. But to return to *Ossi di seppia*: here, the focus is on the poet, the pseudonymous Arsenio, and his beloved. It is she who is able to break the chain of necessity and save herself. The Christological nucleus of Montale's later poetry originates here. The difference is that in *Ossi di seppia* the beloved saves herself; later, in *La bufera e altro*, she will save both herself and the poet. The most important feminine figure in this first volume is Arletta, "tied to the poet by the 'string' of a profound affinity: the obscure presentiment of 'universal evil,' the reciprocal wound, – the sickness of living."[13] She will reappear in Montale's final volumes.

Speaking of Montale's following volume, *Le occasioni*, let us begin with the title of this 1939 volume dedicated (from 1949 onwards) to I.B., that is, Irma Brandeis, or the figure Clizia. As Giorgio Zampa notes, the title refers to "a miraculous event, a miracle: sign, presage, mystical omen, the opposite of repetition and predictability."[14] Here, for example, the sea, a figure of eternal continuity and repetition with its waves and tides, is largely absent (paralleling Montale's move to Florence). Two structural elements underline the collection. First, the autobiographical element fades away. There are fewer romantic outbursts, as Montale notes, because of his need for "objective expression" (*un'espressione oggettiva*).[15] As for the language itself, notoriously described by the poet as "our heavy polysyllabic language" (*nostro pesante linguaggio polisillabico*),[16] in which Montale tries to "dig out another dimension" (*scavare un'altra dimensione*),[17] we find a greater emphasis on rhyme and assonance. Indeed, Montale aimed, as he said, for his own *sprung rhythm*,[18] and he found it strange that none of his critics cited Gerard Manley Hopkins. On the whole, the poetry of *Le occasioni* wasn't pure poetry as Mallarmé and Valéry wished; it was rather, as Montale said, "a fruit which should contain its motifs without revealing them, or better without blurting them out." So, famously, when he was thinking of Clizia, he began a poem "La speranza di pure rivederti / m'abbandonava" (The hope even of seeing you again / was leaving me).[19] Yet Montale concludes this poem with the image "a Modena, tra i portici, / un servo gallonato trascinava / due sciacalli al guinzaglio" (at Modena, between the arcades, / a liveried servant dragged / two jackals on a leash).[20] As the Italian poet afterwards explained, it was the appearance of these "odd animals" (*animali buffi*)[21] that made him associate them with Clizia, and caused him to wonder if they had been sent by her, or if they were just illusory "signs of death" (*segni della morte*).[22]

La bufera e altro (1956), the poet's third volume, is considered by the majority of critics to be the zenith of Montale's poetry. Here, as Montale writes:

> I completed my work with the poems of *Finisterre*, which represent my Petrarchan experience, let us thus say. I projected *la Selvaggia* or *la Mandetta* or *la Delia* (call her as you like) of the *Mottetti* [Motets] on the background of a cosmic and earthly war, without purpose or reason, and I entrusted myself to her, woman or cloud, angel or petrel.[23]

As Gianfranco Contini wrote, the originality of this book resides in the "disruptive and massive eruption of a reality (which I will call 'external') in a [poetic] world ... that had, however, elaborated for itself its distrust in the real." Giovanni Macchia has perceptively called this collection "the novel of Clizia"[24] for the overwhelming importance of the figure of the American Irma Brandeis, the Christ-bearing (*Cristofora*) Beatrice, the "visiting angel,"[25] who bears the imprint and plan of God. From *Le occasioni* to *La bufera e altro*, Clizia has undergone, in Glauco Cambon's words, "an apotheosis": she becomes now "an angelic voice or presence and, eventually, sheer creativity, light's very force, the cosmic antagonist of evil; as a metaphysical source of salvation, she surpasses even Dante's Beatrice; as feminine deity, she tends to supplant the God of Christian orthodoxy. That is Montale's supreme myth."[26] In *La bufera e altro*, Clizia is "projected," as Montale says, into the midst of a universal war. This war, "of all time and of all" (*di sempre e di tutti*)[27] finds Montale and Clizia on opposing sides of the Atlantic. It is Clizia whom Montale addresses in "La primavera hitleriana" (The Hitler spring),

> Guarda ancora
> in alto, Clizia, è la tua sorte, tu
> che il non mutato amor mutata serbi,
> fino a che il cieco sole che in te porti
> si abbacini nell'Altro e si distrugga
> in Lui, per tutti.[28]
>
> [Look again
> Up high, Clizia, it is your destiny, you
> Who conserve, changed, the unchanged love,
> Until the blind sun you bear within
> Dazzles in the Other and is destroyed
> In Him, for everyone.]

Yet *La bufera e altro* doesn't revolve around a single feminine figure; a whole section of it (*madrigali privati* [private madrigals]) is dedicated to another female figure, Maria Luisa Spaziani, "la Volpe," who is a counterpart to the heavenly Clizia. Spaziani is the "Anti-beatrice" (*l'Antibeatrice*), "a very earthly character" who gave Montale "the sense above all of still being alive."[29] No longer is salvation "for all"; rather, as the poet writes, "il dono che sognavo / non per me ma per tutti / appartiene a me solo" (the gift that I dreamed of / not for me but for all / belongs to me alone).[30]

After a long period of poetic silence, Montale published *Satura* in 1971. This volume of poems, which follows several books of prose such as the 1956 *Farfalla di Dinard* (The butterfly of Dinard), the 1966 *Auto da fé*, and the 1969 *Fuori di casa* (Away from home),[31] is a hybrid collection of various styles and languages, written in a completely new style: everyday language dominates. As Marco Forti notes, by using the title *Satura*, Montale "has alluded to a poetic form that, after the highest and icy cosmic reflection of *La bufera*, responded by opening up (apparently becoming simplified) to the factual and conceptual multiplicity and chaos of the world in which we live."[32] The themes vary; indeed, this is a fundamental new trait of Montale's later collections, as Pier Vincenzo Mengaldo perceptively indicated. And yet, two figures return in these final years: first, Arletta, now called Annetta, who reappears as a "paradoxical alter-ego of a poet who died young"[33] and, second, Clizia, who remains the most highly venerated figure in Montale's poetry. As Montale would write in 1980, a year before his death, in "Clizia in '34": "non era amore quello / era come oggi e sempre / venerazione" (that was not love, / it was, as it is today and always, / veneration).[34]

Translation Career

Eugenio Montale is the most problematic poet-translator of modern Italy. He translated frequently for economic reasons. Montale turned to translation work after he was fired from his job as director of the private library *Il Gabinetto Vieusseux* in 1938, for refusing to become a member of the Fascist party. For the next seven years he had to rely on translation work from major publishing houses like Mondadori and Bompiani, some of which ended up in the famous anthology edited by Elio Vittorini, *Americana*: *raccolta di narratori dalle origini ai nostri giorni* (Americana: Collection of narrators from the beginning to the present day).[35] Perennially short of money and pressed for time, he took short cuts, as critics have shown,[36] by subcontracting some of his translations to Lucia Rodocanachi. Likewise – and this has been almost completely passed over by critics – Montale sometimes relied on published or non-published translations of others. His translations of Cervantes's *Entremeses* (Farces) and *Novelas* (Novellas), as well as Christopher Marlowe's *Faust* were rewritings of previous Italian renderings, as he privately admitted, and Montale's versions of Shakespeare's *Timon of Athens*, *The Comedy of Errors*, and *A Winter's Tale* were partially based on the French translations by François-Victor Hugo. In addition, Montale was found guilty by Italian courts of having plagiarized Bice Chiappelli's translation of Eugene O'Neill's *Strange Interlude*, for which he was ordered to pay a stiff fine.[37] This singular fact is omitted in almost all studies of Montale.[38] Antonio Prete sums up this period by stating that "Montale as a translator of narrative and theater, in particular during the years from 1940 to 1943, was only a reviser of translations done by others."

After the Second World War, Montale again relied, at times, on another ghost-translator, namely, Maria Luisa Spaziani. In a recent interview, she revealed that she gave Montale versions of Angus Wilson's novel *Hemlock and After* and Herman Melville's story *Benito Cereno*,[39] both of which Montale published in his own name after minimal corrections.[40] This tendency to depend on others for translations extended to Montale's own journalistic work. He published articles written by Henry Furst under his own name in the newspaper *Corriere della Sera*,[41] about seventy short stories written by Maria Luisa Spaziani in another newspaper, *Corriere dell'Informazione* (signed "*alastor*"), and two prefaces to works by Boccaccio and Defoe that were also written by Spaziani.[42] Montale was not happy with his "second profession" (*secondo mestiere*), and he did all he could to lessen its weight.

Translation Ideology

Like most poet-translators, Montale preached one thing and practised another. He extolled the virtues of literal translations, yet the only poetry he translated literally was his own (into French). He proclaimed certain poets untranslatable (like Yeats), and then proceeded to translate them. He spoke most highly of "marvelous adaptations" (*meravigliosi rifacimenti*), but almost never made such versions. He declared that a translator must know the language from which he translates, while often relying on intermediary texts (other translations or ghost-translators), since he was never fluent in English. Yet these paradoxes are understandable in a poet always forced to eke out time for his own poetry among his various *secondi mestieri* (second professions). We will begin by speaking of Montale's philosophy of translation and then see how this functions in his own self-translation.

When critics speak of Montale's translation philosophy, they generally cite the same well-known passages. Yet an interview the poet gave to Mario Picchi in 1956 for the latter's article devoted to translation in the literary review *La Fiera Letteraria* has been consistently neglected. Indeed, in this interview, Montale laid down two axioms of his own translation activity, which are clearly Crocean. That they are implicitly derived from Croce's own philosophy on translation is proven, in absence of clear indications to the contrary, by the supremacy of Croce's theories on Italian culture of the first half of the twentieth century along with the well-known fact that Montale read Croce's treatises (however skeptical he was about other facets of the latter's philosophic system). As Montale says in the 1956 article, "A good [*buona*] translation is that which doesn't seem [a translation]; that which presents a text which one would call original [*originale*]."[43] And, "Faithful or unfaithful, as it may be, a translation is always *another* thing [*altra cosa*]; it can even better [*migliore*] than the original, but it is different [*diversa*]."[44] Therefore, for Montale, a translation is never a reproduction of the original text. In

Montale's (and Croce's) view, translations are not necessarily worse than the original text, although most often this is the case. Indeed the translation can be *migliore,* and Montale often cites famous versions by Monti and others, not to mention his own translation of *Billy Budd*. Yet such "recreative" versions are not necessary when there is a bilingual text. Two corollaries that Montale also affirms in this interview are that spiritual affinity is not a requisite, noting only that affinity of techniques is helpful, and that a translator should translate into a modern idiom, and not archaize the text (as dal Fabbro does at times).

Montale's translation ideology developed, as we said, under the shadow of Benedetto Croce's own idea of translation. Even so, Montale was not a Crocean, disagreeing with him on many fundamental philosophical issues.[45] If Rocco Montano goes much too far in claiming "one can only think of the Croce-Montale relationship in a direction of antithesis,"[46] it is nonetheless true that there were vital differences between the two. And yet it is also the case, as Franco Contorbia remarks, that the "dialogue" between Montale and Croce is "important … without any question."[47] Moreover, we might say that Montale's complicated relationship with the thought of Croce resides not entirely with Croce's philosophy but also with Croce's acolytes. In truth, Montale was always averse to a systematic philosophy of whatever sort, as he plainly stated, against "every type of systematic philosophy."[48] Nonetheless, Montale's praise of Croce is, at times, unstinting, as we can see in his newspaper article commemorating the philosopher's birthday, where Montale goes so far as to say:

> Today Benedetto Croce turns 85 and from every part of Italy the minds of those who owe to him the best of their intellectual education turn to him. How many are there? It would be impossible to count them, because not only are there intellectuals, let's say, by profession, the intelligentsia, but also those, even more numerous, who received the imprint of his thought through indirect means.[49]

As we have said before, Croce's influence over Italian culture during the first half of the twentieth century was immense. As Contini noted in his *La parte di Benedetto Croce nella cultura italiana* (The role of Benedetto Croce in Italian culture), Croce "conquered"[50] Italian culture with the publication of his *Estetica come scienza dell'espressione e linguistica generale* (The aesthetic as science of expression and general linguistics, 1902) and his editorship of the journal *La critica* (from 1903 onwards). Croce's domination was so extensive, as Montale said, that "at least four generations nourished themselves on his thought."[51]

According to Montale, Croce's influence was both positive and negative: positive in "clearing the terrain from age-old misunderstandings," and negative in "having given an exclusively spiritual character to the creative *fiat*, connoting as 'extrinsic' the material completion of the work."[52] Nevertheless, in Montale's "Intervista immaginaria" (Imaginary interview), he revealingly writes about Croce:

> After the other war, in [19]19, the absolute immanentism of Gentile gave me much satisfaction, however badly I deciphered the most confusing theory of the pure act. Later, I preferred the great idealistic positivism of Croce.[53]

Certainly, here we are dealing with the philosophy of Croce, and not specifically with his poetics; one might add, the philosophy of Croce is indissolubly linked to his anti-Fascist stance that is shared by Montale. Yet Montale's overall view of Croce is certainly not easy to establish: his own record of meetings with Croce is "not exempt ... from internal contradictions, involuntary discontinuities, and memory tailspins of various order and gradation (and therefore irreducible to a perfectly univocal and 'linear' telos)."[54]

The sticking point, of course, is the notion of translation. That Montale knew of Croce's opinion of poetic translation is beyond question: it was well known. We know that Montale additionally read Croce's *Estetica, Breviario di estetica, L'Aesthetica in nuce, La poesia, La letteratura della nuova Italia*, and other assorted essays.[55] Montale, moreover, frequently declared how certain writers were untranslatable. So, whether or not he ascribed his viewpoint on translation to Croce or not, he was definitely in agreement with him.

According to Croce, as we saw, faithful poetic translations are not possible. But this doesn't mean that poet-translators should abandon translation. Rather, Croce asserts that they shouldn't try to translate poetry literally, but they should aim for "a recreation [*una ricreazione*], which would make them live again in their untranslatable personal tone." To achieve this successful recreation – not a successful reproduction of the original, but a successful creation of a new work of art – several things are necessary. First, "the servile [*servile*] observance of the letter must yield before the right [*diritto*] of the spirit." The translator must grasp "the spirit and tone of a poem," and he must have a "large freedom [*libertà*] in variations and eliminations and additions where he feels them necessary." This freedom isn't absolute, however, and isn't based wholly on the translator's will. At best the translations can "transmit" some of the "original vibrations" and "dynamic power of the original inspiration, the line of its interior rhythm." Indeed, "even a beautiful [*bella*] translation is original as much as an original work!"[56] Nonetheless, the eventual failure of the translation is that it cannot "ever attain rest in itself, interior unity, which belongs to original poems, always remaining with a shadow of uneasiness and disquiet."[57]

While Montale drew on Croce's views, this doesn't mean that he would take them to the extreme end of translation: adaptation, or Lowellian imitations. Montale is careful to ask his own translators not to stray into the territory of Robert Lowell: as he writes to Luciano Rebay, "You are authorized to change many things without arriving at the extremes of Lowell."[58] If we use the helpful three-part theoretical division posited by John Dryden in the seventeenth century – metaphrase, paraphrase, and imitation – Montale utilizes the middle term and process in his poetic versions. Neither "ponies" nor imitations, his poetic translations instead carve their own path, guided by the poet-translator's own poetics and inspiration. His versions of lyric poems restore vibrations of the original, but don't reproduce the exact metre (except in rare cases), style, diction, or phraseology.

Nonetheless, despite this (short) interview, Montale seldom explicitly theorized about translation. Indeed, in an article on Montale's translations, Anna Dolfi writes, "It is with a certain shock … that one discovers the almost total absence of Montalian reflections on translation."[59] When Montale passes judgment on a translation, except on very rare occasions, he always praises the Italian version. His highest praise is for *ricreative* translations, "meravigliosi rifacimenti" (marvellous re-writings).[60] Montale approvingly cites, for instance, Vittorini's version of Erskine Caldwell's *God's little acre*: "It is a betrayal [*tradimento*] from top to bottom, and yet whoever reads the book in Italian and turns to the original will not hesitate to favor the ingenious judgment of the translator."[61] Yet, obviously, these *tradimenti* which equal or surpass the original are rare occurrences: "A meeting like Fenellosa-Pound, which marvelously made some Japanese Noh come to life again [*rivivere*], is not a possible event every day."[62] But it does continue to happen, as the French poet Armand Robin shows, "who splendidly translates and recreates [*ricrea*] without bothering to be faithful to the presumed Cartesian genius of the French language."[63]

Yet in general, despite all these commendations, for Montale, "original works are little [*poco*] translatable," and some are by nature untranslatable, namely, the works of Charles Baudelaire[64] and Guillaume Apollinaire,[65] James Joyce and Marcel Proust.[66] Immense and perhaps fatal difficulty lies in translating William Wordsworth's poetry,[67] T.S. Eliot's theatre,[68] and Henry James's late work.[69] Saul Bellow's *Herzog* is described as "untranslatable,"[70] because of the concentration of slang.

Another difficulty lies in translating lyric poetry that is philosophical at its core:

> The poets of the Dolce Stilnovo, Petrarch, Shakespeare in his sonnets, the great Spanish, English, and German metaphysical (or religious) poets, and more recently Hopkins, Valéry, Yeats, Benn and others expressed ideas acceptable [*accettabili*] only in "that" form. Thus the scarce [*scarsa*] translatability of poetry.[71]

Only in a few instances does Montale criticize translations, namely, those "of little importance, which put to a decisive test the fiber [*fibra*] of certain masterpieces."[72] What are the reasons that lead to Montale's dissatisfaction? We can see this more clearly in his appraisal of translations of Eliot:

> Eliot was up till now (except for rare and partial exceptions) served badly by eager interpreters, in perpetual struggle with inadequate expressive means, with languages that inevitably flatten out the lightness of his recitative.[73]

Here, Montale signals three separate flaws: French translations, while conserving *lo sfumato*, nevertheless significantly water down the English originals; Italian versions end up distorted because of the abundance of elisions, caesuras, and uncommon Italian monosyllables that the Italian translator is forced to use to try to replicate the source language; German translations sentimentalize the original text. The French and Italian versions fail because of their language, their form, as Croce would say; the German translations disappoint because the individuality of the translator gets in the way.

If, then, as we have seen, Montale reserves his highest admiration for what we would call imitations, the poet-translator does, on the other hand, frequently praise literal translations. He writes approvingly about Lino Pellegrini's literal translation of Robert Browning, "a literal translation of B[rowning]'s poems is already in itself praiseworthy and a difficult undertaking; and it is necessary to praise Pellegrini for the pleasing [*felici*] results obtained."[74] Montale justifies the need for a literal translation of Browning because the exact nature of these poems, "rambling and intricate" (*divaganti e intricati*), necessitates a version that helps the reader understand the text. Likewise, Montale asserts that Aurora Ciliberti's "excellent" (*ottima*) translation of Auden couldn't be anything other than literal: it is a "literal version, nor could it be otherwise."[75]

In other cases, he commends Mario Pasi's rendition of the untranslatable Apollinaire, "translated to the letter with great scrupulousness [*scrupolo*],"[76] as well as approving Carlo Izzo's *Poesia inglese contemporanea da Thomas Hardy agli Apocalittici* (Contemporary English poetry from Thomas Hardy to the Apocalyptic poets), which the translator "translated well [*bene*], literally, luckily [*per fortuna*], because every other form of translation was condemned [*condannata*] to failure."[77] One of the defining characteristics of the literal translation in a bilingual edition is its aid to the reader. As Montale notes about translations of Gottfried Benn, "*Aprèslude* published by Scheiwiller: these [poems] in the difficult original text with a useful [*utile*] facing Italian version."[78] The difficulty of the original texts, for Montale, demands a literal translation – in Croce's words, "strumenti per l'apprendimento delle opere originali."[79]

Self-Translation

Montale's view on translation should also be examined in the light of his translation of his own work into other languages. No one has analysed in depth, for instance, Montale's own translation of his *Ossi di seppia* poem entitled "Ripenso il tuo sorriso" (I am thinking again of your smile) into French. This poem, inspired by the dancer Boris Kniaseff, whom Montale met at the home of Bianca and Francesco Messina, was written in 1923, and translated a year later into French, so that the dancer, who didn't know Italian, could read it.[80] This translation was unpublished until Laura Barile's edition of Montale's letters to the Messinas, so clearly it was not considered a polished work of art by the poet himself. Indeed, Montale was unsure how he wished to translate the last word of the poem. Yet it is a precious document, nonetheless, of how Montale actively translated into a language, French, which he always knew better than English (see table 2.1 below).

Evidently, this translation attempts to translate the poem word-for-word into French; the emphasis, indeed, is more on the semantic and

Table 2.1 "Ripenso il tuo sorriso"

Eugenio Montale **"Ripenso il tuo sorriso"**	**Eugenio Montale (self-translation)** **"Je repense à ton sourire"**
Ripenso il tuo sorriso, ed è per me un'acqua limpida [I think again of your smile, and it is for me a clear water]	Je repense à ton sourire, et c'est pour moi comme une eau limpide [I think again of your smile, and it is for me like clear water]
scorta per avventura tra le petraie d'un greto, [glimpsed by chance among the heap of stones of a riverbed,]	par hasard trouvée parmi les tas des pierres d'un grève, [by chance found among the mass of stones of a bank,]
esiguo specchio in cui guardi un'ellera i suoi corimbi; [narrow mirror in an which an ivy watches its corymbs;]	petit miroir dans lequel une lierre regarde ses corymbes; [small mirror in which an ivy watches its corymbs;]
e su tutto l'abbraccio d'un bianco cielo quieto. [and over all the embrace of a calm white sky.]	et au dessus la caresse d'un blanc ciel quiet. [and above the caress of a calm white sky.]
Codesto è il mio ricordo; non saprei dire, o lontano, [This is my memory; I wouldn't be able to say, o distant one,]	Voilà mon souvenir; je ne saurais dire, o lointain, [Here is my memory; I wouldn't be able to say, o distant one,]
se dal tuo volto s'esprime libera un'anima ingenua, [if from your countenance a candid soul expresses itself freely,]	si de ta mine se dégage libre une âme ingénue, [if from your appearance a candid soul liberates itself freely,]
o vero tu sei dei raminghi che il male del mondo estenua [or else you are [one of] those wanderers whom the evil of the world exhausts]	ou si tu est de[s] ces errants que le mal du monde exténue [or if you are of those wanderers whom the evil of the world exhausts]
e recano il loro soffrire con sé come un talismano. [and carry their suffering with them like a talisman.]	et qui portent avec-eux leur souffrance, comme un talisman. [and who carry with them their suffering, like a talisman.]
Ma questo posso dirti, che la tua pensata effigie [But this I can tell you, that your considered effigy]	Mais je peux te dire ça, que la pensée de ton effigie [But I can tell you this, that the thought of your effigy]
sommerge i crucci estrosi in un'ondata di calma, [submerges the fanciful worries in a wave of calm,]	submerge les chagrins bizarres dans une ondée de calme, [submerges the strange sorrows in a wave of calm,]

Eugenio Montale "Ripenso il tuo sorriso"	Eugenio Montale (self-translation) "Je repense à ton sourire"
e che il tuo aspetto s'insinua nella mia memoria grigia [and your appearance insinuates itself in my gray memory]	et que ta figure se glisse dans ma mémoire grise [and your figure slips into my gray memory]
schietto come la cima d'una giovinetta palma ... [pure like the top of a very young palm tree ...]	adroite comme le sommet d'un très-jeune palmier ... [clever like the summit of a very young palm tree ...]
	ou d'une très-jeune palme... [or of a very young palm leaf ...]
Source: Montale, *L'opera in versi*, 30	Source: Montale, *Lettere e poesie*, 161

syntactic replication rather than a recreation or poetic adaptation. The first verse, for example, renders the syntax and lexical original as closely as the two different languages permit. The French version is studded with cognates (which Montale often chose to avoid in his own translations of foreign poetry): "non saprei dire, o lontano" becomes "je ne saurais dire, o lointain"; "in un'ondata di calma" becomes "dans une ondée de calme"; "il male del mondo estenua" becomes "le mal du monde exténue." Phrases like "bianco cielo quieto" and "mia memoria grigia" are all literally translated into French. There are a few situations where Montale did not select the corresponding existing cognate, but chose a French synonym: "sommet" instead of "cime" (It. *cima,* height); "se glisse" in the place of "s'insinuer" (It. *si insinua,* insinuate itself); "petit" and not "exigu" (It. *esiguo,* small). But on occasion, Montale opted for a French word that does not exactly reproduce the meaning of the Italian, having a different nuance entirely: "trouvée" ("scorta"); "caresse" ("abbraccio"); "voilà" ("codesto"); "souci" ("crucci"); "bizarres" ("estrosi"); "adroite" ("schietto"). Out of forty possible cognates (for nouns, verbs, and adjectives),[81] Montale chose thirty-two, which is an impressive number. Eight of the Italian verses rhyme, while only two of the verses in the French translation rhyme (not counting the final, uncertain verse).[82]

The literalism of this translation is consistent with Montale's own penchant for having his poetry be translated in a faithful manner. This is because he wants his poetry to be read and understood: he prefers Croce's "ugly translation," the *commento* (commentary), which helps the reader decipher the text. One case rises above all: Mario Praz's version of Montale's "Arsenio," which was published in T.S. Eliot's 1928 *Criterion*. This translation, "surprising" (*sorprendente*), as Montale called it, is, in his words to Valery Larbaud, a "tour de force of literal translation [*traduction littérale*] and truly … literary [*littéraire*]. It is an uncommon success."[83] Yet an opposing tendency appears in other letters of Montale. For a French translation of "Arsenio," he suggests that it be translated in blank verse, as he tells Nino Frank, a verse he defines as "preoccupied with a more intrinsic than extrinsic musicality, a greater adherence to the shades of spiritual life, a certain pathetic linear aridity, apt to suggest echoes and fantasies of the intelligence, more than the weeping music ... of the early symbolists."[84] In line with following – more the spirit than the letter – are Montale's recommendations to Luciano Rebay, who translated some of his poems into English. As we saw earlier, the Italian poet specifically suggests a non-literal translation method, which nevertheless shouldn't be as free as Robert Lowell's *Imitations*:

> You will see that it is very difficult and a literal version wouldn't do. It is full of hypermetrics, hypometrics, hiatuses, alliteration, faux exprès, questionable caesuras, at the limit (but not beyond) of every possible regular Italian metrical system. Can one find equivalents? I don't know if this is a problem for English and American poets. You are authorized to change many things without arriving at the extremes of Lowell.[85]

Likewise, speaking of his poem "Quando si giunse al borgo del massacro nazista" (When one arrived at the village of the Nazi massacre), Montale informs Rebay that it is not "necessary" (*necessario*) for each translated verse to correspond to an English verse. In fact, if need be, he can take "all possible liberties" (*tutte [le] libertà possibili*).[86] And even more clearly, Montale advises a German translator to completely rewrite some of the stanzas of "Elegia di Pico Farnese" (Elegy of Pico Farnese): "If you can, even if you change everything, make a syncretic *canzonetta* where god and phallus appear ambiguously."[87]

So what does Montale prefer, then, a literal translation of his works, or a freer version? The answer is that even if the Italian poet-translator translates his "Ripenso il tuo sorriso" pedantically, and commends Praz's "tour de force literal translation," he particularly wants artistic translations. Indeed, the fundamental word in his estimation of Praz's version is not *traduction littérale* (literal translation) but *littéraire* (literary). Montale desires Crocean *ricreazioni*: translations that have all the natural rhythm, tone, and subtlety of the original.

Quaderno di Traduzioni

In a 14 November 1941 letter to Contini, spurred on by a recent proposal by his friend Giuseppe De Luca, Montale for the first time raises the question of creating a volume of translations. As the poet informed Contini,

> It wouldn't displease me to do twenty poetic translations for 3000 lire etc., etc. *Doing* [*fare*], not collecting; because besides 2 Eliot [poems] I have nothing decent [*nulla di decente*]. I would therefore need a lot of time. To choose English, some Spanish and maybe two or three not too Buddhist Chinese. The selection would take longer than the execution.[88]

There are a couple of interesting things to note here: first, the possible inclusion of (not too Buddhist) Chinese poets, whom Montale would have read in Giorgia Valensin's translations of Chinese poetry, to which he contributed a notable preface;[89] and second, the fact that Montale considers his previous lyric translations "nulla di decente" besides Eliot, which presumably includes his translations of William Shakespeare, Léonie Adams, and Jorge Guillén.

Montale wrote to Contini at least three other times about his forthcoming volume, in 1947 and 1948. On 13 November 1947, he spoke of "a small volume of my poetic versions (20/22 poems) which is being published in Milan";[90] on 8 January 1948, he noted that "La Meridiana should have sent you a while back a *Cahier* of translations of mine, but they sent it to Domo[dossola]; did you receive it?"[91] And on 20 July of the same year, he wrote to the Italian critic, "My book of transl[ations] is almost ready."[92] In the end, 1,500 copies of the volume were published in September of that year (a large number for the small art house publisher, Meridiana).[93]

The title of Montale's volume of translations is a curious case. On only one other occasion did Montale use the word *quaderno* in his own poetry, and once again as a book title: *Quaderno di quattro anni* (Notebook of four years).[94] There, however, it was the publisher who chose the title and not Montale, who preferred another title.[95] Thus, we might say, the lemma *quaderno* is a hapax legomenon in Montale's oeuvre, which would afterwards become the canonical name for the new genre of volumes of translated lyric poetry. It is certainly meant to indicate less an organic poetry book or a *canzoniere*, than a humble notebook of translation exercises, or "crumbs" (*briciole*). Montale's introduction to the 1948 *Quaderno* explains these "briciole" in part:

From the banquet – certainly not Lucullian – of my greatest translations (which were, between 1938 and 1943, the sole pot boilers allowed to me) some crumbs had fallen under the table that I hadn't thought about collecting. The brotherly care of my friend Vittorio Sereni, to whom I dedicate my *Quaderno*, helped me find them. Some of these exercises – the lyrics of Guillén and two of the poems of Eliot – date back to 1928–29. The rewritings of the three Shakespearean sonnets also come before 1938. The passages from *Midsummer* are from '33; some of them were to be adapted to pre-existing music, and here it would be useless to expect a literal fidelity to the text. In any case, I wanted to publish the original text of all versions for reasons of uniformity.[96]

This book of translations can be fruitfully read in a couple of different ways: first, as a contemporary volume to his own *La bufera e altro*. It is true that Montale's *Quaderno* was published in 1948, eight years before his extraordinary poetic work; yet it does share several key themes with "Silvae," one of the sections of *La bufera e altro*, as highlighted by Romano Luperini:

The collection of these versions brings into the open the same plot of motifs and suggestions that we met in the *Silvae* of *La bufera*: the renewed interest in Eliot, the remoteness and the foreignness of the Muses to the present time (such that Blake's text seems to confirm the Foscolian escape of the *Grazie* or the Hölderlinian departure of the gods), the return of the dead (in Hardy's "Garden seat").[97]

Thus, it is demonstrably the case that many of Montale's predominant poetic themes do return in his *Quaderno di traduzioni*. Indeed, Montale's choice of translations is inevitably guided by his own poetic inclination and inspiration.

Along with reading the *Quaderno di traduzioni* together with "Silvae," as Luperini has masterfully done, one could also focus on the dominance of Anglo-American poetry in the *Quaderno*: a rarity in Italian poetry. This is, of course, in contrast to the Francophilia so apparent in the majority of other Italian poets, from Campana to Ungaretti, Luzi to Caproni. French poetry was the most studied and imitated, by Italian poets up until Montale (and even beyond), and among foreign languages it was well known. Montale was indeed an exception (Attilio Bertolucci, Franco Buffoni, and Giovanni Giudici would later follow him in his Anglophilia) in his appreciation and love for American and English poetry. However this was not due to an *amor de lonh* (love from afar), as Russian and Czech poetry attracted Giudici, but owing to the affinity between Montale's poetics and English poetry. Laura Barile rightly notes that "perhaps no other poet of our twentieth century had such an intense, lively, and modern tie with Anglo-Saxon poetry."[98] This Anglophilia explains, for example, the inclusion of predominantly modern poets. He was not imbued with devotion to classical poetry, like others of his generation (e.g., Quasimodo). It therefore follows, as Pier Vincenzo Mengaldo writes, that Montale chose authors, except for Shakespeare, not in the distant past (namely, Greek and Roman antiquity). In other words, Montale lacks "the 'archaeological' component, of self-disguise in 'someone distant' whose mask can be worn, which occupies such a great part of twentieth-century translating."[99] A case of the latter is Edoardo Sanguineti's *Quaderno di traduzioni*, whose three translated authors are Lucretius, Shakespeare, and Goethe.

Montale opted to open his volume of translations with Shakespeare's sonnet 22, translated most likely for Irma Brandeis.[100] The Italian poet-translator was about forty-five years old when he translated this sonnet, and fifty-two when the *Quaderno* was first published. This emphasis on youth is even more intensified in the translation; while Shakespeare's original phrases the sentence in a negative fashion, "My glass shall not persuade me I am old,"[101] Montale changes this to the positive "Allo specchio, ancor giovane mi credo" (In the mirror, I still think I am young). By now, Montale and Brandeis have not written to each other in a decade (since 1938); their romantic relationship is concluded, but she remained a touchstone for Montale's poetic output. We will analyse in more detail the translation of Shakespeare's sonnets when we later compare Montale's and Ungaretti's translation methods.

Why Montale selected to include several fragments of *A Midsummer Night's Dream* can be ascribed to his impish spirit (*spirito folletto*) of which Glauco Cambon speaks;[102] but there is one particular passage that surely resonated with his own poetry, with the theme of revenants: the dead returning and present among the living. This is Shakespeare's Puck speaking:

...Ecco l'ore notturne
in cui le tombe s'aprono e i fantasmi
scivolan via dall'urne
dei camposanti.[103]

[Here are the nocturnal hours
when the tombs open up and the ghosts

> slip away from the urns
> of the graveyards.]

It recalls the poem of Thomas Hardy, also included by Montale in his *Quaderno*, "The Garden Seat": "At night when reddest flowers are black / those who once sat thereon come back ..."[104] The same fragment of *A Midsummer Night's Dream* also is tied, in Montale's translation, to two other translations in the *Quaderno*. In this fragment, Puck says "Ora i tizzoni consumati splendono ..."[105] (Now the spent embers shine). This recalls Hopkins's "Pied Beauty," where Montale translated "fresh-firecoal" as "crollo di tizzi giovani nel fuoco"[106] (fall of young embers into the fire). Likewise, the verb "rugge" (roars) in Puck's "Rugge il leone affamato" (The famished lion roars) recurs as a rhyme in Montale's translation of Djuna Barnes's "Transfiguration": "Rugge e fugge Lucifero"[107] (Lucifer roars and flees). These lexical ties are important, since they indicate the idiolect of Montale, his specific diction, and they help to make the *Quaderno* cohere.

More ink has been spilled on the relationship between Eugenio Montale and T.S. Eliot than on Montale's relationship with any other foreign poet. Yet there is not a sufficiently clear description of the relationship of the two poets. Part of this is due to Montale's own ambiguous and changing statements throughout the years. As a young poet, he claimed to be influenced by the most important English poet. Yet as Montale achieved recognition and fame in his own right, he began downplaying the role of Eliot in his own poetry. For instance, in 1960, when he had become one of the most famous Italian poets, Montale wrote:

> Someone criticized me for having here [in *Le occasioni*] adopted the Eliotian method of the objective correlative: which is providing an object (the poem) in which the cause is included in the form of a suggestion, not, however, explained or commented on in psychological terms. The truth is that in 1929 I had translated two brief poems of Eliot, but I knew nothing else of that poet; while many pages of mine of the previous years already were imposing that path on me.[108]

In a 1974 interview, Montale spoke briefly of his involvement with Eliot's poetry:

> I translated three poems by Eliot brought to me by Mario Praz, who asked me to make an attempt at translation. I did it. Afterwards I met Eliot, with

> a lot of pleasure on both sides. But I mean, I didn't go deep into the rest of his production. Especially the *Four Quartets*, I have never approached them. He is certainly an important poet ... It's only the early Eliot that I approached.[109]

Indeed, Eliot and Montale were both influenced by French symbolism and Robert Browning's innovative dramatic monologues. In 1948, Mario Praz made the first important attempt to show Eliot's influence on Montale.[110] Substantially, Praz hypothesized three things. First, that Montale and Eliot shared the same "message" (*messaggio*).[111] Second, that Montale utilizes some of the same stylistic traits as Eliot. Third, that their poetry lives in the same "arid landscape" (*arido paesaggio*).[112] This article was written before Montale's *La bufera e altro*, and the whole *verso* (after the *recto*) of Montale's career. It would be necessary now to update the references. Montale's work underwent three separate phases of Eliotian influence. First, Montale's *Ossi di seppia* was similar in landscape and negative message to *The Waste Land*. His volume *Le occasioni* was based on the concept theorized by Eliot as the "objective correlative," where objects become "in the poetic metamorphosis, an 'occasion' for poetic recollection and genesis."[113] His *La bufera e altro* is infused with the "Christian symbology" as well as other important symbols in Eliot's *Four Quartets*.[114] And Montale's *verso*, his later work, as Laura Barile contends, is influenced by Eliot's ability to "disguise himself" (*travestirsi*), his "'dressed up' attitude, in falsetto, of his final books."[115]

As for Montale's translations of Eliot – in the *Quaderno* are three, "Canto di Simeone" (A song for Simeon), "La figlia che piange," and "Animula" – the first is a genuine masterpiece, rightfully anthologized by many. Here, "la leggerezza del suo recitativo" (the lightness of his recitative) cited by Montale as indicative of Eliot's verse is conveyed in the translation. The poem, as George Talbot maintains, attracted Montale for "its tone of renunciation, consonant with the tone of his own poems"[116] from *Ossi di seppia*. While Eliot infused this poem with the structure and diction of the Anglican version of the "Nunc dimittis," Montale made three fundamental alterations in the poem that complicate its religious interpretation as intended by Eliot.[117] First, Montale eliminated the liturgical repetition of "Grant us thy peace,"[118] by rephrasing it every time ("Accordaci la pace"[119] [grant us (thy) peace], "dacci la pace tua"[120] [give us your peace], and "Concedimi la pace"[121] [bestow on me (your) peace]). Second, he modified "the stations of the mountain of desolation,"[122] with the key theological references to the Stations of the Cross and Golgotha, into "la sosta nei monti desolati"[123] (the stop in the desolate mountains). And lastly by adding the indefinite article "un" and removing the adjective "certain," Montale generalized into abstraction the allusion to the Virgin Mary: "the certain hour of maternal sorrow"[124] becomes "l'ora di un materno dolore"[125] (the hour of a maternal sorrow). The explanation for these substantial ideological changes has to do, as Ernesto Livorni states, with the fact that "Montale's secular ideal cannot correspond with Eliot's faith."[126] That Montale's ideology, along with his own poetics, adapts Eliot in this way, can be seen in Croce's own words, quoted earlier, explaining why a translation is never a replica of the original: "ogni traduzione, infatti, o sminuisce e guasta, ovvero crea una nuova espressione."[127]

Montale's volume of translations is, as critics have noted, predominantly English; only Jorge Guillén, Joan Maragall, and Oskar Milosz break this monolingualism. The case of Guillén is rather surprising. Here is a poet whose pure poetry lies diametrically opposed to Montale's own, as Roberto Gigliucci finely puts it,

> To summarize: Guillén, supreme twentieth-century poet of the "pure" and abstract-emblematic style, even if at the service of an exclamatory praise of the real; Montale, the exceptional representative, in Italy, of the physical-metaphysical tradition, impure in a modern way and simultaneously tensed towards an impossible and impoverished transcendence.[128]

Montale's translations of Guillén, cold, and somewhat desultory, have curiously and occasionally been marred by a few textual errors. First, there is a notable Montale gaffe, due to a "false friend," in a translation of Guillén's "Presagio." In 1931, Montale translated "Eres ya la fragancia de tu sino" (you are the fragrance of your destiny) as "Tu sei come il profumo del tuo seno"[129] (You are like the fragrance of your breast). He later corrected this in the first, 1948 edition of his *Quaderno di traduzioni* to "In te si fa profumo anche il destino"[130] (In you, even destiny becomes fragrance). Yet in the same poem, a typographical error crept in. Montale's 1931 version of Guillén's Spanish verse "Te sostiene / la unidad invasora y absoluta" (Invasive and absolute unity / supports you) reads "ti sostiene / l'irrompente unità dell'assoluto"[131] (the irruptive unity of the absolute / supports you). When this version is printed in Anceschi's and Porzio's 1945 anthology of translations, *Poeti antichi e moderni tradotti dai lirici nuovi*, a typist's error changes Montale's version to "ti sostiene / un'irrompente verità di assoluto"[132] (an irruptive, absolute truth supports you). *Unità* (unity) became *verità* (truth). Montale, however, keeps the error, incorporating it into his 1948 *Quaderno*, simply changing the word order: "un'irrompente / verità di assoluto ti sostiene"[133] (an irruptive / absolute truth supports you).

While it is true, on a metrical level, that "in his translation of 'El Cisne' [The swan] Montale gives proof of his exceptional technical bravura, rendering the text in the same original metrical system,"[134] there still seems to be something artificial or unnatural in Montale's translations. That scholars have found similar phrasings to Ungaretti, whose poetics are so divergent from Montale's own, raises the question of whether, in fact, Montale was himself translating Guillén into a foreign hermetic language. Here, then, is the point. As scholars have noted, the bridge between *Ossi di seppia* and *Le occasioni*, was, in part, built on a utilization of the type of purified syntax and language used by Guillén. Indeed, we would not expect any other motivation for translating such a diverse figure, and Montale, in 1975, stated that he translated the poems not from a spiritual affinity but because "they seemed to me easily translatable."[135] That is, translating them allowed him to incorporate Guillén's language, and the focus on the symbol that would become not isolated, as in the tradition of pure poetry followed by the Spanish poet, but "defeated by the discourse."[136] In Piero Bigongiari's words, the symbol "becomes correlative."[137] Yet Montale's versions of Guillén are often paraphrastic (*parafrastiche*), as Croce would say, and could be described as "simple commentaries on the original."

As for Catalan, Montale translated both Joan Maragall's poem "El cant spiritual" (The spiritual song) as well as the Catalan libretto of Manuel de Falla's *Atlantida* (Atlantis), based on Jacint Verdaguer's eponymous poem. Montale's decision to translate a poem by Maragall has surprised more than a critic or two. Leonardo Sciascia justifies it with the term "contraddizione" (contradiction):

> The "Cant" is one of the least Montalian things which Montale went near in his activity as translator ... At a certain moment of his life, on a certain day, he felt the need to translate, to make his own, yielding to what we might call contradiction (*la contraddizione*).[138]

Indeed, Montale said that Maragall was a "mestre de gay saber" (master of cheerful knowledge), which the Italian poet never managed to become. As Montale wrote in a late poem, "A Leone Traverso" (To Leone Traverso),

Sognai anch'io di essere un giorno mestre
De gay saber; e fu speranza vana.
Un lauro risecchito non dà foglie
Neppure per l'arrosto ... Mai fu gaio
Né savio né celeste il mio sapere.[139]

[I too dreamt of one day being a master
Of cheerful knowledge; and it was a vain hope.
A dried out laurel tree doesn't even shed leaves
For a roast ... never cheerful
Nor wise nor celestial was my knowledge.]

It will become obvious how this difference in personality (and philosophy) moved the translation away from the original Pantheistic religious meaning.

In the preface to his version of Maragall, Montale revealingly explains his translation and its inevitable flaws:

> It is not difficult to transport the Catalan hendecasyllables of the most famous lyric of Maragall, the "Cant espiritual" [Spiritual song], into Italian hendecasyllables. A diligent literal version is enough, or so it seems. Suppressing then, as I have done, a pleonastic verse and a half and some useless exclamations, the poem even seems to us to gain [*guadagnare*] something. When the work is done, however, one sees that the best part of it has been lost, that crackling sound of green pine cones thrown in the fire, which is particular to all of Catalan poetry. But it would be vain to try to obtain such effects with complicated alliteration and displays of unusual accented words. With this, one would give an affected and baroque idea of an extremely simple poet.[140]

In other words, in Montale's view, what can be reproduced – the metrical structure of hendecasyllables – is little in comparison with what is lost, the particular phonetics of Catalan. A diligent literal version (*diligente versione letterale*) doesn't make up for the distinctive crackling of the original. As Loreto Busquets notes, the Maragall poem has no fewer than eighty monosyllabic words, and the Italian version, in most cases, has to be translated with at least two-syllable words.[141] This challenge is even more pressing than the translation of English monosyllabic verse like Hopkins's.

Montale removes much of the repetition of the original Catalan text, especially its colloquialisms.[142] Besides the suppression of a verse and a half, he eliminates numerous words, from verbs ("que passa" [which passes], "es" [is], "cercant" [searching]), to adverbs and adjectives ("tan" [so much], "tot" [all], "aquest" [this], "sempre" [always]) and nouns such as "Senyor" (Lord). We can notice, as well, his tendency to drop definite articles (a typical hermetic practice) in an attempt to replicate the velocity of the Catalan verse, resulting in "eterna pace" (eternal peace), "morte" (death), "ombra" (shadow), "fede" (faith), and "stelle" (stars). On several occasions, Montale significantly alters the terminology of the poem. First, when Maragall speaks of the earthly illusion of the far and the near ("lluny" and "prop"), these are turned by Montale into "qui" (here) and "laggiù" (down there).[143] "Laggiù" highlights, indeed, the terrestrial nature of the "inganno" (deceit); rather than the horizontal emphasis on what is near and far away, Montale focuses on the vertical nature of down here / there, as opposed to up there, in the sky, in the heavens.

Montale's rendition of two verses of the poem, in particular, suggests how his poetics differ from Maragall's. In the original, the last two verses of stanza three are

> I el compte de lo molt, i el poc, i el massa,
> Enganyador, perquè ja tot ho és tot?
>
> [And (would) the calculation of the much, and the little, and the too much
> (be) deceitful, because everything is everything?]

Montale renders them as:

> E il calcolo del poco e il molto e il troppo
> Solo un inganno, perché il tutto è il nulla?
>
> [And the calculation of the little and the much and the too much
> (is) only a deceit, because all is nothingness?]

As Mario Puppo first noted,[144] Montale translated "tot ho és tot" as "il tutto è il nulla" (all is nothingness), instead of a literal Italian translation like "il tutto è il tutto" (all is all). For, as Puppo suggests, "For Montale, but certainly not for Maragall, everything [*il tutto*] can coincide with nothingness [*nulla*]."[145] Indeed, Maragall uses *tot* five times in his poem, while Montale translates it only once, shunning it on the other occasions. Another point bears mentioning: Montale transforms the adjective *enganyador* (deceitful) into a noun, *inganno* (deceit/illusion), that brings to mind his "Forse un mattino andando": "Poi / come s'uno schermo, s'accamperanno di gitto / Alberi case colli per l'inganno consueto"[146] (Then / as if on a screen, / Trees, houses, hills will encamp due to the normal illusion). Likewise, he underlines this noun by adding *solo* (only) to the translation: *solo un inganno*. Indeed, that Montale translated "tot ho és tot" as "il tutto è il nulla" makes sense now, considering his own poem, where "vedrò compirsi il miracolo: / il nulla alle mie spalle"[147] (I will see the miracle take place: / nothingness at my back).

By dint of reducing extraneous elements in the poem – including a verse and a half – and in certain cases purposely translating the opposite semantic meanings, Montale creates a new poem, which recalls the original but has a different philosophical and religious expression at its core. As with his version of Eliot's "Canto di Simeone," Montale does not hesitate to draw the poem away from dogmatic religious beliefs towards a drastic scepticism. This "buona" translation, as Croce would say, is an "approximation [*approssimazione*], which has the original value [*valore originale*] of a work of art and can exist by itself."[148]

The only translation that Montale called an "adattamento" (adaptation) was his version of Djuna Barnes's "Transfiguration," which Montale published in *Corriere della Sera* on 17 February 1974, and then included in his revised 1975 *Quaderno di traduzioni*.[149] While Montale doesn't speak anywhere of Barnes's poetry, he does say that her novel *Nightwood* is "judged untranslatable."[150] In Montale's "Trasfigurazioni" (Transfigurations) the first thing to be noticed is the transformation, the *transfiguration*, of the title into the plural, a stylistic trait frequent in Italian poetic tradition.

The metrical structure of the original is iambic tetrameter with frequent end rhymes. Montale's version, with irregular rhythm, does away with the end-rhymes, but does have some half-rhymes ("orizzonte" / "morte" [horizon / death]), assonance ("Profeta" / "sgretola" [prophet / crumble to dust]), and alliteration ("farfuglia" [mumble] / "pendaglio" [pendant]). As he said in an interview, "Instead of rhyme I have used assonance and alliteration, which replace it. I couldn't keep the rhyme." Indeed, he said that the rhyme would have made the Italian "horrible!"[151] The original poem's alliteration and assonance is often paralleled in Montale's Italian: the alliterative *s* in "Un *s*ole furibondo, ar*s*o di *s*ete" (A wrathful sun, burning with thirst), or *g* in "Ru*gg*e e fu*gg*e Lucifero" (Lucifer roars and flees), or the double *l* (that tic of Montale noted by Rebecca West)[152] in "la coccine*ll*a ... la rose*ll*ina" (The lady bug ... the little rose).

As for the content of this poem, Barnes imagines the cosmos going back in the opposite direction: time and causality are turned upside down. Insects turn back into larva, Abel returns to life, Lucifer comes up from below, Eden is restored as a pristine paradise, and all the future days are eaten by the first day. Montale, on the other hand, does not follow the poem's meaning. Both poet and translator have Abel rising from the dust, but Barnes has Cain lifting his knife "from the thrust," while Montale has "La lama di Caino ha vibrato il colpo" (Cain's blade let fly the blow). These are two opposing actions: Barnes's Cain, instead of lowering the knife for the thrust, "lifts from the thrust." Montale's Cain, on the other hand, has already killed Abel. So Barnes's cause and effect reversal is not respected by the Italian poet. Or, when Barnes imagines Adam's rib being placed back, and Eve returning inside Adam, Montale keeps the meaning of the first verse and not the second: "accanto a questa piaga c'è una donna che piange" (Next to this wound there is a woman who weeps). Instead, Eve is pictured as standing next to Adam's "piaga." Finally, the last couplet in Barnes's poem reinforces the fiction of time working backwards: the last day feeds on the first. But in Montale it is actually the sun that performs the action, an action that is no longer a chronological reversal. Rather, now the sun "sugge l'ultimo giorno e insieme il primo" (sucks up the last day together with the first). While in Barnes's poem time returns to its origins, in Montale's translation the end of time is hastened and the (solar) apocalypse has come.

Despite the vast semantic differences between the poem and the translation, there are evident points of contact. Most importantly, the couplet structure is retained – even with a different rhythm – and many Italian cognates or near-synonyms are used in the poetic "adattamento." Indeed, we might say of this adaptation, with Croce, that "a translation, however different from the original, is still always inspired by that work and is founded on its re-evocation [*rievocazione*]." Montale has *transfigured* the original poem, leaving a recognizable structure and semantic frame; what has changed is the coherent spirit and intention of the poem that (only) in English imagines the grand reversal of the arrow of time.

The most substantial additions to the 1975 edition of the *Quaderno* were the three poems of Yeats. The Irish poet, "a completely untranslatable poet,"[153] fascinated Montale, despite Yeats's overly fanciful mythologies ("esoteric wisdom in which he did not believe").[154] Montale's choice of including additional poems gives Yeats the largest place in the *Quaderno* after Shakespeare and Guillén. These new translations should be seen in the light of Montale's own advanced age, and inevitably, cannot fail to conjure up the phantom of Irma Brandeis, of their youth, and of Montale's own poetic power to reflect on the past. The two key themes of Yeats's poems, as Éanna Ó Ceallacháin notes, are Eros and poetry, within the context of old age.[155]

In this Italian translation of "When You Are Old" (the original text, of course, being Pierre Ronsard's French poem "Quand vous serez bien vieille, au soir, à la chandelle" [When you are old, at night, at candlelight]), the poet tells his beloved to read his own love poetry, in which she figures so prominently, so that she can remember her "occhi d'un tempo e le loro ombre" (eyes of long ago and their shadows). Emilio Guariglia's acute analysis reveals the following changes in Montale's version.[156] First, our poet-translator suffuses the translation with references to a "tu": there are ten references, four more than the original, reinforcing the link between the poet and the beloved, as well as that between the beloved and the personified "Amore." Second, Montale uses a marked style that purposely recalls Stilnovistic poetry in language ("dolcezza" [sweetness], "dolce" [sweet], "amore" [love], "bellezza" [beauty], and "volto" [visage]) quite foreign to his own poetic production. The acme of this return to the Italian "dolce stil novo" (sweet new style) is found in the final stanza, where Montale turns Yeats's indirect discourse into direct speech: the beloved now speaks directly to the personification of "Amore." Here Guariglia aptly brings up Dante's sonnet "Un dì si venne a me Malinconia" (One day Melancholy came to me), where Dante writes that "guardai e vidi Amore, che venia ... / e certo lagrimava"[157] (I watched and I saw Love, who came ... / and certainly was crying). Montale's own belief in the *Donna angelo* has been explored in various studies,[158] but at least one quote from Montale's sister Marianna should bring this well into focus. As she wrote to a friend of hers about her brother, "[Montale] speaks of glances: he says that he needs only one glance to penetrate into the depths of a soul, to have its definitive, perfect impression, the intuition that doesn't go wrong. He speaks of eyes that he has seen and which have revealed everything to him."[159] It should therefore be evident that this poetic version can be read as a confirmation of Croce's dictum that "even a beautiful translation is original as much as an original work!"

In these versions from Yeats, Fiorenzo Fantaccini suggests that "the characteristic that one immediately observes in these translations is the all in all substantial faithfulness to the form [*fedeltà alla forma*]."[160] Yet it is unclear why a modification in the number of verses of the original, combined with a removal of regular rhyme (substituted by assonance and alliteration) and a shift in poetic metres, along with a change in the punctuation should be called "fedeltà alla forma." In Montale's versions from Yeats, we clearly hear what Croce called "the spirit and the tone" of the originals.

Montale chose to end his 1975 edition of his *Quaderno di traduzioni* with the Italian poet Fernando Bandini's "Nimbus," a Latin translation of Montale's poem "La bufera."[161] While the editors of Montale's *Opera in versi* didn't include it, even though by all rights it should have been incorporated for its structural significance, the poem ends the *Quaderno di traduzioni* on a specific note. The final Latin verse, "gestu iussisti, tenebras initura, valere" (With a gesture you said, entering the darkness, farewell), translating the Italian "mi salutasti – per entrar nel buio"[162] (you greeted me – to enter into the dark) is addressed to Clizia. The Italian poem, "La bufera," composed many years back, thus returns with a heightened meaning. So much time has passed, and Clizia is by now a myth that no longer, except in certain moments, recurs in Montale's verse. And yet the post–Clizia world, the post-war world, inevitably has her as a fundamental referent. As Montale wrote in 1979, in "Poiché la vita fugge" (Since life flees), "Fummo felici un giorno, un'ora un attimo / e questo potrà essere distrutto?"[163] (One day we were happy, an hour an instant / and can this be destroyed?).

Montale Versus Ungaretti

That Montale and Ungaretti, the two most famous modern Italian poets, differ so much in their own poetics, is reinforced by their vastly contrasting translation methods. We will now compare the versions by Montale and Ungaretti of Shakespeare's Sonnet 33. Before we begin, however, it is necessary to say a few words about Ungaretti as translator. Indeed, though Montale was the first poet-translator to entitle his volume of translations a *Quaderno di traduzioni*, Ungaretti's collection of poetic translations in 1936, entitled simply *Traduzioni* (Translations), was among the most important precedents for Montale's own *Quaderno*.

Ungaretti shared both Croce's and Montale's belief that the translation of poetry is impossible. As he explains,

> Poetry is individual and inimitable to such a degree that it is untranslatable. Translation is the crucial test [*la prova del fuoco*] of how much it [poetry] is individual and inimitable. The rhythm is not translatable, each language deriving the groupings of its rhythm from its specific character and length of its specific words in the most untransferably particular way. The syllabic quality is not translatable, the first sensible difference between two languages residing mainly in phonic values. The content is not translatable, since each content is animated and involved in the secret of a personality. It wouldn't otherwise be a unique personality, as is, fatally, every human person. The content will thus be subject to interpretation too. At last neither the form nor the style is translatable, in which everything else adds up, is fused together and lives, and becomes moving (*commovente*), if all the rest wasn't and couldn't be translatable.[164]

For Ungaretti, then, the rhythm, phonic texture, content, and style of a poem cannot be faithfully transported into another language. Despite this pre-announced failure, "there are no other roads to follow if not that of literal translation. In some way, always badly [*malamente*], one can give an idea of the original text, respecting its meanings, respecting them however much is possible."[165] So why does Ungaretti translate? "Simply to make an original work of poetry" (*fare opera originale di poesia*).[166] Ungaretti and Montale both wish to make such a work with their translations, but their methods of translation are incredibly different. Ungaretti opts for "traduzione letterale" (literal translation), while Montale prefers to recreate Shakespeare in Italian dress.

Shakespeare attracted Ungaretti immensely, and it took him fifteen years to publish his *40 sonetti di Shakespeare* (40 sonnets of Shakespeare).[167] Indeed, as the Italian poet writes, it was "a great adventure of my literary life,"[168] and it helped him in his own "investigations" that formed a bond between Petrarch and later European poetry, like that of the Bard. The adventure lasted so long, since he needed to find what he considered to be the correct style, tone, and metrics. First of all, in his opinion, "to translate a poem especially means trying to capture its expressive sign, of style, which distinguishes it and reveals it."[169] Second, he aimed for "a tone that in my text seemed to me to have derived the accent, and even the unfolding in the phrasing of the articulations, from Petrarch in his energetic moments."[170] Third, considering that English and Italian have different rhythms, "the difficulty was resolved by itself, keeping in mind that in a same group of words, the quantity of Italian syllables is superior to English syllables in the relation of about 16 to 10 or 11."[171] For this reason Ungaretti eschewed hendecasyllables and used longer verses. Yet this a priori metrical choice did not imply that the metrical patterning was preset:

> Nine-syllable, seven-syllable, eleven-syllable, five-syllable lines, never being mere rules for me, aren't therefore born in me from preconceived ideas, after I have found the words; but they are born inside me together [*insieme*] with the words, naturally shifting the meaning of the latter. When there is a hendecasyllable in my translation, it is because the sense of the translation, that is the words themselves of the original, dictated that movement, and none other, to the translation that attempted to be exact in meaning.[172]

In general, Ungaretti wanted to free himself and Shakespeare from previous encrustations. As he wrote, "It was important for me to provide, above all to myself, an interpretation of Shakespeare that wouldn't deceive me; and I had to avoid many types of blunders: of words; or of an entire orientation: that emphatic one of the Romantics, that gossipy one of twentieth-century writers, that muffled one of so many others."[173]

Table 2.2 shows the two translations, with Shakespeare's original text.

Two things are immediately clear, one of which we already referred to. While Ungaretti uses a mixture of long verses, Montale translates into hendecasyllables. Likewise, Ungaretti refuses to use rhyme which Montale on the other hand uses in a minor key, with some off-rhymes, along with assonance and alliteration. Thus, Ungaretti puts aside the traditional structures of a poem: metre and rhyme. While the distinguished professor Agostino Lombardo judged Ungaretti's version as among the most "scrupulous,"[174] the same translation contains blemished verses such as the final couplet, as critics have noticed.[175] Montale, on the other hand, aims for the "maximum concentration"[176] of the poetic text, while Ungaretti seems more concerned with reproducing the semantic meaning of the text. In doing so, Ungaretti frequently alters the word order of the original English in a search to "express with supreme exactness" the original. He aims for direct, "secret contact"[177] with the author. And yet his version leaves much to be desired. Rather than "a compromise between two spirits" as Ungaretti ideally conceived of translation, his translation is more a serviceable pony than a happy offspring. It is, like some of Montale's translations of Guillén, "un commento" (a commentary), in Croce's terminology.

Table 2.2 "Sonnet 33"

William Shakespeare "Sonnet 33"	**Eugenio Montale "Sonetto XXXIII"**	**Giuseppe Ungaretti "Sonetto XXXIII"**
Full many a glorious morning have I seen	Spesso, a lusingar vette, vidi splendere [Often, while it flattered peaks, I saw shine]	Ho veduto più d'un mattino in gloria [I saw more than a morning in glory]
Flatter the mountain-tops with sovereign eye,	sovranamente l'occhio del mattino, [in a sovereign manner the eye of morning,]	Con lo sguardo sovrano le vette lusingare, [Flatter the peaks with its sovereign gaze,]
Kissing with golden face the meadows green,	e baciar d'oro verdi prati, accendere [and kiss green meadows with gold, kindle]	Baciare d'aureo viso i verdi prati, [Kiss with a golden countenance the green meadows,]
Gilding pale streams with heavenly alchemy;	pallidi rivi d'alchimie divine. [Pallid streams with divine alchemies.]	Con alchimia di paradiso tingere i rivi pallidi, [With paradisiacal alchemy dye the pallid streams,]
Anon permit the basest clouds to ride	Poi vili fumi alzarsi, intorbidata [Then (I saw) vile fumes rise up,]	E poi a vili nuvole permettere [And then permit the vile clouds]
With ugly rack on his celestial face,	d'un tratto quella celestiale fronte, [suddenly that celestial forehead suddenly clouded,]	Di fluttuargli sul celestiale volto [To float on his celestial visage]
And from the forlorn world his visage hide,	e fuggendo a occidente il desolato [and the desolate world escaping to the west,]	Con osceni fumi sottraendolo all'universo orbato, [With obscene fumes withdrawing it from the blind universe,]
Stealing unseen to west with this disgrace:	mondo, l'astro celare il viso e l'onta. [(I saw) the star hide its visage and shame.]	Mentre verso ponente non visto scompariva, con la sua disgrazia. [While towards the west it disappeared unseen, with its disgrace.]
Even so my sun one early morn did shine	Anch'io sul far del giorno ebbi il mio sole [I too at daybreak had my sun]	Uguale l'astro mio brillò di primo giorno [Likewise my star twinkled early]
With all triumphant splendour on my brow;	e il suo trionfo mi brillò sul ciglio: [and its triumph gleamed on my eyebrow:]	Trionfando splendido sulla mia fronte; [Triumphing splendid on my forehead;]

Table 2.2 "Sonnet 33" (*Continued*)

William Shakespeare "Sonnet 33"	Eugenio Montale "Sonetto XXXIII"	Giuseppe Ungaretti "Sonetto XXXIII"
but, out! alack! he was but one hour mine,	ma, ahimè, poté restarvi un'ora sola, [but, alas, it could remain there a sole hour,]	Ma, ah! Non fu mio che per un'ora sola, [Ma, alas! It was not mine except for a sole hour,]
The region cloud hath masked him from me now.	rapito dalle nubi in cui s'impiglia. [kidnapped by the clouds in which it gets tangled up.]	Il nuvolo della regione già lo maschera a me. [The region cloud already hides him from me.]
Yet him for this my love no whit dis-daineth;	Pur non ne ho sdegno: bene può un terrestre [Yet I don't have disdain for it: well might an earthly]	Non l'ha in disdegno tuttavia il mio amore: [Yet not in disdain does my love have it:]
Suns of the world may stain when heaven's sun staineth.	sole abbuiarsi, se è così il celeste. [sun darken, if such is the celestial one.]	Astri terreni possono macchiarsi se il sole del cielo si macchia. [Earthly stars can be stained if heaven's sun is stained.]
Source: Montale, *Quaderno di traduzioni*, 18	Source: Montale, *Quaderno di traduzioni*, 19	Source: Ungaretti, *Vita d'un uomo: traduzioni poetiche*, 167

It is impossible, on the other hand, to forget while reading Montale's translation that we are reading a poem and not prose, because of the poetic elements (rhythm, rhyme, assonance, alliteration, and poetic concentration). His version is meant as music for our ears, and it succeeds admirably in such a goal. Certainly the familiarity with this sonnet form must be factored in, since, as scholars have long noted, Montale used the Elizabethan sonnet form in four of his own poems in *La bufera e altro* (in *Finisterre*).[178] In this particular translation of Shakespeare, as in his other translations generally speaking, Montale often removes repetition. "Sun," "world," "stain(eth)," "cloud(s)," and "face" appear two or three times in English. Yet Montale doesn't translate any word identically – either he omits it the second (or third) instance (as with "cloud[s]," "face," and "sun"), or he translates it differently ("mondo" and "terrestre," or "fumi" and "nubi"). On a metrical level, he varies the hendecasyllable through added enjambment, like "desolato / mondo" (desolate / world) and "terrestre / sole" (earthly / sun). Moreover, he diminishes explicit personifications, eliminating "face" in "kissing with golden face" ("baciar d'oro")[179] or "permit." As Rachel Meoli Toulmin states, "Montale eludes every anthropomorphic eco."[180] This is not a philological word-for-word translation, but a Crocean "recreation."

Translation Techniques

We have read Montale's translations in the light of Croce's theory of the impossibility of translating poetic texts. Montale, by shunning a literal, word-for-word approach to translation, instead strove to create an independent poem in Italian. One repeated axiom in studies of Montale's translations, originally posited by Gilberto Lonardi, is that he "loves to find for himself an already-given *form* with which he can reckon, meaning that form will be respected, in substance, by the translator."[181] This is hardly accurate and is a misleading characterization. Montale rarely uses the equivalent metre of the original. Indeed, he almost always avoided metrical and analogical translations (e.g., either imitative or functional metrical equivalence) in his versions. Indeed, there are twenty foreign poems in the *Quaderno* that use rhyme as a structuring device. Yet, there is not one translation in which Montale end-rhymes every verse, in contrast to the English, French, and Spanish originals. In only four of these twenty poems does he even rhyme half of the verses; in more of these poems, his versions have no end-rhymes at all. Overall, quantitatively speaking, he end-rhymes under 20 per cent of their verses (80/435). Although Montale does not conserve the identical pattern of rhymes, he does, nevertheless, hint at them, and substitutes their phonic texture through the use of prolific assonance, alliteration, half-rhymes and internal rhymes. So, for example, in Barnes's "Transfiguration," we see the alliteration in "farfuglia" / "pendaglio," the assonance in "Profeta / sgretola." In his translation of Hopkins, as Laura Barile points out, Montale translates Hopkins's curtal sonnet of ten and a half verses into fourteen, turns Hopkins's *sprung rhythm* into almost all hendecasyllables, breaks up the syntactical layout of the original through massive enjambment, and omits the prevalent end-rhyming of the English.[182] All of this is done in the "battle to dig another dimension into our heavy polysyllabic language."[183]

As for the syntactical and lexical elements of Montale's poetic versions, his use of variation has been remarked upon by many critics: a classic example is his version of Hardy's "Garden seat," which has been analysed by Mengaldo.[184] There, Montale breaks up the massive anaphora and refrains: for instance, Hardy's "for they are as light as upper air, / they are as light as upper air!" becomes "perché sono leggeri come l'aria / di lassù, perché sono fatti d'aria!"[185] (because they are light like the air / up there, because they are made of air!). Here, we see two other prominent characteristics of Montale the translator: the use of added enjambment ("l'aria di lassù"), and the change in punctuation, which is another case of Montale's predilection for variation. Along with these structural and stylistic changes, Montale often adapts the ideological content and context of the original poem according to his own philosophical tastes. He removes the religious specificity in Eliot; he voids Maragall's pantheist conclusions; and he elides the theosophy of Yeats. He openly domesticates the French poem by Milosz, where the "Polish-Lithuanian world"[186] becomes Italianized. His domesticating approach does not attempt to bring the reader towards the text, but the text towards the reader.

Conclusion

This chapter has ranged wide and far in treating a poet-translator of the first order whose translation career was both influential and notorious. Translations of first-caliber stand next to signed translations actually done by others. There is no question that Montale excelled at poetic translation and that his best translations are lyric poems, not prose or drama. It is not coincidental, then, that Montale signed his name to translations of prose (and dramatic) works done by others. His frenetic period of translation, dating from 1938 to about 1945, resulted both in fine and inadequate translations. Montale's version of *Billy Budd* is recognizably a refined piece of work, as is his co-translation of Steinbeck's novel *La battaglia* (In dubious battle).[187] On the other hand, his solo version of Steinbeck's *Al dio sconosciuto* (To an unknown God) and his Shakespearian dramas done for Mario Praz's collection are of lesser worth. Yet his poetic translations, which he included in his *Quaderno di traduzioni*, are almost uniformly distinctive.

Montale doesn't aim, in his poetic translations, for a commonly sought goal: the "foreignization" of the translation, where the translation becomes infused with the source text's linguistic structures and culture. His preference, to adapt and domesticate the foreign text, derives from the influence of Benedetto Croce. Translation should result in the creation of a new, independent work of art. Thus, the reader does not sense that the original text was Spanish, English, or French. For Montale there is no true tête-à-tête with the original poet or poem: as Lonardi astutely notes, "The total enslavement to the object to translate is missing in Montale."[188] Montale strives to create a poem, not a translation: "a translation is always *another thing*," as he writes. His Italian sounds natural, and not forced or strange (except in his versions from Guillén). As we already read in his 1956 interview, in words that are Crocean to the core, "A good translation is that which doesn't seem [a translation]; that which presents a text that one would call original."[189] His translations do not reflect back the original in a sustained way: as Maria Pia Musatti remarks, he does not attempt "a mechanical and meticulous imitation of formal solutions."[190] He never repeats the original rhyme patterns, and he always uses fewer end-rhymes; he almost never conserves the metrical scheme of the original, or its Italian equivalent. He departs from religious dogma. His versions, then, are not Nabokovian "ponies," meant to be as faithful to the source text's language, style, and content as possible; yet neither are they Lowellian "imitations." Indeed, his sole *adattamento*, "Trasfigurazioni," is similarly structured to the original, and its liberties are not as extensive as might be supposed from its subtitle.

If we are to consider the poets Montale translated, it must be said that many of them are not in a recognizable poetic canon: Melville, Maragall, Joyce, Milosz, Barnes, and Adams. And even some of the poems of the canonized poets are less-known, or in a lower key: Blake's "To the muses," Dickinson's "The Storm," Hardy's "The Garden seat," and Yeats's "After long silence." In other cases, however, Montale's eye did fall upon the most recognizable poem of a particular poet, or a particularly representative one: Dylan Thomas's "Poem Fifth"; Eliot's "A Song for Simeon"; Guillén's "El cisne" (The swan); Pound's "Hugh Selwyn Mauberley"; Yeats's "Sailing towards Byzantium"; Hopkins's "Pied Beauty"; Cavafy's "Περιμένοντας τους βαρβάρους" (Waiting for the barbarians); and Shakespeare's "Sonnet 33."

Montale translates poems that share stylistic affinities with his own verse (e.g., Eliot's "A Song for Simeon") and poems that differ from his preferred style (e.g., Guillén's compositions, or Hardy's "The Garden Seat" with its obsessive repetition, refrains, and parallel syntax). Moreover, on several occasions, Montale chose poems whose messages or religious nuances were far from his own. A case in point is Maragall's "Cant espiritual," where Montale ends up overturning the religious certainty of the Catalan poet: instead of a Pantheistic "tot ho és tot," Montale's translation asserts "il tutto è il nulla."

Montale's poetic translations are "occasions." He is, as Bigongiari noted, a translator of "poems," as opposed to a translator of "poets."[191]

While Ungaretti, for example, published volumes of translations from Shakespeare and Góngora, Montale translated at most six poems of an individual poet. Texts that are less than poetic masterpieces gave him even more freedom, perhaps, more room for his poetic craft. As he wrote to Guglielmo Petroni about his own version of Milosz's "La Berline arrêtée dans la nuit" (Berlin carriage motionless in the night), "It is like an original poem (of mine), maybe better."[192] Montale's *Quaderno*, we said, established a genre. After his *Quaderno di traduzioni*, many poet-translators borrowed this title for their poetic anthologies of foreign poetry. Indeed, that Montale chose such a title attests once more to his focus on texts, on "a notebook of *translations*": occasions and epiphanies.

3 Giorgio Caproni: Translation, *Vibrazioni*, and *Compensi*[1]

This chapter focuses on the Francophile poet Giorgio Caproni, whose translations stand out from many of his Italian contemporaries on account of their euphony and naturalness. Despite the fact that Caproni's translations have been studied by a number of scholars,[2] there remains no integral overview of his translations coupled with a detailed analysis of his *Quaderno di traduzioni*. I will argue that Caproni's translation ideology is based, like Montale's, on the Crocean idea that poetry is untranslatable. What can be transmitted, at most, are simply poetic *vibrazioni* (vibrations), as the Italian philosopher maintained. Therefore, the poet-translator must attempt a recreation, either in formal verse, or in free verse. If the source text is in formal verse, Caproni's domesticating, imitative translation method seeks to reproduce the original poem's musical *vibrazioni*. If the poem is written in free verse, Caproni attempts to attain "maximum fidelity," and compensate for inevitable loss through the addition of assonance and alliteration, a process Franco Fortini described as compensation.

After an introduction to Caproni's poetic career, translation career, and translation ideology, we will spend the rest of the chapter discussing his *Quaderno di traduzioni*, followed by his translation techniques. Through comparisons of his translations of Charles Baudelaire, René Char, and André Frénaud with those by other notable Italian poet-translators (Giuseppe Ungaretti, Vittorio Sereni, and Giovanni Raboni), we see how similar translation philosophies can give rise to far different results.[3]

Poetic Career

Giorgio Caproni was born in Livorno in 1912, moved to Genoa at the age of ten, and then to Rome in 1939, where he lived as a writer, translator, and teacher, until his death in 1990. His poetry followed an idiosyncratic path through the twentieth century, entering late into critical consciousness, as noted by scholars.[4] He saw himself excluded from the most influential poetic anthology of the mid-twentieth century – Luciano Anceschi's 1943 *Lirici Nuovi* (New lyric poets), perhaps because, as Giuseppe Leonelli says, his full maturity only began to be seen in his 1952 book *Stanze della funicolare* (Funicular stanzas).[5]

The first stage of Caproni's poetry, covering the volumes *Come un'allegoria* (Like an allegory, 1936), *Ballo a Fontanigorda* (Dance at Fontanigorda, 1938), and *Finzioni* (Fictions, 1941), was impressionistic in nature. He later described the beginning of his career: "At the origin of my poetry … I would say that there is youth and the almost physical enjoyment of life, shaded by a … continual warning of the presence, in everything, of death."[6] His verse is synaesthetic, full of continual tactile sensations. The title of his first volume refers to the fact that the natural landscape is an objective correlative for his feelings. The surface meanings give way to what Caproni called "my uneasiness and that of others."[7] In the following verses from *Come un'allegoria*, the earth is both itself and a figure of the poet:

La terra, con la sua faccia
Madida di sudore,
Apre assonnati occhi d'acqua
Alla notte che sbianca.[8]

[The earth, with its face
Damp with sweat,
Opens sleepy, watery eyes
On to the whitening night.]

The second stage is opened up by Caproni's *Stanze della funicolare*,[9] which is then included in Caproni's *Il passaggio d'Enea* (The passage of Aeneas, 1956), "his most metrically-rich volume,"[10] signalling the full maturity of the poet.[11] One critic goes so far as to say that no other Italian poet equals him for his "devotion to and his pleasure in rhyme, with their fundamental value (like pillars for the architrave), a devotion and pleasure integrated by subtle inventions and metrical variants, enjambments, ellipses, alliteration, diminuendos, and lengthening of notes."[12] An example is his small masterpiece, "1944," with the startling opening lines:

Le carrette del latte ahi mentre il sole
Sta per pungere i cani. Cosa insacca

La morte sopra i selci nel fragore
Di bottiglie in sobbalzo?[13]

[The milk wagons, ouch, while the sun
Is about to sting the dogs. What is Death
Bagging on the paving stones in the crash
Of rattling bottles?]

The poem begins with the anacoluthon *le carrette del latte* (the milk wagons), followed by the exclamation *ahi* that imparts a nuance of indescribable sadness. These first four verses have three enjambments, breaking down the continuity of the poetic verse, rendering it staccato.

In Caproni's next book, *Il seme del piangere* (The seed of weeping, 1959), his poetry reaches an apex, in a *canzoniere* dedicated to his deceased mother:

"Preghiera"

Anima mia, leggera
va' a Livorno, ti prego.
E con la tua candela
timida, di nottetempo
fa' un giro; e, se n'hai il tempo,
perlustra e scruta, e scrivi
se per caso Anna Picchi
è ancor viva tra i vivi.[14]

["Prayer"

My soul, lightly
Go to Livorno, I beg of you.
And with your timid
Candle, at night
Go around; and, if you have time,
Search and scour, and write
If by chance Anna Picchi
Is still alive among the living.]

With Caproni's *Congedo del viaggiatore cerimonioso e altre prosopopee* (The farewell of the ceremonious traveller, and other prosopopoeias, 1965), his poetry entered his final stage. As the poet-translator

Giovanni Raboni noted (and I will return to this poet-translator later on in this chapter),

> From a certain point onwards – let's say, and not only because of the title, from the 1965 collection – Caproni has done nothing other than "taking leave" (with his dry, "ceremonious," terrible irony) from the earth and from hope, as if the moment of "asking halt" had come for him, poet-traveller ... but in truth, that taking leave began with the very beginning of his poetry and, at least for us, will never have an end.[15]

In the poet's eponymous allegorical poem, "Congedo del viaggiatore cerimonioso," the poet-traveller asks *congedo* from everyone and everything, even if he doesn't "know well the hour of / arrival" or "the train stations preceding mine."[16]

Congedo alla sapienza
e congedo all'amore.
Congedo anche alla religione.
Ormai sono alla destinazione.
Ora che più forte sento
Stridere il freno, vi lascio
Davvero, amici. Addio.
Di questo, sono certo: io
Son giunto alla disperazione
Calma, senza sgomento.
Scendo. Buon proseguimento.[17]

[I take leave of wisdom
And I take leave of love.
I take leave also of religion.
By now I am at the destination.
Now that I hear more loudly
The break screech, I leave you
Truly, friends. Adieu.
Of this, I am sure: I
Have arrived at calm
Desperation, without dismay.
I'm getting off. Enjoy the rest of your journey.]

In the next volume, *Il muro della terra* (The wall of the earth, 1975), the form and metrics of Caproni's verse decisively transform into shorter verses, packed with enjambments and rhymes: this will hold true for the rest of Caproni's final period. We come across aphoristic poems, like the following:

"Deus Absconditus"

Un semplice dato:
Dio non s'è nascosto.
Dio si è suicidato.[18]

["Hidden God"

A simple fact:
God didn't hide.
God committed suicide.]

Or, in a poem that gave rise to the volume's title:

"Anch'io"

Ho provato anch'io.
È stata tutta una guerra
d'unghie. Ma ora so. Nessuno
potrà mai perforare
il muro della terra.[19]

["I too"

I tried, I too.
It was a complete war
of fingernails. But now I know. No one
will ever be able to drill through
the wall of the earth.]

Caproni's following volume, *Il franco cacciatore* (The freeshooter, 1982), named after Weber's opera *Der Freischütz*, was defined by Giovanni Testori as "one of the summits (*vertici*) ... of our poetry: a summit that is simultaneously [a sensation of] vertigo (*una vertigine*)."[20] This book of poems shares with the next volume, *Il conte di Kevenhüller* (The count of *Kevenhüller*, 1986), the literal and allegorical subject of hunting, *la caccia*. The themes of these books have been aptly described as "being searched for where one is not; the arrival at a place where one has never arrived; the rejection of the 'noise of history.'"[21] The shortened verses often become "epigrammatiche" (epigrammatic). In *Il conte di Kevenhüller,* Caproni makes use of a frame story: an eighteenth-century count who proclaimed a general *caccia* and a subsequent reward for the killing of a "ferocious beast" (*feroce Bestia*) who was terrorizing the countryside.[22] Caproni explained that, in his view, critics were wrongly assuming the Beast was God, or only God: "We, too, are the beast ..." It can also be understood, the poet continues, "as a symbol (or metaphor) of Evil (*Male*), in all its various forms."[23]

In Caproni's final, posthumous volume, *Res amissa* (Lost thing, 1991), the title suggests its predominant theme. If the previous two books investigated *Il male* (evil), as the poet himself declared, this final volume, *Res amissa,* "the lost thing," searches for *Il bene* (The good). As Caproni writes, "All of us receive something precious as a gift, which then we lose irrevocably."[24] Caproni goes literally beyond all he has written before:

Son già oltre la morte.
Oltre l'oltre.
    Già oltre
(in queste mie estreme ore corte)
l'oltre dell'oltremorte ...[25]

[I am already beyond death.
Beyond the beyond.
    Already beyond
(in these brief final hours of mine)
the beyond of the beyond-death ...]

To conclude, as Giulio Ferroni suggestively says, "an absolute lightness, far from any intellectualism, which brushes up and caresses the forms of a fragile and delicate reality, leads Caproni to a wisdom and a capacity for knowledge that are able to touch the most vertiginous abysses of culture and contemporary daily life."[26]

Translation Career

Giorgio Caproni came relatively late to translation. His first book-length translation – in 1951, at the age of thirty-nine – was Marcel Proust's *Il tempo ritrovato* (Time regained).[27] By then, he had already published his first four poetic volumes – *Come un'allegoria* (1936),[28] *Ballo a Fontanigorda* (1938),[29] *Finzioni* (1941),[30] and *Cronistoria* (Chronicle,

1943).[31] The bulk of Caproni's translations were published in the 1960s and 1970s:[32] René Char (1962),[33] Charles Baudelaire (1962),[34] Louis-Ferdinand Céline (1964),[35] Guy de Maupassant (1965),[36] Blaise Cendrars (1967),[37] André Frénaud (1967 and 1971),[38] Jean Genet (1971 and 1975),[39] Federico García Lorca (1972),[40] Wilhelm Busch (1974),[41] and Guillaume Apollinaire (1979).[42] During these two decades, Adele Dei notes,

> His work on writing and the word, the test of the mixture of levels and languages, in this period becomes put into practice with the demanding translations, which continue in a quick rhythm, becoming a real parallel profession and probably slowing down poetic activity.[43]

Often, indeed, the poet-translator complained about having to translate, not having the time to write his own poems. As he wrote to his friend, the poet Carlo Betocchi, "I am at work. Poems, zero. But how to work for oneself when one is working for others? I, poet with a thin voice, don't have so much energy."[44] And again, "Verses, I haven't written any more of them. Solely and only translations and translations."[45] And once more, now writing to André Frénaud: "I have written only a few short poems, alas, and I too am depressed. The translations are killing me (*Les traductions me tuent*)."[46] Indeed, Caproni, like Giudici and Montale, published *more* translations than original verse. This, too, is a clear example of just how important and necessary translation was to his own work (though this fact has not been noticed by critics). Moreover, Caproni introduced or helped introduce Céline,[47] Frénaud,[48] Genet,[49] Char,[50] and Proust[51] to Italians and Italian literature.

Translation Ideology

To begin with, like many other poet-translators such as Vittorio Sereni, Giovanni Raboni, and Mario Luzi, Caproni claims ignorance of translation theories, not considering himself an "expert" or "professional translator." He explains that he has "no mental laboratory equipped for [this] purpose" and that it is impossible for him to propound any theories on translation.[52] Again, Caproni doesn't consider translation as a praxis that can be readily defined, and whatever positive work he has accomplished remains "a mystery to my very eyes."[53] His many successes and new creations do not lend themselves, in his view, to theoretical formulations about how to translate a particular style or a specific genre.

Yet there are three obvious principles underlying Caproni's translation ideology. First, faithful poetic translation is impossible. Second, translation is best when the translator selects an author whose poetics are foreign to his own. And third, translation allows the translator himself to engage in self-discovery. These axioms determine his particular relationship with the original text: translation necessitates a profoundly personal and artistic engagement with the original poem. His methodology of translation is fundamentally binary, depending on whether he's translating formal or non-formal verse. In the former case, as with Apollonaire, he focuses on finding an equivalent metre, domesticating the text; in the latter, as with Frénaud and Char, he searches for the maximum of "fidelity," and introduces assonance and alliteration in a process of compensation.

Caproni was no doubt influenced, in the first case, by Dante's pronouncement on translation in the *Convivio* (Banquet), which the modern Italian poet repeatedly cites: "E però sappia ciascuno che nulla cosa per legame musaico armonizzata si può de la sua loquela in altra transmutare sanza rompere tutta sua dolcezza e armonia" (Everyone should know that nothing harmonized according to the rules of poetry can be translated from its native tongue into another without destroying all its sweetness and harmony).[54] The original can never, in all its identical value, be reproduced in another language. Caproni's favourite and most recurring metaphor about the untranslatability of poetry is as follows:[55]

> Words run between men like coins – they are the coins of a trade as important and base [*vile*] as victuals and other things strictly (physiologically) necessary. And one knows that foreign coins are foreign currency – in this case, always currency that loses in exchange, due to that unavoidable right of usury [*diritto d'usura*] that, in such trade, always goes against original purchasing power. Thus this is why one commonly says that translating is equivalent to impoverishing [*impoverire*] a text.[56]

Words, like currencies, lose in exchange value, because of *usura*, or the transaction fees. Usury, here, refers to the failure in translation to transfer the exact connotations and phonetic elements of the original word, resulting in the inevitable loss. This occurs, for Caproni, only with poetry. As he says elsewhere, repeating the metaphor of currency exchange, prose is "always translatable," while poetry is translatable only "paying a very large (and often ruinous) discount rate [*tasso di sconto*]."[57]

Montesquieu seems to have originated this metaphor in his *Lettres persanes* (Persian letters):

> Translations are like those copper coins which have the same value as a piece of gold, and are even more used by people, but are always light and of a bad alloy. You want, you say, to make these illustrious dead be reborn among us; and I aver that you definitely give them a body; but you do not give them life.[58]

For Caproni, in translating poetry, this "struggle with the lion," one loses as soon as one starts. For all it takes is the wrong word, the false note, the cacophonous syllable to render the whole attempt futile (a point likewise made by Ungaretti, as seen earlier). Caproni constantly notes that merely changing a word or even an accent breaks the music's "charm." The poem "is pulverized [*polverizzata*]."[59] Here we can think of Roman Jakobson's argument for the untranslatability of poetic translation, which Caproni would have certainly subscribed to.

If Caproni is in agreement with Dante and Jakobson about the untranslatability of poetic works, there is one poem in particular that is a paradigmatic case of an untranslatable poetic text. Caproni purposely did not attempt to translate it either, this classic of French symbolism, rendered many times into Italian in the twentieth century, and a touchstone for Italian hermetic poets from Mario Luzi to Alessandro Parronchi: namely, Valéry's *Le cimetière marin* (The graveyard by the sea). As Caproni writes in a review of a translation of the French poet by Mario Tutino,

> I too have committed many sins [*peccati*] as a translator. Sins that I would call sins of greed, or better of desire: desiring the stuff of others, at bottom. But it has never crossed my mind to test myself (only to test myself) in translating Paul Valéry's "Le cimetière marin" … For me, "Le cimetière" will always remain the most crystal clear example – the most extreme example, if we'd like – of the nearly absolute impossibility of translating poetry.[60]

And if he does positively review Tutino's version, it is even clearer that he considers it an ultimate proof that poetry is finally untranslatable, an opinion, Caproni remarks, held by Valéry himself. Indeed, Caproni even refuses the nomenclature of translations. As he says in a radio interview, he never calls his versions translations, "but rather, after the example of Leopardi, I call them imitations."[61] Therefore, when Caproni includes several translations from Apollinaire, Prévert, and Lorca at the end of his volume of original poems, *Il seme del piangere*, he calls them "Imitazioni." He explains that his *imitazioni* are not translations, because perfect translations, as we have seen, are impossible due to the nature of poetic language. Each sign has a nearly infinite number of overtones, namely tonal vibrations that arise from the specific word:

> While in practical language the acoustic or graphic sign of the word remains tied to the letter and the pure and simple information, in poetic language the word itself conserves, yes, its own literal meaning, but also is laden with an almost infinite series of "harmonic" meanings (and I say "harmonic," using the term as it is used in physics and music) that shape its particular expressive form.[62]

Caproni is well aware of how language shapes poetry, referring on several occasions to how Racine couldn't have composed specific verses (*la fille de Minos et Pasiphaë* [the daughter of Minos and Pasiphaë]) in Italian and how Ugo Foscolo couldn't have created certain verses in French: the infinitesimal overtones or vibrations of a word change from one language to another. The specific source language, then, has certain characteristics that do not allow for an easy transfer to the target language. To repeat what Giuseppe Ungaretti wrote, "The syllabic quality is not translatable, the first sensible difference between two languages precisely residing in their phonic values."[63] Thus, the translator must find a way to bring across or imitate the original music. Here, Caproni, who played the violin from childhood onwards, makes the interesting analogy, which he returns to again and again: "The translator ... [is like] someone who must transcribe for violin, let us say, what has been written for the flute."[64] In musical composition, transcription for a different instrument inevitably causes massive changes from the original score. What this indicates, moreover, is that translation is not technically a process of replication: the resulting translation is different in kind from the original. Caproni is therefore in agreement with those who consider the translator fundamentally an interpreter of texts: "The translator, some affirm, is an interpreter, like the violin or piano virtuoso. It is a rather simplistic general idea, but at bottom, acceptable."[65] The translator, like the musician, interprets the composer's work, but the interpretation can never exactly coincide with the written score. This is where the necessary third element comes in, between the original text and the poet: what Caproni requires from a poetic translator is not only "profound historical, critical and philological knowledge," but an "active gift for song [*canto*], that is, knowledge and experience of that third language [*terza lingua*] which is conversing in poetry."[66] The "terza lingua" allows the transfer of similar value from one poetic language to another to occur. The poet needs a refined ear, capable of finding the most subtle nuances and poetic vibrations of words: only such an *orecchio* (ear) will be able to help the translator "save [*salvare*] ... the literal meaning [*senso letterale*] without destroying the vibrations [*le vibrazioni*] of the poem."[67] These *vibrazioni* were theorized by Croce as the only thing that can be faithfully transmitted (*trasme[sse]*) in a poetic text from one language to another. For Caproni, as well, these *vibrazioni* are the only traces of the original, and they are marks of a successful poetic *ricreazione* (recreation).

The key for Caproni is to find the correct pace and metre. As he tells Carlo Betocchi, his translation of Théophile de Viau's poem will be ready soon: he just needs to "find the rhythm."[68] On another occasion, Caproni describes translating Verlaine's magical rhythm as "a hard nut" (*un osso duro*). Caproni would later say in his address upon winning the *Premio Monselice* (Monselice Award) for translation that he agrees with those, like Iginio de Luca and Elio Chinol, who maintain that the translator must "privilege the movement" and that "rhythm must be sustained at any cost."[69] If we recall, Nietzsche, in *Beyond Good and Evil*, spoke of this same feature of rhythm in translation: "What is most difficult to render from one language into another is the *tempo* of its style."[70]

This doesn't mean that the translation's metre is necessarily reflective of the metre of the original, "mimetic" in James Holmes's terminology; often Caproni translates into a different metrical structure. Rather, the metre, which can change gradually during the translation, must respond to the poetic elements at work, ensuring that the *vibrazioni* are given free rein. Indeed, Caproni consistently translates formal verse this way, except in his prose translations from Baudelaire (which we will come to later). When Caproni deals with non-formal verse, like that of Frénaud or Char, where there is no regular rhyme or metre, he makes use of what the poet-translator Franco Fortini called "compensi."

According to Fortini, "compensation and substitutions"[71] (*compensi e supplenze*) are involved in every translation, but especially in versions of lyric poetry, where the translator can use all the riches offered by phonosymbolism. For Fortini, compensation is a process to be used especially when the translator cannot or does not wish to reproduce the rhyme; likewise, for Caproni, the general process of compensation, which does apply to all of his versions, has special significance for poems that do not have a poetic framework of regular metre and/or rhyme. For both Fortini and Caproni, the translator should select words that originate a series of overtones through assonance and alliteration. Indeed, that "third language," which Caproni mentioned, implies the skilled and expert use of such phonosymbolism that creates "a series of diverse harmonics from the sound ... which approach, however, the original value [*valore*] as much as possible."[72] Ideally, then, the created overtones in the target language will retain a similar *valore* as in the original: the new vibrations should not be, in other words, random or insignificant, but should bear a similar relationship with the semantic content of the words themselves.

Consequently, the poet-translator must first be a poet in order to successfully translate poetry (a tenet Caproni shares with Dryden), even if certain poems, like Valéry's *Le cimetière marin*, elude translation. The translator performs a subjective task – a personal and intimate transference from the original text to the new translation (or imitation, as we saw that Caproni prefers to call it). The task, while being a *techne*, like "constructing a piece of furniture, painting a picture, sculpting a statue, or composing a sonnet or a novella"[73] is anything but trivial. Rather, translation is a task invested with supreme existential importance. Poets, as Caproni explains in his essay "L'arte del tradurre" (The art of translating), are not so much inventors as they are discoverers: they descend within themselves and discover unknown regions of their soul. In turn, they offer the same sort of experience for their translators (and their readers). The poet "investing the translator with his power, stirs up and renders diurnal [*diurno*] in [his] translator what was already sleeping, nocturnal, and therefore ignored."[74] This allegory is, in fact, as Caproni suggests, the fairy tale of Sleeping Beauty. It is, then, thanks to the author, that the translator (and reader) experiences a marvellous expansion of self-knowledge:

> And all the translator's pleasure (if it can be called pleasure); all the compelling attraction that pushes him onwards consists in feeling, thanks to a certain text, an enlargement of his very experience or consciousness (of his own being or existence, more than of knowledge), precisely because such a text compels him to explore zones of his self that otherwise – perhaps – he wouldn't have known.[75]

This is why, as Caproni states in an interview, he translates dissimilar authors: the encounter between him and the original text is not a meeting but a clash of consciousness. He is convinced that

> The enriching or enlargement of consciousness [*coscienza*] to which I alluded is much more probable the more difficult or even hostile a certain reading is and therefore its transfer [*traslazione*]. [This is] a difficulty that forces us to lower ourselves, like good miners [*buoni minatori*], always lower; not only into the text but into ourselves, first of all, specifically to perceive and capture in ourselves, in the clearest way, the genuine force of the text demanding our voice.[76]

The more difficult it is to translate a text, the more translators, "da buoni minatori" (like good miners), can engage in a process of self-revelation. This is similar to Vittorio Sereni's reasoning in his own *quaderno di traduzioni, Il Musicante di Saint-Merry* (The musician of Saint-Merry). There, Sereni shows his faith in both principles shared with Caproni: first, that translators often translate authors specifically foreign to their own sensibilities, and second, that translating texts illuminates the translator's own mind:

> One also translates, if not just for opposition, also for comparison. In translation, one doesn't appropriate for oneself someone else's text or make it one's own, as much as it is this [foreign] text that absorbs an area in our sensibility, indefinite until then, and illuminates it – and one learns more from someone who doesn't resemble us.[77]

Indeed, Sereni gave a copy of this *quaderno* to Caproni, and next to this quote Caproni annotated: "I said this."[78] Thus, for both poet-translators, translating awakens the soul, especially when the poet translated is not similar to the translator. As Caproni argues, the translator is therefore forced to "explore zones of one's consciousness, of one's experience … that otherwise would probably have forever remained asleep."[79]

The metaphor of a soul and mind rising from their slumber is chosen by Caproni in the previous quote and in discussions on translation. As Lorenzo Flabbi notes,[80] it is also what René Char (whom Caproni translated) called "la mission d'éveiller" (the mission of awakening). If this is the poet's mission, the translator shares it, imitating it both actively and passively. The poem causes the translator-reader to look deeply within just as the writer does when creating a text. So Caproni's *imitations* refer not only to a style of translation that brings about an independent work, but also to the process of self-searching undergone by the translator.

Despite Caproni's belief in the inevitable diminution of the poetic text in translation, what results from a poetic translation should not always be considered a failure. When the translator of poetry truly succeeds, the translation acquires an independent life of its own (the afterlife or *Überleben* of Walter Benjamin):[81] this can only come from the poet who knows how to use that "third language" of poetic language. For Caproni, the translations done by poets, "just as they are always 'another thing' [*un'altra cosa*] are, forgive the tautology, another thing: that is, something more that is added to the patrimony of our literature, and to literature in general."[82] This "altra cosa" is called a "ricreazione" by Croce and a "creative transposition" by Jakobson.[83] It is "other" because the new translation belongs to neither the author nor the translator. In Caproni's preferred metaphor, this translation is a child of both parents: "a child [*figlio*] is born who resembles a little both one and the other."[84]

We can reassume, then, Caproni's translation praxis, which aims to create this "figlio." He strives first to maintain the poetic quality of the text, through imitating or choosing a new metre and rhyme scheme. For Caproni, rewriting the text is often required, especially when dealing with formal poems (such as Apollinaire's "Les Cloches" [The bells]). Second, if the original poem has no specific metre or rhyme – as in the poetry of Frénaud – he "compensates," using additional assonance, alliteration, apocope, stylistic inversions, and repetition. In analysing Caproni's translations, we will see how Caproni's "terza lingua" functions through a combination of metre, rhyme, and phonosymbolic elements. And we will also see how it is that the only failure of Caproni as a translator – his prose translations of Baudelaire – can be explained by the choice to translate the French poet mostly into prose.

Quaderno di Traduzioni

This volume, sketched out by Caproni, but edited by Enrico Testa, was published posthumously by Einaudi in 1998. Caproni had intended to publish his *Quaderno di traduzioni,* following personal requests by Giulio Einaudi, but due to illness and then his death, he was unable to finish the volume himself. He left enough notes to allow Testa to form a reasonable approximation of what the final plan would have looked like.

Caproni selected Apollinaire to open the *Quaderno*, since he (along with Prévert) dominates one pole of the volume. Indeed, Apollinaire's importance to Caproni as a poet was significant, owing to the "extraordinary emotional charge, and I mean even passionate (*passionale*) charge, of his texts."[85] Indeed, as Caproni goes on to say, the figure of Apollinaire posed a dichotomy for Italian poets of his generation, forcing them to choose either "him (daily life) or the axis Mallarmé-Valéry (the sublime)."[86] Caproni obviously chose the former. Even if Apollinaire represents the "quotidiano della vita" (daily life), this doesn't in any way imply that his verse is prosaic. Rather, "Apollinaire's greater charm is born from the music," even when the French poet seemingly uses the most prose-like (*prosastico*) verse.[87] Yet it is not merely music that incites Caproni but the French poet's fantastic mixture of styles, a combination of modern and ancient, neologisms and archaisms, which "makes the translator, not in his turn as much an *artiste* and philologist, go crazy."[88]

Caproni then goes on to describe his procedure in translating the French poet, asserting that his overarching goal was to rewrite the French poems as though Apollinaire had written them originally in Italian. Certainly, the poet-translator always tried "to keep, as much as possible, faithful [*fedele*] to the letter [*lettera*]." But this fidelity was not of the highest priority:

> But when such faithfulness would have damaged the music [*la musica*], that is the spirit or linguistic brio which animates the poetic discourse with his exquisitely French *trovate*, I didn't hesitate to intervene with ideas and inventions of my own, trying to restore that music into Italian: that inspiration, that brio. In other words, I played with a foil (thrust against thrust, invention against invention), in the rather presumptuous attempt, in truth, to rewrite the chosen texts (and I refer above all to the *chansons*, which would lose all flavor removed from their metrical structure) as if Apollinaire had written them in Italian, and with the resources of the Italian language (and tradition). Without, obviously, deluding myself into thinking that I had given the perfect copy.[89]

As we see, "la musica" (music) is more necessary to get across into Italian than "fedeltà" (faithfulness). And Caproni indeed prefers to translate, above all, the "*chansons*, le canzoni, le canzonette" of Apollinaire.[90] The poet-translator proudly uses the resources of Italian, domesticating the text:

> How to behave in front of a *chanson* like "Les cloches" (*Le campane* [The bells]), which draws all of its grace precisely and only from its air of *chanson* [a song]? A sole road remains for the translator. To entirely rewrite [*riscrivere*] the text, yet saving its [*salvandone*] literal meaning, just as the very Apollinaire would have written it if he had used Italian instead of French.[91]

For the poet-translator, the French text must be rethought and brought into Italian for the Italian reader. And Caproni does rewrite Apollinaire's "Les cloches" (The bells) to a degree, switching all French names to Italian, transforming whole verses, and shifting their order. He turns the eight-syllable French verse into a predominantly nine-syllable line, and he uses a different rhyme scheme. For example, in the first stanza below in table 3.1, we can see two of the above traits: the second and third verses are exchanged, and the fourth verse is translated much differently. Yet the rhyme pattern – *abba* – is kept the same in the translation as in the original.

If Caproni was singularly at home with Apollinaire's poetry, with Char it was another story. Caproni was not a famous resistance fighter, like Char, and he didn't share the French poet's exalted sense of poetry. As Caproni explains, Char's verse was "involved from head to toe in those *bouts d'existence incorruptibles* [bits of incorruptible existence] which are his poems." The French phrase "bouts d'existence incorruptibles" comes from Char himself, who described his poems as "bouts d'existence incorruptibles que nous lançons à la gueule répugnante de la mort, mais assez haut pour que ricochant sur elle, ils tombent dans le monde nominateur de l'unité" (bits of incorruptible existence which we throw in the repugnant mouth of death, but high enough so that ricocheting onto it, they fall into the world, nominator of unity).[92] Yet Caproni describes the power of Char's poetry coming not from without, but from within the poet himself, "dozing but present, as if the poet hadn't done other than *reawaken it*, not *inventing*, but *discovering* [*scoprendo*]."[93] This is, once more, a confirmation of how Caproni envisioned the poet as a discoverer, and not an inventor.

As with Frénaud, Caproni engaged in correspondence with Char, and visited him at his home a few years before the death of both poets.[94] Caproni was anxious in his translations of Char, above all, with obtaining the utmost fidelity: "I desire the maximum fidelity."[95] For instance, in his translation of "A la désespérade" (To the despairing [woman]), if we were to make a list of all the words translated from French into

Table 3.1 "Les cloches"

Guillaume Apollinaire **"Les cloches" [The bells]**	**Giorgio Caproni** **"Le campane" [The bells]**
Mon beau tzigane mon amant [My beautiful gypsy my lover]	Zingaro bello amore mio [My beautiful gypsy my love]
Écoute les cloches qui sonnent [Hear the bells that ring]	Ci siamo amati storditamente [We loved each other giddily]
Nous nous aimions éperdument [We loved each other utterly]	Senti che razza di scampanio [Hear such pealing of bells]
Croyant n'être vus de personne [Believing not to be seen by anyone]	E vuoi che non lo sappia la gente [And you want people not to know]
Source: Caproni, *Quaderno di traduzioni*, 32	Source: Caproni, *Quaderno di traduzioni*, 33

Italian that are cognates, it would not only be a long list but it would make up most of the vocabulary of the entire poem. Not taking account of pronouns, prepositions, negations, or articles, thirty-three of the forty-six French nouns, verbs, and adjectives are replaced by Italian cognates. This is an extraordinary number: over 70 per cent. Whole verses are translated into Italian cognates: for example, "Je ne désire plus que tu me sois ouvert"[96] (I desire no more that you be open for me) is rendered as "Non desidero più che tu mi sia aperto" (I desire no more that you be open to me); "Puits de mémoire, ô coeur, en repli et luttant"[97] (Well of memory, oh heart, in retreat and fighting) as "Pozzo di memoria, oh cuore, che ripiega e che lotta" (Well of memory, oh heart, which retreats and fights); and "Laisse dormir ton ancre tout au fond de mon sable"[98] (Let your anchor sleep at the very bottom of my sand) as "Lascia che la tua àncora dorma in fondo alla mia sabbia" (Let your anchor sleep at the bottom of my sand). This contrasts with Caproni's practice with other poets, like Apollinaire: in his version of "Les cloches,"[99] Caproni used seventeen cognates out of forty-one similar words (nouns, verbs, etc.), or 40 per cent: about a half as many as here. Naturally, this rudimentary quantitative measurement does not take into account syntactical, grammatical, or metrical changes. When Caproni chooses not to use cognates, he generally accentuates alliteration and assonance. Here are three examples of this from his translation of Char's poem, "A la désespérade." The Italian poet translates "sous ta face profonde" (under your deep face) as "sotto il tuo volto profondo" (under your deep countenance), rendering "face" not as "faccia" but "volto," in order to create the assonance of *o* in "sotto," "tuo," and "profondo";[100] he turns "Poète confondant et sois heureux" into "poeta sconcertante, e sii contento,"[101] which plays on the consonants *s*, *c*, and *t* and vowels *o* and *e*; and he translates "m'attache" as "m'occupo" in the final verse, to draw out the alliterative *p* in the phrase "m'occupo dei tuoi preparativi."[102] His translation of "A la désespérade" is more concise than the original, a tenet which also holds in many other versions of Caproni's. For instance, in Char's "Congé au vent"[103] (Farewell to the wind), there are ninety-eight words in French and only eighty-eight in Caproni's "Addio al vento" (Adieu to the wind).

We will see some of these traits in another poem he translated by Char, "A ***" (To ***), which was also translated by Vittorio Sereni (see table 3.2 below). Indeed, Caproni was, along with Sereni, the most important translator of the French poet into Italian. Their collective volume, *Poesia e prosa* (Poetry and prose), appeared in 1962 and was the first volume of translations of Char that was published in Italian.

Caproni generally translates verse for verse, and his translation contains the same number of verses as the original. Sereni, on the other hand, often has extra verses: in his second volume of Char translations (after the 1962 volume, which was reissued by Einaudi separately in 1968),[104] *Ritorno sopramonte e altre poesie* (Return to the mountain and other poems),[105] eleven of Char's twenty-four poems in verse are translated with at least an extra verse, if not two (or three).[106] A recent article by Giuseppe Scaglione has analysed the translations by Caproni and Sereni of this powerful love poem.[107] Both poets translate word-for-word, though Sereni follows the syntax more closely, using more lexical cognates. Yet it is Caproni's version that is surely the most valuable as a poetic text, and this is due both to strength of expression and musicality, achieved through Fortinian compensation. As for specific poetic techniques, Caproni utilizes apocope (*amor*, *ciascun*, *vien*), eschewed by Sereni, along with inversions ("Da tanti anni sei l'amor mio," which inverts the French "Tu es mon amour depuis tant d'années") and repetitions (*nemmeno ciò che / nemmeno ciò che*; *alfine / alfine*; *nella ... della nostra / nel ... della nostra*; *"dico fortuna" / "dico fortuna"*), rarely found in Sereni's version.[108] Caproni's alliteration – the *s* in *senza spanderne il segreto* and the *n* in *Nella cuore della nostra nuvolaglia* – is more profuse than Sereni's and strengthens the phonosyllabic fibre of the translation. Sereni's slower rhythm is prosy at times, for example in "E il dolore che vien d'altrove / Trova alfine separazione," and less harmonious. Indeed, much of the music in his version comes from the borrowed words of

Table 3.2 "A ***" (To ***)

René Char "A ***"	Giorgio Caproni "A ***"	Vittorio Sereni "A ***"
Tu es mon amour depuis tant d'années, [You have been my love for so many years,]	Da tanti anni sei l'amor mio, [For so many years you have been my love,]	Da tanti anni sei il mio amore, [For so many years you have been my love,]
Mon vertige devant tant d'attente, [My vertigo before so much waiting,]	Il mio capogiro in così lunga attesa, [My vertigo in such a long wait,]	La mia vertigine davanti a tanta attesa, [My vertigo in front of such a wait,]
Que rien ne peut vieillir, froidir; [Which nothing can age, chill;]	Che nulla può invecchiare, raffreddare; [That nothing can age, chill;]	Che nulla può invecchiare, raggelare, [Which nothing can age, freeze,]
Même ce qui attendait notre mort, [Not even who waited for our death,]	Nemmeno ciò che aspettava la nostra morte, [Not even that which awaited our death,]	Persino chi attendeva che morissimo, [Not even who awaited for us to die,]
Ou lentement sut nous combattre, [Or slowly found out how to fight us,]	O lentamente seppe combatterci, [Or slowly found out how to fight us,]	O lentamente ci seppe combattere [Or slowly found out how to fight us]
Même ce qui nous est étranger, [Not even that which is foreign to us,]	Nemmeno ciò che ci è estraneo, [Not even that which is foreign to us,]	Perfino chi ci è estraneo, [Even whoever is foreign to us,]
Et mes éclipses et mes retours. [and my disappearances and my returns.]	E le mie eclissi e i miei ritorni. [And my disappearances and my returns.]	E le mie eclissi e i miei ripensamenti. [And my disappearances and my second thoughts.]
Fermée comme un volet de buis [Closed like a box-wood shutter]	Chiusa come un'imposta di bosso [Closed like a box-wood shutter]	Chiusa come un'imposta di bosso [Closed like a box-wood shutter]
Une extrême chance compacte [An extreme solid luck]	Un'estrema fortuna compatta [An extreme solid fortune]	Un'estrema fortuna compatta [An extreme solid fortune]
Est notre chaîne de montagnes, [Is our mountain range,]	È la nostra catena di monti, [Is our mountain range,]	È la nostra catena di montagne, [Is our mountain range,]

Table 3.2 "A ***" (To ***) (*Continued*)

René Char "A ***"	Giorgio Caproni "A ***"	Vittorio Sereni "A ***"
Notre comprimante splendeur. [our compressing splendor.]	Lo splendore che ci comprime. [The splendor that compresses us.]	Il nostro comprimente splendore. [Our compressing splendor.]
Je dis chance, ô ma martelée; [I say luck, o my hammered woman;]	Dico fortuna, o mia martellata; [I say fortune, o my hammered woman;]	Dico fortuna, oh mia martellata; [I say fortune, oh my hammered woman;]
Chacun de nous peut recevoir [Each of us can receive]	Ciascun di noi può ricevere [Each of us can receive]	Ognuno di noi può ricevere [Each of us can receive]
La part de mystère de l'autre [The mysterious part of the other]	La parte di mistero dell'altro [The mysterious part of the other]	La parte di mistero dell'altro [The mysterious part of the other]
Sans en répandré le secret; [Without spreading its secret;]	Senza spanderne il segreto; [Without spreading its secret;]	Senza spargerne il segreto; [Without spreading its secret;]
Et la douleur qui vient d'ailleurs [And the grief that comes from elsewhere]	E il dolore che vien d'altrove [And the grief that comes from elsewhere]	E il dolore che del resto ne deriva [And the grief that derives from the rest of it]
Trouve enfin sa separation [Finds at last its separation]	Trova alfine separazione [Finds at last separation]	Finalmente ritrova la sua separazione [Finally finds its separation again]
Dans la chair de nôtre unité, [In the flesh of our unity,]	Nella carne della nostra unità, [In the flesh of our unity,]	Nella carne della nostra unità, [In the flesh of our unity,]
Trouve enfin sa route solaire [Finds at last its solar route]	Trova alfine il suo corso solare [Finds at last its solar course]	Trova finalmente la sua strada solare [Finally finds its solar path]
Au centre de notre nuée [At the centre of our dense cloud]	Nel cuore della nostra nuvolaglia [In the heart of our cloud mass]	Al centro del nostro nembo [At the centre of our storm cloud]
Qu'elle déchire et recommence. [Which it tears open and rebegins.]	Che squarcia e ricompone. [Which it splits over and recomposes.]	Che squarcia e ricomincia. [Which it splits open and rebegins.]

Table 3.2 "A ***" (To ***) (*Continued*)

René Char "A ***"	Giorgio Caproni "A ***"	Vittorio Sereni "A ***"
Je dis chance comme je le sens. [I say luck as I feel it.]	Dico fortuna così come sento. [I say fortune just as I feel.]	Dico fortuna come lo sento. [I say fortune as I feel it.]
Tu as élevé le sommet [You have elevated the summit]	Tu hai alzato la vetta [You have elevated the peak]	Tu hai elevato la vetta [You have elevated the peak]
Que devra franchir mon attente [Which will need to cross my waiting]	Che la mia attesa dovrà superare [Which will need to overcome my waiting]	Che dovrà oltrepassare la mia attesa [Which will need to go beyond my waiting]
Quand demain disparaîtra. [When tomorrow it disappears.]	Quando domani sparirà. [When tomorrow it disappears.]	Quando domani sparirà. [When tomorrow it disappears.]
Source: Caproni, *Quaderno di traduzioni*, 118	Source: *Caproni, Quaderno di traduzioni*, 119	Source: *Poesia francese del Novecento*, 362–5

Caproni. As Scaglione notes, Sereni, who translated this poem a decade or so after Caproni,[109] keeps six of Caproni's verses identical in his own rendering (and the poem is only twenty-five verses long), presumably since he couldn't improve on Caproni's version. But this should not be surprising if Sereni himself wrote that "there exists, or at least existed for me, a further moment in which one doesn't translate any longer, simply, a text, but rather one translates the echo, the repercussion that text has had in us."[110]

Sereni's translation reveals how much he heard Char in the echo of Caproni: Sereni is in dialogue here not only with the French poet, but with his Italian friend and fellow translator as well. Yet, it comes down, finally, to this. Caproni is more suited to translate Char's rhythmical verse than Sereni: Caproni is more able to make the most of the resources of Italian phonosymbolism and musicality (rhyme and rhythm). Sereni was never able to match Caproni in this aspect of poetics. Sereni, rather, excels with the staccato verse of William Carlos Williams or the prose poems of Char that are less formally structured.

If Apollinaire was stylistically the most congenial for Caproni, and Char the most dissimilar in terms of poetics, Frénaud was the poet who shared the closest philosophical similarities with Caproni of any of the poets he translated. Caproni judged him one of the greatest living

French poets.[111] Frénaud played a key role for Caproni, and their correspondence is extensive. Caproni also dedicated a poem to him: "Lasciando Loco" (Leaving Loco).[112] The Italian poet-translator explains his interest in Frénaud, showing that their difference in poetic styles was compensated by their philosophical affinity:

> What magnetized me in him behind the great wall (the obstacle) of a style so far from my own, and beyond the dross, here and there, of his rhetoric? Certainly his religious atheism and his scorched stoicism played their role.[113]

Yet it is not only a question of philosophy, but also a question of imaginative similarity that tied them together: it was certain similarities, for instance, between Caproni's *Stanze della funicolare* (Funicular stanzas) and Frénaud's *Le silence de Genova* (The silence of Genoa).[114] The fact is, as Mengaldo notes, that Frénaud does not tread the line laid down by symbolist poets – which Caproni, as we saw with Mallarmé and Valéry, generally avoided translating. Nor, however, does Frénaud follow in the footsteps of Apollinaire.

Nonetheless, Caproni maintains that it is not so much a closeness that draws him to Frénaud's poetry but a sense of distance, of *diversità*: "The authentic spur [*molla*] that gave me the start, also for Frénaud, was the rapid recognition, in him, of that *diversity* [*diversità*] that I have always profitably looked for." This *diversità* resides above all in Frénaud's style. As Fabio Scotto writes, Frénaud's poetry is characterized by its "long verse, oriented towards semantic elaboration," while Caproni aims for a

> desertification of the text, the melodic despotism of his "moderately short" verse, his parodic rhyme, the spatial wandering of the words and the punctuation on the page, his epigrammatic fragments piercing like dagger blows.[115]

In Caproni's unrhymed and unmetered translations of Frénaud (matching the French poet's lack of form), the Italian poet thus transforms the French text not according to a predetermined rhyme scheme or metrical pattern, but at the lexical level itself. As Elisa Bricco observes, "The lexical transformations are the base, the fundamental element of this translation."[116] Caproni himself writes that he tried to remain faithful to the French (as opposed to rewriting it as in his Apollinaire translations):

> Within the limits of the possible, except for a few cases, I have tried not to stray too much [*non scostarmi troppo*] from the literal meaning, and always to keep myself on the edge of prose, according to what seemed to me the genuine spirit of the originals.[117]

It has been duly noted that in his translations of Frénaud, Caproni draws closer and closer to the French text as time goes by.[118] This is a constant feature of Caproni's variants in translations, both in poetry and prose, namely that he arrives at an even-greater literalism. But now let us look at his translation of Frénaud's "Epitaphe" (Epitaph), which was also translated by Ungaretti, and will therefore offer a means of comparing the two poet-translators' methods. (See table 3.3 below.)

According to Ungaretti, as we saw earlier, translation is theoretically impossible – as for Caproni. In the opinion of Ungaretti, the rhythm, syllabic quantity, content, form, and style are not transferable from one language to another. Thus, in essence, a translation is, in Ungaretti's words, "always the result of a compromise between two spirits."[119] Or, as Caproni would say, the translation is the child of the poet and translator. So, for Ungaretti, with poetic translation theoretically impossible, the reason for translation is "simply to make an original work of poetry."[120]

The first thing to be noted is the difference in title: while Caproni translates it literally, Ungaretti reprises a verse from the poem. The length of the two translations differs because of syntactic modifications. While Caproni's translation consists of thirteen verses, just like the French, Ungaretti's translation contains fifteen: two more than the original. This is due to Ungaretti's frequent verbal dislocations, from the first verse ("morto sarò") to the last ("per voi, permane"). This syntactic torsion is absent from the French and from Caproni's version, and is explainable by the date of the translation, namely, 1954. By this time Ungaretti had long been writing poetry with an eye to Petrarch, whose own verse was filled with syntactical inversions. Indeed, we can see the infiltration of Ungaretti's poetics already in the first verse, as Carla Gubert indicates:[121] Frénaud descriptively describes himself as dead, with "poussière / sur les buis" (dust / on the box trees); the Italian poet changes this to a simile: "sarò come sopra i bossi / polvere" (I will be like dust / above box trees). For Ungaretti it is not a question so much of changing lexical meanings but of changing the structure of the poem and the syntactical sequence. Indeed, there are about a dozen

Table 3.3 "Epitaphe"

André Frénaud "Epitaphe" [Epitaph]	**Giorgio Caproni "Epitaffio" [Epitaph]**	**Giuseppe Ungaretti "Tutto sarà in ordine" [Everything will be in order]**
Lorsque je serai mort avec de la poussière [When I am dead with some dust]	Quando sarò morto, insieme con un po' di polvere [When I will be dead, together with a bit of dust]	Quando morto sarò come sopra i bossi [When dead I will be like dust]
sur les buis – et les chiens joueront avec les enfants, [on the box trees – and the dogs will play with the children,]	sui bossi – e i cani giocheranno coi bambini, [on the box trees – and the dogs will play with the children,]	Polvere e con i bimbi i cani ruzzeranno, [On box trees and with the children the dogs will romp about,]
personne n'est en faute – le soleil [no one is at fault – the sun]	nessuno è in colpa – il sole [no one is to blame – the sun]	Nessuno è in fallo. Il sole nello stagno [No one is at fault. The sun in the pond]
luira dans l'étang pour se délasser, [will shine in the pond to relax,]	Brillerà nello stagno per svagarsi, [will shine in the pond to relax,]	Splenderà per svagarsi. [Will shine to relax.]
au matin sur les plates-bandes une buée perle; [in the morning on the flower beds the mist pearls;]	un umidore imperla al mattino le aiole; [a dampness will pearl the flower beds in the morning;]	Sui margini di aiuole di mattina [On the edges of the morning flowerbeds]
emmêlé avec les plantes je croîtrai parmi elles, [mixed with the plants I will grow among them,]	mescolato con le piante crescerò in mezzo a loro, [mixed with the plants, I will grow among them,]	S'imperla appannamento. [Misting becomes pearled.]
éparpillé avec les graines, délivré. [scattered with the seeds, freed.]	sparso coi semi, liberato. [scattered with the seeds, freed.]	Frammischiato alle piante tra di esse crescerò, [Mingled with the plants among them I will grow,] Sparso con la semente, liberato. [Scattered with the seed, freed.]

Table 3.3 "Epitaphe" (*Continued*)

André Frénaud "Epitaphe" [Epitaph]	**Giorgio Caproni "Epitaffio" [Epitaph]**	**Giuseppe Ungaretti "Tutto sarà in ordine" [Everything will be in order]**
Tout sera en ordre ni plus ni moins. La nature [All will be in order neither more nor less. Nature]	Tutto sarà in ordine, né più né meno. La natura [All will be in order, neither more nor less. Nature]	Tutto sarà in ordine, né più né meno. La natura [All will be in order, neither more nor less. Nature]
brouille les pistes, poursuit ses jeux, elle rit. [covers its tracks, continues its games, she laughs.]	imbroglia le piste, persegue i suoi giochi, ride. [covers its tracks, pursues its games, laughs.]	Le piste imbroglia, i giuochi suoi persegue, ride, [Covers its tracks, pursues its games, laughs,]
Bienveillante avec d'autres il le faut croire [Benevolent with others it is necessary to think of her	Benevola con altri, dobbiamo crederlo, [Benevolent with others, we must believe it]	Benevola con altri, occorre crederlo, [Benevolent with others, it is necessary to believe]
jusqu'à les lâcher quand il lui plait. [until Nature abandons them when she wants to.]	fino a mollarli quando le farà piacere. [until it abandons them when it wants to.]	Sino a mollarli quando le parrà. [Until it abandons them when it pleases.]
Mais quel tremblement dans vos voix sera-t-il demeuré [But which trembling in your voices will have remained]	Ma quale tremito nelle vostre voci sarà rimasto, [But what trembling in your voices will be left,]	Ma nelle vostre voci quale tremito [But in your voices what trembling]
de ma voix qui avait parlé pour vous? [of my voice that had spoken for you?]	della mia voce che aveva parlato per voi? [of my voice that had spoken for you?]	Della mia voce che parlato aveva [Of my voice that had spoken]
		Per voi, permane? [For you, remains?]
Source: *André Frénaud tradotto da 15 poeti italiani, e da Elio Vittorini*, 32	Source: *Frénaud, Non c'è paradiso*, 205	Source: *André Frénaud tradotto da 15 poeti italiani, e da Elio Vittorini*, 33

instances of the above-mentioned shiftings, almost one in each verse of his translation. Ungaretti makes up for the lack of formal metre and rhyme through this pattern of inversions. Caproni, on the other hand, doesn't make use of shiftings here, even if he frequently utilizes stylistic inversion in other translations. For example, in verse 9, the poet-translators use identical verbs and nouns, but in a different order: Ungaretti has "Le piste imbroglia, i giuochi suoi persegue, ride," while Caproni has the more faithful "imbroglia le piste, persegue i suoi giochi, ride." Caproni does use phonosyllabic effects here, such as the alliterative *p* in "un *p*o' di *p*olvere," *s* in "*s*parso coi *s*emi," and he uses the assonance of *i* in "su*i* boss*i* – e *i* can*i* giocheranno co*i* bamb*ini*." Ungaretti uses assonance with the *s* of "*s*ole," "*s*tagno," "*s*plenderà," and "*s*vagarsi."

This translation is one of the few instances where Caproni comments on the differences between his version and another's. He justifies his translation of the final verses in the following way:

> It is one of the rare cases in which the conjunction between two languages is such as to render sufficient – and even musically productive – the pure and simple literal transposition, and it is to this, in fact, which here I kept myself, finding again almost intact in my Italian version, together with the movement, the same vibrations [*le stesse vibrazioni*] of the text.[122]

We note here that he uses the same (Crocean) terminology as we saw before: "le stesse vibrazioni del testo" (the same vibrations of the text). Caproni then remarks that Ungaretti chose to translate differently, "with a completely other ear, I repeat, and perhaps with the intention of integrating the text with a *tradition* more of our own: Petrarchan."[123]

In the end, both translations effectively read as poems. The final verse in Ungaretti's version is powerful by its brevity as a pentasyllabic line, with "permane" (persists) lingering in the air as an unanswered question, as though the existence of the poet – the "tremito / della mia voce" – were hanging in the balance. On the other hand, Caproni's rendering focuses on the interlocutors: "nelle vostre voci … / … per voi?" as though interrogating the existence of others.

We now come to the final poet in Caproni's *Quaderno*, Baudelaire, whose verse was certainly the most intractable to translate for our Italian poet. Caproni writes to Betocchi in 1954 about some initial translations of Baudelaire: "I am racking my brains on them."[124] In 1962, Caproni's translation of Baudelaire's *Fleurs du mal* (Flowers of evil) was published by Curcio. But, due to editorial cuts and revisions, Caproni's version was so massively altered by the editor that he publicly renounced it, writing that "a Baudelaire with my name is circulating, which is not mine at all, so much has it been revised and 'wronged,' perhaps on the model of the most prized translations."[125]

Indeed, up until Caproni's death he had been working on a new translation of *Les Fleurs du mal*, which has recently been published.[126] Caproni originally decided to translate *Les Fleurs du mal* into prose, except for the poems in the last two sections of the book, *Révolte* (Revolt) and *La mort* (Death). His choice of translating most of Baudelaire's verse into prose was rather startling, considering how many French poets Caproni had already translated into Italian verse – from Prévert and Apollinaire to Éluard and Char. Caproni himself states that he chose prose because Baudelaire, like "all true poets" (*tutti i veri poeti*), is "practically untranslatable" (*pressoché intraducibile*). So, lacking "the presumption" (*presunzione*) for "a rewriting [*rifacimento*] in Italian verse (which would require a new Vincenzo Monti), we have preferred the simple translation into prose."[127]

Certainly another factor is that Caproni admired Baudelaire's poetry to such a degree that it was inconceivable to think about adapting it in the same way he translated Apollinaire, Verlaine, or Prévert. He couldn't simply rewrite it in Italian as if Baudelaire had been born Italian. He had too much respect for the prestige of his verse, and not enough *presunzione*.[128] So, Caproni used prose in a higher literary register than the French itself and filled his translation with archaic poetic diction like "procella" (tempest), "dittamo" (dittany), and "bombito" (rumble).[129] The Italian poet-translator turned back to the Italian poetic tradition, more magniloquent than the French one, which gives a different flavour to his version. On the rhetorical front, Caproni has recourse to alliteration and assonance to try to compensate for the missing metre and rhyme. Yet Caproni's prose, heavy with rhetorical effects like inversions and hyperbatons, clearly lies at a distance from Baudelaire's own prose poems in the *Spleen de Paris* (Paris spleen).

Meanwhile, as we said, Caproni translated the final two sections of *Les Fleurs du mal* in verse. The Ligurian poet found these poems "too closely tied to certain of our personal adventures for us to be able to resist the temptations of the siren."[130] Indeed, as Luca Pietromarchi remarks, the "poetic universe" of Baudelaire and Caproni are very close,[131] especially with Caproni's poetry beginning with *Congedo del viaggiatore cerimonioso*.[132] As critics have long observed, Caproni's own verse deals with the idea of travelling. Pietromarchi rightly observes, noting the version of the last stanzas of Baudelaire's poem, "Le voyage," that

> Caproni ... repudiates that extreme romantic tremor, which illuminated a light of hope at the bottom of the abyss ... conferring on the voyage, not the Baudelarian sense of an orphic adventure, but the sense of an inexorable dissolution of knowledge and hope in the unknowable. [133]

In other words, Baudelaire's *nouveau* (new) is enwrapped in the *inconnu* (unknown), at the end of the *viaggio* (voyage), the end of life. We will look specifically now at the final two stanzas of "Le voyage" in translations by both Giorgio Caproni and the significant poet Giovanni Raboni (see table 3.4 below). Before we begin, let us see what Raboni says about his own translation techniques. Raboni translated twenty works in his career, more than almost all poet-translators. He translated predominantly from French, and he is best known for his versions of Proust's *À la recherche du temps perdu* (In search of lost time),[134] Flaubert's *L'Éducation sentimentale* (Sentimental education),[135] and the poetry of Baudelaire,[136] Apollinaire,[137] and Jacques Prévert.[138] Like Caproni, Raboni considers himself a translator, but not a "theorist of translation" (*traduttologo*).[139] Both poet-translators believe in the impossibility of perfect translations. As Raboni says, translating a literary text is something "totally impossible, from a conceptual point of view, which, however, at times, one must do and which is all the same necessary to do."[140] In Raboni's view, one must try to understand the author's style "intimately, and be intimately (and tirelessly) faithful to it," keeping in mind, however, that "the literal meaning" is only one of a series of factors. Since "it is absolutely, obviously, categorically impossible to be faithful to everything," it is necessary to select "from time to time something to which one must be faithful, or better, less unfaithful."[141] In other words, "one can be faithful only making a meticulous and rigorous system of 'programmed' infidelities."[142] These "programmed infidelities" (*infedeltà programmate*) changed through Raboni's translations of Baudelaire, a "work in progress ... practically interminable," stretching out through multiple editions,[143] like Giudici's version of *Eugenio Onegin*, for more than twenty years. In the first version, published in 1973,[144] Raboni says he aimed for two things, "prosiness" (*prosasticità*) and "transgression" (*trasgressione*). Thus, he came to publish his 1975 laudatory preface to Attilio Bertolucci's prose translation of *Les Fleurs du mal*. In contrast, in

Table 3.4 "Le voyage"

Charles Baudelaire "Le voyage" [The voyage]	**Giorgio Caproni "Il viaggio" [The voyage]**	**Giovanni Raboni "Il viaggio" [The voyage]**
O Mort, vieux capitain, il est temps! levons l'ancre! [O Death, old captain, it is time! Let us raise the anchor!]	Andiamo, Morte, vecchio capitano! è ormai l'ora! [Let's go, Death, old captain! It's now time!]	Su, andiamo, Morte, vecchio capitano! [Come on, let's go, Death, old captain!]
Ce pays nous ennuie, ô Mort! Appareillons! [This country bores us, o Death! Let's cast off!]	Questa terra ci aduggia: è tempo di salpare! [This land bores us: it is time to set sail!]	Salpiamo, è tempo, via da questa noia! [Let's set sail, it's time, away from this boredom!]
Si le ciel et la mer sont noirs comme de l'encre, [If the sky and the sea are black like ink,]	Tu sai che i nostri cuori sono pieni d'aurora, [You know that our hearts are full of dawn,]	Son neri come inchiostro terra e mare, [They are black like ink, land and sea,]
Nos coeurs que tu connais sont remplis de rayons! [Our hearts that you know are full of rays!]	Anche se nero inchiostro sono il cielo ed il mare! [Even the sky and sea are black ink!]	Ma i nostri cuori, vedi, sono colmi di luce. [But our hearts, see, are filled with light.]
Verse-nous ton poison pour qu'il nous réconforte! [Pour us your poison so that it comforts us!]	Mescici il tuo veleno, giacché ci riconforta! [Pour us your poison, since it comforts us!]	Versaci per conforto il tuo veleno! [Pour us, as comfort, your poison!]
Nous voulons, tant ce feu nous brûle le cerveau, [We want, so much does the fire burn our brain,]	Vogliamo, tanto ci arde il cervello un tal fuoco, [We want, so much does such a fire burn our brain,]	Quel fuoco arde il cervello: giù nel gorgo profondo, [That fire burns the brain: down in the deep whirlpool,]
Plonger au fond du gouffre, Enfer ou Ciel, qu'importe? [To plunge into the bottom of the abyss, Hell or Heaven, what does it matter?]	Naufragar nel gorgo, Cielo o Inferno, che importa? [To shipwreck in the whirlpool, Heaven or Hell, what does it matter?]	Giù nell'Ignoto, sia L'Inferno o il Cielo, [Down in the Unknown, whether Hell or Heaven,]
Au fond de l'Inconnu pour trouver du nouveau! [At the bottom of the Unknown to find something new!]	Per trovare del nuovo sul fondo dell'Ignoto! [To find something new at the bottom of the Unknown!]	Scendiamo alla ricerca di qualcosa di nuovo! [Let us descend in the search for something new!]
Source: Caproni, *Quaderno di traduzioni*, 294	Source: Caproni, *Quaderno di traduzioni*, 295	Source: Baudelaire, *I fiori del male e altre poesie*, 225

the later years of his revisions (the last edition is from 1999),[145] he sought to normalize the metre,[146] reducing, for instance, enjambment.

While Caproni translates *Le Voyage* in double seven-syllable verses (*doppi settenari*), mostly in rhyme (*abab, CxCy*), Raboni doesn't rhyme at all. Yet paradoxically, Caproni's version generally adheres to Baudelaire's text. Raboni's version is decidedly less faithful, because he eliminates words from the French, such as *nous voulons, tant, nous, qu'importe*[147] (all translated in Caproni's version), while he often translates a vastly different semantic meaning or he translates into a different register. The French *ciel* (*cielo* for the Ligurian poet) becomes, for Raboni, a different concept entirely, namely *terra,* and *ce pays* turns into *via da questa noia*. Moreover, there is a colloquial patina in Raboni's translation, evinced in *su* and *vedi,* that is absent both from the French and from Caproni's rendering. On the other hand, Caproni's translation is more literary with its diction (*aduggia* and *mescici,* for instance)[148] that is clearly formal and not colloquial. If Raboni, for example, translates rather literally "Nos coeurs ... sont remplis de rayons" as "i nostri cuori sono pieni di luce,"[149] Caproni has the more poetic (and rooted in literary tradition) "i nostri cuori sono pieni d'aurora."[150] It is Caproni whose version is more markedly a poetic transfusion. This is not entirely surprising, since to translate Baudelaire into verse, the translator must possess a remarkable talent and ear for all the possible sonorities in one's language. We can see this most clearly in the final verses. Here, Raboni emphasizes the descent into the unknown, with *giù* repeated twice, *profondo* added to the Italian version (for *au fond*), and *L'Ignoto* moved up to the seventh verse.[151] Yet his prosaic *sia* in *sia/L'Inferno o il Cielo* destroys the poetic effect of the verse. Finally, Raboni translates *plonger* as the weaker *scendiamo,*[152] putting too much weight on the repeated adverb *giù*. Caproni, meanwhile, uses the Leopardian *naufragar,*[153] which leads us irresistibly to think of the infinite, here in the deepest abyss of the unknown. It is Caproni's version that is both the most faithful to the original, from a grammatical, lexical, and formal point of view, and the most successful as a recreation of the French original. We saw that for Raboni, a faithful translation implies "mettendo a punto un minizioso e rigoroso (anche se, necessariamente, elastico) sistema di infedeltà 'programmate.'"[154] The problem is that here the infidelities do not release an explosion of poetic grace – whereas Caproni's own liberties, as we saw for instance with *aurora,* creates a most potent verse. Then again, it would have been surprising if Raboni, whose own poetry lacks the musical power and rhythm of Caproni's, had been able to achieve a more forceful translation of Baudelaire.

It is with Baudelaire that Caproni ends his *Quaderno*, but not with the French poet's *La mort* but rather with "Les Petites Vieilles" (The little old women). This latter poem is significantly chosen for its concluding verses, by a poet-translator who was in his late seventies: "Ruderi, oh mia famiglia, cervelli congeneri, io ogni sera vi do un solenne addio! Dove sarete domani, Eve ottuagenarie, su cui grava l'artiglio tremendo di Dio?" (Ruins, oh my family, congeneric brains, every evening I give you a solemn adieu! Where will you be tomorrow, eighty-year-old Eves, on whom the terrible claw of God weighs down?).[155] Here, Caproni compares himself to multiple Eves, with God's tremendous claw on his shoulder, an apt image for the poet battling with God (and his absence) in the last period of his poetry. This *Quaderno*, "a real workshop of the translator as imitator,"[156] is finally "a dialogue with many voices among Caproni's poetry, the texts of the chosen poets and the versions of such poets."[157] It is within this volume's translations that we see the opening of Caproni's final poetic phase (begun with the *Congedo del viaggiatore cerimonioso*). Finally, it is through Caproni's translations that, as Giorgio Agamben remarks, "the 'transmutation' was prepared that marks the thematic turning point of Caproni's final poetry."[158]

Translation Techniques

Elisa Bricco has helpfully synthesized the manner in which Caproni translated, which roughly followed five stages:

> He began with a quick draft of a first manuscript version, more or less literal ... following this was a second manuscript version/variation, which was enriched by the search for the meaning of particularly important words, and with a comparison with versions by other translators (he even rewrote poems verse by verse, one by one from the various versions by other translators to make the comparisons); he thus arrived at a first typed version, which he glossed with corrections and starting points drawn from further encyclopedic and dictionary investigations; a second typed version followed, defined in hand "Final," even this glossed, and at last a third typed version which would then be printed.[159]

Indeed, Caproni was very emphatic about seeing his *bozze* (drafts) and having time to correct them. As he asks Betocchi, "Will I be able to see the proofs of the translated pages, when there is time? A rereading with a detached mind will always be of help. I would like to very much."[160] For Caproni, correcting the proofs "means, for me, to compare again everything with the text."[161]

There are a number of constants in Caproni's translation methods of poetry. First, there is almost always an adherence to the original (or equivalent) metre, or rhythmical structure. As Lorenzo Flabbi shows, Caproni's translation of Henri Thomas's poem "'Le village, l'arbre' [The village, the tree] perfectly accounts for the alexandrines and the system of rhymes in the original."[162] Or as Mengaldo notes in Caproni's translation of Frénaud's "Il n'y pas de paradis" (There is no paradise), "Caproni, as usual, conserves with the greatest faithfulness possible, the structure of the original."[163] Indeed, as Laura Dolfi shows in her analysis of Caproni's translation of Lorca's "Llanto por Ignacio Sánchez Mejías" (Lament for Ignacio Sánchez Mejías), a number of verses retain the exact placement of accents as in the original Spanish.[164] Along with this, Caproni aims to reproduce "the rhythm, the sound, above all the tone" of the original.[165] As for the rhyme, a cornerstone of Caproni's technique, he not only tries to preserve equivalent or similar rhyme schemes but also frequently adds internal rhymes. As Mengaldo writes,

> On the whole, one can perhaps say that the faithfulness of Caproni is above all faithfulness to the melodic and singing characteristics, and in some way gnomic, of the original ... The values of repetition, identity, and parallelism are reproduced with all of the means possible.[166]

For, as the Italian poet writes, if the form or simply the cadence of the word is changed, although the "literal meaning" remains "intact" (*intatto*) the "poetic effect" is "completely lost or altered."[167] Moreover, Caproni's use of alliteration and assonance is all the greater when the translation lacks rhyme, as Elisa Bricco and Judith Lindenberg show: he "compensates," to use Fortini's words, with such poetic effects for the inevitable losses in translation.[168]

Frequently Caproni prunes the originals as well, which goes against one of the main translation hypotheses, formulated by Antoine Berman, that "every translation tends to be longer than the original."[169] Yet, Caproni's translation of Théophile De Viau's *Stances* (Stanzas) has 146 words instead of 178 (about 20 per cent fewer words). He drastically cuts out and reduces phrases and words, rearranging the syntax. Likewise, in Victor Hugo's "Elle était déchaussée, elle était décoiffée" (She was barefoot, she had ruffled hair),[170] there are 135 words in French but only 105 in the translation (20 per cent fewer words).[171] Caproni eliminated much: because what was most important for him was maintaining the rhythm and rhyme in this poem (the rhyme scheme *abab/cdcd/efef/ghgh* remains identical in the translation). This rhyme scheme led to the segmentation of the clauses of the original and it inverted the syntax, as we see in the last strophe of the poem. Here is the French text and its gloss, and then Caproni's translation and its gloss:

Comme l'eau caressait doucement le rivage!
Je vis venire à moi, dans les grands roseaux verts,
La belle fille heureuse, effarée et sauvage,
Ses cheveux dans ses yeux, et riant au travers.

[How the water softly caressed the shore!
I saw coming towards me, in the great green reeds,
The beautiful happy girl, alarmed and wild,
Her hair in her eyes, and laughing sideways.]

Molle blandiva l'acqua ora la spiaggia.
E dal canneto folto, lei felice,
vidi, e sgomenta, venire selvaggia
ridendo, fra i capelli, di tralice.[172]

[Softly the water caressed now the beach,
And from the thick bed of reeds,
I saw her happy, and dismayed, coming wild
Laughing, through her hair, sideways.]

The first verse of the translation makes use of Italian freedom in word order: the subject is placed after the verb, instead of before, as in the French. The second and third verses are rather contorted and impossible to render into grammatically faithful English. If Hugo's French in these two lines is rather straightforward, postponing the direct object ("la belle fille"), Caproni's Italian is syntactically complex. The juxtaposition, for example, of the first person "vidi," followed by "e sgomenta," referring to the girl, is quite harsh. Yet Caproni uses many Italian cognates. Meanwhile, in Caproni's translation of Lorca's "Llanto,"[173] the Italian poet-translator also eliminates words in order to keep to a seven-syllable line (*il settenario*), a shorter and quicker metre than the original.

Table 3.5 "Chez la fleuriste"

Jacques Prévert, "Chez la fleuriste" [At the florist's]	**Giorgio Caproni, "Dalla fioraia" [At the florist's]**
Et il tombe [And he falls]	E casca [And (he) falls]
En même temps qu'il tombe [At the same time that he falls]	Nello stesso tempo che casca [At the same time that (he) falls]
L'argent roule a terre [The money rolls to the ground]	I soldi ruzzolano in terra [The coins tumble to the ground]
Et puis les fleurs tombent [And then the flowers fall]	E poi i fiori cascano [And then the flowers fall]
Source: Caproni, *Quaderno di traduzioni*, 170	Source: Caproni, *Quaderno di traduzioni*, 171

There are two more techniques, namely, conserving repetition and adding inversion, which, as Lorenzo Flabbi points out, are some of Caproni's distinctive traits as a translator.[174] We can see (in table 3.5) an example of the first in his version of Prévert's *Chez la fleuriste* (At the florist's). Caproni repeats the equivalent Italian term for *tomber* (*cascare*) in all three verses. This sort of repetition is foreign to other poet-translators like Montale and Buffoni.

In short, Caproni focuses on making an original text: a recreation means finding equivalences in the target language and culture. Domestication is the key idea here, and the text is brought towards the reader. When there is a battle between fidelity to the text and poetic valour of Italian, the Italian poet-translator opts for the latter.

Conclusion

Caproni's translation methods are assuredly domesticating. He doesn't attempt to make his translations sound foreign, so he translates even proper names into Italian. His goal is to make the translation sound as if it were originally written in Italian. So the fact that it is a translation should be invisible. We have seen this similar ideology at work in Montale's versions, which differs from both Giudici's and Sanguineti's practices. Yet there are two different roads that Caproni follows: imaginative equivalencies with rhymed and metered poems (as in Apollinaire); and extreme fidelity, tempered by *compensi*, to a non-metrically regular text (as in Char and Frénaud).

Caproni would surely agree with Joseph Brodsky that "meters are the magnitude of the soul." The search for music is paramount to his translations, and therefore a poet must translate poetry, not a professional translator. When a poet achieves an excellent translation, the translation becomes a work of poetry, and this becomes an addition to the "patrimony of literature." Yet one author overwhelmed Caproni throughout his life: Baudelaire. Caproni came up against a poet whose multifarious rhythmical and rhyming texts challenged his own preternaturally-gifted ability to utilize any number of metrical forms. His translation of the *Fleurs du mal* is, in effect, somewhat disappointing, notably in his prose translations: his selection of different registers creates a strained music. The translations were themselves unsatisfying to Caproni, for which reason he first repudiated them and then didn't publish a new version. But it is clear where his talent led him: his translations of Char, Frénaud, and Apollinaire are often truly marvellous and read as though composed in Italian. With the former two French poets, Caproni had an advantage, I would argue, since his own poetry is more founded on assonance, alliteration, and rhythm than Char's and Frénaud's.

Caproni, in the years preceding his death, was working on three translations: his *Quaderno di traduzioni*, and new versions of Baudelaire's *Fleurs du mal* and Céline's *Mort à credit* (Death on the installment plan). These two French accursed (*maudits*) writers wrote in completely opposite styles: Baudelaire in classical verse, recalling Racine, and Céline in solecism-filled slang. Both authors to some degree accompanied Caproni for the last third of his life, from the early 1960s until 1990. And the Italian poet was unsatisfied with both of his published translations, and both times he was unhappy with the editors' treatment. His Céline was censured, in part; his Baudelaire was amputated and crassly mutated. Yet his dissatisfaction also resided in his own translation methods. His first translation of Céline was filled with archaic Tuscanisms, both idioms and imprecations.[175] His 1962 translation of Baudelaire translated most of the book into prose and into a mixture of styles and registers that was alien to the classical French text. So where was he headed with his revisions of Céline and Baudelaire? The portion that he revised of *Mort à credit*, about fifty pages of Céline's novel, expunges most of the Tuscan slang and adheres more closely to the French, with much more obscenity, vulgarity, and blasphemy.[176] His new version of Baudelaire still kept the majority of poems in prose, and his continual dissatisfaction with it can be seen in his note to Mengaldo about the

Quaderno, in which he says about Baudelaire that "I could [*potrei*] save "Le voyage" (translated into verse) and another two or three poems."[177] The conditional *potrei* shows his reticence to include the French poet.

To conclude, the last phase of Caproni's poetry is marked by the *caccia della lingua* (hunt for language) as Agamben declares, "where the word turns now to its own logical power, it speaks itself." In one of the poems in his posthumous *Res amissa*, composed on a summer Sunday evening in 1988, we see how Caproni visualizes his voice as translated in words, but painfully so, with extreme loss:

Ahi mia voce, mia voce.
Occlusa. Rinserrata.
Anche se per legame
musaico armonizzata.[178]

[Ah, my voice, my voice.
Occluded. Shut in.
Even if by poetic
tie harmonized.]

On numerous occasions Caproni cited Dante's phrase about the impossibility of translation, seen here in the "legame / musaico armonizzata." What Caproni imagines in this poem is his voice obstructed, closed off in words, even if the words are musically assembled and harmonized. The emphasis lies in the action of the two past participles (fatefully past tense): *occlusa, rinserrata*. This poem is a truly imperfect translation, then, and a recognition of the impermanent stability of words and lives. We have already seen how Frénaud questioned, in his *Epitaphe*, whether his voice would survive in the voices of others, or as Caproni translated, "Ma quale tremito nelle vostre voci sarà rimasto, / della mia voce che aveva parlato per voi?" (But what trembling in your voices will be left / of my voice that had spoken for you?) If the last stage of Caproni's poetry is an obsessive search for possible answers to this question, here our poet finds a definitive, negative response. The trembling (*tremito*) will be lost in translation.

4 Giovanni Giudici: Translation, Constructive Principles, and *Amor de lonh*[1]

Giovanni Giudici's translations, many of which are from Russian[2] and Czech,[3] do not reflect common trends among Italian poet-translators. No twentieth-century Italian poet cemented his poetic career with formative translations from these two literatures. Moreover, he translated more Anglo-American poets than any other Italian poet-translator of his generation. Even if Giudici had never written a verse of his own, he would still be known today for his artistic translations from Russian, Czech, and English. The critic Giorgio Manacorda even suggests that "from a cultural point of view Giudici's most important activity is certainly that of a translator."[4]

Giudici's translation of *Eugene Onegin* masterfully wedded an innovative use of poetic registers to a ductile poetic metre, fulfilling his own desire of creating a long narrative poem. Alexander Pushkin became an Italian citizen, so to speak, and now is permanently in the orbit of Italian literature. Giudici's translations of Czech poetry, first gathered together in his *Omaggio a Praga* (Homage to Prague),[5] constituted the first anthology of modern Czech verse published in Italian and Giudici was, moreover, instrumental in introducing several Czech poets to the Italian reading public. His translations of Robert Frost[6] have become canonical; his were the first volumes of Italian translations of Sylvia Plath,[7] John Crowe Ransom,[8] and Hart Crane.[9] Whereas most poet-translators generally composed one *quaderno di traduzioni*, from Montale[10] to Sanguineti,[11] Giudici published three separate *quaderni*: *Addio, proibito piangere e altri versi tradotti (1955–1980)* (A valediction, forbidding mourning and other translated poems),[12] *A una casa non sua*: *nuovi versi tradotti (1955–1995)* (To a house not his own: new translated poems),[13] and *Vaga lingua strana: dai versi tradotti* (Beautiful strange language: from translated poems).[14]

While a few critics have studied Giudici's translations,[15] on the whole they have been relatively neglected, and my analysis of his *quaderni di traduzioni* is the first comprehensive study of them. In particular, I am concerned with situating Giudici's translations at the heart of his work because of their literary and cultural importance. This is certainly not to demean his own poetry, which has played a significant role in Italian letters due to several factors: Giudici's linguistic virtuosity, his alternating high and low styles, his autobiographical verse, and his rewriting and innovation of the Italian literary tradition (*le forme logore* [worn out forms] in Giudici's formulation). Yet his translations are so integral to his own work, as we will see, that reflecting on them allows us to better understand Giudici's own poetry and poetics. I will show that for him translations are not mere appendages to his *oeuvre*, but they are part and parcel of his own work. His *quaderni di traduzioni* reveal a consummate craftsman at work whose books are not randomly organized or casually put together, but woven together in a carefully articulated structure. Not miscellanies of translations, they are new books with original titles, and they offer clear divisions within the volumes. Giudici's translation work is responsible for his poetic consciousness, poetic metres, and some of his most fulfilling verse in Italian. I will demonstrate how Giudici's translations do not, generally, adapt the source work in the target language, but try to "foreignize" Italian through a combination of linguistic factors. My reading will draw on three theorists: Yury Tynjanov, and his theory of poetic language, which helped form Giudici's own poetics; Friedrich Schleiermacher, and his well-known theorization of moving the reader of the translation towards the original text; and Lawrence Venuti, with his reformulation of Schleiermacher's conception into the notion of the "foreignizing" translation. It will become clear that Giudici's own poetics revolve around the foreignness of poetic language itself, which conditions his own translations and renders them poetically foreign for an Italian reader. Thus, Giudici, by means of a judicious choice of a specific "constructive principle" (Tynjanov) inherent in the source text, brings the reader towards the original through an estranging and a foreignizing translation method.

This chapter is organized in several sections. First, I will begin by giving an outline of Giudici's poetic career and poetics; second, I will provide a panorama of Giudici's translations through the years and a description of his translation ideology; and third, I will discuss his trips to Russia and Prague and the resulting translations of *Eugene Onegin* and Czech poets in *Omaggio a Praga*. Then I will analyse his three *quaderni di traduzioni*, and afterwards I will compare his translation of Emily

Dickinson with that of Margherita Guidacci's. I will follow this with a review of Giudici's translation methods and conclude by connecting his translations to his Italian verse.

Poetic Career

Giudici was born in 1924 in Le Grazie, a small seaside village near La Spezia in the northwestern Italian region of Liguria. He spent his formative years in Rome, worked in Milan as a copywriter at Olivetti for many years, and returned to his native town where he died in 2011. His first major work of poetry, *La vita in versi* (Life in verses, 1965), is characterized by the poet's portrayal of himself as a typical bourgeois in Milan, yet it is not so much an autobiographical portrait as a depiction of a (Poundian) *persona*.

Emblematic of this volume are the following well-known verses:

"La vita in versi"

Metti in versi la vita, trascrivi
Fedelmente, senza tacere
Particolare alcuno, l'evidenza dei vivi
...
Inoltre metti in versi che morire
È possibile a tutti più che nascere
E in ogni caso l'essere è più del dire.[16]

[Put your life into verses, transcribe
Faithfully, without silencing
Any detail, the evidence of the living
...
Moreover, put into verses that dying
Is possible for all, more than being born,
And, in any case, being is more than speaking.]

The semi-autobiography (*fedelmente, senza tacere / particolare alcuno*) gives way to the concluding tercet: a person cannot be born (*nascere*) but only die (*morire*), and poetry (*dire*) is unable to achieve being (*essere*). In a subsequent phase, as we will see, Giudici will discover that poetry can in fact *be* and not merely *say*, and that a poet can both inscribe and incarnate himself in his verse.

His poetic career can be divided into two periods: pre- and post-1966. In the first period, his poetry, while ingeniously composed, is structured around specific themes: the condition of a typical middle-class man in Milan during the "economic miracle," the pull of left-wing politics and the search for the divine, nostalgia for his dead mother, guilt of various kinds, and the masks of everyday life. The contradictions within Giudici's work cannot be underlined enough, and they suggest some of the complexities involved in the interpretation of his poetics. As the critic Giovanni Tesio writes, Giudici is a "Catholic without a church, Communist without a paradise, intellectual without a family tradition."[17] Yet two decisive events occurred in his life that irremediably altered his poetics: his 1966 trip to Moscow and 1967 trip to Prague. These two journeys transformed Giudici's consciousness of himself as a poet and translator. The result was not only translations from Czech and Russian poetry but also a different idea of poetry itself. From 1967 onwards, a new conception of poetic language – as a physical body, as the body and blood of the poet, and as the body and blood of the nation itself – dominated Giudici's poetics, greatly impacting both his poetry and his translations. The energy and vitality of Giudici's linguistic virtuosity come to the fore, and content becomes equally dependent on form.

This shift in poetics can be exemplified in Giudici's attachment to the writings of the influential Russian literary critic, Yury Tynjanov. Tynjanov, born in the last decade of the nineteenth century, was "one of the founding members of the school of formalism in Russia"[18] and he was the first to conceive of literature as a system.[19] Giudici learned of him when the critic Giansiro Ferrata mentioned his name in a review of Giudici's volume *La vita in versi*. Procuring a copy of Tynjanov's *The Problem of Verse Language* directly from Tynjanov's family, Giudici set to work translating it with Ljudmila Kortikova upon his return from Russia. Under the influence of Tynjanov's book, Giudici began thinking of language not as a transparent vehicle to transport content but as something that gives meaning itself. Language signifies and creates meaning through its form, as Giudici writes in *Andare in Cina a piedi* [Going to China on foot]: "Tynjanov was not perhaps the first or the only one to discover that a poem is not only what it *means* [*significa*], but above all what it *is* [*è*]; but without a doubt it was his book that helped me become fully conscious of this."[20]

The components of poetic language are not limited to referents, but they include all aspects of the text: grammar and syntax, diction, rhyme, rhythm, sound, rhetorical figures, and layout of the page, all of which combine to form the poem. While Giudici credits Tynjanov with convincing him of this, he also carried this out himself, even if unconsciously, in his contemporary translation of Jiří Orten. Indeed, Giudici did not faithfully translate the opening verse of Orten's poem "Čemu se báseň říká" (What a poem is called): in Czech, *čemu* (what) is a pronoun. Instead, Giudici rendered this as "La cosa chiamata poesia" (The thing called poetry), turning the Czech pronoun into an Italian noun (*la cosa*). As Giudici went on to write in a fundamental 1984 essay, "Come una poesia si costruisce" (How a poem is constructed):

> At the time, in 1968, when Mikeš and I translated this and many other poems of Orten's, I hadn't paid attention to two details that made and above all make this poetic text ["La cosa chiamata poesia"] almost a concentrate [*concentrato*] of an *ars poetica* for me; one of them – which emerges only in translation, since in the original there is only the simple relative pronoun *čemu* – is the definition of poetry as *thing* [*cosa*].[21]

The verse *La cosa chiamata poesia* (chosen by Giudici and Mikeš to be the title of the Italian volume) becomes an *ars poetica* precisely because poetry is asserted as autonomous from its referents and its content. On this basis, spurred on by his experience in the Prague Spring of 1968 and conversations with Mikeš and other Czech writers and intellectuals, Giudici developed more articulated and metaphorical notions of poetic language.

For Giudici, poetic language became something physical, a sort of body, even a person, by virtue of its action on the poet: indeed, in this view, it is co-author of the poem itself. "Language is a person [*una persona*]," Giudici writes on various occasions, with "(almost always) mysterious desires (*volontà*)," and this "person," this "living body" is indeed "co-author of the poem."[22] For Giudici, language "uses us just as we use it." Not only does he consider "Language as a big person" but also he considers language "a species of Superspecies among the many that populate the world, distinguishable and distinguished in those single entities that are linguistic families, national languages, dialects, and slangs."[23] This means that there is a pre-existing language from which poems emerge, almost without any help from the poet himself.

This concept of poetry as a physical body enlarges to include the body of the author himself: poetic language becomes the body (and blood) of the poet, in a process of metaphorical transubstantiation. As Giudici writes: "a poem is a *thing* [*cosa*], born from a mysterious alchemy, from a species (I would dare hypothesize) of Transubstantiation, from a simple *speaking* to a much more complex and concrete *being* [*essere*]."[24] Indeed, if we remember the final verse from Giudici's poem "La vita in versi," "and in any case being is more than speaking," it is clear how the poem achieves the supreme state of being, of existence due to its incorporation of the physical essence of the poet.

Giudici goes on, asking rhetorically, "Isn't writing a projection [*proiezione*] of our body, beginning with the complete sign of the little schoolboy who learns to spell his name, to *write himself* [*scriversi*]?"[25] The poet writes himself into the poem – as Jiří Orten did. As Giudici says, "Orten is the Czech poet who writes himself ... the poet *is* his own text, biology and biography entirely entrusted to writing."[26] The poet immortalizes not merely his words within the poem, as is usually thought, but his body. It is as though in reading a poem, we unspool the DNA of the author that is contained within the poem, strand by strand, verse by verse.

And lastly, poetic language becomes politically and religiously identified with the state itself, with the nation. As Giudici notes in his preface to Jiří Orten's poetry, "Language is in fact the body of the nation [*il corpo della nazione*], and the 'incarnated word' of the community."[27] Once again, it is to the Czech nation that Giudici turns (but he also speaks similarly about Pushkin and the Russians), this time in a review of Jaroslav Seifert's verse:

> I hadn't yet understood to what degree a Bohemian poet is almost naturally delegated to represent and indeed (if he is a true poet) does represent his nation, for whom even when he writes of blouses and underwear lying on a meadow to dry, he is still a civil poet, at the service of Language [*al servizio della Lingua*]. And never did a nation more than the Bohemian nation coincide concretely and with religious viscerality with its own Language.[28]

The adjective *religiosa* is precisely chosen, since for Giudici, as he writes in *Andare in Cina a piedi*, "language is also a religion, in the more proper and secular sense of the term a common value that unites us. The Latin *religio* derives from *religare*: to unite together. Language is the patrimony of the nation, community of past and present people, in whom it (language) is incarnated."[29]

The religious vocabulary of transubstantiation and incarnation as well as Giudici's assertion that "the word is 'the word,' the Word [*il Verbo*] (for whoever is ready to bet on it) of God, the Word that doesn't bear to be called in vain: and this is valid for everyone, believers or non-believers" makes clear that behind his conception of poetic language lies the idea that language is indeed the word of God.

This dramatic shift in poetics is first visible in *Autobiologia* (Autobiology, 1969).[30] Written post-Moscow and, especially, post-Prague, this volume showcases the new identification of poetry and body: in his poem "I segni della fine" (The signs of the end), in fact, Giudici speaks of "mia mania – di pareggiare biografia e biologia"[31] (my obsession – of equating biography and biology). As *La vita in versi* was heavily influenced metrically-speaking by Giudici's translations of Frost, *Autobiologia* contains the first poems in the metre of Pushkin's *Eugene Onegin* (along with some translations of Pushkin's own lyric poems).[32]

Giudici's following poetic volume, *O beatrice* (O beatrice, 1972)[33] is a defining book in his career,[34] since the poet, for the first time, truly lets language take hold of his pen. An example is the eponymous litany "O beatrice," which celebrates, in a cadenced Italian ending in Latin, a beloved with both *stilnovo* and divine attributes (*da sempre nata* [born from eternity]; *mater mea gloriosa* [my glorious mother]), mixed with earthly ones (*senza manto* [without a mantle]; *senza cielo* [without heaven]):

O beatrice senza manto
Senza cielo né canto.
Beatrice da sempre nata.
Beatrice stella designata …
Beatrice pietosa
Filia et mater mea gloriosa.[35]

[O beatrice without a mantle,
Without heaven or song.
Beatrice born from eternity.
Beatrice, appointed star …
Beatrice, merciful
Daughter and glorious mother of mine.]

The following two poetic books, *Il male dei creditori* (The evil of creditors, 1977),[36] and *Il ristorante dei morti* (The restaurant of the dead, 1981)[37] signal a return to the use of masks and characters and were less successful as poetic volumes. In an excerpt from the first one, we see the power of poetry to subdue guilt: "Distruggerla con pazienza; / Per abilità d'ingegno / Sovvertirla in innocenza" (Destroy it with patience; / Through the talent of the mind / Subvert it into innocence).[38] In the second book, *Il Ristorante dei morti*, the titles of the sections of the book clearly evince the focus on masks, such as "Persona femminile" (Feminine person)[39] or "Il piccolo commediante" (The little third-rate actor).[40]

In 1984, Giudici came out with *Lume dei tuoi misteri* (Light of your mysteries), a carefully constructed work that picks up where *O beatrice* left off. Here, Giudici's previous reflections on the nature of poetic language reach a distinctive apex. Language is, as Giudici's biographer, Simona Morando writes, defined more and more as the "the pivot of an 'involuntary poetics' guided by Chance, never static but rather continually boiling."[41] The signifiers continually lead the signified: sound and rhythm orchestrate meaning in verse.

With the following volume of Giudici, *Salutz* (Health, 1984–6),[42] we have a *canzoniere* of precisely 1,000 verses, organized in seven sections of ten pseudo-sonnets each, followed by a *lai* (lay) of twenty verses. This *canzoniere* is, as Giudici explains, "more or less ironically imitating the style of Provençal troubadour poetry and German Minnesang."[43] The beloved, however, takes on the characteristics of Poetry herself. Here is an excerpt from one of the poems of the final section:

"Vii. 9"[44]

Minne – addentata verde mela
Cerva dendròn mia radice
Nome in Praga di maria
Seno in Praunia di beatrice ...
Scritto di me perché si dia
Da verbo carne a cui graffiare
Nostra finale epifania –
Ridere morire dal vivere
Sing mir a Lidele

[My lady – bitten green apple
Doe, tree, my root
Name in Prague of maria
Breast in Praunia of beatrice ...
...

In these fourteen verses imitating a sonnet, there is an almost total lack of punctuation, a mixture of foreign words from German, Greek, and Yiddish, and each verse seems to stand on its own. We can note the important *da verbo carne a cui graffiare / Nostra finale epifania*, which reminds us of the link between body and word for our poet.

The successive volume, *Fortezza* (Fortress),[45] shares with *Salutz* a narrative quality not present in Giudici's earlier volumes, this time based on a central sequence whose protagonist is a prisoner going through the spiritual exercises of St. Ignatius of Loyola in a mysterious time and place that could either be Byzantine Italy, Baroque Spain or Austria, or the Third Reich.[46]

Giudici's last three volumes, *Quanto spera di campare Giovanni* (How long Giovanni hopes to live, 1993),[47] *Empie Stelle* (Impious stars, 1996),[48] and *Eresia della Sera* (Evening heresy, 1999),[49] are much more communicative than *Salutz* or *Fortezza*. Here, for instance, is the beginning of the eponymous poem of "Quanto spera di campare Giovanni,"[50] which, as (Giovanni) Giudici explains, he wrote after having been teased by his cousin for moving back to Le Grazie at his advanced age:

> Mettere su una casa
> Alla sua età – quanto spera di campare Giovanni
> Ti sei domandato:
> E io che non ho osato
> Replicare alcunché
> Nemmeno tra me e me – sui due piedi
> Per quanto approssimato tentando un calcolo
>
> [To set up a house
> At his age – how long does Giovanni hope to live
> You asked yourself:
> And I who didn't dare
> Respond anything,
> Not even to myself – off the cuff
> Attempting a calculation, however imprecise]

Indeed, as the poet writes in an important essay,

> if there is a Muse of the modern poet, and in this case for the writer of poetry who is here confessing, it is exactly Melancholy. But more than this figure, I would say, it is … the chain of failures and miseries to which this feeling is tied and from which the wretched nostalgia [*grama nostalgia*] derives of not having been a man in the fullness of one's very humanity.[51]

We can see this melancholy occasionally and explicitly emerge in his verses: "Unica musa / Nostra fu sempre Melancolia" (Sole muse / of ours was always Melancholy). Melancholy is always there, underneath the surface: he is melancholic about

> not succeeding in being a man in the sense of the fully human, which … pushes us to the 'work table': the hope, that is, if the word, The Word, if (*si parva licet*) the incarnated word of God or whoever speaks for Him, might not be able to break open the thing, the materiality, the complexity of life and relationships, to hook a tiny piece of reality. Vain hope! ... All art, dominion of the Muses, is also the dominion (the declaration!) of this human insufficiency, of this failure.[52]

Giudici's poetry does not fit neatly into any of the various schools or "isms" of modern Italian poetry – nor do his translations. His tone and style are influenced by Giovanni Pascoli, Umberto Saba, Guido Gozzano, and Eugenio Montale on the one hand and Dante on the other. With "an absolutely post-hermetic verse, colloquial and theatrical, singable and repeatable,"[53] his poetry takes its distance from both the neo-avant-garde (*il Gruppo 63*),[54] as well as from the hermetic poets. His poetry was officially canonized from 1965 onwards; it appeared in the influential series "Lo specchio" (The mirror) published by Mondadori[55] and in the most important Italian poetry anthologies, from Pier Vincenzo Mengaldo's *Poeti italiani del Novecento* (Twentieth-century poets)[56] to Cesare Segre and Carlo Ossola's *Antologia della poesia italiana* (Anthology of Italian poetry).[57]

Translation Career

Turning now to his translations, let us begin with the most neglected fact in critical circles: Giudici published more volumes of translations than original poetry, yet we rarely hear (*pace* Manacorda) that his translations are so numerous and important. On the one hand, he published nineteen books of poetry; on the other hand, he published twenty-seven translations or co-translations.[58] His first book of poems, *Fiorì d'improvviso* (It suddenly flowered),[59] came out almost simultaneously with his first translation, *L'Architettura americana d'oggi* (Built in U.S.A.: Post-war architecture). The majority of his translations in the 1950s and 1960s were, in fact, of non-poetic works: a translation of Arthur Schlesinger's book on Kennedy (1960);[60] a book on Algeria (*La tragedia d'Algeria* [Tragedy in Algeria], 1961);[61] Cuba (1961);[62] *La tradizione intellettuale da Leonardo a*

Hegel (Western intellectual history from Leonardo to Hegel, 1962);[63] a book on Hiroshima in 1965;[64] a Swedish novel in 1966;[65] the essays of Edmund Wilson in 1967;[66] a memoir by Stanislaus Joyce about his more famous brother (1967);[67] and, as I have already mentioned, the important book of literary criticism by Tynjanov in 1968[68] (co-translated from Russian). In the same period, Giudici's translations of Pound (1959), Frost (1965), Crane (1966), and Czech poets (1968, 1969) were published, and in the next decade Russian poets (1971), Mao Zedong (1971), J.C. Ransom (1971), Pushkin (1975), and Plath (1976) were published. In the 1980s and 1990s he came out with his translations of Loyola (1984), more Pushkin (1985), Coleridge (1987), and his first two *quaderni di traduzioni*, before starting the twenty-first century with his Shakespeare translation (2002) and his last *quaderno di traduzioni* (2003).

Finally, it should be remembered that Giudici taught classes and held seminars and public lectures on literary translation: in 1975, he was a visiting professor for a semester at the University of Connecticut (Storrs); in 1986, he was again a visiting professor during the autumn and winter terms at the Università di Perugia; in the winter of 1987, he taught a course at the Università di Bergamo, followed by a notable paper – "Da un'officina di traduzioni" (From a workshop of translations) – given the following year at the famous conference "La traduzione del testo poetico" (The translation of the poetic text), organized by Franco Buffoni (and the subject of chapter 6); in 1994, Giudici gave a talk on translation at the Istituto Banfi and held a seminar at the Università di Pisa in 1997.[69]

Translation Ideology

Giudici fleshed out his theory of translation most explicitly in his 1988 lecture "Da un'officina di traduzioni" as well as in the pages of his 1992 volume *Andare in Cina a piedi* (Going to China on foot). To begin with, the motivation to translate for Giudici comes, as he explains in his lecture, from "a strong 'excursion' (or difference) between the language from which one translates and the language into which one translates."[70] In other words, it is the distance between dissimilar languages that excites the curiosity of the translator. This is one of Giudici's idées fixes, and something that no other Italian poet-translator has so explicitly maintained. He compares translation to "a sort of adventure, an advancing into an unknown country, moved by a love from afar [*amor de lonh*], fascinated like Jaufré Rudel by an unseen beauty, by 'hearsay' of it."[71] Likewise, as he writes in *Andare in Cina a piedi*, "If, for example, I think of that great poet who is my favorite, I can't manage to accept that 'Bajo los arcos del puente el agua clara corría' [Under the bridge's arches the clear water flowed] can be translated with 'Sotto le arcate del ponte l'acqua chiara correva' [Under the bridge's arches the clear water flowed], however exemplary this translation might appear."[72] Giudici explains that

> The relative facility of rendering meaning and syntax (the "what-one-means" of the text) has as its counterpart the almost total cancellation of "that-which-is" [*ciò-che-è*]: sound, rhythm, rhyme, and all the other components of poetic language.[73]

In other words, the physical nature of the poem (*ciò che è*), the *body* of the poem, has disappeared in the Italian translation. This is, above all, the reason Giudici did not translate that "grande Poeta da me prediletto" (great and favourite poet of mine), Antonio Machado. "The harsh and incontrovertible exactitude of the letter," Giudici writes, "abuses and destroys the airy grace of the spirit; or, with a different metaphor, the body suffocates the soul [*il corpo soffoca l'anima*] of the original, the very 'rich and strange' that establishes an essential and inalienable distance between everyday language and poetic language."[74]

Specifically speaking, then, from a linguistic viewpoint, Giudici indicates that this translation fails not for lexical reasons but because of prosody and not so much because of the number of syllables or the position of accents but because of the sound of the vowels and consonants in each language:

> One sees right away, in fact, that the series of vowel and consonant sounds of the original is perceptibly different from that of the literal translation which is quite correct according to the language of communication, but not adequate (because *impossible*) according to poetic language.[75]

This distinction between poetic language and everyday (communicative) language, taken from Giudici's reading and translation of Tynjanov, contributes to Giudici's idea that poetic language is fundamentally foreign. This is vital to Giudici's own translation ideology, which is based on translating culturally and linguistically foreign texts (prevalently non-Romance language based). Since Giudici believes in translating verse into verse ("the problem is not in translating from a language into another language, but from a poetic language into a poetic language") and poetic language is by nature foreign, his poetic translations will be foreignizing and not domesticating. For Giudici, poetic language is by nature "a superlanguage, foreign and strange": this is such a fundamental notion for him that it would be tautological to speak of poetic language as a foreign language. The first implies the second, so that he can speak of language involved in that "becoming strange (that is, poetic), which is its sole *raison d'être.*" Any of a number of things will add to the *unheimlich* quality of the translation:[76] yet these are not left up to chance. Giudici decides which factor(s) to emphasize based on the original text. As he writes about Tynjanov's "constructive principles," once more in "Da un'officina di traduzioni":

> Tynjanov says that poetic language results from the interaction of various "constructive principles" like that syntactic-semantic principle, or rhythmical one, or phonic one, or based on rhyme, or on possible contextual references, etc. And in each poem there is (or there should be) one of these constructive principles that is considered *fundamental*, that can be renounced only at the cost of compromising the identity, the existence of the poem itself [*l'esistenza della poesia stessa*]. We know well that in this subject we cannot be too categorical; but generally speaking I think that the suggestion of Tynjanov still constitutes a small, but useful, handbook for the translator of poetry, whose first duty will therefore be to establish what the fundamental "constructive principle" is in the text to be translated.[77]

Thus, to take some examples from Giudici's own translations, these are some "constructive principles" he used in translation: a loose nine-syllable line, simulating the non-canonical *novenario* (Pushkin); a series of alliterations (Coleridge); a specific type of diction (Frost); and a pattern of ironic rhymes (Plath). Giudici, by stressing a specific principle, estranges the reader, by forcibly moving the reader towards the original text.

As we saw earlier, the translator's movement of the reader towards the text was influentially theorized by the theologian and philosopher Friedrich Schleiermacher, whose 1813 seminal paper "On the Different Methods of Translation" paved the way for a modern approach to translation, based not on the classic (Roman) dichotomy of translating according to the letter or the spirit but on the amount of foreign influence exerted on the target text by the source text. By this measure,

Giudici consistently moves the reader of his translations towards the original text and disturbs his "peace." Schleiermacher indicates that the way to move the reader towards the author is to "bend" the translation towards the source text. Indeed, it is in this bending of Italian that Giudici renders the translation foreign. The Italian reader is faced with, alternately, strange and unusual metres spilling over through enjambments, obsessive assonance and alliteration, an explosion of rhyme, syntax wrenched out of place, and foreign words. Schleiermacher's approach was further developed by twentieth-century translation theorists like Lawrence Venuti. As Venuti theorizes,

> Foreignizing translation signifies the difference of the foreign text, yet only by disrupting the cultural codes that prevail in the target language. In its effort to do right abroad, this translation method must do wrong at home, deviating enough from native norms to stage an alien reading experience ...[78]

What Italian readers do not expect from Italian poetry – from Dickinson's unconventional punctuation to an imitation of Pushkin's iambic tetrapody – is offered by Giudici. "Wrong at home" means that the translation will not be fluent, or "invisible," as Venuti calls it. The foreignizing translation will clearly be out of line with the normal expectations of an Italian reader. This is, of course, precisely Giudici's own poetic credo: poetry is fundamentally incarnated in language that estranges the reader.

Given Giudici's preference to translate linguistically and culturally distant texts, it is natural that he doesn't consider a perfect knowledge of another language as necessary to translate its poetry. We will see, for instance, how this contrasts with the view of Vladimir Nabokov and Nabokov's idea of literal translation. Indeed, except on rare occasions, Giudici preferred to translate from languages he either did not know (Czech), knew very little (Russian), or knew only from books (English).[79]

Russia and *Eugene Onegin*

Giudici's brief stay in Moscow in 1966 revolutionized his poetic worldview. Previously, Giudici had been ashamed to call himself a poet:[80] "It was really in Russia that for me the meaning of the word 'poet' was modified: up until then I had almost been ashamed to declare myself, in

Italian, a 'poet.'"[81] Giudici would often return, in later years, to this difficult problem of nomenclature. For more than a decade, then, from 1953 to 1966, Giudici published volumes of verse but could not bring himself to call himself a poet. What changed his attitude was the contact with Russian people. This self-awareness was extremely important, allowing Giudici to consider translating the most beloved poet in Russia, since he was now assured of his own poetic vocation. He would publish *Eugene Onegin* in several different versions, and include a chapter of it in his first *quaderno di traduzioni*. It was the most important translation of his career.[82]

Giudici, after a month in Moscow, came back and started studying Russian, using "a little grammar book in French entitled *Le russe sans peine* [Russian with ease]."[83] He had already conceived of the "utopic project of knowing my Pushkin, a Pushkin at first hand, translating only myself his masterpiece *Eugene Onegin*."[84] Yet it wasn't only a private or "sentimental" interest that drew him to the poem. Giudici wished to

> make an "Italian" *Onegin*, in the sense of acquiring for our perhaps too clever and disenchanted modern poetry that which in *Onegin* seemed to me a freer, more spontaneous, and more nobly ingenuous relationship between the author and the text, as well as a rarely used verse in Italian prosody and the least distant as possible from the enchanting Pushkinian iambic tetrapody.[85]

So what did Giudici know of Russian to translate the 5,541 verses[86] of *Eugene Onegin*? When he began his long, thirty-year translation project of this book, which lasted from 1970 to 1999, he translated

> having as sole instruments the already-mentioned disks of Aksonov [a famous Russian actor], the translations in prose and in verse of Ettore Lo Gatto, the translation in prose and the useful notes of Eridano Bazzarelli, the Russian-Italian dictionary, and my very modest linguistic concepts.[87]

At this point, it is true, he had co-translated the important book by Tynjanov on poetic language, but his co-translation was certainly more in revising a prose crib than translating directly from the Russian.

Pushkin's poem had been translated into Italian several times before, notably by Eridano Bazzarelli and Ettore Lo Gatto. While Bazzarelli's translation was, as Giudici indicated, in prose, Lo Gatto had translated Pushkin twice, once into prose and once into verse (hendecasyllables).

The latter verse translation, by one of the most important Italian professors and scholars of Russian,[88] had (and continues to have) many supporters, especially among Italian Slavists.[89] It is fluent and expansive and shows a scholar-translator who is – more or less – at home in the Italian poetic tradition. Yet Giudici's intention was not to translate in a philological manner. He insisted that he wanted his translation to "take its place in the sphere of Italian literature."[90] Specifically, he considered this translation to be part of his own poetic endeavour: "In its faults and its merits I consider the present translation a stage of [my] poetic pursuit [*ricerca poetica*]."[91] This sounds very much like a Poundian goal of integrating other poems into his own. Yet Giudici has written elsewhere (in a preface to his translation of Sylvia Plath):

> I don't believe much in the legend of the translator (and especially of the translator who is a poet) who "makes his own" the translated text, even if this may happen, for reasons difficult to state, in some rare cases; I rather believe in the concrete possibility of the translator, expert in the practice of poetry, to put at the service of the text his experience as maker of verses, his being able more than others to understand what occurs in poetic language and therefore to project in translation some fundamental characteristics of the original text.[92]

Giudici, then, is clear on how the target language should allow the original text to shine through. As I explained before, he believes not in a domesticating translation method, but in a foreignizing translation, in which the source language indelibly infuses the target language through its own rhythm, diction, and syntax.

As a poet in his own right, Giudici is most interested in constructing stories, dramas, and interior monologues and in juxtaposing characters and masks, all filtered and modified in the crucible of language. Pushkin provided a clear narrative structure for such a task, and Pushkin's metre seemed to confirm that they shared a common "spiritual magnitude" (as Joseph Brodsky would say). Indeed, one of the reasons Giudici translated Pushkin's masterpiece was because he greatly admired its metre. As he wrote, European languages nourished nostalgia and envy of *Eugene Onegin*'s "iambic tetrapodies." He wanted to import it into Italian, selecting it as the main "constructive principle" (Tynjanov) of his translation. For Giudici, the metre of Pushkin's poem is "almost in a joking tone, for which reason the poetic discourse is accompanied to a modern ear by a certain *ironic* nuance, ambiguously open both to comedy and to passion."[93] And Giudici went so far as to say that if one of his poems happened to be read after his death, he would wish it to be in this metre.[94] Yet, to be precise, Giudici did not translate *Eugene Onegin* into strict iambic tetrapody. Rather, as Nicola Gardini intuits, for Giudici the "stressed recurrence," or rhythm, is more important than "syllabic meter."[95] Thus, our poet translates into a *novenario* that isn't a standard *novenario*, but can range from seven to ten syllables:

> An Italian verse oriented around nine syllables with three strong accents, which wasn't and is not a necessarily so-called "novenario" and occasionally varies to meters of eight, ten and sometimes even seven syllables.[96]

As Gardini suggests, Pushkin was, for Giudici, a "model." Yet a model difficult to follow:

> A model full of variants, the ineliminable variant being the dissatisfaction of the translator ... This translation is essentially interminable ... it is part of a work and *mise en abîme* of the same work.[97]

The other main attraction of *Eugene Onegin* was the fact that it was a narrative poem, and this quality particularly appealed to Giudici. Pier Vincenzo Mengaldo explains how Giudici's own poetic ambitions to create a narrative poem (the "search for the lost masterpiece"[98] mentioned by critics) found an equally ambitious text:

> Giudici transfers into his version of *Onegin* that aspiration to abundantly narrative meters, still possible in different cultures ... but which he, as producer, can only brush up against or follow with sketches and fragments.[99]

Indeed, the poetic volumes of Giudici that are concentrated on specific plots or themes – such as *Fortezza* or *Salutz* – do not actually have clearly defined narrative structures.

On the whole, Giudici's metrical translation of *Eugene Onegin* was enthusiastically received by Italian poets and critics (from Giovanni Raboni, Maurizio Cucchi, and Fernando Bandini to Gianfranco Contini and Gianfranco Folena), while it was generally disparaged by Italian scholars of Russian literature.

The poet Giovanni Raboni suggested that Giudici's translation proposes the *vera musica* (true music) of the original, by means of his "mimetic" imitation of Pushkin's metre, foreign to Italian ears:

> An undertaking of astounding novelty and stylistic compactness, which through a bold phonosyllabic imitation of the original's iambic tetrapody adds an unprecedented kind of metrical system to our tradition and, I would dare to say, to our ear.[100]

Likewise, Gianfranco Contini wrote that Giudici was the only translator who succeeded in conveying "something of the extraordinary thrill of that apparently light and futile work, but of a sublime futility, which is *Onegin*."[101]

Criticism of Giudici's translation by Italian Slavists took two main forms.[102] Some Italian scholars of Russian criticized Giudici for his choice of metre, since *il novenario* isn't used in Italian poetic tradition. They preferred the more popular hendecasyllable, namely, an "analogical" form. The other main critique was of Giudici's language and style, which they considered too colloquial.

One of the lone dissenters among Italian poets was Franco Fortini (former friend of Giudici), who argued that Giudici's translation was too adaptive, idiosyncratic, and resolutely postmodern, labelling it a "conscious and almost cynical work of parody and of 'carnevalization,' whose result is a sarcastic little book of a postmodern *Onegin* for drums and harmonica."[103] As I wrote, while Fortini had once promoted "artistic" translations, he came to believe that a classic should be rigorously translated by a group of specialists in a word-for-word manner. Giudici did not share this belief, since he thought that translation should be done by an individual writer inspired with curiosity or passion for the foreign text.

Nonetheless, Giudici's translation of Pushkin – or the "Moscow Dante," as Contini called him[104] – was influential precisely because it was an iconoclastic rendering of the Russian. Giudici's translation offered another interpretation that was more powerful and perhaps more ambiguous than previous efforts by translators, and it was in a more highly-stylized poetic form than any other translation. As Folena argued: "He hasn't given us an Italianized Pushkin, but, *si licet*, an Italian (as poetic language) Pushkinized."[105] In other words, Pushkin has not been standardized in a generic foreign language but Italian has been brought closer to Pushkin and Russian through linguistic devices, especially through the importation of the Russian rhythm into Italian. This is precisely what Schleiermacher meant when he spoke about his preferred method of translation: bringing the reader closer to the author and text (as Giudici does). As an example, here are the final verses of

Giudici's *Eugene Onegin*, where we can clearly hear the idiosyncratic Italian metre:

Beato chi lasciò il festino
Della vita senza bere
Tutto il vino del bicchiere.
Non lesse il suo romanzo fino
In fondo e seppe dirle addio
D'un tratto, come a Onieghin io.[106]

[Blessed he who left the banquet
Of life without drinking
All the wine in the glass.
He didn't read his novel to
The end and was able to bid it farewell
At once, like I to Onegin.]

This is a mixture of *novenari* and *ottonari* that alludes to the Russian iambic tetrapody, replicates Pushkin's rhyme structure (in this case, *effegg*), and includes the notable half-rhyme of *addio / io*, internal rhymes (*lasciò / io; vino / festino / fino*) and four enjambments.

Now this idea of poetic (and metrical) translation could not be further removed from that of the most famous and notorious translator of *Eugene Onegin*, Vladimir Nabokov. Nabokov strove for a severely "literal" translation, shorn of all poetic elements. As he memorably wrote, "The term 'literal translation' is tautological, since anything but that is not truly a translation but an imitation, an adaptation or a parody."[107] He abhors the fact that so much poetry "still languishes in 'poetical' versions, begrimed and beslimed by rhyme."[108]

His goal was to provide a "pony" for readers who could lean on his English translation and come closer to understanding Pushkin's Russian text. Nabokov explains his axioms as follows:

> In transposing *Eugene Onegin* from Pushkin's Russian into my English I have sacrificed to completeness of meaning every formal element including the iambic rhythm, whenever its retention hindered fidelity. To my ideal of literalism I sacrificed everything (elegance, euphony, clarity, good taste, modern usage, and even grammar) that the dainty mimic prizes higher than truth. Pushkin has likened translators to horses changed at the post houses of civilization. The greatest reward I can think of is that students may use my work as a pony.[109]

He translated into non-rhyming generally iambic verse, since he considered iambic verse the normal speech pattern of English. Two volumes of commentary accompanied his translation, consisting of more than 1,000 pages of textual, metrical, literary, and historical notes.

For Nabokov, the literal sense could only be achieved by understanding the literary, historical, and cultural milieu in which Pushkin's masterpiece was born. A translator must be familiar with "the *Fables* of Krilov, Byron's works, French poets of the eighteenth century, Rousseau's *La Nouvelle Héloïse*, Pushkin's biography, banking games, Russian songs related to divination, the difference between cranberry and lingenberry … and the Russian language."[110]

There are several key similarities and differences. Both Nabokov and Giudici do not believe in domesticating the original. For both, the translation should reproduce certain aspects of the original: for Nabokov, the semantic content and syntax; for Giudici, the metre. Yet, as we see from the quote above, Nabokov insists on the complete and encyclopedic knowledge of the source language and the literary tradition surrounding it. Not coincidentally, he unearthed a whole series of French verse alluded to by Pushkin as well as successfully emending the text in a few places. Conversely, Giudici wanted to dive into the unknown, into the totally foreign source language. Giudici chose metrical equivalence by choosing to use a metre similar to Pushkin's, whereas Nabokov opted for a loose and erratic iambic verse with no regular amount of syllables. One of the most significant differences lies in the question of tone (even Robert Lowell in his *Imitations* attempted to transmit the same tone as an original text): Giudici sustained an even tone through *Eugene Onegin*, while Nabokov's mixture of registers and archaic syntax combined to produce a farrago of styles. Nabokov himself remarked that "I do not care if a word is 'archaic' or 'dialect' or 'slang'; I am an eclectic democrat in this matter, and whatever suits me, goes."[111] Here, Nabokov is disregarding the norms and poetics of the target text entirely in favour of the source text.

Let us compare a stanza (chapter 3, stanza 17) in Nabokov's and Giudici's translations (and the original Russian) so that we can see the differences. (See table 4.1 below.)

That Nabokov more closely patterns the original Russian in diction is clear; there aren't any lexical blunders. In contrast, Giudici's translation doesn't adhere to the Russian. He doesn't translate здесь (here) (verse 1), мне (to me) (verse 9), and худая (sorry) (verse 11); and his diction is imprecise in verse 2 (*rimani* instead of sit down [сядь]), verse 4

Table 4.1 *Eugene Onegin*

Literal version ***Eugene Onegin***	**Giovanni Giudici** ***Eugenio Onieghin***	**Vladimir Nabokov** ***Eugene Onegin***
«Не спится, няня: здесь так душно! ["(I) can't sleep, nurse: here (it's) so stuffy!]	"Non dormo, njanja: che afa! Apri ["I can't sleep, nanny: what mugginess! Open]	"I can't sleep, nurse: 'tis here so stuffy!
Открой окно, да сядь ко мне». [Open (the) window and sit down by me."]	La finestra e con me rimani." [the window and stay with me."]	Open the window and sit down by me."
Что, Таня, что с тобой? – «Мне скучно, ["What, Tanja, what (is wrong) with you?" "I'm bored,]	– Tanja, cos'hai? – "Sono annoiata. [– Tanja, what's wrong? – "I am bored.	"Why, Tanya, what's ails you?" "I'm dull.
Поговорим о старине». [Let's talk of olden (times)."]	Parlami dei tempi lontani." [Talk to me about the olden days."]	Let's talk about old days."
– О чем же, Таня? Я бывало, [About what, then, Tanja? I used]	– Ma di che? Una volta a memoria [– But about what? Once by heart]	"Well, what about them, Tanya? Time was, I
Хранила в памяти не мало [to keep in (my) memory not (a) few]	Sapevo molte vecchie storie, [I knew many old stories,]	Kept in my memory no dearth
Старинных былей, небылиц [Old tales, fables]	Alcune vere, altre inventate, [Some true, others invented,]	of ancient haps and never-haps
Про злых духов и про девиц; [about evil spirits and about maidens;]	Di brutti spiriti e ragazze; [Of ugly spirits and girls;]	about dire spirits and about maidens;
А нынче всё мне темно, Таня: [But now all to me (is) dark, Tanja:]	Ma adesso tutto è buio, Tanja: [But now all is dark, Tanja:]	but all to me is dark now, Tanya:
Что знала, то забыла. Да, [what (I) knew, that (I) have forgotten. Yes,]	Quel che sapevo l'ho scordato. [That which I knew I have forgotten.]	What I knew I have forgotten. Yes,
Пришла худая череда! [things have come to a sorry turn!]	Anche il mio turno è ormai arrivato! [My turn too has now arrived!]	things have come now to a sorry pass!

Table 4.1 *Eugene Onegin* (*Continued*)

Literal version **Eugene Onegin**	**Giovanni Giudici** **Eugenio Onieghin**	**Vladimir Nabokov** **Eugene Onegin**
Зашибло ... – «Расскажи мне, няня, [(I'm) fuddled ... " "Tell me, nanny,]	È finita. – "Ma dimmi, njanja, [It is over. –"But tell me, nanny,]	My mind is fuddled." "Tell me, nurse,
Про ваши старые года: [about your old years:]	Della vostra vita trascorsa [in your past life]	about your years of old.
Была ты влюблена тогда?». [Were you in love then?"]	Fosti innamorata una volta?" [Were you once in love?]	Were you then in love?"
Source: Rosengrant, "Nabokov, Onegin, and the Theory of Translation," 8	Source: Giudici, *Eugenio Onieghin*, 60–1	Source: Cited in Rosengrant, "Nabokov, Onegin, and the Theory of Translation," 9

(the second person imperative *parlami* instead of the first person plural imperative "let's talk" [Поговорим]), verse 6 (*sapevo* instead of keep [Хранила]), verse 7 (the tales and fables are not *vere*), verse 10 (*anche* instead of "yes" [Да]), verse 11 (the whole verse is shifted from the third person to the first person), verse 12 (*è finita*, instead of *[I'm] fuddled* [Зашибло]; he adds *ma*), and verse 13 (*vita* instead of *years* [года]; he adds *trascorsa*).

Yet Nabokov's word choice is extremely problematic and, as Judson Rosengrant remarks, it

> can only strike the native ear as strange, if not downright bizarre. There is, moreover, the matter of Nabokov's evident desire to concoct out of a hybrid of modern British and American English (with Gallic and archaic admixtures) a pastiche of Pushkin's early nineteenth-century Russian, a desire that very likely led to the above-mentioned "'tis," "dull," "haps," and "never-haps," as well as "dearth" (for the pedestrian "nemalo") and "dire" (for the much more common "zloj").[112]

Indeed, it is fair to say, as Edward Brown does, that "Nabokov has drained the poetry out of Pushkin's lines in his translation."[113] In Nabokov's version there is no rhyme or additional enjambment, but there is erratic iambic rhythm, and amalgamated diction. Meanwhile, Giudici's translation is recognizably a poetic artefact with a series of rhymes (*effe*), assonance and alliteration (e.g., the *e* in *storie, inventate,* and *ragazze*; the *t* in *fosti innamorata una volta*?), and added enjambment (*Apri/la finestra*); they are all within the pronounced framework of the *novenario*. On the other hand, the semantic content of the Russian has come across in Nabokov's translation, but it is shorn of its essential poetic elements. In the opinion of his fellow émigré, Alexander Gerschenkron, "Nabokov's translation can and indeed should be studied, but despite all the cleverness and occasional brilliance it cannot be read."[114]

Giudici profited enormously from his translation of Pushkin, by learning how to use a metre similar to the Russian iambic tetrapody. The same thing happened with his earlier translation of Frost, as he wrote, when he learned how to free himself from the tyranny of hendecasyllable verse, allowing him to vary the syllable count from eleven up to seventeen:

> From the experience of the versions of Frost and Pushkin depend, respectively, the emancipation from the hendecasyllable and the adoption, beginning with *O beatrice*, of the verse modelled on the Russian iambic tetrapody, a prosody that if only one poem of mine survived, I would hope, after all, that it would be the norm and meter of such a poem.[115]

The fact that Giudici learned how to free himself from a rigid hendecasyllable and how to use a verse "modelled" on the metre of *Eugene Onegin* is quite noteworthy. Rarely do poets change their poetic metres by basing them on foreign models. Giudici's receptiveness to the structure and style of foreign poetry, as nourished through translation, allowed his own poetic skills to be refined.

Prague and *Omaggio a Praga*

The first collection of foreign poetry translated by Giudici – before his three *quaderni di traduzioni* – is his *Omaggio a Praga* (Homage to Prague). In truth, it is a collection of Czech poetry with some of Giudici's own poetry preceding it. It is not technically a *quaderno di traduzioni*, owing to the presence of his own verse, but it is what Rodolfo Zucco has elsewhere described as a "satura": a volume containing both poetry and translations.[116]

Giudici explains the importance of Prague in the preface to *Addio, proibito piangere*, which excerpts many poems included in his *Omaggio a Praga*:

> Prague wasn't an accident of my many, too many and insane trips: it was a place of my life [*un luogo della vita*], it was first of all a language of black stone, blind and impenetrable, which I wanted to penetrate to resuscitate (*rivivere*) in it words and thoughts of people who suddenly had become close to me.[117]

Giudici was never an art-for-art's sake writer. He was too influenced by Umberto Saba's verses, Giacomo Noventa's teachings, communism, and Catholicism. But there in Prague in 1967 he had multiple revelations. One of his Czech friends, Vladimír Mikeš, helped him translate Czech poetry. Giudici's discussions with Czech writers, like Mikeš, many of whom desperately aimed to leave the country, were inspiring and extremely influential:

> There were endless and nocturnal conversations about language, about language that was the body of that Bohemia, of writing as a body [*sulla scrittura come corpo*], of the body that soars ... and what did I know until then about language lived as a drama, as tragedy? It was the ephemeral hope of Dubçek, coinciding with the hopes and illusions of individual lives.[118]

Giudici's grand idea was the idea of language's physical existence: the physicality of words, metre, and rhyme. Language, in Giudici's view, is not static and passive: a writer does not use simply a set of predetermined symbols. Men and women write in language and are written by language in a reciprocal relationship.

He describes the process of translation when working with his friend Vladimír Mikeš:

> Mikeš would read the Czech, telling me the literal meaning in Italian and (where necessary) he specified for me the various further implications of poetic language: rhyme, rhetorical figures, semantic ambiguity, etc. I followed him and I went forward step by step, as though proceeding in a dense forest, blindfolded and held by my hand.[119]

Here, he stresses the importance of the various components that make up the *lingua poetica*: rhyme, rhetorical figures, semantic ambiguity, and torsion of Italian. Below, we will examine these elements in Giudici's translations, since they are key elements of his translation method.

Giudici later wrote, in the preface to *A una casa non sua*, about the circumstances surrounding the publication of *Omaggio a Praga*. Having returned in the autumn of 1968 with the editor Vanni Scheiwiller, they decided to "improvise in a few weeks" this book as a "symbolic protest" against the regime that was installed there after the Soviet invasion in August.[120] The Italian poet-translator emphatically sets the conception of this volume, then, in the political tumult of the time. As Massimo Bacigalupo writes, for Giudici,

> the Czech poets are therefore the defenders of language against every totalitarian invasion (Nazism, Stalinism, consumerism), unyielding personal voices, light and very robust, even if strong only in intuition and passing fancies and games.[121]

Giudici would note in 1985 that his view of Czech poetry at that time was partial: he missed important figures like Jaroslav Seifert, whom he met briefly in 1967. Why? First, because Giudici knew next to nothing about his poetic career; then, as we saw earlier, because he didn't understand how naturally Bohemian poets "rappresent[ano]" (represent) their nation through their language.

In the panorama of foreign literature, Czech poetry had never received much attention in Italy.[122] Sporadic translations of modern Czech poetry appeared in magazines, but aside from "popular" Czech poetry, there were no anthologies of this verse before Giudici's 1968 anthology.[123] Although Vítězlav Nezval, Vladimír Holan, František Halas, and Jaroslav Seifert had been previously translated into Italian, Giudici introduced the poetry of Orten,[124] Ivan Blatný, and Jiří Kolář into the Italian literary world.[125]

Quaderni di Traduzioni

Let us turn now to Giudici's official *quaderni di traduzioni*. Both his *quaderni* and his own poetic volumes are often composed and arranged according to a macrotext. As Niccolò Scaffai notes, Giudici emphasized the "structural-organizing aspect" of his volumes. "The book must, that is, reveal, before analysis and already at a paratextual or even typographical level, its very status as a complex work elaborated according to an authorial project."[126]

This profound degree of organization is evident in many of Giudici's volumes of original poetry. The same is true of his first two *quaderni di traduzioni*. This is what Giudici has to say about the structure of *Addio, proibito piangere*:

> Curious destiny, how this book is made, deferentially ordered by chronology: it begins with a metaphysical (the type of poet that, for the sheer suggestiveness of the epithet, I would have liked to have been then) and ends with a romantic (the type of poet who, at this point without any more suggestions, I will regret not having been able to become).[127]

While Giudici begins with John Donne, whose poem gave rise to the title of the volume, and ends with Coleridge, the volume is not chronological according to the age of the poets. Were it chronological, Coleridge wouldn't be the final poet but the second poet, immediately following Donne. As it is, the order of the book is John Donne (b. 1572), Hart Crane (b. 1899), Emily Dickinson (b. 1830), Ezra Pound (b. 1885), Robert Frost (b. 1874), John Crowe Ransom (b. 1888), Jiří Orten (b. 1919), František Halas (b. 1901), Jiří Kolář (b. 1914), Alexander Pushkin (b. 1799), W.B. Yeats (b. 1865), and Samuel Taylor Coleridge (b. 1772).[128] So why does Giudici assert that it is "deferentially ordered by chronology"? It is ordered almost chronologically by the date(s) of translation.[129] This is fascinating since it indicates that for Giudici the chronology of the book is formed not by the history or biography of the translated poets, but by the literary encounters that he had with them. The volume's structure is thus subjective and personal. As he indicates, this *quaderno* is structured around an idea of himself as poet. Giudici opens the volume with Donne, as metaphysical poet, followed by Dickinson, another metaphysical-type poet. Then he includes Pound, Frost, and Ransom, the latter two engaged in formal verse. Then there are the sensual and "baroque" Czech poets, followed by Pushkin's romantic hero (read and translated, however, ironically); the two most romantic poets, Coleridge and Yeats, end the volume. The excerpt from Pushkin is from the last chapter of *Eugene Onegin*, which Giudici modified the least throughout his translation-in-progress and which he was most satisfied with. Both Coleridge and Yeats are translated only in part – Giudici explained how he couldn't translate all of Yeats even though he was commissioned to do so – proving Giudici's difficulty in being a "romantic poet" as he so desired.[130] It is thus clear that this *quaderno* was specifically ordered and arranged by Giudici.

The *quaderno* is tilted towards Giudici's beloved Pushkin, who has more pages devoted to him than anyone else. The majority of poems are, however, English and American. Giudici once again emphasizes the corporeal nature of their words in speaking of how the defunct translated poets would have been oblivious to his "future handling (*maneggi*) of the body of their words."[131] Why did he choose to translate them? "Because of passion; or for practice; or more humbly: because of the infatuation from having heard [about them]."[132] Yet it is important to note that Giudici had already translated these poets: his translation collection is a new project. By collecting them in a volume, he is giving them a textual relationship that they did not have as separate translations.

Giudici's second *quaderno, A una casa non sua,* was published in 1997. The title of the book was not a casual choice of Giudici's. This volume is entitled after a verse from Robert Graves's "Frightened Men." Massimo Bacigalupo, in his afterword to the book, acutely describes Giudici's use of Robert Graves's verse "To a house not his own," translated as *A una casa non sua,* in the following way:

> In Giudici ... the expression *A una casa non sua* evidently alludes to the work of the translator, who visits, comes, to a house, a language, not his own, renders homage to it, moves inside of it with circumspection, commits a small adultery, but also creates a passage between that house and his. Language is always a space, a body. And it is always truly alien, *unheimlich*.[133]

This goes along with our initial hypothesis that Giudici does not domesticate but foreignizes, both when he writes poetry and when he translates it: he brings the reader towards an alien reality.

As Giudici indicates in his preface,

> The translations reunited here descend, for the most part, from motives of affection or recreation or simple practice: the height, as one can see, of "dilettantism" and with all its merits and demerits.[134]

Here, once again, there is a preponderance of English poetry, and sixteen out of twenty poets are new to the second *quaderno.* Despite the overwhelming majority of English verse, the *quaderno* begins with a Latin philosopher (Aquinas) and ends with a Chinese ruler (Mao). As Rodolfo Zucco perceptively notes, Giudici's translations often deal with the theme of writing, as in Aquinas's "Pange lingua" (Tell, tongue), Shakespeare's sonnets, Yeats's "Sailing to Byzantium," Pound's "Hugh Selwyn Mauberley" and "Greek Epigram," and Orten's "La cosa chiamata poesia."[135] This isn't, perhaps, surprising. For Giudici, translation inevitably fosters reflection on poetics. Translation is not done spontaneously.

Poetry depends on tweaking and modifying language until it appears foreign to us; so does the art of translation. A translation that does not betray any sign of foreignness is not acceptable for Giudici. The notion of poetics is central to Giudici's own verse: his poetry is extremely self-conscious. For instance, as Massimo Bacigalupo observes, Giudici's translation of Aquinas's verse "Svela, o Lingua, del glorioso / Corpo il mistero" (Reveal, o Language, the mystery / of the glorious body) truly synthesizes his own poetics.[136] From Prague to the Christian Saint, there is a clear poetic ideology at play. Aquinas's meditation on the sacraments becomes Giudici's meditation on the power of language: this is signalled by something as little as Giudici's explicit invocation to language "O lingua," which in Latin lacks the vocative *o*. The reason is clear, then, why Giudici chose this poem to begin his *quaderno*.

This volume does not only have a metapoetic theme, but it also has a cosmological panorama. With John Milton and John Dryden, we visit the beginning and the ending of the universe: the "big bang and black hole." After these cosmological poems, Giudici placed a poem in praise of women's bodies, which opportunely preludes the final Czech poems. In fact, the line stretching from Milton's *Paradise Lost* to Halas's "Le donne giovani" (Young women) is anything but coincidental: it is almost a theological reversal. From the apple and the sin of the flesh to the guilt-free sensual *notti frizzanti* (sparkling nights) in which

l'aria è piena di piccole
ragazze spogliate
danzanti fra i mulinelli
dei nostri desideri ... [137]

[the air is full of young
girls undressed
dancing among the whirlwinds
of our desires ...]

Giudici's translations from Chinese poets, which he retranslated from English, are an interesting case. These versions are not philologically precise, then, but are twice removed from the originals. They are, more precisely, poetic exercises that are less renderings from Chinese than poetic compositions straddling the line between original verse and translation.

In the event, Giudici chose for his purposes a poem by Po Chu-Ï and two by Mao Zedong. The former poet's lament at the end, his shame of not having participated actively in society as a poet, is shared by Giudici:

> Ed io oggi: per quali meriti
> Non ho mai lavorato in un campo, né abbattuto albero?
> Il mio stipendio statale è trecento misure,
> A fine anno il grano mi avanza.
> Pensandoci, mi vergogno in segreto:
> E tutto il giorno non me ne posso scordare.[138]
>
> [And I today: for what reasons
> Haven't I ever worked in a field, or cut down a tree?
> My government salary is 300 measures,
> At the end of the year I have grain left over.
> Thinking about this, I am secretly ashamed:
> And all day I can't forget about this.]

The volume concludes with Mao Zedong's poem with its cautious hope for the future, with peasants lighting candles and paper boats to chase away malign spirits ("Candeline e barchette di carta accese rischiarano il cielo" [Little candles and burning paper boats light up the sky]). Once more, the organization of Giudici's collection is not left to chance.

Giudici's third and final *quaderno di traduzioni*, *Vaga lingua strana: dai versi tradotti*, had a very troubled editorial history, as is clear from the private correspondence between Rodolfo Zucco – who expertly edited Giudici's *I versi della vita* (in the *Meridiano* series) in 2000 – and the publisher Garzanti. After Zucco had sent in the corrected proofs for *Vaga lingua strana*, the publisher changed his mind and drastically altered the plan and framework of the volume; instead of a four-part structure containing *Addio, proibito piangere*, *A una casa non sua*, *Eugenio Onegin*, and other translations, the volume contained only a selection of translations from the first two *quaderni di traduzioni*. A selection, let us note, that was carried out by the publisher and not by the poet or the putative editor.[139]

The title of the *quaderno*, *Vaga lingua strana*, derives from one of Giudici's own poems, "Ritratto (I)" (Portrait [I]) from *Fortezza*. In other words, we have a progression in the titles of the three *quaderni*: from the poetry of Donne to Graves to Giudici. It has been noted by Zucco that Giudici's adjective *Vaga* comes from Leopardi. Moreover, like Leopardi,

Giudici wanted to keep the foreignness of the language in translation – the Greekness of the Greek or the Frenchness of the French. As Leopardi writes, "The perfection of a translation consists in this, that the translated author is not, for example, Greek in Italian, Greek or French in German, but the same in Italian or in German as he is in Greek or French."[140] Likewise, Giudici shared Leopardi's underlying belief that a "perfect" translation is impossible. The *Verfremdungseffekt* (distancing effect), theorized by Brecht, defines *tout court* the role of poetic language for Giudici. Translation, then, would be grade zero of this alienation: where two different poetic languages meet. As Giudici wrote of the dialect poet Biagio Marin:

> Marin ... is the author who puts himself at the service of language [*al servizio della lingua*], the poet who submits to the service of poetry, continually and uninterruptedly available for it, almost obeying the tormenting anxiety of translating, but the right word would be *transubstantiating* [*transustanziare*], one's own body into the written word, the totality of one's reality.[141]

It is clear that Giudici is also describing his own poetics. To write poetry means not only to translate (*tradurre*), but really transubstantiate (*transustanziare*): to take a biblical metaphor, to turn the communion wafer and wine into the body and blood of Christ. Indeed, as Alberto Cadioli observes, the use of the loaded theological term has a double meaning. If poetic verses are, on the surface, communicative, on the other hand, they affirm their own autonomous existence, their own "ontological dimension."[142]

On the whole, Pushkin dominates the first *quaderno* and Plath the second. What leaps out in the third *quaderno* is the attention devoted to Pound, who occupies more pages than any other poet. Yet for Giudici, his favourite Pound is the early, pre-*Cantos* poet. He doesn't translate any of the *Cantos;* he prefers to remain with the Pound who wrote *A lume spento* and "Hugh Selwyn Mauberley," in which the personas are more recognizable and the language is less fragmented and allusive. The version of "Mauberley" attests to Giudici's identification with a foreign text. For instance, as Giudici remarks in his "Note di un traduttore del 'Mauberley'" (Notes by a translator of "Mauberley"), when he translated Pound's poem, it was in large part due to his "almost self-identification with the character Mauberley, defined by critics 'a minor artist' and presented by the poet as one *out of key with his time*. And who more than me is *out of key*, then as now, with this time and with this present into which we sink?"[143]

The other poet with an impressive presence in this *quaderno* is the Czech Jiří Orten: he has (or ties for) the largest number of poems in both *Addio, proibito piangere* and *Vaga lingua strana*. This Jewish poet was randomly run down on a street by a Nazi truck at the age of twenty-two during the Second World War. Orten wouldn't seem likely to be another alter ego of Giudici; yet he incarnates Giudici's longing to believe himself of Jewish origins. We have already come across this quote; it is vital as a picture of Giudici's poetics, which connect the body to the nation through poetry: "Orten is the Czech poet who writes himself ... In this nation which is its own language, the poet *is* his own text, biology and biography entirely confided to writing."[144]

This is, in a way, the fundamental idea of Giudici, that the poet is his own particular language writing him, that a poet's life is not merely in his language but is his language. And yet Orten is also, biographically, "a poet without irony, a poet innocent before literature: like a 'cruelly young' boy who could write his first authentic love letter, even composing it entirely from remembered quotes."[145]

Giudici versus Guidacci

Let us turn to a comparison of Giudici's translation style with that of another major post–Second World War Italian poet, indeed, the most prolific poet-translator of twentieth-century Italy: Margherita Guidacci. Her translations have been poorly studied because she has been unfairly neglected as a poetic figure. Yet she has translated more than any other twentieth-century Italian poet, and this in itself deserves study.

Guidacci, born in Florence in 1921, translated both from English and Slavic languages, and she originally learned English owing to her "immense desire to be able to read Shakespeare in the original."[146] She was an English high school teacher and then became a professor of English literature at the University of Rome. For her, translation was an important creative experience, which meant finding "a new language" for the translation. While "the ideal always remains having beautiful and faithful [*belle e fedeli*] translations," she maintained that one of the two terms must be sacrificed. Yet Guidacci considered the notion of "fidelity" very reductive if only applied to lexical "adherence."[147] Indeed, she states, since the text is composed of three elements, meaning, rhythm, and sound,[148] a translation obeying only the first element would only be faithful to one of the three components of the poetic text.

Rather, as she claims, one must aim to provide an equivalent rhythm and phonic texture in the translation: not "overlapping" (*sovrapposizione*) but "equivalence" (*equivalenza*). After all, it is clear that the rhythm of the original along with its phonic texture is rarely reproducible (and here, we see a link with Ungaretti's pronouncements on the impossibility of translation). What the translator should aim for is, therefore, a rhythm (and music) that performs the same function in the target language as the source language. This cannot be achieved through a "slavish transposition."[149] A similar-functioning rhythm and sound contribute to the overall goal of every poetic translation, which, in Guidacci's view, is to affect the reader in the same way that the reader of the original translation was affected. For Guidacci, this parallelism, the similar effect on the reader of the original and the reader of the translation is the "true and unique faithfulness" (*vera e unica fedeltà*) that counts. It is truly the "essence of translation." The final result should "move [*commuovere*] the reader almost like the original."[150] To succeed, the poet-translator must inhabit and live with the text: the original poem must be "relived [*rivissuto*]." Naturally, this doesn't always occur, since there are certain texts (like Keats's "Ode on a Grecian Urn") that, in Guidacci's words, refuse to be translated by a poet.[151]

Guidacci published various translations of Emily Dickinson's poetry – later included in the recent *Meridiano* volume *Tutte le poesie* (Complete poems) – which came from different original English editions. It was only in 1955 that T.H. Johnson published the first critical edition of Dickinson's poems,[152] many of which had been egregiously altered or amputated (beginning with the elimination of Dickinson's dashes) by previous editors. It is not clear what adulterated text Guidacci used for her 1947 volume of Dickinson's translations,[153] but she added poems from the Johnson edition for her updated 1961 volume of translations from Dickinson, while generally keeping the poems she translated in 1947 unaltered, as Barbara Lanati shows.[154] As we will see, this means that Dickinson's original punctuation is not respected by Guidacci, thus creating a different sort of poetic rhythm. Table 4.2 shows poem 718 translated by Guidacci and Giudici with the original side by side.

Since it is not evident which text Guidacci translated from, it is not appropriate to go into a detailed lexical analysis of her version in comparison with Giudici's. Rather, we can comment on some underlying metrical and syntactical differences that have to do with their particular translation methods.[155] Guidacci translates this poem into a poetic structure based on hendecasyllables, alternating with some *settenari* and *novenari*. As Bianca Tarozzi writes,[156] this metrical variety, also used

Table 4.2 "I meant to find Her when I came"

Emily Dickinson	Giovanni Giudici	Margherita Guidacci
I meant to find Her when I came –	Pensavo di trovarla – quando venni – [I thought of finding her – when I came –]	Io volevo trovarla al mio ritorno, [I wanted to find her on my return,]
Death – had the same design –	La Morte – pensava lo stesso – [Death – thought the same –]	e lo stesso pensiero ebbe la morte; [and death had the same thought;]
But the success – was His – it seems –	Ma – sembra – fu suo il successo [But – it seems – it was his the success]	ma fu sua la vittoria a quanto sembra, [but it was his the victory as it seems,]
And the *Discomfit* – Mine –	E la rassegnazione – fu per me – [And the resignation – was for me –]	E fu mia la sconfitta. [And mine was the defeat.]
I meant to tell Her how I longed	Pensavo di dirle quanto atteso – [I thought of telling her how]	Volevo dirle quanto desiderio [I wanted to tell her how much desire]
For just this single time –	Avessi proprio questo solo attimo – [I had awaited just this sole instant –]	avevo anche di questo solo incontro; [I had even of this sole meeting;]
But Death had told Her so the first –	Ma la Morte l'aveva detto prima – [But Death had told her before –]	ma glielo aveva già detto la morte, [but death had already told her it,]
And she had *hearkened Him* –	E lei se n'era andata, con la Morte – [And she had gone away, with Death –]	essa le aveva dato ascolto. [she had listened to him.]
To wander – now – is my Repose –	Vagabondare è – adesso – mio riposo – [To wander is – now – my rest]	E la mia vita è in un perpetuo errare; [And my life is in a perpetual wandering;]
To rest – To rest would be	Fermarmi – fermarmi sarebbe [To stop – to stop would be]	il riposo sarebbe [rest would be]

Table 4.2 "I meant to find Her when I came" (*Continued*)

Emily Dickinson	Giovanni Giudici	Margherita Guidacci
A privilege of Hurricane	Un privilegio d'uragano – [A privilege of hurricane –]	un privilegio d'uragano [a privilege of hurricane]
To Memory – and Me.	Per la Memoria – e me. [For Memory – and me.]	per me, per la memoria. [for me, for memory.]
SOURCE: Dickinson, *Tutte le poesie*, ed. Marisa Bulgheroni, 808	SOURCE: Dickinson, *Tutte le poesie*, ed. Marisa Bulgheroni, 1650	SOURCE: Dickinson, *Tutte le poesie*, ed. Marisa Bulgheroni, 809

in Guidacci's translations of Elizabeth Bishop and T.S. Eliot, contributes to the "rhythmic flexibility," creating a "naturalness of the poetic text" that allows Guidacci's fundamentally domesticating (to use Venuti's term) translations to be read with pleasure a generation later. Likewise, "the very strong relationship with the tradition of Italian verse"[157] leads her to frequently invert the noun and verb (most clearly in vv. 2, 4, 7, and 9), a practice common in Italian poetry. Here, indeed, we don't hear the "spasmatic" rhythm of the original Dickinson. Guidacci utilizes the technique that Antoine Berman called "rationalization":

> this bears primarily on the syntactical structures of the original, starting with that most meaningful and changeable element in a prose text: *punctuation*. Rationalization recomposes sentences and the sequence of sentences, rearranging them according to a certain idea of discursive *order*.[158]

By not respecting Dickinson's punctuation, Guidacci modifies the "discursive order" of the source text. She constructs sentences according to her own poetic style. Giudici, meanwhile, follows the original syntax more closely, and he maintains the authentic punctuation that creates such an unfamiliar reading experience both in the original and in the translation. Keeping the foreignness of the original in Italian means conserving, as one of Tynjanov's "constructive principles," the idiosyncratic punctuated syntax of the poem. Thus, using Venuti's terminology, Giudici "foreignizes" the text, in contrast to Guidacci.

Translation Techniques

Let us now look into Giudici's translation practices in more detail. Overall, as we have seen, he tries to move the Italian reader closer to the foreign poet: as Antonio Prete writes of Giudici's translation ideology, "Familiarize the foreigner, without having him lose his distance."[159] Giudici's method of foreignizing the target language is primarily linguistic (syntactical, lexical, and metrical). He focuses on one or two of Tynjanov's "constructive principles." For instance, we have seen how he translates Pushkin into an unusual Italian rhythm. This in itself makes the translation sound strange and foreign. With Frost, he strives to keep the precise naming of plants and to respect his colloquialisms that in their precision are "terrifying, at times, for the translator."[160] So, in "Mending wall," Giudici conserves the first verse's colloquial syntax: "Something there is that doesn't love a wall" is rendered as "Qualcosa c'è che non sopporta un muro" (there's something that doesn't put up with a wall).[161] In "Reluctance," Giudici translates the unfamiliar New England botanical aster and witch hazel faithfully as *astro* and *hamamelis*.[162]

In Coleridge's "The Rime of the Ancient Mariner," Giudici aims to load the translation with a similar concentration of alliteration and assonance possessed by the original (e.g., in English verses like "The furrow followed free"). We can see this in a few examples, as in the *s* in "Il sole sorgeva a sinistra"[163] (The sun rose in the west); the *u* and *i* in "tutto ululii, ruggiti e schianti"[164] (everything was howling, roaring, and cracking); the *f* and *ccia* in "fai quella faccia? Con una freccia"[165] (you make that face? With an arrow); and the *a* in "che fa la nebbia calare"[166] (which makes the fog descend). In Plath, he conserves the abundance of rhymes in translation, where he adds more separate rhyme-words than in the English original.

Along with these constructive principles, we can classify at least six different secondary linguistic aspects of Giudici's translation practice (which can also become primary constructive principles of translation in their own right): the conservation of the same amount of verses in a poem; enjambments; raising the register for poetic power; added assonance and alliteration; omission of words; and the foreignization of Italian syntax and the introduction of foreign vocabulary into Italian.

It is unusual for Giudici to alter the number of verses in translation. Even when he omits or changes words, he generally keeps the same number of verses, which is "an almost inalienable precept."[167] It is this principle that prompted Giudici to experiment with new types of hendecasyllable lines, since it was only by increasing the verse horizontally that Giudici could conserve the same number of verses as the original English poems. Thus, the normal eleven-syllable line at times reached seventeen syllables. The fact that Giudici most often translates into the same number of verses goes against one of the tenets of modern translation theory that was formulated by Shoshana Blum-Kulka: namely, the explicitation hypothesis, according to which translations are always longer than the originals regardless of the languages, genres, and registers.[168] And when Giudici goes beyond the verse count of the source text, it is often not for reasons of explicitation, but because of poetic devices like enjambments.

For instance, in his translation of Pound's lovely "Nel biancheggiar," he adds two verses to one line by using three enjambments. "It wills not die to leave us desolate" is transformed into "... non vuole / Morire lasciando / Le nostre anime sole"[169] (it doesn't want / to die, leaving / our souls alone). The enjambments underline the semantic content of this verse: they draw out the desire not to die by stretching out one verse to three verses.

Giudici is a poet who even in his own verse favours enjambments to capture the reader's attention and focus on a specific word, or to create significant ambiguity. All of his poems contain them; likewise, his translations generally have more enjambments than the source text. His translation of Pushkin, for example, has twice as many enjambments in the first chapter (forty-seven versus twenty-four).[170] Giudici uses them regularly in other translations, from Donne ("la sorte / mia"[171] [my / destiny]) to an anonymous French poem ("fondo / Del bene"[172] [depth / of the good]).

Second, Giudici often prunes the original. A particularly significant omission is the noun "tree" in his translation from Milton: "... the fruit / of that forbidden tree" becomes "il frutto / proibito"[173] (the forbidden fruit). Most likely the elimination of "tree" was due to the assonance and alliteration of *frutto* and *proibito*. Other omissions abound: for instance, in Coleridge's "Kubla Khan," *stately* is not rendered in the verse *Un duomo di delizia fabbricare*[174] (To fabricate a dome of delight) and *vláčný*[175] (soft) is not translated in Seifert's "Viaggio di nozze" (honeymoon). Generally speaking, these omissions make the Italian translation tighter and more compact and allow Giudici to respect his precept of keeping the verse count the same.

Third, Giudici frequently modifies words or phrases for poetic impact: he raises the register. For instance, in a famous poem of Dickinson's, *ground* becomes *prato* (meadow) and the phrase *the Horses' Heads/Were towards* becomes *i cavalli/correvano verso*[176] (the horses / ran towards). Other examples are *spasmo*[177] (spasm) for *heartburn* in Hopkins and *po nemoci* (literally, "after sickness"), which becomes *le ossa rotte*[178] (broken bones) in Seifert's poem "Tra le righe" (between the lines). Analogous instances can be found in many pages of *Eugene Onegin*, and they are evidence of Giudici's intention to translate from one *poetic* language into another. This clearly runs counter to widespread translation practices of domestication.

The poet-translator Franco Fortini theorized the idea of "compensation" in translation, as we saw in a previous chapter:[179] the new target language can increase alliteration and assonance, providing a more complex system of phonic texture. This is on display in Giudici's translations from Coleridge, as noted, and is moreover present in almost all of his other versions. For example, in Donne, the alliteration of *l* is compensated by an assonance/alliteration of *av*: "And lawyers find out still / Litigious men, which quarrels move / though she and I do love" becomes in Giudici's version "e querelanti / Avranno gli avvocati avvegnanché / si faccia io e lei l'amore"[180] (and plaintiffs / will have lawyers, although / she and I make love). Likewise, in Orten's "O assorti occhi" (O absorbed eyes), the assonance in *o* and the alliteration of *c* is evident: "O assorti occhi – occhi al di là degli occhi"[181] (O absorbed eyes – eyes beyond eyes), imitating the original Czech "O oči civící o oči za očima."[182] Giuseppe Ghini has noted that Giudici uses assonance in his version of *Eugene Onegin* when he is unable to find an exact end-rhyme, such as *economista / arricchisca*[183] (economist / enrich).

Giudici alienates the reader by using foreign words (as he does frequently in his own poetry) or by altering Italian syntax to fit the source text. In his translation of *Eugene Onegin*, Giudici kept many of the foreign words used by Pushkin (in French, English, Latin, and German), but he also maintained some of the Russian terms[184] and translated some Russian words into other languages like French.[185] In addition, as Massimo Bacigalupo has noted, Giudici keeps two Latinisms in his translation of Aquinas's hymn "Pange lingua" (Tell, tongue): *Et in mundo conversatus* and *Cibum turbae duodenae* remain substantially the same as *E nel mondo conversato* (And dwelling in the world) and *Cibo alla turba duodena*[186] (Food for the crowd of twelve), except for the Italian morphological endings. Likewise, Giudici leaves the original German *Ach, du* (Oh, you) of Sylvia Plath in his translation of "Daddy."[187] These are instances in which the reader notices that he is reading a translation, because the original text erupts into view, either directly in the source language, or in a calque. Likewise, on numerous occasions, as pointed out by Rodolfo Zucco,[188] Giudici alters the normal Italian syntax to accommodate the foreign text. First, he uses an intransitive Italian verb transitively in a poem by Ransom: *beat the air* becomes *annaspa il vuoto*[189] (grasping the void) and similar cases can be found in his other translations (e.g., *Sospirando ricordi*[190] [breathing memories] in Halas's "Accordi"). Second, Giudici makes use of the Italian present participle as in Pound's poem: *credenti in menzogne di vecchi* (believing in old men's lies). And third, he utilizes archaic Italian vocabulary, like *rossità* (which translates the common *redness*).[191]

It is clear from these observations that Giudici does not aim to domesticate his author and his text for the Italian reader. His goal is to alienate the reader who reads his translations as much as the reader who reads his own alienating verse (written in a seemingly foreign language [*una lingua strana*]). From keeping foreign words in the text, to introducing new foreign words (translating a Russian word by a French word, for instance, in his translation of Pushkin), to the frequent use of rhetorical figures (assonance and alliteration, above all) that emphasize the linguistic texture of the translation, and to enjambments that break the normal syntax and other grammatical twisting or archaic vocabulary, Giudici is consistent in the foreignizing translation strategies theorized by both Schleiermacher and Venuti. Indeed, rather than adding words to enable him to fill out a particular rhyme or metre scheme, Giudici eliminates them. For Schleiermacher (and Venuti), as we have seen, the ideal is a translation that is "towards a foreign likeness bent" (*zu einer fremden Ähnlichkeit hinübergebogen*).[192] Giudici bends Italian both in his poetic translations and his original verse in order to procure that aura of strangeness inherent in poetry.

Conclusion

Giudici wrote clearly about the relationship between his poetry and his Italian translations that

> Someone could now raise the knotty problem of how and how much a poet can be influenced by the poets that he happens to translate or, vice versa, can transfer onto these poets a certain patina of his own style. I will say, for however much it regards me, that I hope to have been fairly exempt from the former and the latter; yet immediately adding that, without a doubt, my "mode of translating" poetry of others has influenced my writing.[193]

In terms of poetic metre, we have already seen how translating Frost enabled Giudici to use the hendecasyllable more freely and less rigidly. Giudici adopted a preferred metre while he was translating Pushkin and it pushed him towards a prolific use of rhyme. The structure of Giudici's own poetic language was thus profoundly influenced by his translations. Likewise, his *Fortezza* draws considerably on his interest in and translation of St. Ignatius of Loyola. *Salutz* would be inconceivable without the background of the troubadours, Dante, and Petrarch. His reworking of Dante's *Paradiso* drew on many of his favourite authors, as Simona Morando has noted, from St. Augustine and St. Francis through Giacomo Noventa and Kafka to Eliot and Pound.[194] As we saw at the beginning of this chapter, Giudici's own poetry varied considerably in form, content, and style during his career. Yet his use of the same rhetorical figures, from assonance and alliteration to enjambments and etymological figures is widely encountered in both his own work and his translations, even when his translated authors do not use them.

Of major Italian twentieth-century poets, no one but Giudici has translated Russian or Czech authors. Giudici has reintroduced Pushkin in Italy and made a strong case for *Eugene Onegin* in Italian as a brilliantly structured and styled poem. Giudici brought Czech poets like Jiří Orten, Ivan Blatný, and Jiří Kolář into the Italian literary field. His translations of Plath, Frost, and Ransom quickly became authoritative.

For Giudici, translation is ultimately the description of poetry itself: translation is a form of transubstantiation; it is the way to incarnate reality. Translation, then, is not merely a poetic exercise, or an effort to create an autonomous aesthetic object, but a method of incorporating the totality of one's body into words. Indeed, this is how Giudici sees Kafka's whole enterprise, as well as his own: "Writing (or, more precisely, the process of writing, the material act of writing, hand and pen, ink and paper) is therefore for Kafka life itself, the mortality of the body exorcized [*la mortalità del corpo esorcizzata*], made aseptic and finally invulnerable."[195] Or, in Giudici's own verses, from *Salutz*, where body and word have finally become fused through a process of *essere*, going beyond the act of *dire*:

A voi mi scrissi quasi più che morto
Essendo la mia lettera il mio corpo
Parola per virtù transustanziale:
In seno a voi riposto
Io pergamena – e inchiostro[196]

[To you I wrote myself almost more than dead
My body being my letter
Word in its very nature transubstantial:
Placed in your breast,
I am parchment – and ink]

5 Edoardo Sanguineti: Translation, *Travestimento*, and Foreignization[1]

"It is I who translate: it is I who am speaking."[2]

–Edoardo Sanguineti

Edoardo Sanguineti (1930–2010) was a pre-eminent Italian poet, writer, and intellectual. He published novels and numerous books of poetry, plays, and essays, along with a copious number of translations. Indeed, no modern Italian poet, excepting Salvatore Quasimodo, translated as much foreign drama as Sanguineti. He translated plays by Aeschylus, Aristophanes, Brecht, Corneille, Euripides, Ionesco, Molière, Seneca, Shakespeare, and Sophocles.[3] He also translated Petronius's *Satyricon*,[4] Goethe's *Faust*,[5] as well as lyric poems from several languages.[6]

This chapter is divided into several sections: first, an overview of Sanguineti's poetic career; second, an introduction to his translation ideology; third, an examination of his translations and adaptations, culminating in his *Quaderno di traduzioni*; next, a review of his translation techniques; last, a comparison of Sanguineti's and Giovanni Giudici's translations of a sonnet by Shakespeare. We will show how the Italian poet-translator's conception of translation both draws on Bertolt Brecht's idea of theatrical alienation and appropriates Walter Benjamin's notion of interlinear translation. For Sanguineti, translations of classical works are fundamentally *travestimenti* (travesties). His *travestimenti* are not all alike: the role of colloquialisms, foreignisms, metre, and rhyme shift, as will become evident. Yet they all share the important and essential characteristic of being composed by an individual poet with distinctive poetics. Therefore, even if Sanguineti's *travestimenti* differ in their reflection and refraction of the original texts, they are always works defined by characteristic features of his own style.

Poetic Career

Sanguineti first made his mark on the Italian literary scene with his 1956 *Laborintus* (Labyrinth),[7] a highly experimental and innovative long poem that would form one of the cornerstones of the Italian neo-avant-garde's 1961 poetic anthology *I Novissimi: poesie per gli anni '60* (*I novissimi*: Poetry for the sixties).[8] Sanguineti described his poetic career as being dominated by three consecutive literary styles: tragedy, elegy, and comedy:

> As a young man, I began by writing tragic verse; then, for a few years I wrote elegiac poems; now I write comic poems ... In some readings and debates, I've happened to say that I write "comically," this being the only way to approach the "tragic."[9]

His *Laborintus*, a watershed in post-war Italian poetry, was an example of tragic verse; its subject matter dealt with the protagonist, Laszo Varga, and his immersion in the *Palus Putredinis* (Filthy swamp), or, in other terms, writing poetry in an era threatened with nuclear annihilation. Sanguineti's elegiac period began with his 1971 *Reisebilder* (Travel pictures),[10] continuing through his 1981 *Scartabello* (Notebook),[11] where his new style of poetry incarnated itself in a diaristic, ironic treatment of daily life, starting from small facts, in "petites proses en poème" (little narratives in a poem),[12] as he writes in an untitled poem:

> Per preparare una poesia, si prende "un piccolo fatto vero" (possibilmente
> fresco di giornata): c'è una ricetta simile in Stendhal, lo so, ma infine
> ha un suo sapore assai diverso: (e dovrei perderci un'ora almeno, adesso,
> qui a cercare le opportune citazioni: e francamente non ne ho voglia):[13]
>
> [To prepare a poem, one takes "a little true fact" (if possible,
> newly-hatched): there's a similar recipe in Stendhal, I know, but ultimately
> it has a quite different taste: (and I should lose an hour at least, now,
> here in looking for the appropriate citations: and frankly I'm not in the mood):]

His third phase, a comic phase, opened with his 1982 *Cataletto* (Coffin) and continued up until his death, is characterized by a plurality of styles and themes that share a downward stylistic thrust. An example is his apocalyptic alphabet, signalling the infernal turn followed by Sanguineti in this period (well noted by commentators), when he adapted Dante's *Inferno*[14] as well:

anime amiche all'aspro astro afroditico,
abnepoti dell'albero adamitico,
audite le mie antifone acide & ascetiche,
arche di angui & di anguille arcialfabetiche:
apro abissi di aleppi apocalittiche,
ansimo ansie di angosce & di asme asfittiche:
adattatemi auricole atte & attente,
annunzio un acre, acerrimo accidente:[15]

[souls friendly with the bitter aphroditic star,
descendants of the Adamic tree,
hear my acidic & ascetic antiphonies,
arks of snakes & of arch-literal eels:
i open abysses of apocalyptic aleppos,
i pant anxieties of anguish & asphyxial asthmas:
adapt for me auricles apt & attentive,
i announce a pungent, most bitter fit:]

While his poetics changed through time, the underlying political impulse behind them remained the same. As Sanguineti noted about himself in the essay "I santi anarchici: la mia poesia" (Anarchic saints: My poetry):

> The problem of a poet, today, still remains for me, as for its readers, transforming the impulse to revolt into a proposal for revolution, and making a feasible project out of one's lack of faith.[16]

Sanguineti thus yearns to inspire revolution through words. In the same article he alludes to an episode in Charlie Chaplin's *Modern Times*, where Chaplin finds himself unknowingly in the middle of a (Communist) demonstration, waving a banner, and he is hauled away by the police. Chaplin is a "marvelous allegory of the happy destiny [*felice destino*] of the poet," Sanguineti writes. Like a poet

> he waves a rag of words, unaware and courteous, it doesn't matter, but he finds a mass of strangers at his back, following him, transforming the sense of his poor verbal operations into action, and charging them with a collective value: a mass who wants, as has long been said, and as one perhaps always dreams, to modify the world, and change life.[17]

This faith and hope in political change through words will accompany Sanguineti all of his life.[18] Indeed, for this self-described last Marxist (*ultimo Marxista*), translation provides an ideal way to implement this change. Each individual reader or audience member, rather than being force-fed specific dogma or being inculcated into passivity, can be ideally required to interpret the text, to criticize and form judgments, to dream collectively of another type of society that will take the place of the current one, and to change life as it is into something freer, more just, and more equitable for all. This heady political project, as evinced in Sanguineti's words, is generally latent in the Italian poet's translations, but sometimes it explicitly comes to the foreground (as in his version of Lucretius' *De rerum natura*, his *travestimento* of *Faust*, and his adaptation of Carlo Gozzi's *L'amore delle tre melarance* [The love of three oranges]).[19]

Translation Career

Sanguineti's first translation was a collective version of James Joyce's lyric poetry with Alfredo Giuliani, J. Rodolfo Wilcock, and Alberto Rossi. In 1968, he published his first of many dramatic translations: Euripides's *Bacchae*. The following year, he published a noted translation of Petronius's novel *Satyricon*, which came out in tandem with Federico Fellini's own film version of the *Satyricon*. Sanguineti spent the next three decades mostly translating for theatre: Seneca's *Phaedra* (1969), Euripides's *The Trojan Women* (1974) and *Hippolytus* (2012),[20] Aeschylus's *Choephori* (1978) and *Seven against Thebes* (1992), Sophocles's *Oedipus Rex* (1980) and (partial) *Antigone* (1993), Molière's *Don Juan* (2000), Aristophanes's *Thesmophoriazusae* (2001), Brecht's *The Caucasian Chalk Circle* (2003), Corneille's *The Comic Illusion* (2005), Shakespeare's *King Lear* (2008) and an unfinished version of *Measure for Measure*. He also published a version of Goethe's *Faust* (1985), and in the last decade of his life he published three volumes of verse translations, including volumes by Goethe (2003) and Shakespeare (2004), and his *Quaderno di traduzioni* (2006).

Translation Ideology

In Sanguineti's seminal 1978 article "Il traduttore, nostro contemporaneo" (The translator, our contemporary),[21] alluding to the Polish writer Jan Kott's *Shakespeare Our Contemporary*,[22] Sanguineti begins his discourse by speaking of pseudo-translations, specifically the famous nineteenth-century Italian poet Giacomo Leopardi's "Cantico del gallo silvestre" (Canticle of the sylvan rooster). It might seem paradoxical to focus on pseudo-translation in an essay on translation, but it is through this concept that Sanguineti reveals his core thinking. According to our poet-translator, in a belief constant through the years, "there is no difference between a translation and a pseudo-translation."[23] Therefore, as Sanguineti writes, "all true translations are false documents."[24] Consequently, a translation has no authentic relationship with the original text. To call it a translation, Sanguineti argues, is to insinuate a false relationship with the original. Translations, strictly speaking, do not exist. Nothing can be transferred from the source to the target text, although Sanguineti's translations occasionally repudiate this belief, as we will later see with those of Shakespeare: "every translation, willingly or not, burns up the text, leaving no residue." Not only does Sanguineti make this claim, he goes even further by saying that in translation "there is truly no other speaker than the translator."[25] When you read Homer in translation, you are not reading the Greek poet, but his translator. The translator moves from being a medium to being the original author. It is the translator who is "our contemporary." It is the translator who tries to speak to us through "his living language, into our living language." It is the translator who hides behind the "phantasmal and phantasmagorical clothes of fabled *personae*, like Aeschylus, Sophocles, and Euripides."[26]

Thus the translator, a magician and a deceiver, speaks through the mask of the author he translates and the characters he resuscitates. And here is the relevance of Sanguineti's term *travestimento*, which we could render as travesty, adaptation, or disguise, depending on the context. Our poet-translator would begin to use this term starting with his 1985 adaptation of *Faust*. *Travestimento*, which was prevalently used in the Baroque period, signifies two separate notions. It can refer to a parody of a classical theatrical text (whence the English *travesty*). As Gérard Genette observed in *Palimpsests*, burlesque travesty in the seventeenth century

> rewrites a noble text by preserving its "action," meaning its fundamental content and movement (in rhetorical terms, its invention and disposition), but impressing on it an entirely different elocution, or "style," in the classical sense of the term.[27]

The second meaning of *travestimento* is "disguise." Actors are *travestiti*, transvestites: they are in disguise. Indeed, the translator bears a fundamental similarity to the actor: both act out, linguistically, a text. In general, for Sanguineti, the concept of *travestimento* embraces all aspects of writing, from translation to normal authorship: "in truth translating is writing [*far scrittura*]. And therefore it is always adaptation [*travestire*]."[28] This term, then, becomes for our Italian poet-translator a fundamental lens through which to approach the idea of theatrical translation, his favoured genre. While all translations are *travestimenti*, by nature, given that the translator is the author in disguise, not all of Sanguineti's translations parody the original text. His *Faust* lowers the style of the original to a great degree, but his version of Corneille's *L'Illusion comique* (The comic illusion) does not. As Sanguineti said in a 2008 interview, *un travestimento* can be a literal version or a free version or anywhere in between:

> Sometimes, the *travestimento* can even be taken to the limit of total rewriting [*riscrittura*]. But this is only one of the poles within which the translator's activity reveals itself. The other pole is constituted by a sort of superstition of faithfulness: this too is obviously legitimate, but ultimately always veined with hypocrisy.[29]

In considering Sanguineti's conception of *travestimento* further, it is necessary to speak of Brecht and Benjamin, both of whom were important figures for Sanguineti. While their influence on Sanguineti's verse has been traced to some degree, their impact on his translation ideology has generally gone unnoticed. Indeed, it is my contention that Brecht oriented Sanguineti's translation method towards a particular aim – that of alienating (*Verfremdung*) the audience – while Benjamin offered a possible style of translation, namely interlinear, that Sanguineti would pursue by using extensive syntactical and lexical calquing.

Brecht's own idea of theatre revolved, then, around *Verfremdung*. As he wrote in *A Short Organum*, "The exposition of the story and its communication by suitable means of alienation [*verfremdungen*] constitute the main business of the theater."[30] This alienation is brought about in the following way: "Alienating an event or character means first of all stripping the event of its self-evident, familiar, obvious quality and creating a sense of astonishment and curiosity about it."[31] This estrangement, while similar to what the Russian formalists described as *ostranenie*, goes beyond linguistic defamiliarization. As Sanguineti says, Brecht's idea of theatre "implicated, through estrangement [*straniamento*], a critical attitude on the part of the spectator."[32] The Italian poet classified him as "a great transformer [*travestitore*]. Think of the *Threepenny opera* which originates from a text by John Gay, or *Coriolanus*."[33] Through alienation, Sanguineti seeks to estrange his reader, and he accomplishes this through his linguistically challenging translations. Readers (and spectators) are forced to grapple with the texts. The less difficult or resistant the original text (e.g., *The Satyricon*), the more Sanguineti problematizes it in his translation through contorted syntax; the more revolutionary or challenging the text, the less Sanguineti transforms it (e.g., *King Lear*).

While he was influenced by Brecht's idea of alienation and the German author's own *travestimenti*, Sanguineti found the concrete method for his *travestimenti* in Benjamin's classic essay on translation. There, Benjamin extolled interlinear translations. As he asserts in "Die Aufgabe des Übersetzers" (The task of the translator), the "true translation" (*Die wahre Ubersetzung*) can be done through "a literalness in the rendition of the syntax, which exactly proves the word, not the sentence, as the Ur-element of the translator."[34] Hölderlin's Greek translations are the "prototypes" of this type of literary translation, but the ideal interlinear translation, according to the German philosopher, is not of a poetic text. As Benjamin continues,

> For to some degree (*Grade*) all great writings, but holy writings the most, contain their potential (*Virtuelle*) translation between the lines. The interlinear version of holy texts is the prototype (*das Urbild*) or ideal (*Ideal*) of all translation.[35]

The interests of Sanguineti, a declared Marxist, lie elsewhere. He will appropriate this method for his "travestied" versions of purely literary works. As the Italian poet-translator comments, "my ideal remains interlinear translation; not in the sense of a merely dictionary-type interlinearity, but also rhythmic, syntactic, and acoustic interlinearity."[36] Sanguineti follows this dictum by a variety of methods: imitating, as much as possible, the syntax of the original, and imitating the sound and cognates of the original (even going so far as to use "false friends" that nevertheless maintain a close phonetic resemblance). While Sanguineti does not usually reach the same extreme and contorted effects of Hölderlin's translations, he does often "Hellenize"[37] (or Latinize, for instance) the Italian text. Through an interlinear approach, Sanguineti infuses his translations with his own idiosyncrasies, his own verbal idiolect – excessive punctuation, superfluous pronouns, solecisms, alliteration, and cacophony.

Such a method clearly shows an adherence to Lawrence Venuti's foreignizing ideology, where the reader is decisively brought towards the text and not vice versa. Yet such a reading experience is obviously not natural for the reader. This alien reading experience, this Brechtian alienation, is intensely felt in Sanguineti's versions. It should not be surprising, then, that Sanguineti's translations have been neglected by classicists.[38] This is due, in no small part, to Sanguineti's particular approach, in which the translations are not smooth, "invisible"[39] creations but works that are written in an idiosyncratic Italian. The notion of interlinearity fits Sanguineti's own manner of composition perfectly, because it enables him to justify the use of his particular poetics. After all, a line by line and even word for word rendering will naturally cause a translation to be filled with unnatural syntax and diction. Add to that the search for phonetic reproduction or imitation, and you have the Sanguinetian cocktail of virtuoso translation.

Nonetheless, before looking at his translations, it will be helpful to examine his rewritings of Italian texts, since they, too, constitute *travestimenti.*

Translations and Adaptations

Italian Adaptations

In Sanguineti's view, his reworkings and adaptations of Italian texts constitute the highest grade of *travestimenti.* This would seem counterintuitive, since such adaptations are only intralingual translations rather than interlingual translations (in Roman Jakobson's terminology). They belong to the category of a "rewording," instead of "translation proper."[40] Moreover, Sanguineti borrows whole octaves, for instance, in his adaptation of Ariosto, or multiple verses in the case of Dante, so at times it is simply the same text in a different context. Yet when Sanguineti performs collages with other texts, or riffs on the original, we see a higher grade of *travestimento.*

His version of the first canticle of the *Commedia* is certainly more measured and faithful to the text than other rewritings Sanguineti composed. Often, Sanguineti abbreviates Dante: Cavalcante de' Cavalcanti's famous lines about his son are shortened by about half, although with no insertions of foreign material. Other times, however, his treatment of Dante is oriented towards collage: for example, Sanguineti's portrayal of Paolo and Francesca includes a whole medley of voices: Dante, Giacomo da Lentini, Andreas Capellanus, and Chrétien de Troyes. On the whole, however, his adaptation of *Inferno* remains quite tied to the text because of the fibre of the Dantean tercets.

Yet the same cannot be said for Sanguineti's 2001 version of Carlo Gozzi's *L'amore delle tre melarance*. Here, the Italian poet-translator doesn't have an original text in verse: only Gozzi's plot sketches, his *canovaccio*. Sanguineti thus has the license to invent the dialogue *ex novo*, reinterpreting the theatrical fable in a modern key (e.g., "Silvio re di Coppe" [Silvio, King of cups] becomes the recent Prime Minister Silvio Berlusconi). Gozzi writes in his *canovaccio* that Pantalone, servant to the King,

> fantasticando sull'origine della malattia chiedeva al Re in secreto, per non essere udito dalle guardie, che circondavano il Monarca, se la Maestà sua avesse acquistato nella sua giovinezza qualche male, che comunicato al sangue del Principe ereditario lo riducesse a quella miseria, e se il mercurio potesse giovare.[41]
>
> [imagining the origin of the sickness (of Silvio's son), he asked the king in secret, so as not to be heard by the bodyguards, who surrounded the Monarch, if His Majesty had acquired in his youth some disease, which, passed on to the blood of the hereditary prince, had driven him to this misery, and if mercury could help.][42]

Sanguineti expands this into the following:

> Sire, parliamo piano. Se qui non c'è chi ci ode,
> vigilante, gorilla, corazziere, custode,
> mi dica, in confidenza, in tutta verità,
> questa atroce astenia non è un'eredità?
> Quando voi foste giovane, altissima maestà,
> vi godeste la vita, si racconta, si sa:
> *chemin di fer*, champagne, ostriche, e ballerine:
> nigeriane, albanesi, polacche, e parigine.
> Oggi un omo, domani un etero, un pedofilo,
> sadico, masochista, scambista, iperzoofilo,
> sempre impetuoso, incauto, schiavo di ogni capriccio,
> senza un preservativo, scopaste come un riccio.
> Non foste, forse, voi, voi macho tanto ardente,
> anche un poco, soltanto, immunodeficiente?[43]
>
> [Sire, let us speak quietly. If no one can hear us here –
> neither a sentry, nor a gorilla, a cuirassier, nor a guard –

tell me, in confidence, completely truthfully,
is this atrocious asthenia not an inheritance?
When you were young, most noble majesty,
you enjoyed life, it is told, one knows:
baccarat, champagne, oysters, and ballerinas:
Nigerian women, Albanians, Poles, and Parisians.
Today a man, tomorrow a hetero, a pedophile,
sadist, masochist, swinger, zoophilist,
always impetuous, incautious, slave to every fancy,
without a condom, you screwed like a hedgehog.
Weren't you, as macho as hot-blooded,
also a little immune-deficient?]

Clearly Sanguineti's low style, full of slang, bears no resemblance to Gozzi's; the only similar element is that Sanguineti composes fourteen-syllable verses (*martelliani*), the same type of verse that Gozzi occasionally intersperses in his prose sketches. Indeed, Sanguineti's rewriting of Gozzi goes far beyond his translations of foreign texts, even such adaptations as *Faust*.

Now that we have seen two separate forms of *travestimenti* from Italian texts, we can move on to Sanguineti's *travestimenti* of foreign authors, which are in all cases more adherent to the source texts.

Petronius

We begin with Petronius's *Satyricon*, Sanguineti's second translation after Euripides's *The Bacchae*. His version of Petronius is more imitative than his drama translations, so much so that critics justly call it "a real rewriting."[44] That it might be a *travestimento* (*avant-la-lettre*) like *Faust* seems at first sight excluded by Sanguineti's own words that describe it as a "translation with facing text":

> I translated Petronious in a manner extremely faithful, on the one hand, almost literal I would dare to say (except, as one says, for errors and omissions), which could even count as a sort of translation with "facing text," if not absolutely interlinear.[45]

Here is another reference to Benjamin's notion of interlinear translation. Let us take two examples from the text to glimpse what Sanguineti says. The *Satyricon* begins:

Num alio genere furiarum declamatores inquietantur, qui clamant: "haec vulnera pro libertate publica excepi, hunc oculum pro vobis impendi; date mihi [ducem] qui me ducat ad liberos meos, nam succisi poplites membra non sustinent"?[46]

[For by another type of furies are the public speakers disturbed, who cry out: "these wounds I received for popular liberty; this eye for you I sacrificed: give me a guide, who leads me to my children, for slashed hamstrings do not hold up (my) limbs"?]

Sanguineti turns this into:

Ma sono di questo genere, proprio, per me, quelle Furie che agitano quelli che declamano, quando proclamano: "Queste mie ferite le ho subite per la libertà della repubblica, questo mio occhio l'ho perduto per voi. Datemi una guida, che mi guidi dai miei figli, che ci ho i tendini tagliati, che non mi tengono su il corpo."[47]

[But they are of this type, truly, in my opinion, those Furies who agitate those who declaim, when they proclaim: "these wounds, these I have suffered for the freedom of the republic, this eye of mine I have lost for you. Give me a guide, who can guide me to my children, because I have slashed hamstrings, which don't hold up (my) body."]

Another excerpt from further on in the *Satyricon*:

Postquam lustravi oculis totam urbem, in cellulam redii osculisque tandem bona fide exactis alligo artissimis complexibus puerum fruorque votis usque ad invidiam felicibus.[48]

[After that I traversed with my eyes the whole city, I returned in (my) little room and I bind in the closest embraces the boy and enjoy (my) desires so as to cause envy in the happy.]

Sanguineti translates this as:

Me la sono esplorata con i miei occhi, la città, tutta. Poi, sono ritornato nella mia camera, che finalmente mi prendo regolarmente i baci miei, dal ragazzo mio, che me lo stringo nei miei strettissimi abbracci, che mi godo la voglia mia, con un piacere da fare l'invidia.[49]

> [I explored it with my eyes, the city, all of it. Then I returned to my room, so that finally I get for myself as usual my kisses, from my boyfriend, who I hold tight in my most tight embraces, so that I enjoy my desire, with an enviable pleasure.]

These aren't mere interlinear translations that are impartial and objective; rather, Sanguineti's hand is everywhere, and this is apparent in the following transformations that infuse the translation with popular Italian elements: the pleonastic pronouns and adverbs *mi, ci, si*; the colloquial *che*; and the left and right shiftings. As the Italian poet-translator noted, he treated Petronius's text "with excesses of colloquiality, and blunders that were in truth calculated and sophisticated."[50] He did not merely abundantly calque the syntax of the Latin, but he moulded his version according to his individual stylistic aim, "with my search for impressions of spoken speech, very near to that so little dignified, so irregular, and so lively Latin."[51] Indeed, Sanguineti summed it up well, when he said that

> in translating him, in some way, I came to restore (*restituire*) in Petronious that sort of Petronian manner, pseudo-Petronian (*pseudo-Petroniana*), which I had fabricated for myself, in some way, starting from him.[52]

The interesting paradox here is implicit in the word "restituire." Sanguineti is restoring to Petronius the very model of writing – "pseudo-Petroniana" – that the Italian writer fabricated for his own literary use in his novels. Sanguineti's prose style is both indebted to and yet creditor of Petronius's poetics. The source (Petronius) and the imitation (Sanguineti) combine here into a virtuoso version of the *Satyricon*. While later translations from the classics will make use of the same translation technique of calquing, none, except for *Faust*, will have the proliferation of colloquial elements present here.

Classical Drama

In this section we will examine Sanguineti's translation of *Oedipus Rex*. For this theatrical translation, this "splendid and terrible experience," Sanguineti found himself between the commissioning director, Benno Besson, and Hölderlin's translation of Sophocles. As our poet-translator recounts,

> with Besson, everything was complicated by the fact that, in the German production, Hölderlin's text was used, and so he looked at my translation through the lens of Hölderlin. Naturally, I was terrorized by a similar archetype.[53]

In this drama, Sanguineti's propensity for a foreignizing approach finds an even more rigid example in Hölderlin's version. For example, let us look at two verses spoken by Tiresias to Oedipus. In Greek, the verses are "ἆρ' οἶσθ' ἀφ' ὧν εἶ; καὶ λέληθας ἐχθρὸς ὢν / τοῖς σοῖσιν αὐτοῦ νέρθε κἀπὶ γῆς ἄνω"[54] (Do you know of whom you are? And hated, unbeknownst to you, / by those of yours under and above the ground?). The German runs, "Weißt du, woher du bist? du bist geheim / Verhaßt den Deinen, die hier unten sind, / Und oben auf der Erd"[55] (Do you know, whence you are? You are hidden / hated by yours, who are here under / And on top of the earth). In Sanguineti's Italian, they read, "Ma sai, tu, di chi sei, tu che non sai che sei orribile, / per i tuoi, per chi è giù, e per chi è sopra la terra, qui?"[56] (But do you know, you, whom you come from, you who do not know that you are horrible, / for yours, for who is under, and for who is above the earth, here). Here, Hölderlin has closely hewed to the Greek, adhering as closely as possible to the literal syntactical category: the German pronoun *den Deinen*, for example, translates the Greek pronoun, αὐτοῦ. Sanguineti's version follows Hölderlin, for example, in translating αὐτοῦ as the pronoun *i tuoi*, and in translating the general grammatical flow of the verse. Sanguineti keeps his translation in two verses, in contrast to Hölderlin's three verses, marking it with syntactical parallelism and anaphora ("per chi è") and strong alliteration and assonance (*sai/sei/sai/sei*). He sets off the harsh *ἐχθρὸς* with his *orribile*, which is the only polysyllabic word in these two lines, and thus it stands out in Italian (while in Hölderlin's version, the Greek term is highlighted by its corresponding German word at the end of the verse). These two translations are profoundly different from Salvatore Quasimodo's rendering: "Conosci la tua origine, / e come sei odioso ai tuoi morti e ai tuoi vivi?"[57] (Do you know your origin, / and how hateful you are to your dead [relatives] and your living [relatives]?). The discrepancies between Hölderlin/Sanguineti and Quasimodo are clear. Quasimodo's translation flows well and sounds completely natural to an Italian ear brought up on the standard Italian poetic tradition. Yet in return he doesn't follow the Greek syntax, rephrasing the initial question, while paraphrasing the final four Greek words. Indeed, Quasimodo's translation makes no mention of place (νέρθε κἀπὶ γῆς ἄνω), which is present in the original Greek.

Sanguineti's effort (as well as Hölderlin's), on the other hand, is a stuttering, haltering verse. Our poet-translator has broken the verse into several pieces, and with the repetition of *sei/sai* and the alliteration of (*per*) *chi* and *che*, and *tu/tuoi*, he creates a new style for his translation: what he called "oracolese" (oracularese). If, for Sanguineti, "that which in the phantom of the Greeks should arouse passion in us ... is a feeling, it seems to me, of insurmountable distance ... it is not a pardonable error to stir up a dominating feeling of nearness and familiarity,"[58] it is clear that his translation fits into this category. None of Sanguineti's various translations contains what is commonly indicated as a mark of a good translation, namely, smooth and fluid writing; neither does his own verse. His translations are always marked by their discontinuity and their interrupted discourse. This alerts the reader that he is reading a foreign text, one that doesn't naturally seem written by an Italian, which imitates the halting rhythms of speech and thought.

Quaderno di Traduzioni

Sanguineti's *Quaderno di traduzioni* didn't arise independently. Rather, as the poet wrote to the author of this book,

> Some years ago, I signed a contract with Einaudi for a "Trip to Italy," which I would have completed in places and epochs chosen by myself (and my wife); but since I was caught up in a thousand engagements, nothing came of it; Einaudi, to resolve the old problem, proposed to me that I gather together, according to the custom of the white Einaudi series of poetry, a *quaderno di traduzioni*, in great part already published.[59]

In his 2006 *Quaderno di traduzioni*, Sanguineti assembled versions from three authors and passages from four works: Lucretius (*De rerum natura* [On the nature of things]), Shakespeare (*Sonnets*), and Goethe (*Römische Elegien* [Roman elegies] and *Venezianische Epigramme* [Venetian epigrams]). None of these belongs to the Italian poet's favoured genre of translation: drama. And both Shakespeare's and Goethe's works are lyric poems, a genre which Sanguineti generally avoided translating. The *Quaderno* itself is ordered chronologically,[60] beginning with Lucretius, passing through Shakespeare, and ending in Goethe. As Sanguineti noted, "I put together what I had at my disposal (Lucretius, Shakespeare, Goethe: three epochs, three languages, three cultures)."[61] This *Quaderno* is not a final, definite image of Sanguineti at work. It is one of the many snapshots or anthologies that he scattered in his wake. In contrast with other *quaderni di traduzioni* – from Eugenio Montale's to Vittorio Sereni's – this *Quaderno* is not an assembling together of a career's work of translations. It is simply a work from Sanguineti's *officina* (workshop) of translations, one of the innumerable macrotexts that Sanguineti organized throughout his career.

Lucretius

Lucretius, the Latin father of materialist philosophy, is the most ideologically similar poet to Sanguineti. For both, religion is an illusion and a delusion. Yet the fact that Lucretius wrote in verse must not be forgotten, as he is (in Sanguineti's words) "poetically, an author ... of absolute greatness."[62] Although Sanguineti never finished translating the whole of *De Rerum Natura*, it was "a late utopia of mine ... an experiment in perpetual growth."[63] When this author met the Italian poet two weeks before his sudden death in 2010, Sanguineti repeated this desire, unaware that his wish would never be fulfilled.

Sanguineti arranged his translations of Lucretius into three thematic categories: *Natura* (Nature), *Amore* (Love), and *Morte* (Death). *Natura*, the largest section, begins with "questo terrore dell'animo e queste tenebre" (this terror of the mind and this darkness). Sanguineti ends his anthology of Lucretius's poem (in the section *Morte*) with verses describing the Athenian plague and the survivors preferring to fight to carry away their dead instead of leaving them behind: "combattendo / con molto sangue, piuttosto che abbandonarli, i loro cari cadaveri" (fighting / with much blood, rather than abandoning them, their dear corpses). We thus begin with *terrore* and we end with *terrore*. This is quite at variance with Lucretius's *De Rerum Natura*, which begins with the invocation of Venus – not with the anguish of humans unable to understand how nothing can come of nothing.

Stylistically, Sanguineti's rendition is full of assonance and alliteration: the *t* in "un solo giorno sven*t*ura*t*o *t*i ha *t*ol*t*o via i *t*uoi *t*an*t*i piaceri della vi*t*a" (one sole unfortunate day took away your numerous pleasures of life"), and the left and right shiftings in "quando lo colpisce, quello, un ragazzo che ha membra muliebri" (when it strikes him, the boy who has feminine limbs).[64] As for the ideological lens of historical materialism, we can see it in Sanguineti's handling of a particular Lucretian verse: "vitaque mancipio nulli datur, omnibus usu." A literal translation would be "and life is given to none to possess fully, but for all to use." Sanguineti, though, translates it somewhat differently: "e a nessuno è data in proprietà privata, la vita, ma è un valore d'uso, per tutti" (and to no one is it – life – given as private property, but it is a use-value, for all). The key distinctions are the translations of the words *mancipio, omnibus,* and *usu. Mancipio*'s principle meaning here is of full possession, but Sanguineti alters it to emphasize the Marxist tenet of rejecting private property. In addition, he renders the Latin *usu* as the anachronistically Marxian concept of "use-value." Likewise, by situating "per tutti" (*omnibus* [for everyone]) at the end of the sentence, he underlines that life should be used *on behalf of* everyone, not merely individually. Inspired first of all by Karl Marx, but also by his own love for artistic collaboration, Sanguineti thus makes the Italian version signify that people should not live as isolated monads in capitalistic societies, but they should actively seek out others with whom to live and work for a common and better future.[65]

Shakespeare

After Lucretius comes Shakespeare, whose *Macbeth,*[66] *King Lear,*[67] and *Measure for Measure*[68] Sanguineti elsewhere either explicitly adapted (the first in *Macbeth Remix*) or translated (the latter two in *La tragedia di Re Lear* and *Misura per misura*). In 1998, Sanguineti, together with the musician Andrea Liberovici, published *il mio amore è come una febbre e mi rovescio* (my love is like a fever and i fall over), which includes a *travestimento* called *Sonnet*. This piece is based on works by both Shakespeare (Sonnets 2, 20, 23, 43, 91, 129, 144, and 147) and the Italian poet (*Animali elementari 1–4* [Elementary animals 1–4], *Glosse: 15* [Glosses: 15], *Canzonetta pietrosa* [Stony pop-song], and *Catasonetto* [Downsonnet]). Generally, the sonnets by Shakespeare are spliced together and not recited whole, giving rise to passages like the following that combine Shakespeare's Sonnets 20 and 23 and Sanguineti's poem "Animali elementari 2":

Voce 2: mi sento mancare
sopraffatto
Coro: amore, amore, amore,
Voce 2: dal peso della potenza stessa del mio stesso amore:

Coro: master, master
Voce 1: quando vedo il tuo fuoco, tutto sciolto
sotto gli aculei del tuo sterno, e colo
tra le tue tibie, dentro
Coro: master, mistress[69]

[**Voice 2**: i feel myself fainting
overwhelmed
Chorus: love, love, love
Voice 2: by the weight of the very potency of my own love:
Chorus: master, master
Voice 1: when i see your fire, all melted
under the spines of your sternum, and i drip
between your tibias, inside
Chorus: master, mistress]

In cases like this, the "text is a montage of texts," as our Italian poet-translator has said. Here, Sanguineti stylistically reinterprets Shakespeare's Sonnet 23 "As an unperfect actor on the stage," in a key of feverish sexuality ("amore è una febbre"), through the juxtaposition of his own poems.

Turning now to Sanguineti's *Quaderno di traduzioni*, the sonnets by Shakespeare included therein were first published independently in Sanguineti's 2004 *Omaggio a Shakespeare* (Homage to Shakespeare). The translated sonnets provide an exercise in rhetorical virtuosity, as critics have remarked. The Italian poet's extraordinary version of Sonnet 43, for instance, will remain a testament to his poetic valour. Sanguineti's abiding faithfulness to the meaning of each word separates this translation from his *travestimenti* (such as *Faust*). Here is a passage from this translation, followed by a gloss, and then Shakespeare's original text:

come sarebbero, io dico, beatificati i miei occhi,
guardando in te, nel giorno vivente,
quando, nella morta notte, la tua bella ombra imperfetta,
attraverso il sonno profondo, ai miei ciechi occhi appare![70]

[how would, I say, my eyes be blessed,
looking at you, in the living day,
when, in the dead night, your beautiful imperfect shade,
through deep sleep, to my blind eyes appears!]

How would, I say, mine eyes be blessed made,
By looking on thee in the living day,
When in dead night thy fair imperfect shade
Through heavy sleep on sightless eyes doth stay![71]

Even more than in his translation of Lucretius the translation imitates, as much as possible, the tone and register of the original. The selection of sonnets displays Sanguineti's desire to deal with both the intense rhetorical texture of the English text, as in Sonnet 43, and his interest in the florid descriptions of lust, as in Sonnet 129 with its famous opening "th'expense of spirit in a waste of shame,"[72] masterfully rendered as "spreco di spirito in uno squallore di vergogna" (a waste of spirit in a squalor of shame).[73]

We have seen Sanguineti's firm belief in the impossibility of translation. Yet Fausto Curi, one of his best readers, rightly suggests that "the version of the *Sonnets* implicitly puts into question Sanguineti's doctrine of translation, since who we have in front of us is certainly not a 'betrayer.'"[74] Indeed, the reason that Sanguineti's version is less evidently a *travestimento* than his other translations is owing to Shakespeare's complicated rhetorical and syntactical structure. To a degree, the poetic grammar of the Elizabethan English is already "foreignized" from the point of view of modern-day speech. Therefore our poet-translator only adds some punctuation to further slow down the verse and break it up into fragments. In general, however, his interlinear approach is clearly evident. On the whole, the English word order is maintained in Sanguineti's translations and to great effect.

Goethe

While Shakespeare's style was the special attraction for Sanguineti, it was the final author of the *Quaderno*, Goethe, who had a long and profound influence on Sanguineti's own ideas of poetry and modernity. As Pieter de Meijer has shown,[75] Sanguineti's books, often with German titles (*Wirrwarr* [Chaos], *Reisebilder* [Travel pictures], *Postkarten* [Postcards], and *Traumdeutung* [Interpretation of dreams]), are studded with quotations from many different works of Goethe that "often lead to the center of the poet's subject." In particular, *Faust* is truly "an obsession"[76] for Sanguineti. As the Italian poet writes, the myth of *Faust* is the myth of modern man that "every modern author has dreamed of retelling." It is all the more appropriate, then, with this "myth *par excellence* of modernity" that Sanguineti for the first time, as we have seen, explicitly applies the word "travestimento" to his translations. What is particularly striking is Sanguineti's own explanation of his personal relationship with this text: "probably, in dealing with this legendary and fundamental figure, it is the text in which my personal projection was the strongest; that is, while in other texts no one corresponds to myself."[77] In his translation, as the critic Niva Lorenzini writes, Sanguineti attempts to create "the last *Faust* possible."[78] As part and parcel of the *travestimento,* the Italian poet-translator selects and elides passages from the original German. For example, Fausto Curi describes the dramatic changes in the Italian version, which eliminate the whole second part of *Faust,* including the triumphal conclusion that assures immortality for the protagonist.[79] Sanguineti, as a historical materialist, gives us a work shorn of any religious optimism.[80] Altering and abbreviating the original text, he makes the work fundamentally nihilistic and pessimistic. While Sanguineti carves a new ideological breach in the play, he also plays with the various styles therein, using, as he explains,

> an impudent mixture of styles ... from one moment to another, and all together, the screenplay and epic theater, pathetic comedy and curtain-raiser, tragedy and operetta, melodrama and farce.[81]

Let us look closely at the verbal texture in Sanguineti's *Faust.* What immediately strikes the eye is his incorrigible, idiosyncratic syntax that is full of pleonasms like personal (and reflexive) pronouns and particles (like *ci*). We can see, for example, Sanguineti's colloquial grammar in translating the German "Mich dünkt, die Alte spricht im Fieber" (It seems to me that the old woman speaks in a fever)[82] to "Ci ha una febbre che ci delira, quella, per me"[83] (She has a fever that makes her delirious, that one, for me). In the Italian translation there is the low-register *ci ha*, a right-shifting (*quella*), and the colloquial syntax *che ci*. It is much less straightforward and smooth than the German.

This alienating syntax reproduces both colloquial Italian grammar heard in the streets and expressions in *stare* (to be), reflecting the speech of southern Italy, appropriate for this version of *Faust* originally commissioned by the Neapolitan theatre group, Alfred Jarry. As for the diction, there are many foreign words (e.g., "telenovelas" [soap operas]), slang words ("rockettaro" [rock singer]), obscene words and expressions ("Ha da fottersela il Dracula, il senza màcula, quella / il Dràcula, che se la incula ... " [Dracula must fuck her, / Dracula the spotless, that one / Dracula screws for himself]),[84] and a plethora of anachronistic objects and terminology that refer to the post-Goethean world (from

"Barbie" to "paninoteche" [sandwich shops]). On the one hand, then, we have Sanguineti shifting Goethe's lexicon to the utter depths of language, to the lowest of the low (obscenities), and to its origins (babble and onomatopoeia). On the other hand, Sanguineti transforms the ideological environment to the late twentieth century and deliberately skews the cultural and political frame of reference (using words such as "democristianamente" [like the Christian Democrats]).

Turning to the Italian poet's versions of Goethean elegies and epigrams in his *Quaderno di traduzioni*, his mode of translation is different. Here there is no longer parody, cultural adaptation, or extensive colloquial elements. For example, let us look at a Venetian epigram from the *Quaderno*, first in the original German (with an English translation in brackets), and then in the Italian translation (with a gloss afterwards):

> Zürnet nicht ihr Frauen daß wir das Mädchen bewundern:
> Ihr genießet des Nachts was sie am Abend erregt.[85]
>
> [Do not be angry, women, that we admire the girl:
> You enjoy at night what she arouses in the evening.]
>
> Non arrabbiatevi, donne, che ci ammiriamo, noi, la ragazzina:
> Vi degustate, di notte, quello che lei ci stimola, di sera:[86]
>
> [Do not be angry, women, that we admire, we do, the girl:
> You taste, at night, what she stimulates in us, in the evening:]

We immediately note a few things besides the general faithfulness of Sanguineti's translation (excepting the addition of *ci* in the second verse). First of all, there are no commas in the German text, but there are seven commas in the Italian version. This is important because commas indicate how the poem should be read and recited, almost word for word. They break the Italian discourse into nine separate parts through verbs and phrases ("non arrabbiatevi" / "che ci ammiriamo" / "vi degustate" / "quello che lei ci stimola"), nouns and addressees ("donne" / "noi" / "la ragazzina"), and temporal adverbs ("di notte" / "di sera"). The unfolding of the discourse has the effect of emphasizing the words that flow from the poet's (translator's) pen. It is no longer a crisp two-verse epigram as in the German, but in Italian it has become rhetorically complicated and syncopated. The famous colons that end Sanguineti's verse also contribute a retarding effect and a lack of closure: the last translation of the *Quaderno,* in fact, ends with a colon, instead of with a period. One could say, indeed, that this punctuation also reflects Sanguineti's own theory of translation, namely, that a classic never is definitively translated, but it is always retranslated for each generation.

In these Venetian epigrams chosen by Sanguineti, one word especially recurs no less than five times: "saltimbanco" (acrobat). This semantic field of acrobatics alludes to Goethe's lithe lover, Bettina. For Sanguineti, a keen reader of the Italian poet Aldo Palazzeschi and his idea of the *saltimbanco,* the repetition of this key term is notable. Poets and *saltimbanchi* (acrobats) are close relatives for Goethe, for Palazzeschi, and for our poet, Sanguineti. As Sanguineti said in an interview with Antonio Gnoli, in Goethe's epigrams

> for the first time the figure of the acrobat emerges ... So Goethe invents this figure and makes it into a privileged erotic object. The imagination with which he describes certain gymnastic evolutions is extraordinary. After the Greeks nothing similar had been written. And I find it very stunning that he relates the acrobat's work to the poet's. Goethe is indeed the first of the moderns to intuit this.[87]

Indeed, the theme of the (erotic) *saltimbanco* fundamentally relates to the major theme that runs through the entire *Quaderno,* namely Eros, which is visible from different perspectives. For Lucretius, love is an unquenchable desire (to be avoided), since lovers, in Sanguineti's translation, cannot "con tutto il corpo, in quel corpo penetrare, né perdersi"[88] (with all one's body, penetrate in that body, nor lose oneself). For Shakespeare, too, love is often excoriated, as in the famous Sonnet 129, in which it is described as

> A bliss in proof, and proved a very woe
> ....
> All this the world well knows, yet none knows well
> To shun the heaven that leads men to this hell.[89]

Yet with Goethe everything changes. The first Roman elegy (in Sanguineti's version) says it eloquently: "Un mondo davvero sei tu, o Roma: senza l'amore, però, / Il mondo non sarebbe il mondo, e nemmeno Roma sarebbe più Roma" (A world truly you are, o Rome: without love, however, / the world wouldn't be world, and not even Rome would any longer be Rome).[90] In another elegy, Goethe tells how famous kings would gladly give him half of their glory, if only he would permit them to share his beloved's bed for one night. And it is Goethe who, from a quantitative point of view (endorsed by Sanguineti),[91] dominates the *Quaderno di traduzioni*, occupying more than half of it, while Shakespeare and Lucretius share the rest. The *Viaggio in Italia* (Travel to Italy) originally intended by Sanguineti, has turned into something quite different, yet Goethe's travels nevertheless strongly define the *Quaderno*, culminating in the figure of Bettina. She dominates Goethe's *Venetian Epigrams* and the *Quaderno* as a whole, and she is Sanguineti's main object of fascination. She incarnates the character of the *saltimbanco*, whose agility in games of life is inimitable and rivals the poet's own agility in using language. The key adjective that describes her is indeed "agile," and she rocks up and down, exposing herself to Jove and the underworld with equal facility. She is both the poetic muse and the erotic muse. This erotic theme doesn't just occur in these translations or the *Quaderno*, though. Eros is a dominating feature in all of Sanguineti's texts: as he noted, "thematically, the theme of desire runs through all my work, texts or imitations."[92]

Translation Techniques

Sanguineti, as we have seen, uses an interlinear approach to translation, reproducing rhetorical and syntactical structures as much as possible. He calques grammatical and lexical traits of the original, and he frequently lowers the register of the text by introducing colloquial syntax and diction. A number of other characteristics predominate, which are present in Sanguineti's own poetry as well: a lack of rhyme and a lack of traditional metre (with the exceptions noted below) that are substituted by copious assonance and alliteration that often verge on cacophony; solecisms; superfluous use of pronouns, conjunctions, and adverbs; and obsessive punctuation.[93] Foreignisms are included in freer versions or adaptations like his *Faust*. In brief, Sanguineti's interlinear method is always shaped by his own poetics.

In two translations, Sanguineti replicated the original metre: Corneille's *L'Illusion comique* (and here the rhyming scheme as well) and Euripides's *Hippolytus*. Yet these constraints do not alter the foreignizing method of Sanguineti. The pronounced syntactical shiftings and syncopation are evident in both works. Indeed, it is necessary for us to take a moment to discuss this latter work of Euripides, which was Sanguineti's final staged translation. As he said in a 2010 lecture, there are two "diabolic" (*diabolici*) elements[94] in his translation of *Hippolytus*, namely, the usage, as much as possible, of the same Italian word for the same Greek word in the same position of the verse, along with the "calqued model" of the original metrics. What he aimed for was "a translation (based) on calquing" (*la traduzione a calco*): "the final landing place (*approdo*) where I have arrived."[95] And yet this final landing place is not unlike his previous moorings or translation methods. He writes about translating specifically from Greek, although any foreign language can fill this role: "translating means importing a foreign language into one's language, and not adapting Greek to our language. One must Hellenize Italian, not Italianize Greek."[96] He remained generally faithful to this approach throughout his entire career as translator, from both classical and modern languages.

Sanguineti versus Giudici

Let us see how these two different poets, who both shared such similar translation philosophies, translated Shakespeare's Sonnet 23.

Table 5.1 shows the two Italian translations next to Shakespeare's original with back translations in brackets.

To begin with, both poet-translators are concerned with faithfulness to the text: both respect the number of verses. Yet they differ with regards to rhyme and metre. Giudici translates Sonnet 23 in hendecasyllables, while Sanguineti translates it into free verse. While not preserving the original rhyme scheme, Giudici nonetheless translates the last rhyming couplet as a rhyming couplet in Italian, in contrast to Sanguineti (who does, however, use slightly more end-rhymes). Thus, Giudici attempts a more functionally equivalent translation. In addition, Giudici's version is much more rapid than Sanguineti's. This can be seen in two specific ways. Giudici uses fewer words (93 to Sanguineti's 120) and less punctuation (2 commas to Sanguineti's 22 commas). Moreover, he achieves his velocity by abbreviating or eliminating English expressions or words: "fear of trust" becomes "timidezza" (timidity), phrases like "learn to," "look for," "that more," and words like "strength," "burden," and "might" are removed, as are connectors and pronouns like "so," "and," and "who." Sanguineti, meanwhile, leaves nothing untranslated, although a few times the change in emphasis or syntax is notable: "heart" instead of the English "books" is the subject of verse 12 in Sanguineti's text, "fear of trust" becomes "per timore e sconforto," and "the perfect ceremony of love's right" becomes "il perfetto rituale della cerimonia d'amore."

Table 5.1 "Sonnet 23"

William Shakespeare "Sonnet 23"	Giovanni Giudici "Sonetto 23"	Edoardo Sanguineti "sonetto 23"
As an unperfect actor on the stage,	Come un mediocre attore sulla scena [Like a mediocre actor on the stage]	come un attore inesperto, sulla scena, [like an inexpert actor, on the stage,]
Who with his fear is put besides his part;	Che per panico esca fuori parte [Who from panic steps out of his role]	che, con il suo timore, dimentica la sua parte, [who, with his fear, forgets his role,]
Or some fierce thing, replete with too much rage,	O un esaltato gonfio di furore [Or from an exaltated swelling of fury]	o come un essere feroce, pieno di una rabbia eccessiva, [or like a ferocious being, full of an excessive anger,]
Whose strength's abundance weakens his own heart;	Cui troppa foga renda il cuore fiacco [Whose excessive impetus renders the heart weak]	che, per l'abbondare dell'impeto, indebolisce il suo cuore, [which, due to the abundance of the impetus, weakens his heart,]
So I, for fear of trust, forget to say	Per timidezza io non so recitare [Due to timidity I am unable to recite]	così io, per timore e sconforto, dimentico di pronunciare [so I, from fear and discomfort, forget to pronounce]
The perfect ceremony of love's rite,	La ceremonia d'amoroso rito [The ceremony of loving rite]	il perfetto rituale della cerimonia dell'amore, [the perfect ritual of the ceremony of love,]
And in mine own love's strength seem to decay,	Onde l'amore mio sembra scemare [By means of which my love seems to fade]	e nell'impeto stesso del mio amore mi sento mancare, [and in the very impetus of my love I feel myself die,]
O'ercharged with burden of mine own love's might.	Per troppa forza del mio stesso amore. [By excessive force of my own love.]	sopraffatto dal peso della potenza stessa del mio stesso amore: [overcome by the weight of the very potency of my very love:]

Table 5.1 "Sonnet 23" (*Continued*)

William Shakespeare "Sonnet 23"	**Giovanni Giudici "Sonetto 23"**	**Edoardo Sanguineti "sonetto 23"**
O let my books be then the eloquence	Oh sian dunque i miei libri mia eloquenza, [Oh may my books therefore be my eloquence,]	oh, possano essere l'eloquenza, i miei scritti, [oh, may eloquence, my writings, be]
And dumb presagers of my speaking breast,	Muti profeti del parlante petto, [Mute prophets of a speaking breast,]	muti profeti del mio cuore che parla, [mute prophets of my heart that speaks,]
Who plead for love and look for recompense,	Chiedono amore e giusta ricompensa [They ask for love and just recompense]	che invoca amore e chiede ricompensa [which invokes love and asks for recompense]
More than that tongue that more hath more expressed:	Più di quanto la lingua mai abbia espresso. [More than however much my tongue has expressed.]	più di questa lingua, che più si è più espressa: [more than this language, which exists the more it is expressed:]
O learn to read what silent love hath writ!	Oh leggi quel che ha scritto il muto cuore: [Oh read what (my) mute heart has written:]	oh, impara a leggere quanto ha scritto il silenzioso amore: [oh, learn to read what silent love has written:]
To hear with eyes belongs to love's fine wit.	Udir con gli occhi è il genio dell'amore. [To hear with eyes is the genius of love.]	conviene, al sottile spirito dell'amore, ascoltare con gli occhi: [it becomes the subtle spirit of love to hear with eyes:]
Source: Shakespeare, *Sonnets*, ed. Katherine Duncan-Jones, in *Complete Works*, 21	Source: Giudici, *Vaga lingua strana*, 13	Source: Sanguineti, *Quaderno di traduzioni*, 33

In conclusion, Giudici's version is more polished and crisp, and it is in a higher register. Yet it does not exactly produce the effect of reading *Shakespeare's* sonnet, by dint of its omissions and abbreviations. What it does create is a highly charged autonomous poetic text, with its assonance and alliteration. Nevertheless, the "foreignness" that is frequently in Giudici's translations is little present here. His translation is, in fact, an anomaly in this respect. Here, Giudici has chosen the poetic metre as a dominant constructive principle, in Yury Tynjanov's words, specifically the hendecasyllable, as prestigious and traditional in Italian as the iambic pentameter in English. This poetic metre is natural for an Italian reader and doesn't create a sense of foreignness or alienation.

On the other hand, Sanguineti's version is clearly a translation; it doesn't aim to be a poetic recreation through massive additions or omissions to the text, and it doesn't fall into any specific poetic metre. The semantic content is faithfully reproduced and there is even more assonance and alliteration and end-rhyming than there is in Giudici's version. If we hadn't known that Sanguineti considers poetic translation impossible, we wouldn't be able to guess it. As we remarked above, this uncommon faithfulness to the original syntax and diction is owed to the fact that the original English text is already so highly "foreignized" with its turns of phrase and artful rhetorical style. Therefore, neither poet translates here in a truly "foreignizing" manner: each poet betrays his normal translation method.

Conclusion

Besides being a poet, Sanguineti was also a linguist of sorts, and he edited the *Supplemento* (Supplement) to the most prestigious Italian dictionary, *Grande dizionario della lingua italiana* (Comprehensive dictionary of the Italian language). As he wrote in his 2004 preface,

> An imposing mass of words, in every language, are imposed through translation ... and not only linguistically. Language speaks, as it should, to the enormous existential and practical conquest, both ideological and cultural ... Let us exaggerate a little, and say that, in the beginning, there is always an act of translation.[97]

This passage perfectly illustrates that for Sanguineti translation is at the root of all literature,[98] as we saw before: "Tradurre è fare scrittura."[99] And while every language has its own portion of "translationese," Sanguineti's translations explore the other side of this: the freedom to create an idiolect into which to translate. After all, every Italian translator is faced with the perennial problem of which language to translate into: from higher to lower registers, northern, central, or southern dialects, slang or pre-language babbling. Sanguineti's epigraph, which I quoted at the beginning of the chapter, "It is I who translate: it is I who am speaking," is pertinent here. This citation, which prominently ends the poet-translator's introduction to his collection of theatrical translations, could helpfully be read in the context of the Saussurian difference between *langue* and *parole*. Saussure famously wrote,

> La langue n'est pas une fonction du sujet parlant, elle est le produit que l'individu enregistre passivement ... La parole est au contraire un acte individuel de volonté e d'intelligence.[100]

> [Language is not a function of the speaking subject, it is the product which the individual registers passively ... The word is, on the contrary, an individual act of will and intelligence.]

In effect, what Sanguineti affirms in all his writing is that writers stand out by their usage of *parole*, their individualized and iconoclastic speech. Nowhere, perhaps, is this clearer than in this Italian poet's translations, which theoretically ("there is really no other speaker than the translator") and practically (in terms of the traits we have already discussed) are defined by his idiolect. Rather than translating into a general standardized *langue*, Sanguineti turns the words of others into his own stylized, syncopated, and fragmented speech. It is Sanguineti who speaks through the masks of dead playwrights, poets, and novelists.

We have seen, in the course of this chapter, that Sanguineti intends to estrange the reader and audience through his translations, or *travestimenti*. He is helped along by his own idiosyncratic writing style, yet not all of his translations follow the same route or pattern. Indeed, he insists that his translations not be lumped together or considered identically fashioned: "all have in common the fact of being different from a certain mode of translating, but this doesn't make them all the same." In other words, the fact that Sanguineti rejects a domesticating, reader-centred approach does not mean that his translations are identically conceived. So, for instance, he translates Greek tragedies into a higher register than other genres: while abundant calquing takes place, there is nonetheless an absence of egregious colloquialisms and foreign words. Yet his translation of Corneille's *L'Illusion comique* has specific constraints like the imitative metrical and rhyme schemes. If, for example, his versions of Catullus' poems are more colloquial than most of his other translations, his *Faust* is in even a lower stylistic register that is filled with obscenities and slang of all sorts. Nonetheless, the glue binding them together is the overall interlinear approach that is filtered through Sanguineti's own poetics.

In closing, Sanguineti stands out in the panorama of twentieth- and twenty-first-century Italian poet-translators for two reasons: first, the number of theatrical translations (although neither generally recognized nor appreciated, he has innovatively adapted much of classical drama for the Italian stage); and second, his innovative translation methods. His replication of syntactical structures of the original text and his own idiolect combine in a unique foreignizing translation approach. When the history of modern Italian poet-translators is written, Sanguineti will occupy a most prominent and well-deserved position.

6 Franco Buffoni: Translation, Translation Theory, and the "Poietic Encounter"

Franco Buffoni was born in Lombardy, northern Italy, in the city of Gallarate, in 1948. During his thirty-five-year teaching career, he taught English literature, literary criticism, and comparative literature at the universities of Bergamo, Cassino, Milan (IULM), Parma, Trieste, and Turin. As a poet he has thirteen volumes to his name;[1] as a fiction writer, three volumes of narrative;[2] and as a scholar, eight volumes of literary criticism.[3] Moreover, Buffoni edited the important volumes on translation: *La traduzione del testo poetico* (The translation of the poetic text, 1989);[4] *Ritmologia: atti del convegno Il ritmo del linguaggio: poesia e traduzione* (Rhythmology: Papers from the conference "The rhythm of language: poetry and translation," 2004);[5] *Traduttologia: la teoria della traduzione letteraria* (Translation theory: The theory of literary translation, 2005);[6] *Testo a fronte* (Parallel text), the most important journal dealing with translation in Italian (and certainly one of the most important in all of Europe); six anthologies of Italian poetry in translation (in Arabic,[7] Chinese,[8] Hebrew,[9] Portuguese,[10] Russian,[11] and Spanish[12]); and eleven anthologies of Italian poetry, where he has diligently brought forth and nourished a younger generation of Italian poets.

Buffoni is, along with Franco Fortini, the most important poet-theorist of translation in modern Italy. We spoke of Fortini earlier and his theory of compensation. While Fortini was somewhat on the edges of the academic world (he became a university professor of Italian very late in his career), Buffoni is a full-fledged academic with a doctorate in American literature and numerous professorships. While Fortini opened up translation studies for Italian poets, Buffoni revolutionized the field of Italian translation studies by broadening its theoretical framework. From Anceschi, Buffoni's "ideal mentor," the Italian poet internalized the primacy of the *poietic* encounter, while incorporating other concepts in his theory of translation – from Julia Kristeva's intertextuality and Friedmar Apel's notion of the movement of language in time to Henri Meschonnic's idea of rhythm and Jean Bellemin-Noël's avant-text. Buffoni's paradigm of translation is both a framework for interpreting translation and a method for translating poetry. He is clearly at variance with the other four poet-translators in this study for whom translation is, at core, an impossibility. Buffoni sets out to overturn this conception by framing the issue of translation not as reproduction of content (or "equivalence") but as a meeting of different *poetics*. Translation is thus always possible. Naturally, Buffoni's own translations do not always equally privilege all five aspects: namely, the poietic encounter, intertextuality, movement of language in time, rhythm, and avant-text. If the *poietic* encounter is, at heart, the standpoint from which Buffoni analyses others' translations, it is also the standard by which his own versions ask to be interpreted. Thus, in this chapter, while I will draw on the other four notions mentioned above, which at times provide crucial interpretative guidance, I will rely on the *poietic* encounter between the translator and the original text.

Poetic Career

Critics have divided his work into three main periods.[13] The first stage includes his first three books. In this phase, as noted by Franco Brevini,[14] what ties Buffoni's work together is his ironic "vocazione da fantaisiste"[15] (clown-like vocation) that was inspired by Aldo Palazzeschi and Jules Laforgue. This stage is characterized, in the main, by "lightness." Here, for instance, is the opening of the poem "Italiano" (Italian) from *I tre desideri* (The three desires), where Eliot's famous "this is the way the world ends / not with a bang but a whimper" turns even more sarcastic, even playful:

Il mondo non finirà con un gran botto,
Ma con un piagnisteo, un uggiolio,
Un piagnucolio[16]

[The world will not end with a great bang,
But with a moaning, a whining,
A whimpering]

In Buffoni's subsequent 1987 volume, *Quaranta a quindici* (40–15), he adapts Pound's "Lake isle" (itself a parody of Yeats's "Lake Isle at Innisfree"):

Oh Mercurio dio della truffa
Dammi un tavolo e un'antologia,
E venti ragazzi davanti.[17]

[O Mercury god of thievery
Give me a table and an anthology
And twenty boys in front of me.]

The following passage from Buffoni's successive book, *Scuola di Atene* (School of Athens, 1991), illustrates the lightness spoken of by critics. It is a charming piece that recalls, for instance, Sandro Penna's poetry, and it is musically graceful with its assonance, alliteration, and rhyme:

Ma lo vedevano gli altri al mattino
Bruno perfetto come Apollo
Provare la chiave del casello
E lento posare la catena?
Aveva mai pensato il Bruno
D'essere dio almeno per uno?[18]

[But did the others see him in the morning
Bruno perfect like Apollo
Try the key of the tollbooth
And slowly put down the chain?
Did he ever think, Bruno,
Of being god at least for one?]

A change comes after his provisional self-anthology *Adidas: poesie scelte 1975–1990* (Adidas: Selected poems, 1975–1990, 1993). He starts to structure his individual lyrics together in micro- and macro-narratives (whether in an individual book of poetry or in a trilogy), which are no longer in an ironic and *fantaisiste* vein. Rather, the tone is more objective, more focussed. For example, in his *Suora carmelitana e altri racconti in versi* (Carmelite nun and other tales in verse, 1997), the first volume of a trilogy, he explores a startling new theme within a different genre – a tale in verse – as shown here from the beginning of the eponymous poem:

Il convento di Via Marcantonio Colonna
È del trenta. E mia zia
Che aveva lavorato nella ditta
E quando è entrata la guerra era finita

È lì dal quarantasei.
Da allora è uscita tre volte per votare
(Divorzio, aborto e quarantotto)
E due per andare in ospedale.
Per votare ci vuole la dispensa
E anche per l'ospedale.

[The convent on Via Marcantonio Colonna
Is from (19)30. And my aunt
Who had worked in the company
And when she entered the war was over
Has been there from (19)46.
Since then she has left three times to vote
(Divorce, abortion and [19]48)
And twice to go to the hospital.
To vote one needs a dispensation
And also for the hospital.]

One word in this poem would have been inconceivable in Buffoni's earlier work, and it shows how his style is no longer tied to high literary models: namely, the English term that is left untranslated by the poet: *fist fucking*. The utilization of such a term in a poem about a protagonist-nun demonstrates how far Buffoni has gone towards a forthright public repudiation of the Church, which will become more and more pronounced as time goes on.[19]

After this book is the autobiographical volume, *Il profilo del Rosa* (The profile of [Mount] Rosa, 2000) that is defined by the poet himself as a "long trip through the four decades of my life, from childhood to full maturity, but also through the places where it principally occurred." Returning to his childhood home, Buffoni finds that

Una radice ha rotto il vaso
Nell'atrio della casa riaperta
La pianta è sempre stata bagnata
Dal vetro rotto dal vento.[20]

[A root has broken the vase
In the atrium of the re-opened house
The plant has always been bathed
By the glass broken by the wind.]

The last volume of the self-described trilogy, *Theios* (Uncle, 2001), is another type of *bildungsroman* in verse, this time of Buffoni's young nephew, Stefano, to whom the volume is dedicated: "A Stefano a quei suoi / Dentini appena incominciati" (To Stefano, to his recently emerging baby teeth). The book ends with a Shakespearean invocation to fecundity from the pen of a poet whose own sexual identity prevents such a succession: "Procrea, procrea / Ragazzo mio, che la tua bellezza non si perda" (Procreate, procreate / My boy, so that your beauty is not lost).[21]

After the parenthesis of the curious volume *Del maestro in bottega* (About the maestro in his workshop, 2002), an interesting collection of original poems and translations (a genre belonging to what Rodolfo Zucco calls a *satura*),[22] Buffoni published *Guerra* (War, 2005). This poetic volume, focussed on his father's experience in the Second World War as a prisoner of war in Germany, marks a striking shift in Buffoni's work, according to the critic Andrea Cortellessa: from "'pure' poet, a light and wandering thing – to engaged intellectual, demonstrating and intransigent."[23] The following verses show an undeniable break with his past verse, including the poetry from his previous trilogy:

"Sono ostriche, comandante?"
Chiese guardando il cesto accanto al tavolo
Il giovane tenente.
"Venti chili di occhi di serbi,
Omaggio dei miei uomini," rispose sorridendo
Il colonnello. Li teneva in ufficio
Accanto al tavolo. Strappati dai croati ai prigionieri.[24]

["Are they oysters, commander?"
Asked the young lieutenant,
Looking at the basket next to the table.
"20 kilos of Serbian eyes,
homage from my men," responded, smiling,
the colonel. He kept them in his office
next to the table. Torn from the prisoners by Croatians.]

This political perspective will be furthered in the poet's following book, *Noi e loro* (We and they, 2008), concentrating on the double exile from normal society of homosexuals and immigrants. Some of the most piercing verses deal with Mehmet, the poet's lover:

Ho gli occhi di dolore e sono turco
...
In prigione mi hanno torturato
Con gli elettrodi
Ho i segni sotto il mento e sui ginocchi
Anche i piedi mi hanno massacrato.[25]

[I have eyes of sorrow and I am Turkish
...
In prison they tortured me
With electrodes
I have scars under my chin and on my knees
They massacred my feet too.]

In Buffoni's most recent volume, *Roma* (Rome, 2009), he turns his gaze to Italy's capital. As a poet who grew up and matured in Lombardy, with its well-known Enlightenment traditions that influenced him in his progressive politics, he approaches Rome with foreign eyes. Here is a capsule poem that neatly shows a linkage between ancient and modern (Fascist) Rome:

Negli Horti Caesaris il dittatore ospitò Cleopatra,
A Villa Torlonia Mussolini, Hitler.
Quattro intestini ancora impauriti
Per le dimensioni dell'Oceano Esterno
Da placare con sacrifici.[26]

[In Caesar's gardens, the dictator welcomed Cleopatra,
At Villa Torlonia, Mussolini did the same for Hitler.
Four intestines, still frightened,
at the dimensions of the External Ocean
to be soothed with sacrifices.]

If we recall what Buffoni wrote in 1993 about the role of verse, a shift towards the political is not truly foreign to his poetics: "Poetry [is] never tired of repeating, particular to the youngest, those two or three essentials concerning ethics and aesthetics that one no longer has the force or the courage to repeat in a loud voice."[27]

Through the course of his career, as Buffoni remarked, his poetry can be categorized in the following four groups: texts that have a "long stratification," "gifts of the gods," "associative," and "stories in verse."

It is only when he realizes how to juxtapose these "poetic fragments" that he can create a book: they become "the tesserae of a mosaic."[28] Only once they all come together (and here Buffoni quotes Pier Paolo Pasolini's phrase about the difference between an unedited film and the finished film) does a "story (*storia*) become moral."[29] The function of the macrotext, the book, the canzoniere, and the *quaderno di traduzioni* has more and more assumed importance in Buffoni's outlook. Yet if he arranges his original poems only after he has written them, to compose a retrospective whole, he translates a poem thinking about how it will fit in a future *quaderno di traduzioni*. In contrast to his original verse, his translations are born with a specific plan and intention.

Translation Career

Franco Buffoni began his career in the 1970s in a rather unlikely manner: by translating poems by the American minimalist writer Donald Barthelme that were included in the American writer's novel *Snow White*,[30] and also by translating a volume on Henry Kissinger[31] (and ghost-translating other political texts). Little here would hint at the massive works that he would translate down the road. True, Buffoni also edited two works of eighteenth-century Scottish poets (Robert Fergusson and Allan Ramsay) during the same period, but it was only in 1981 that our poet-translator translated a book of poems (by Keats) with the (new) title *Sonno e poesia* (Sleep and poetry). In fact, it was in the 1980s that Buffoni acquired the bulk of his experience, translating Keats (1981),[32] Byron (1984),[33] Coleridge (1987),[34] Kipling (1989),[35] and the canonical and beautifully translated two-volume *Poeti romantici inglesi* (English romantic poets, 1990)[36] that summed up a decade's work. In the following years, he would turn his hand to translating works from the twentieth century, such as Seamus Heaney's poetry (1991),[37] many of which were included or excerpted in in Buffoni's 1999 *Songs of Spring*.[38] In 2012, thirteen years later, his next book of translations appeared: *Una piccola tabaccheria* (A small tobacco shop). In the same year he published more translations of Shelley (*Come un fruscio d'ali: Percy B. Shelley*)[39] and Byron (*I giullari del tempo: George Gordon Byron*).[40] While he translated often by commission during the 1980s, his translations from Heaney onwards were all by choice. No longer forced to translate, Buffoni has spent the last twenty years translating lyric poetry that is most congenial to his poetic temperament, which would fit together in a structured whole (i.e., a *quaderno di traduzioni* or a more general anthology).

The role of translation in Buffoni's career is not secondary to his own creative work, rather, it is totally (*totalmente*) connected to it. Reflecting on translation allowed him to join the two "branches of [my] work," namely, his work as a literary scholar and poet. Buffoni goes so far as to state that it was precisely "the theory of translation which allowed me to construct a personal theory of literature."[41] Therefore, let us now move on to his specific translation ideology.

Translation Ideology

To best grasp the difference in translation philosophies between Buffoni and older Italian poets, one name makes the difference: the Italian phenomenologist Luciano Anceschi. Buffoni, the "ideal disciple" of both Luciano Anceschi and Emilio Mattioli, thus did not grow up under the dominion of Croce, like earlier generations of Italian poets. Anceschi, a follower, in his turn, of Antonio Banfi, sought to free the study of poetry from rigid a priori definitions. Contrary to Croce, Anceschi held that poetry is defined, from individual work to work, by looking at the system of relations structuring it. Poetry is not, despite what Croce argued, simply defined by what poetry is and what it is not: form and content are not inviolable entities. Moreover, the history and criticism of poetic works must, according to Anceschi, be predicated on the role of poetics, expressed and latent, within the poet's works. The reflection on poetics is a vital hermeneutic guide to the poet's own practice. This category will provide the most fundamental guide to examine Buffoni's translations. If Anceschi's phenomenological philosophy was decisive for Buffoni's own growth, so were the philosopher's pronouncements on translation, such as his preface to the translations of the *Lirici nuovi* (New poets). Here, Anceschi wrote "in truth, untranslatable texts do not exist."[42] This maxim would always hold true for Buffoni.

Indeed, for our poet-translator, translations are not photocopies of the source texts. They constitute an independent literary genre, as Buffoni consistently repeats, following in the steps of other modern translation theorists like Jiří Levý. The focus, for Buffoni, is neither on an impossible reproduction of the original text nor on a free adaptation. His previously quoted statement, "There are two great diseases always necessary to try to eradicate [*debellare*]: the idea that the translation can be the reproduction of a text, and the idea that it is a recreation [*ricreazione*]"[43] clearly indicates how Buffoni brushes aside the historical dichotomies of translation theory. It is not, then, a question of "fidelity" or "infidelity": the famous oppositions, such as Cicero's *ut orator/ut interpres* (like an orator/like an interpreter), the Baroque French *les belles infidèles* and *les laides fidèles* (unfaithful beauties / ugly faithful [ones]), the modern-day target-oriented/source-oriented translations, and Lawrence Venuti's concept of invisibility/visibility, are no longer valuable concepts, according to Buffoni.[44] Instead, translations are seen as "poietic encounters" (*incontri poietici*). In these encounters, our poet-translator insists on "loyalty":

> The term loyalty [connotes] two eyes that gazing into other eyes declare love, admitting a momentary "betrayal." I have been loyal to your poetic loftiness [*altezza*], betraying you here and here and here: I did it to remain the most loyal possible to your loftiness [*altezza*]. This is what I say every evening to the poets alive and dead with whom I try to interweave poietic dialogue.[45]

Ideally, this loyalty leads to "this small miracle which as a translation theorist I like to define 'loyal recreation' [*ricreazione leale*]."[46] In his prefaces to the anthologies that he edited of Italian poetry in various languages, Buffoni expressly indicates what he considers a pernicious translation method. This occurs when a translator "turns … to the job, to 'poetese,' to trite themes of pseudo-lyrical or pseudo-experimental satisfied fulfillment."[47] Rather, Buffoni's self-described method of translation depends on finding the "prevalent element" of the text, "that inalienable one," and starting from there. Here, indeed, is a similarity between Giudici's and Buffoni's translation theories, both of whom rely on the theoretical notion of the "constructive principle" that was propounded by Tynjanov. Even if Buffoni doesn't explicitly mention the Russian theorist in his writings, owing to his friend Giudici's "abundant … use"[48] of him, Tynjanov plays a key role in the theoretical framework. Buffoni combines this approach with Ezra Pound's threefold category of melopoeia, logopoeia, and phanopoeia. Analysing a poem for translation, Buffoni selects as a "constructive principle" either Pound's first category ("the rhythmical-melodic inlay"), his second category ("the distinctly formulated thought"), or his third category ("the illumination … the epiphany, that flash, which by itself constitutes the profound meaning of the text").[49] Having decided on a method, Buffoni then knows where he can "eventually carry out a sacrifice," or in other words, where to be loyal and where to betray the author.

Buffoni's five interpretative categories of translations – rhythm, avant-text, intertextuality, movement of language through time, and poetics – also serve as his own guide for translating. We will treat them in order.

To begin with, as the poet quotes the innovative theorist and Bible translator Henri Meschonnic, the rhythm of a text is its fundamental element (*l'elemento fondamentale*).[50] For Buffoni, a poet must first find a rhythm: once he has found a rhythm, he has found his subject. If the poet doesn't find the right rhythm, "you can have the most beautiful things in the world to say but what you write can be at most a newspaper article." Rhythm, which can be heard in both the "the rhythm of the heart of our mother" and "our internal breath," "precedes the appearance of the human species." In the last analysis, rhythm and diction come from the same source: "poetry is born when these two elements are so fused that the difference is no longer seen: as when a ballerina dances so whirling about that the ballerina cannot be distinguished from the dance, because it has become a single thing. Poetic writing, when it is successful, no longer distinguishes the meaning of words from their musicality."[51] It is rhythm, which, according to our poet-translator, allows us to resolve the apparent conflict between, for instance, an Italian poet with a quantitative metre translating a British poet with an accentual-syllabic metre like Keats, Coleridge, or Byron. We will point out specific instances of this when Buffoni offsets words (carving a new rhythm into the translation) or changes metre entirely. It is such an essential component for Buffoni that he even edited a whole volume that was devoted to poetic rhythm.[52]

Next, the avant-text, a term coined by Jean Bellemin-Noël, embraces all of the materials and drafts of the final text. The originality of this concept is that "what is *before* the published *text* is *already text* and *already the text*."[53] Buffoni finds this useful in reflecting on the genesis of the poem. Rather than seeing a text as an indissoluble whole that is born from the head of Athena, as it were, this is a method to "translate in depth, to negate that translation is a process of decoding and recoding, source language, arrival language. The reflection on the avant-text makes one reflect on the formativity – which sometimes can last decades – of a text."[54] Buffoni has on several occasions used such preparatory material in his translations – whether in his versions of Bernard Simeone, Eddy van Vliet,[55] or Seamus Heaney. If the avant-text was popularized in Italian textual criticism, it wasn't linked up to translation theory until Buffoni did so. We will observe a clear example of how the Italian poet-translator makes use of it in his translations of Seamus Heaney's poem "North."

The notion of the movement of language through time was first elaborated by the German theorist Friedmar Apel, whose volume was translated into Italian in the series edited by Buffoni for Marcos y Marcos.[56] Buffoni had "intuited" this concept before reading Apel, but he hadn't "formalized"[57] it. This concept refers to the underlying instability of the target text and especially of the source text. If the target language is always in a state of flux, at a particular moment of time, so is the source language, and, consequently, the source text. In the years, decades, or centuries since the composition of the original poem, the linguistic structures of the original, from syntax and grammar to lexis and pronunciation, have changed. As Buffoni notes, "the so-called 'original' text is not an immobile reef in the sea, but rather a floating platform ... How can one therefore think that this text has remained the same?"[58] This specific category applies most when the translated text belongs to a different period of time, as in Shakespeare's sonnets or in English romantic poetry. We might add that Buffoni has strongly criticized a book on translation theory written by Umberto Eco, *Dire quasi la stessa cosa* (To say almost the same thing), for not taking this concept into account.[59] Equally, the target text, the translation, is determined by its historical and linguistic background. So a retranslation will change according to its temporal moment. As Buffoni noted about his translations of *Songs of Spring*, when he was gathering them together, he ended up retranslating many of the poems, since "almost none of the lexical and syntactical 'solutions' formerly devised worked any longer."[60] In other words, he was forced to retranslate because his own language and that of the world around him had changed in the past ten to twenty years.

Intertextuality, the term originated by Julia Kristeva, refers to the fact that there is no completely original literary creation. Literature is born from literature. Sanguineti, a friend of Buffoni's, also thought the same way about translation, as we saw in chapter 5. Translation, in this light, is not an impossible reproduction of the source text, but (as Kristeva wrote) it is an "absorption and transformation of another text."[61] The formerly hierarchical relationship in translation studies, as Buffoni explains, between the source text and target text "acquires another dimension: it becomes dialogic, and no longer in rank but in time."[62] We will later examine two separate forms of intertextuality in Buffoni's translations: that between Buffoni's and other poets' verses, and that between Buffoni's poetry and his own translations. The concept of intertextuality naturally leads to a discussion of poetics because poets do not create absolutely original works, as indicated above, but they reinterpret literary tradition "in the light of [their] poetics."

This final category, the *poietic encounter*, is the most important category, and to a certain degree it includes the rest. For Buffoni, "translating literature signifies a meeting between the poetics of the translator and the poetics of the translated author."[63] This concept links up with the notion of the movement of language in time, since this encounter occurs in "a point x in time and space that is unique and unrepeatable, since unique and unrepeatable is the status of the languages of the two works that meet in that moment."[64] As Buffoni states, "The sole way I know of relating myself to another poet is that of meeting him 'poietically' in a given text. A meeting that, on one hand, takes advantage of the connection between two poetics, the poetics of the translated author and the poetics of the translator."[65] Essentially we will look at this *poietic* relationship between Buffoni and the original poet by commenting on the different methods used by our poet-translator in conformity with his own poetics.

Yet there is nonetheless a difference in Buffoni's treatments of texts, which he has pointed to by indicating that his second *quaderno di traduzioni* includes both "traduzioni e imitazioni" (translations and imitations): certainly a version of Baudelaire's "A une passante" (To a female passerby) that changes gender and becomes in translation "Lui passava" (He was passing by), manifests a great alteration, enough so that Buffoni calls it an "imitazione" (imitation).[66]

In conclusion, for Buffoni, at core, there are two effective strategies in poetic translation. First, there is the search for "a larger and loftier poetic language, anonymous by definition."[67] To this group belong the important translators and translator-poets (not poet-translators) of, for instance, the "great season of Florentine hermeticism," from Carlo Bo to Renato Poggioli. Buffoni is extraneous to this category. The second translation method is usually followed by poet-translators. This, indeed, is Buffoni's own method, where the translator

> aims to make the most of [*valorizzare*] the encounter / clash between the poetics of the translator and that of the translated author, with the consequence, in the happiest cases, of producing a text worthy of entering into the poet-translator's *quaderno di traduzioni*; then of becoming part in every respect, of his work, of the canon.[68]

Buffoni incorporates translations into his own work: above all in his two *quaderni di traduzioni* along with *Del maestro in bottega*. No other poet has so greatly insisted on *quaderni di traduzioni* forming an integral part of the poet-translator's own *oeuvre*. Yet, if Buffoni, for all intents and purposes, wishes to appropriate poems through translation, he doesn't seek to massively adapt the original, like Robert Lowell who spliced and added where he saw fit.

Quaderni di Traduzioni

Buffoni named his first volume of translations *Songs of Spring*, after a phrase from Keats's ode "To Autumn." With this title, Buffoni aimed to underline two aspects: that his volume is a homage to nineteenth-century romantic poetry, and his close spiritual ties to Keats, the poet whom he has translated most completely. Indeed, as the poet-translator noted, "to say that Keats influenced me would be like saying ... that your mom influenced you."[69] It makes sense then that Buffoni chose to place on the front cover a passage from Keats's "Song":

To know the change and feel it,
When there is none to heal it,
Nor numbed sense to steel it,
Was never said in rhyme.[70]

Percepire il mutamento, sentirlo,
Sapere che nessuno può sanarlo,
Che i sensi non possono indurirlo.
Questo mai è stato detto in poesia.

[To perceive the change, feel it,
To know that no one can heal it,
That the senses cannot harden it.
This has never been said in poetry.]

Buffoni, in his translation of these verses, emphasizes the knowledge that the past is lost and that the mind knows this. While Keats mentions that no one can heal this *change*, Buffoni speaks of the subjective process of *knowing* (*sapere*) that no one can heal it (*sanarlo*). The Italian is more final, more disconsolate. This feeling is also underlined by the conspicuous alliterative roles of the *p* and *s* in the translation: *P*ercе*p*ire (to perceive), sa*p*ere (to know), *p*uò (can), *p*ossono (can), and *p*oesia (poetry) alternate with *s*entirlo (feel it), *s*apere, *s*anarlo (heal it), *s*en*s*i (senses), *p*o*ss*ono, que*s*to (this), *s*tato (been), and *p*oe*s*ia. This alliteration ties together the whole discourse, signalling the painful inexorability of time.

Songs of Spring, published in 1999, consists of thirty-eight poets and 125 poems. It is ordered chronologically[71] and drawn from poetic traditions as diverse as Dutch, French, Icelandic, Greek, Hebrew, Latin, Scottish, Spanish, and Swedish, though the vast majority of the poems are from English. Keats, fittingly, is the most represented poet in terms of quantity of pages, although Tomas Tranströmer ("absolutely one of the greatest living poets")[72] has the greatest number of poems with ten. Other prominent poets represented are Oscar Wilde and Heaney with eight poems, Coleridge and Spender with seven poems, and Byron and Kipling with six poems apiece.

More than thirty of Buffoni's translations in this volume are excerpts from longer works (either individual poems or epic poems). These range from fragments of single poems like Spender's "Ultima Ratio Regum" and e.e. cummings's "enter no (silence is the blood)" to passages from Byron's *Manfred*, Coleridge's *The Rime of the Ancient Mariner*, and Keats's *Endymion*. This is an innovative practice for *quaderni di traduzioni*, which generally include complete poems and not fragments. But this double-anthologizing, both in selecting a poem and in choosing a portion of the poem, matches up with Buffoni's own predilection for the poetic fragment: and let us not forget that *Songs of Spring* opens up with seven true fragments of ancient poetry (Euphorion and Varro Atacinus). It is also a sign of Buffoni's own appropriation of the foreign poem – a way to possess a little piece of the original. We might add that excerpting poems is a common practice of Buffoni's that is followed both in his anthology of English romantic poets and in his self-anthology, *Adidas*.

Within the *quaderno* itself, Buffoni creates certain intertextual echoes. For instance, the two poems by English poet Caroline Anne Bowles ("Conte à mon chien") and the French poet Marie-Claire Bancquart ("Toi petit bâtard" [You, little mutt]) both deal with the same subject, dogs, and form what Buffoni calls "an ideal leitmotiv." In addition, Bancquart's same poem, with its phrase "Notre eau des yeux" (Our water of the eyes) translated as "la nostra acqua degli occhi" (our water of the eyes), recalls Buffoni's first collection of poetry, *Acqua degli occhi*, creating in the Italian poet's words, "a small intertextual short circuit."[73] Another intertextual reference to Buffoni's volume *Acqua degli occhi* is created by Jaime Siles's poem "Variación barocca sobre un tema de Lucrecio" (Baroque variation on a theme by Lucretius) with its verse "Los ojos en el agua son espejos"[74] (The eyes in the water are mirrors) transferred into Italian as "nell'acqua gli occhi sono specchi"[75] (in water the eyes are mirrors). Indeed, the image of eyes as mirrors in water reflects the very same intertextuality where words mirror each other in books through time. Other examples of intertextual links within *Songs of Spring* are easily visible, as in the succession of Coleridge fragments about the moon, for example.

Songs of Spring contains two special examples of translation that I will focus on now. First, Buffoni's translation of the Scottish poet Robert Fergusson's "The Daft Days" into both Milanese dialect and Italian,[76] and second, Buffoni's retranslation of Seamus Heaney's poem "North."

Buffoni's translation into dialect marks a significant linguistic shift, which is all the more remarkable for its singularity. No other Italian poet in *quaderni di traduzioni* translates into dialect.[77] The Milanese and Italian translations of Fergusson reveal different specific techniques but are both united in their strategy of adaptation ("imitation" as Buffoni describes it) of the Scottish text, beginning with the title (*The Daft Days*[78] / *I ultim dì de l'ann*[79] [the last days of the year] / *Gli ultimi giorni dell'anno*[80] [the last days of the year]). Daft, in Scots, means "frolicsome," so the Milanese and Italian translations neutralize the tone. Both renditions are more concise than the original, and if they both retain some of the original exuberant tone, they are less markedly festive. The ornamental flourish of Fergusson's verse is little imitated in the translations, especially the Italian one. As Buffoni explains, "My version in Milanese dialect really turned into an imitation."[81] Then, he turned his "Fergussonian imitation" into Italian, at which point, "I couldn't stop continuing to actualize the text, detaching myself little by little from a translation of an imitation, and falling into an imitation of an imitation."[82]

In the end, Buffoni's Milanese version is much more effusive than the Italian translation, both more personal and more expansive. This isn't clear from the opening stanzas, where, for example, the first stanza is almost exactly identical in Milanese and Italian. Yet, proceeding onwards, the contrast between the two versions becomes great. For instance, if in the fourth stanza, the Milanese runs "Alura, alura sì che ti te se bèl / Te se grand, te se còld, paës"[83] (Well, well, yes, you are so beautiful, / You are so big, you are so warm, country), the Italian turns the direct invocation into an impersonal "Allora sì che il mio paese è grande e caldo / E bello"[84] (So, yes, my country is big and warm / and beautiful). Likewise, Buffoni renders the Milanese "Un'aria che te la sentet subet / S'ciopà denter de ti"[85] (An aria that you immediately feel / explode inside of you) as the Italian "canzoni / Che scoppiano subito dentro"[86] (songs that explode inside immediately). In general, the Italian translation (in comparison with both the original Scots and the Milanese versions) is veined with sadness. The matter-of-fact

Milanese in the fifth stanza, "E se sta tucc insemma / A cuntàss su i ball de l'ann passaa"[87] (And everyone is all together, recounting the things of the past year) becomes in Italian "Poi ci si mette insieme a raccontare / Le cose dell'anno che muore"[88] (Then one gathers together to recount the things of the dying year). The Milanese version speaks of the past (*trascorso*) year, while the Italian speaks more sadly of the year that dies (*muore*). So, if Buffoni in his Milanese translation concludes that there is *nient de pussee bell*[89] (Nothing more beautiful) than the last days of the year (an explicit statement absent from the original), this is completely removed from the Italian, as is the sensation of being together (*Insemma, inozent*[90] [together, innocent]). Rather, the penultimate stanza of the Italian translation finishes with the premonitory *come bambini che non si pensa a dopo* (like children who don't think about afterwards), which is much more threatening than the Milanese *i fioeu … pensà no a l'ann che vegn* (children who don't think of the coming year). Finally, it isn't coincidental that Buffoni consistently uses *alegher* (cheerful) in dialect and *festa* (party) in Italian: in his Milanese version, people are fundamentally *alegher*, while in Italian they are only happy at *feste*: their happiness is conditioned and temporary.

With his translation of Seamus Heaney's poems in 1991, Buffoni was responsible for the introduction of Heaney to the Italian reader. When Heaney won the Nobel Prize for Literature, Buffoni was asked to translate several poems. Not having his own volume nearby, he retranslated them.[91] Thus we have examples of first[92] and second versions of a major poem like "North." The second translation of Heaney's "North"[93] contains only five identical verses out of the forty total verses of his first translation. Buffoni brings the newer version more in line with the literal meaning: through adjectives such as *measured*,[94] translated first as *accanto*[95] (next to) and then *misurabili*[96] (measurable); nouns such as *althing*,[97]which is rendered first *all'interno della comunità*[98] (within the community) and subsequently *vecchi parlamenti*[99] (old parliaments); the verb *were*,[100] which is first rendered as *divennero*[101] (became), and then becomes *erano*[102] (were); the phrase *voices … lifted again in violence and epiphany*[103] is first translated as *voci che risorgevano in violente visioni*[104] (voices that rose up in violent visions) and then *voci sollevate nella violenza e nell'epifania*[105] (raised up in violence and in epiphany); and, perhaps the most momentous translation change is the rendering of *Lie down in the word-hoard:*[106] first this is turned into *custodisci in dispensa*[107] (keep in the cupboard) and next into *sdraiati nel tuo tesoro di parole*[108] (lie down in your treasure of words). Notable here, as well, is Buffoni's concept of the avant-text. As he explains in a lecture, he had no access to Heaney's preliminary versions of "North" for his first translation, while Heaney sent them to him for his later retranslation. So, for example, Buffoni newly translates "violence and epiphany" as "nella violenza e nell'epifania," which is far removed from the first translation's "violente visioni." Moreover, Buffoni's usage of the historic past tense in the second translation, e.g., *ritornai*[109] (I returned) and *trovai*[110] (I found), reflects his own movement in time and language. After an upbringing in Lombardy where such a past tense is eschewed in oral speech, he spent many years in Rome where the *passato remoto* is often used. The retranslation, then, is a more semantically correct translation that is closer to the English and more aesthetically pleasing besides. Buffoni's long acquaintance with Heaney, his immersion in his poetry, and his common poetics with Heaney that are based (as Buffoni notes) on the earthly nature of their verse work together to make his later translation of "North" a more successful autonomous poem that recalls the original even more deeply.

Curiously enough, the poem that Buffoni calls the most beautiful lyric in nineteenth-century English, Byron's "So we'll go No-More A-roving" (a debatable claim itself), is translated rather ineffectively. Perhaps this is owing to anxiety of influence, or simply to the English rhythm, which combined with its particular lightness of tone, is hard to get across in Italian. But, as the opening of the Italian version shows, the translation is marred by heaviness of touch: "So, we'll go no more a-roving / So late into the night"[111] is rendered as "Così, più non andremo / In giro senza meta / Nella notte fonda" (So, no more will we roam / Around without an aim / Late in the night).[112] Amplified into three verses, the Italian "andremo in giro" catches a dissonant note that is too colloquial; likewise, "in giro senza meta," which occupies a whole verse, is simply "a-roving" in English. The English velocity is unmatchable, but this type of failure is rare in Buffoni's translations.

Songs of Spring's concluding text is the prose poem by Bernard Simeone, "Madonna del Parto." This is one of only two poems in the volume that directly deal with an Italian subject. Its special significance here, confirmed by Buffoni,[113] placed at the end of the volume, resides in the classic Socratic metaphor of giving birth to works. Here, the Virgin Mary is nearly at the point of giving birth, yet she hesitates, "vertiginosa e placida" (*vertigineuse et placide*) [vertiginous and calm].[114]

Una piccola tabaccheria, which was published in 2012, includes thirty-eight poets and sixty-one poems, but it is not ordered chronologically like the previous volume. The title is drawn from Pound's "The Lake Isle," which was previously translated by Buffoni in his volume *Quaranta a Quindici* (thus forming another intertextual tie in Buffoni's work between his poetic volumes and his *quaderni di traduzioni*). Pound had originally parodied Yeats's "Lake Isle of Innisfree"; now Buffoni adapts the American poet. In his translation of Pound, Buffoni excises the two references to divinities (*God* and *Venus*) other than Mercury. While keeping the important anaphora of *O Mercury, patron of thieves,* he eliminates repeated words (like *loose, little, bright*, and *profession*) and adjectives (like *damned*). He turns the poem from an impersonal direction to a personal direction: "che mi costringe a concentrarmi sempre" (which always forces me to concentrate) translates "where one needs one's brains all the time." Buffoni's Italian version is more concise. For instance, Pound uses twenty-three words in the final two verses of the first strophe, while Buffoni uses only eleven. The alliteration here is quite intense, as though Buffoni were attempting to rival Pound in melopoeia: the *c* sound dominates in Mer*c*urio (twice) (Mercury), pi*cc*ola taba*cc*heria (twice) (small tobacco shop), *c*on le s*c*atoline lu*cc*i*c*anti (with the shining little boxes), s*c*affali (shelves), taba*cc*o (tobacco), *c*ustoditi nel ban*c*o (kept underneath the counter), *c*apelli (hair), *c*hia*cc*hierando (chatting), *c*omunque (however), *c*he (which), s*c*rivere (to write), *c*ostringe (forces), and *c*oncentrarmi (to concentrate); likewise, the "d" in "*d*io *d*ella truffa, / *d*ammi a tempo *d*ebito" (God of theft, give me in due time) creates melopoeia. This is Buffoni putting Fortini's *compensi* into practise.

In this *quaderno*, Larkin has the greatest number of poems (six), followed by Heaney, Shakespeare, and Eddy van Vliet with four. Once again, there are a wide variety of languages represented: English, Dutch, Arabic, Portuguese, French, Welsh, and Spanish. Once more, English poetry dominates the volume. Yet one of the most interesting thematic centres of this volume involves a series of French (and English) poems: Baudelaire's "A une passante" (To a woman passerby), Verlaine's "L'Apollon de Pont-Audemer" (The Apollo of Pont-Audemer), Rimbaud's "Le dormeur du val" (The sleeper in the valley), Byron's "She Walks in Beauty," and Pound's "Gentildonna." All five poems speak of a person seen either on the street, in the country, or in the mind's eye. One of them, the translation of Verlaine, will be examined here (see table 6.1 below).[115] Already adapted in the title of the version, "Il dio di Roserio" (The god of Roserio), this powerful translation cuts to the bone.

Table 6.1 "L'Apollon de Pont-Audemer" (The Apollo of Pont-Audemer)

Paul Verlaine **"L'Apollon de Pont-Audemer"** **[The Apollo of Pont-Audemer]**	**Franco Buffoni** **"Il dio di Roserio"** **[The god of Roserio]**
Un solide gaillard! Dix-huit ans: larges bras; [A robust guy! Eighteen years: large arms;]	Diciotto anni, e che spalle solide, che mani [Eighteen years, and what solid shoulders, what hands]
Mains à vous arracher la tête de l'épaule; [Hands to tear off your head from your shoulder;]	Pronte a fare a botte appena capita, [Ready to come to blows, as soon as it happens,]
Sur un front bas et dur, cheveux roux, coupés ras. [Over a low and hard forehead, red hair, cut short.]	Capelli corti e rossi sulla fronte [Short, red hair over his harsh]
Puis, à la danse, il a, ma foi, crâne air, le drôle! [Then, at the dance, he has, well, a bold look, the rascal!]	Dura. Devi vederlo quando si scatena [Forehead. You must see him when he lets loose]
Les enfants poussent drus aux filles qu'il enjôle, [The children crowd around the girls that he flatters,]	In discoteca: nessuna gli resista! [In clubs: nobody can resist him!]
Dans la puberté fière et fauve, le beau gas [In his proud and tawny puberty, the handsome fellow]	Ed egli va sentendosi guardare [And he goes, aware of being watched,]
Va, comme dans sa pourpre un roi qui sait son rôle [Walks, like a king in his purple who knows his role]	Nell'ora della fiera giovinezza [In the hour of his proud youth]
Et parle à voix humaine, et marche à vastes pas. [And speaks with a human voice, and walks with immense steps.]	Come un dio nel suo ruolo [Like a god in his role]
Plus tard, soit que le sort l'épargne ou le désigne, [Later, whether destiny spares or designates him,]	Passa. Più tardi, in là con gli anni, [Who passes by. Later, well on in years,]
On le verra, bon vieux, barbe blanche, oeil terni [One will see him, nice old man, white beard, clouded eye]	Anche se la sorte lo risparmia, [Even if destiny spares him,]

Table 6.1 "L'Apollon de Pont-Audemer" (The Apollo of Pont-Audemer) (*Continued*)

Paul Verlaine "L'Apollon de Pont-Audemer" [The Apollo of Pont-Audemer]	**Franco Buffoni "Il dio di Roserio" [The god of Roserio]**
S'éteindre doucement, comme un jour qui finit; [Extinguish softly, like a day that ends;]	Lo vedrai vecchio e malandato spegnersi, [You will see him, old and in poor health, pass away,]
Ou bien, humble héros; martyre de la consigne, [Or, humble hero; martyr of the mission,]	O peggio, umile eroe, martire in missione, [Or worse, humble hero, martyr on a combat mission,]
Au fond d'une tranchée obscure ou d'un talus [At the bottom of an obscure trench or an embankment]	In fondo a una trincea o in un fossato [Into the bottom of a trench or ditch]
Rouler, le crâne ouvert par quelque éclat d'obus. [Roll, the skull opened by some shrapnel.]	Rotolare con il cranio sfondato. [Rolling with a smashed-in skull.]
Source: Buffoni, *Una piccola tabaccheria*, 56	Source: Buffoni, *Una piccola tabaccheria*, 57

While the French begins with an exclamation about the boy, "Un solide gaillard!" Buffoni cuts to the chase with *Diciotto anni*. With a combination of enjambments (*mani / pronte, fronte / dura, come un dio nel suo ruolo / Passa, in un fossato / Rotolare*) and more expressive language (owing to concision) than the original as in "il cranio sfondato" (instead of "le crâne ouvert par quelque éclat d'obus"), and "Lo vedrai vecchio e malandato spegnersi" in place of "On le verra, bon vieux, barbe blanche, oeil terni, / S'éteindre doucement, comme un jour qui finit," colloquial language such as "Devi vederlo quando si scatena / In discoteca: nessuna gli resiste" and the highly effective final rhyme (the only one of the translation) "In fondo a una trincea o in un fossato / Rotolare con il cranio sfondato," the translation takes on an autonomous life. The numbers tell the story too: if Verlaine's poem contains 126 words, Buffoni's has only 88, or nearly one-third fewer words. The Italian version is stronger than Verlaine's original: the poem has been pared down and tightened. This same tendency is present everywhere in Buffoni's translations, but particularly noticeable here. In his own words, in fact,[116] he considers this translation an "imitation," for it takes liberties with the original. A similar argument could be made for Buffoni's version of Baudelaire's "A une passante," which in Buffoni's hands turns into "Lui passava"

(He was passing by). The erotic subject is no longer a woman, but a man. This translation, too, is classified by Buffoni as an "imitation."[117]

The overall contrast between *Songs of Spring* and *Una piccola tabaccheria* is clear. Although each volume contains thirty-eight poets, the first volume is more of a collection of translations that are "the best of twenty years," as its back cover recites. The second volume that is slimmed down by more than half, from 368 pages to 150 pages, is a more cohesive *quaderno di traduzioni*. Confirmation of this comes from Buffoni who writes of how in contrast with past years, he now translates "in great part from empathy, from harmony (*consonanza*)": "there must be a connection."[118] Therefore, two particular criteria – poetics and friendship – determine the shift from the first to the second volume. If Buffoni's main areas of poetic inspiration lie in the English romantics (present in both volumes) and French symbolists, it is only in the second volume that the latter appear (Baudelaire, Rimbaud, and Verlaine). Buffoni acknowledges this in his notes to the volumes. In *Una piccola tabaccheria*, he describes cohesive links between his translations of twenty-one poets, sometimes with multiple connections: Verlaine with Byron, Baudelaire, Pound, and Rimbaud; Rimbaud with Verlaine and Wilde; Heaney with Joyce and Neruda; and Spender with Verlaine and de Ibarbourou.[119] Yet in the first *quaderno*, equivalent connections described by Buffoni are limited to only three out of the thirty-eight poets.[120] Moreover, if fourteen poets in *Songs of Spring* are included partly out of friendship and esteem,[121] only two such poets are found in the later *Una piccola tabaccheria*.[122]

There are seven poets in common between the first and the second *quaderni di traduzioni*: Auden, Byron, Heaney, Wilde, Feinstein, Shakespeare, and van Vliet. The first four have formed nodes in Buffoni's work, in his translations and his critical studies. The presence of Feinstein and van Vliet can be accredited to Buffoni's friendship with them and his esteem of their work. Shakespeare is the outlier, who, with his *Sonnets* remains a crucial poetic model for the Italian poet-translator.

Buffoni Versus Luzi

Here we will compare the translation practices of Buffoni with Mario Luzi. Luzi (1914–2005) was an influential poet, as well as a translator of eleven works from French, English, and Spanish.[123] His main translation activity centred on French poetry that he gathered together in two *quaderni di traduzioni*: *Francamente* (Frankly) and *La Cordigliera delle Ande*

(The Cordillera of the Andes). The latter spanned Pierre Ronsard to André Frénaud. Translation and poetry were symbiotic for Luzi. Antonio Prete notes about the Italian poet that "translating wasn't an exercise, but an essential foundation of his very writing."[124] Luzi explains how "the most difficult translations I have done were when I was, also as a writer, doing something that required an experience of this kind, a comparison [*confronto*] with that author, not with an author, but with that author, with that proposal that each author brings along."[125] Thus, he turned to Coleridge's lyrics when he was searching for "nuance" in his own poetic tongue;[126] he translated Shakespeare when his poetic powers were ripe for such an encounter; he translated Mallarmé late in life when he was "digging into the rhythmic and verbal substance of my Italian";[127] searching for an "edenic exile of form and perfect harmony"[128] from his despair after the Second World War he translated Louise Labé; and he translated Tirso de Molina when he needed to "dissolve a little bit my theatrical language in a species of liturgy, also scenic, simpler ... but more collective, if you like, choral."[129]

Luzi, as we have noted, admits that he doesn't theorize about translating: "I have never truly thought of being able to theorize about an eminently empirical object like translation that, whatever way you look at it, always appeared such to me."[130] Even so, he affirms, like Buffoni, that translation is an ideal encounter between the original poet and the translator: "the translation of a poet is a meeting [*incontro*], a meeting given in certain moments, at certain levels of convergence or of friction with the original."[131] Thus, for instance, when Luzi was translating Coleridge, he describes himself as "alone with the text."[132] Indeed, taking up one of the most important images of the Ancient Mariner, he suggested that "it is necessary for you to be in the open sea when you translate, alone with your man."[133] The fact that Luzi, as a Francophile, didn't know English well, allowed him the freedom to translate differently than he would have translated a French author: "truly that distance, between mythic English and the language I was forced to use, was a territory susceptible of many adventures that I never would have permitted myself to run with a language more obliging like French."[134] This is, of course, the same line of reasoning that Giovanni Giudici put forth for why he chose to translate from languages structurally different from Italian. Yet, we should remember that Luzi's translation of Mallarmé's *Plusieurs sonnets* (Several sonnets) segmented and decomposed the French poet's ductile verse, even though French is so close to Italian.

According to Luzi, the meeting between poet and translator, this "subtle duel," is freighted with ambiguities. Poetic translation by its nature is an "obscure negotiation of concessions, resistance, claims without proof of legitimacy between author and author,"[135] so much so that at the end it is not clear who comes out the winner, or loser. Luzi remarks that "one will never know who was the victim and who the executioner [*carnefice*]."[136] In the best of cases – with no "brawl" (*colluttazione*) – there is a "lucky, happy marriage" (*felice connubio*). A new text is born, "an autonomous text," in which the translator has managed to "burn off the difference, the distance."[137]

For our comparison, I have chosen two passages from Buffoni's and Luzi's translations of Coleridge's *The Rime of the Ancient Mariner* (as shown in tables 6.2 and 6.3 below).

The most striking contrast between Buffoni's and Luzi's translations turns on the use of poetic tradition. Luzi inserts Coleridge not into contemporary twentieth-century Italian poetry, but earlier. Through a frame of end-rhyming, abundant hendecasyllables (along with occasional *settenari* [seven-syllable verses]), and archaic and elevated diction, Luzi's *Ancient Mariner* is indeed rendered ancient. For example, Luzi utilizes an exclusive and aulic poetic register with the following words drawn from the first passage: *volto, raggia, esangue, stillare,* and *inferna.* Likewise, the second excerpt shows how Luzi's rhymes require additions or modifications to the text. In rhyming *respira/mira* and *guida/rida,* he had to add, for example, *quasi rida,* which was absent from the English, and use the archaic *mira.* In general, Luzi's translation retains more than a whiff of the archaic, whether through poeticisms (even such adverbial locutions like *al cospetto di*), or apocope (*conoscer*). This antique patina is, on the other hand, generally foreign to Buffoni's version. Rather, Buffoni focuses more on the "rhythms of the original rather than the meter,"[138] and he doesn't use end-rhyming. His free verse is studded with alliteration and assonance. In the first three verses of the second passage, the recurring *o* marks the *oceano,* which gives way in the fourth verse to the vowel *a* in *luna* (fiss*a* l*a* lun*a* silenzios*a*-mente): the contrast between the ocean and the moon is thus emphasized down to the very phonemes of each word. We can notice half-rhymes as in *guida/guarda,* or *occhio/silenziosamente.* Although Buffoni doesn't dye his version in classical tradition, he does explicitly draw on Dante and Leopardi. For instance, the second verse recalls their "senza vento," and his use of *guazza* in the first passage is assuredly archaic (also used, for instance, by Mario Praz in his purply,

Table 6.2 *The Rime of the Ancient Mariner* (vv. 203–211)

Samuel Taylor Coleridge, "The Rime of the Ancient Mariner"	**Franco Buffoni, "La ballata del vecchio marinaio"**	**Mario Luzi, "La ballata del vecchio marinaio"**
We listened and looked sideways up!	Noi ascoltavamo e scrutavamo intorno! [We listened and peered around!]	Noi ascoltavamo e guardavamo fisso! [We listened and stared!]
Fear at my heart, as at a cup,	La paura nel cuore, mi sembrava, [The fear in (my) heart, it seemed,]	Al cuore come al fondo di una coppa [From (my) heart as at the bottom of a cup]
My life-blood seemed to sip!	Stesse a succhiarmi il sangue! [Would suck out my blood!]	La paura attingeva tutto il sangue! [Fear drew up all the blood!]
The stars were dim, and thick the night,	Densa la notte con le stelle opache [Thick the night with opaque stars]	Le stelle cupe, densa era la notte, [The dark stars, thick was the night,]
The steersman's face by his lamp gleamed white;	E bianco il viso del timoniere alla lanterna: [And white the face of the steersman in the lantern light:]	Il volto del nocchiero raggia esangue [The visage of the helmsman shines wanly]
		presso la sua lanterna; [in his lantern light;]
From the sails the dew did drip –	Dalle vele la guazza cola lenta. [From the sails dew drips slowly.]	Dalle vele stillava giù rugiada [From the sails trickled down dew]
Till clomb above the eastern bar	Ad un tratto si leva sopra a oriente [At once arose in the East]	Finché s'alzò sul ciglio dell'oriente [Until on the edge of the East arose]
The horned Moon, with one bright star	Una falce di luna, ed una stella [A crescent moon, and a star]	Col corno della luna una splendente [With the horn of a moon a resplendent]
Within the nether tip.	Risplende sulla punta, in basso. [Shines at the tip, below.]	Stella vicino alla sua punta inferna. [Star near its lowest tip.]
Source: *Poeti romantici inglesi*, trans. Franco Buffoni, vol. 1, 318	Source: *Poeti romantici inglesi*, trans. Franco Buffoni, vol. 1, 319	Source: Coleridge, *Poesie e prose*, trans. Mario Luzi, 33

Table 6.3 *The Rime of the Ancient Mariner* (vv. 414–421)

Samuel Taylor Coleridge, "The Rime of the Ancient Mariner"	**Franco Buffoni, "La ballata del vecchio marinaio"**	**Mario Luzi, "La ballata del vecchio marinaio"**
"Still as a slave before his lord,	"Come schiavo dinanzi al suo padrone ["As a slave in front of his master]	"Come schiavo al cospetto del signore ["As a slave in the presence of (his) master]
The ocean hath no blast;	Immobile è l'oceano e senza vento: [Immobile is the ocean and without wind:]	sta immobile l'oceano e non respira; [the ocean is immobile and does not breathe;]
His great bright eye most silently	Con l'occhio grande e luminoso [With an eye great and luminous]	il suo grande occhio luminoso mira [its great luminous eye]
Up to the moon is cast –	Fissa la luna silenziosamente ... [It stares at the moon silently ...]	fissa la luna silenziosamente – [stares at the moon silently –]
If he may know which way to go;	Se può sapere quale via seguire: [If it may know what road to follow:]	per conoscer la strada da seguire; [to know the road to follow;]
For she guides him smooth or grim.	Perché, calmo o infuriato, è lei la guida. [Because, calm or raging, she [the moon] is the guide.]	perché, quieto o infuriato, essa lo guida. [because, quiet or raging, she (the moon) guides it.]
See, brother, see! How graciously	Ma guarda, fratello, guarda con che grazia [But look, brother, look with what grace]	Vedi, fratello, vedi con che grazia [See, brother, see with what grace]
She looketh down on him."	Dall'alto lo osserva." [From up high she observes him."]	dall'alto essa lo guarda quasi rida." [From up high she watches him, as if laughing."]
Source: *Poeti romantici inglesi*, trans. Franco Buffoni, vol. 1, 330	Source: *Poeti romantici inglesi*, trans. Franco Buffoni, vol. 1, 331	Source: Coleridge, *Poesie e prose*, trans. Mario Luzi, 53

archaizing version of the *Ancient Mariner*).[139] There is one last point to be made: while Luzi was a Francophile through and through, whose command of English was very shaky,[140] Buffoni spent his academic career as a professor of English literature. Evidence of this is seen in Luzi's misinterpretation of the final verses in Table 6.1. Luzi speaks of the *splendente stella* rising, while Coleridge has the "horned Moon" (Buffoni's *Una falce di luna*) as the subject of this verb. Possibly the archaic *clomb* caused problems for Luzi. Yet the fact that Luzi was not well versed in English, as Buffoni rightly suggests,[141] and that he therefore relied on previous Italian versions such as Mario Praz's *in primis*, contributed to making Luzi's translation even more antiquated.

Despite all this, Luzi's version was, as Edoardo Zuccato justly notes, "the first significant poetic translation of the text." Its poetic power was rendered sympathetically by an Italian poet whose own use of symbols drew on both the later French symbolists and Coleridge. Luzi's translation was, indeed, the "turning point that made Coleridge a permanent presence for both the intellectual circles and the general reading public."[142] Still today, after many other translations, Luzi's remains a valid translation (as Buffoni called it, "that classic one").[143] Yet, I would argue that it is in danger of becoming a period piece due to its reliance on aulic diction and syntax, which by now sounds somewhat outdated. Buffoni's free verse version, on the other hand, is fresh and, despite lacking the formal structure of metre and rhyme, it succeeds in creating a considerable amount of poetic grace in Italian. Two poetics as different as Luzi's and Buffoni's have given rise to two divergent modes of translating Coleridge.

Translation Techniques

In general, Buffoni's practices a subtle art of variation. For instance, in e.e. cummings's scandalous poem (for his time) "the boys I mean are not refined," which uses the eponymous refrain four times, Buffoni alternates "Quelli che intendo io non sono raffinati" (Those whom I mean are not refined), the title of his translation "Ai ragazzi che ho in mente io stasera" (To the boys I have in mind tonight), and "Quelli che dico io sono dei duri" (Those whom I mean are tough ones). Here, due to the idioms and obscene language, Buffoni finds both euphemisms and equivalent vulgar Italian expressions. The first category includes the Italian rendering of *They do not give a fuck for luck* ("E non lo fanno così tanto per farlo" [And they don't do it just for the sake of doing it]), *They do not give a shit for wit* ("Non gliene frega niente di nulla" [they don't care about anything]), and *they kill like you would take a piss* ("Ti ammazzano se gli gira" [they kill you if they feel like it]). Other times, Buffoni replicates the force of the vulgar original, whether translating *tit* as *tetta*, "masturbate with dynamite" as "masturbandosi con la dinamite," *they hump thirteen times a night* ("Ma vengono anche sette volte in fila" [But they even come seven times in a row]), or even intensifying the vulgarity, as in rendering *behind* as *culo* (ass), or translating *they do whatever's in their pants* as "E scopano quando gli tira" (And they screw when they get hard-ons).

Nevertheless, not all of Buffoni's translations are such adaptations: the most faithful versions, almost calques, are his translations from the French of Marie-Claire Bancquart's "Toi, petit bâtard" (You, little mutt) and Bernard Simeone's "Madonna del parto": the first is a lyric poem; the second is a prose poem. This can naturally be explained by the closeness of Romance languages, French and Italian, as opposed to the differences separating Italian from a Germanic language like English. Yet even in many of Buffoni's versions of English poetry, he strictly follows the original. Sometimes the very structure of Italian manages to better the original: an example is Buffoni's translation of Kathleen Raine's "Lachesis," where the assonance of *sogno* (dream) and *sonno* (sleep) give birth to a richness that is unavailable to the original. Here is Raine's poem, followed by Buffoni's translation, and then a back-translation of Buffoni:

Our life a play of passion, says Raleigh's madrigal,
"Only we die, we die"; but older wisdom taught
That the dead change their garments and return,
Passing from sleep to sleep, from dream to dream.[144]

La nostra vita una commedia di passione, dice il madrigale di Raleigh;
"Solo noi moriamo, noi moriamo," ma la saggezza più antica insegna
Che i morti si cambiano d'abito e ritornano,
Da sonno a sonno passando, da sogno a sogno.[145]

[Our life a play of passion, says Raleigh's madrigal;
"Only we die, we die," but the most ancient wisdom teaches
That the dead change clothes and return,
From sleep to sleep passing, from dream to dream.]

We can hear (and see) the dead "chang[ing] their garments and return[ing]" through the near phonetic identification of *sogno* and *sonno* (but not in the vastly different English words "sleep" and "dream").

If Buffoni normally avoids rhyme, he does use it in certain cases to end the poem, generally as a concluding couplet or epigram: for instance, in the triple rhyme (absent from the original) that ends the same poem "Lachesis": "You and I, / my love, must suffer patiently what we are, / Those parts of guilt and grief we play / Who must about our necks the millstone bear" is turned by Buffoni into "Amore, dobbiamo soffrire con pazienza ciò che siamo, / Queste parti di colpa e di dolore recitiamo, / Noi, che sul collo la macina portiamo"[146] (Love, we must suffer with patience what we are, / These parts of guilt and grief we play, / We, who on our neck bear the millstone). The same use of rhyme is evident, for example, in Byron's "Stanzas for music," where Byron's "Nor can we be what we recall / Nor dare we think on what we are" becomes "Non siamo più quel che ricordiamo, / Né osiamo pensare a ciò che siamo"[147] (We are no more what we remember, / Nor do we dare think of what we are). As is clear, his recourse to rhyme occurs especially to emphasize a specific message.

Buffoni, like Montale, frequently shortens the poem. The overall concision (or excision) is clear in a poem like the following from Oscar Wilde's "Panthea": "For man is weak; God sleeps: and heaven is high: / One fiery-coloured moment: one great love; and lo! we die."[148] is turned into the powerfully staccato "L'uomo è debole. Dio dorme. / Il cielo è in alto. Una scintilla. / Grande amore. Morte."[149] (Man is weak. God sleeps. / The sky is high up. A spark. / Great love. Death.) Often the concision comes from Buffoni's cropping of filler adjectives, as in a poem by Walter Savage Landor, "Ternissa! You are fled!" Landor writes, "And your cool palm smooths down stern Pluto's cheek." Buffoni translates it as "E la tua mano rasserena Plutone" (And your hand calms down Pluto). So, the Italian poet-translator eliminated both adjectives, *cool* and *stern*, as well as the noun *cheek*. In a few consecutive verses of Swinburne's "The Garden of Persephone," he also removes filler adjectives: "blind buds"[150] ("i germogli"[151]), "wild leaves"[152] ("le foglie"[153]), "ruined springs"[154] ("primavere"[155]). He uses this technique again in a line by Oscar Wilde (from the poem "Panthea"): "through the hot jungle where the yellow-eyed huge lions sleep"[156] ("nella giungla fino ai leoni / Addormentati"[157] [through the jungle as far as the lions / asleep]).

Another frequent modulation of Buffoni's consists in his setting off the end of the translation with an adjective or phrase: for example, in Shelley's "Ozymandias," the final Italian verses are "Null'altro resta. Intorno alle rovine del relitto / Colossale, nuda infinita informe la sabbia si distende / Solitaria"[158] (Nothing else remains. Around the ruins of the colossal wreck, / naked, infinite, and formless the sand extends / isolated). The original poem, of course, has no such emphasis. The same approach is founded in a fragment of Coleridge where Buffoni highlights the final two adjectives:

When the new or full Moon urges
The high, large, long, unbreaking surges
Of the Pacific main.[159]

Come quando la luna nuova o piena
Le onde grandi e infrangibili sospinge
Dell'immenso Pacifico.
E alte, lunghe.[160]

[As when the moon, new or full
Drives the big and unbreakable waves
Of the immense Pacific.
And high, long (ones).]

By forefronting the adjectives *solitaria* (isolated) and *alte, lunghe* (high, long), Buffoni effectively refers to their substantives: the solitary sand and the tidal surges of the Pacific. Setting off single words like this is analogous to enjambment; in fact, Buffoni often highlights isolated words by using enjambment at the end of the verse, just as he does when he ends a poem with them. Both the techniques of forefronting and enjambment alter the rhythm of the source text and create a new rhythm.

Conclusion

Franco Buffoni is assuredly the most important Italian translator of modern English poetry.[161] His majestic anthology of English romantics will be read for generations to come (it has already been reprinted several times). He has also been a leader in advancing new theoretical approaches to translation in Italy through his important critical essays, his editorship of *Testo a fronte* and the multiple series of poetry for *Marcos y Marcos*, and through his role as a conference organizer. What brings together the different activities of his life – poet, critic, and translator – is the concentration on the written text and its diverse formulations in numerous languages. This threefold aspect of his personality (poet, critic, and translator), which Mengaldo has elsewhere cited as the distinctive mark of modern Italian poets, indubitably enriches each of his individual vocations. Buffoni has eloquently shown how a translator must interpret a poem with a poet's eye. Perhaps most vitally, he has insisted on claiming authorial status for poetic translations that are not free imitations or adaptations, but are philologically accurate poetic representations. The autonomy of the translated poem thus doesn't become unmoored from its source text, but it retains artistic independence due to Buffoni's intense *poietic* dialogue with the original author and text, where translation is not a mere *esperimento formale* (formal experiment) but "an existential experience intended to relive the creative act that inspired the original."[162] At best, this experience will lead the poet-translator to create a text that can be a part of his or her *quaderno di traduzioni* – as in Buffoni's *Songs of Spring* and *Una piccola tabaccheria*. In such a volume, as Buffoni remarks, this translation will become a canonical part of the poet-translator's own verse and live on as long as his or her own poetry.

Appendix

Catalogue of Translations by Modern Italian Poets, 1900–2012

1. *Poets*

Since this is the first complete catalogue of translations published by a selection of modern Italian poets, I have tried to err on the side of inclusion, rather than exclusion. There are 251 poets included, 154 of whom have translated volumes. Spanning more than a century, the catalogue of Italian poets begins chronologically with Giovanni Pascoli (b. 1855) and ends with Paolo Maccari (b. 1975). I have included all of the poets from the following eleven anthologies:

- *Lirica del Novecento*. Edited by L. Anceschi and S. Antonielli. Florence: Vallecchi, 1953.
- *Antologia della poesia italiana. 1909–1959*. Edited by G. Spagnoletti. Parma: Guanda, 1959.
- *Poesia italiana del Novecento*. Edited by E. Sanguineti. Turin: Einaudi, 1969.
- *Donne in poesie. Antologia della poesia femminile in Italia dal dopoguerra*. Edited by B. Frabotta. Rome: Savelli, 1976.
- *Poeti italiana del Novecento*. Edited by P.V. Mengaldo. Milan: Mondadori, 1978.
- *Poesia italiana del Novecento*. Edited by P. Gelli and G. Lagorio. Milan: Garzanti, 1980.
- *Poeti dialettali del Novecento*. Edited by F. Brevini. Turin: Einaudi, 1987.
- *Poesia italiana del Novecento*. Edited by E. Krumm and T. Rossi. Milan: Mondadori, 1995.
- *Poeti italiani del secondo Novecento*. Edited by M. Cucchi and S. Giovanardi. Milan: Mondadori, 1996.
- *Antologia della poesia italiana. Novecento*. Edited by C. Ossola and C. Segre. Turin: Einaudi, 1999.
- *Parola plurale. Sessantaquattro poeti italiani fra due secoli*. Edited by G. Alfano, A. Baldacci, C.B. Minciacchi, A. Cortellessa, M. Manganelli, R. Scarpa, F. Zinelli, and P. Zublena. Rome: Sossella, 2005.

2. *Translations*

This bibliography includes the following translations:
i) Published translations (including chapbooks).
This bibliography does not include the following:
a) Unpublished works.
b) Translations published in newspapers or magazines.
c) Translations published in anthologies.
d) Translations that are published with other original works in the same volume.
e) New, revised, or amplified editions of previous published volumes with the same editor and the same title.
f) Translations with three or more attributed translators.

3. The main source for the translations is the online OPAC SBN catalogue of the Italian library system (opac.sbn.it). The first published editions are cited here whenever possible. Since the aim is not to describe the publishing history for the volumes themselves but rather to offer a comprehensive overview of all of the translations published by these poets, no further editions (revised or amplified) of translations are included, except when there is significant, new material translated.
4. 154 poets translated at least one book, and they are listed in the catalogue. The ninety-seven poets who did not publish a volume of translation are the following:

Libero Altomare [1883–1942]
Gaetano Arcangeli [1910–1970]
Gian Carlo Artoni [1923–]
Mariano Baino [1953–]
Raffaello Baldini [1924–2005]
Angelo Barile [1888–1967]
Luigi Bartolini [1892–1963]
Silvia Batisti [1949–]
Umberto Bellintani [1914–1999]
Mario Benedetti [1955–]
Ferruccio Benzoni [1949–1999]
Marco Berisso [1964–]
Alberto Bevilacqua [1934–2013]
Umberto Boccioni [1882–1916]
Vito M. Bonito [1963–]
Lorenzo Calogero [1910–1961]
Ernesto Calzavara [1907–2000]
Dino Campana [1885–1932]
Antonella Carosella [1948–]
Anna Cascella [1941–]
Bartolo Cattafi [1922–1979]
Enrico Cavacchioli [1885–1954]
Luciano Cecchinel [1947–]
Carolus L. Cergoly [1908–1987]
Carlo Chiaves [1883–1919]
Vittorio Clemente [1895–1975]
Girolamo Comi [1890–1968]
Sergio Corazzini [1886–1907]
Michelangelo Coviello [1950–]
Stefano dal Bianco [1961–]
Claudio Damiani [1957–]
Gabriele D'Annunzio [1863–1938]
Eugenio De Signoribus [1947–]
Nino De Vita [1950–]

Lorenzo Durante [1959–]
Farfa [Vittorio Tommasini] [1881–1964]
Paolo Febbraro [1965–]
Fillia [Luigi Colombo] [1904–1936]
Edoardo Firpo [1889–1957]
Luciano Folgore [1888–1966]
Enrico Fracassi [1902–1924]
Giovanna Frene [1968–]
Florinda Fusco [1972–]
Paolo Gentiluomo [1964–]
Vera Gherarducci [1928–1979]
Luca Ghiselli [1910–1939]
Corrado Govoni [1884–1965]
Guido Gozzano [1883–1916]
Franca Grisoni [1945–]
Francesco Leonetti [1924–]
Fabrizio Lombardo [1968–]
Gian Pietro Lucini [1867–1914]
Paolo Maccari [1975–]
Giancarlo Majorino [1928–]
Anna Malfaiera [1926–1997]
Sandra Mangini [1940–]
Alda Merini [1931–2009]
Carlo Michelstaedter [1887–1910]
Giampiero Neri [1927–]
Luciana Notari [1944–]
Giacomo Noventa [1898–1960]
Rossana Ombres [1931–2009]
Tommaso Ottonieri [1958–]
Nino Oxilia [1888–1917]
Pinin Pacot [1899–1964]
Remo Pagnanelli [1955–1987]
Enrico Pea [1881–1958]
Nino Pedretti [1923–1981]
Giuseppe Piccoli [1949–1987]
Lucio Piccolo [1901–1969]
Rosa Pierno [1959–]
Michele Pierri [1899–1988]
Albino Pierro [1916–1995]
Antonio Maria Pinto [1955–]
Antonia Pozzi [1912–1938]
Paolo Prestigiacomo [1947–1992]
Emilio Rentocchini [1949–]
Vittorio Reta [1947–1977]
Tiziano Rossi [1935–]
Roberto Roversi [1923–2012]
Umberto Saba [1883–1957]
Beppe Salvia [1954–1985]
Gregorio Scalise [1939–]
Scipione [1904–1933]
Rocco Scotellaro [1923–1953]
Gabriella Sica [1950–]
Sandro Sinigaglia [1921–1990]
Michele Sovente [1948–2011]
Aldo Spallicci [1886–1973]
Delio Tessa [1886–1939]
Eugenio Tomiolo [1911–2003]
Trilussa [1871–1950]
Giacomo Trinci [1960–]
Gian Mario Villalta [1959–]
Lello Voce [1957–]
Paolo Volponi [1924–1994]
Valentino Zeichen [1938–].

BIBLIOGRAPHY OF 154 MODERN ITALIAN POET-TRANSLATORS

Elio Filippo Accrocca, 1923–1996

1. Beniuc, Mihai. *La vita della vita.* Co-translated by Dragos Vrănceanu. Rome: Edizioni Rapporti Europei, 1962.
2. Jebeleanu, Eugen. *Il sorriso di Hiroshima e altre poesie.* Co-translated by Dragos Vrănceanu. Parma: Guanda, 1970.

Sibilla Aleramo, 1875–1960

1. La Fayette, Madame de. *La principessa di Cleves.* Milan: Mondadori, 1934.
2. Musset, Alfred de, and George Sand. *Le lettere di Alfred de Musset e George Sand.* Rome: La Bussola, 1945.

Antonella Anedda, 1958–

1. Jaccottet, Philippe. *Appunti per una semina: poesie e prose.* Rome: Fondazione Piazzolla, 1994.
2. *Nomi distanti.* Rome: Empiria, 1998.
3. Jaccottet, Philippe. *La parola Russia.* Rome: Donzelli, 2004.
4. Carle, Barbara. *Non guastare la mia bellezza.* Co-translated by Barbara Carle. Marina di Minturno: Caramanica, 2006.
5. Anvar, Leili. *Malek Jan Ne'mati: la vita non è breve ma il nostro tempo è limitato.* Rome: Empiria, 2010.

Riccardo Bacchelli, 1891–1985

1. Urfé, Honoré d'. *La Fontana dell'Amor verace.* Milan: Mondadori, 1934.
2. Voltaire. *Romanzi e racconti.* Milan: Mondadori, 1938.
3. Baudelaire, Charles. *Lo spleen di Parigi e altre traduzioni da Baudelaire.* Milan: Garzanti, 1947.
4. *Traduzioni.* Milan: Mondadori, 1964.

Tolmino Baldassari, 1927–2010

1. *Quaderno di traduzioni.* Forlì: Nuova compagnia editrice, 1990.
2. García Lorca, Federico. *Maria Maddalena e altri inediti.* Forlì: Nuova compagnia editrice, 1991.

Nanni Balestrini, 1935–

1. Simon, Claude. *Trittico.* Turin: Einaudi, 1975.
2. Lyotard, Jean-François. *Il muro del Pacifico.* Milan: Multipla, 1985.
3. Beckett, Samuel. *Soprassalti.* Carnago: SugerCo, 1992.
4. Jandl, Ernst. *Altrove: opera parlata in sette scene.* Udine: Campanotto, 1995.

Fernando Bandini, 1931–

1. Virgil. *Tre ecloghe.* Vicenza: Neri Pozza, 1981.
2. Horace. *Il libro degli epodi.* Venice: Marsilio, 1992.
3. Murer, Franco. *Memoire di Arthur Rimbaud.* Treviso: Antiga, 1992.
4. Baudelaire, Charles. *I fiori del male.* Milan: Nuages, 1994.
5. Arnaut Daniel. *Sirventese e canzoni.* Turin: Einaudi, 2000.
6. Rimbaud, Arthur. *Le bateau ivre.* Vicenza: Errepidueveneto, 2007.

Giorgio Bassani, 1916–2000

1. Voltaire. *Vita privata di Federico II*. Rome: Atlantica, 1945.
2. Cain, James M. *Il postino suona sempre due volte*. Milan: Bompiani, 1945.

Dario Bellezza, 1944–1995

1. Bataille, Georges. *Simona: Histoire de l'oeil*. Rome: L'airone, 1969.
2. Bataille, Georges. *Madame Edwarda*. Rome: L'airone, 1972.
3. Rimbaud, Arthur. *Poesie*. Milan: Garzanti, 1977.
4. Rimbaud, Arthur. *Opere in versi e in prosa*. Milan: Garzanti, 1989.

Giovanna Bemporad, 1928–2013

1. Novalis. *Inni alla notte*. Brescia: Morcelliana, 1952.
2. Goethe, Johann Wolfgang von, and Charles Du Bos. *Trilogia della passione/ L'ultimo amore di Goethe/L'elegia di Marienbad*. Brescia: Morcelliana, 1952.
3. Hofmannsthal, Hugo von. *Elettra*. Florence: Vallecchi, 1956.
4. *Gli eroi: antologia dell'epica per la scuola media*. Bologna: Patron, 1963.
5. Homer. *Odissea*. Turin: ERI, 1968.
6. Virgil. *Dall'Eneide*. Milan: Rusconi, 1983.
7. Novalis. *Inni alla notte; Canti spirituali*. Milan: Garzanti, 1986.
8. *Cantico dei cantici*. Brescia: Morcelliana, 2006.

Attilio Bertolucci, 1911–2000

1. Balzac, Honoré de. *La ragazza dagli occhi d'oro*. Guanda: Parma, 1946.
2. Lawrence, D.H. *Classici americani*. Milan: Bompiani, 1948.
3. Peacock, Thomas Love. *L'abbazia degli incubi*. Guanda: Parma, 1952.
4. Hemingway, Ernest. *Verdi colline d'Africa*. Co-translated by Aldo Rossi. Turin: Einaudi, 1953.
5. Baudelaire, Charles. *I fiori del male*. Milan: Garzanti, 1975.
6. *Imitazioni*. Milan: Scheiwiller, 1994.

Carlo Betocchi, 1899–1986

1. Lafon, André. *Mattutino: L'élève Gilles*. Milan: Istituto di Propoganda Libreria, 1936.
2. Thérèse of Lisieux. *Poesie di Santa Teresa di Lisieux*. Milan: Editrice Ancora, 1968.

Mariella Bettarini, 1942–

1. Weil, Simone. *Lettera ad un religioso. Risposta alla Lettera ad un religioso*. Co-translated by Carmen Montesano. Turin: Borla, 1970.

Elisa Biagini, 1970–

1. Olds, Sharon. *Satana dice*. Florence: Le lettere, 2002.
2. Clifton, Lucille. *Un certo Gesù*. Milan: Medusa, 2005.
3. Haddon, Mark. *Il cavallo parlante e la ragazza triste e il villaggio sotto il mare*. Turin: Einaudi, 2005.
4. *Nuovi poeti americani*. Turin: Einaudi, 2006.
5. Harding, Stephan. *Terra vivente: scienza, intuizione e gaia*. San Sepolcro: Aboca, 2008.
6. Dickinson, Emily. *"Ho sentito la vita con entrambe le mani."* Co-translated by Domenico de Martino. Milan: Biblion, 2010.

Libero Bigiaretti, 1905–1993

1. Becque, Henri. *La parigina*. Rome: Delfino, 1945.
2. Flaubert, Gustave. *Madame Bovary*. Turin: Einaudi, 1949.
3. Gide, André. *La scuola delle mogli*. Milan: Mondadori, 1949.
4. Maupassant, Guy de. *Pietro e Giovanni*. Milan: Feltrinelli, 1952.
5. Giraudoux, Jean. *La bugiarda*. Milan: Mondadori, 1970.
6. Stevenson, R.L. *L'isola del tesoro*. Florence: Giunti-Marzocco, 1977.
7. Twain, Mark. *Le avventure di Tom Sawyer*. Florence: Giunti-Marzocco, 1984.
8. Verne, Jules. *Il giro del mondo in 80 giorni*. Florence: Giunti-Marzocco, 1987.
9. Verne, Jules. *Le tribolazioni di un cinese in Cina*. Florence: Giunti-Marzocco, 1989.

Piero Bigongiari, 1914–1997

1. Rilke, Rainer Maria. *Poesie francesi*. Co-translated by Giorgio Zampa. Milan: E. Cederna, 1948.
2. *Il vento d'ottobre: da Alcmane a Dylan Thomas*. Milan: Mondadori, 1961.

Giovanni Boine, 1887–1917

1. *Traduzioni inedite da R. Llull e dal Lazarillo*. Fiesole: Opus libri, 1984.
2. Boine, Giovanni. *Inediti: appunti per un articolo sulla psciologia e del misticismo. Traduzione di un capitolo di Arische Weltanschauung*. Rome: Bulzoni, 1987.

Massimo Bontempelli, 1878–1960

1. Tillier, Claude. *Lo zio Beniamino*. Florence: Casa editrice italiana, 1911.
2. Stendhal. *Il rosso e il nero*. Milan: Istituto Editoriale Italiano, 1913.
3. De Quincey, Thomas. *L'assassinio come una delle belle arti*. Milan: Istituto Editoriale Italiano, 1916.
4. Stendhal. *Dell'amore*. Milan: Istituto Editoriale Italiano, 1916.
5. Courier, Paul Louis. *Scritti di battaglia*. Milan: Istituto Editoriale Italiano, 1917.
6. Renard, Jules. *Storie naturali*. Milan: Istituto Editoriale Italiano, 1917.

7. Taine, Hippolyte. *Lettere*. Milan: Istituto Editoriale Italiano, 1917.
8. Constant, Benjamin. *Adolfo*. Milan: Bietti, 1923.
9. Molière. *L'avaro*. Macerata: Bisson e Leopardi, 1925.
10. Gautier, Theodore. *Il capitano Fracassa*. Milan: Istituto Editoriale Italiano, 1927.
11. Dumas, Alexandre. *La signora dalle camelie*. Florence: G. Barbera, 1928.
12. Chateaubriand, François-René de. *Atala; Renato; Le avventure dell'ultimo Abenceragio*. Milan: Mondadori, 1931.
13. Sartre, Jean-Paul. *Le Mosche; Porta chiusa*. Co-translated by Giuseppe Lanza. Milan: Bompiani, 1947.
14. Montherlant, Henri de. *Il gran maestro di Santiago; La regina morta; Malatesta*. Co-translated by Camillo Sbarbaro. Milan: Bompiani, 1952.
15. *Cantico dei cantici*. Venice: Neri Pozza, 1952.
16. Mauriac, François. *Le vie del mare; Il male implacabile*. Co-translated by Renzo Tian. Milan: Verona, 1957.
17. *Traduzioni dalla Bibbia*. Milan: Mondadori, 1971.
18. Apuleius. *L'asino d'oro: le metamorfosi*. Milan: Longanesi, 1972.
19. *Apocalisse di Giovanni*. Milan: SE, 1987.
20. *Il Vangelo di San Giovanni; Lettere di Giovanni*. Co-translated by Salvatore Quasimodo. Milan: SE, 1989.
21. Tacitus. *La Germania*. Milan: SE, 1990.
22. Apuleius. *Amore e psiche*. Palermo: Sellerio, 1992.
23. *Il libro di Giobbe*. Milan: SE, 2009.

Aldo Borlenghi, 1913–1978

1. Israel, Esther Joffe. *Vagone piombato*. Milan: Mondadori, 1949.
2. Poulaille, Henri. *I dannati della terra*. Milan: Mondadori, 1949.

Silvia Bre, 1953–

1. Labé, Louise. *Il canzoniere*. Milan: Mondadori, 2000.
2. Manguel, Alberto. *Stevenson sotto le palme*. Rome: Nottetempo, 2007.
3. Lurie, Alison. *Verita e conseguenze*. Rome: Nottetempo, 2008.
4. Manguel, Alberto. *L'amante puntiglioso*. Rome: Nottetempo, 2009.
5. Connell, Rebecca. *L'arte di dirsi addio*. Turin: Einaudi, 2010.
6. Dickinson, Emily. *Centoquattro poesie*. Turin: Einaudi, 2011.
7. Walker, Alice. *Non restare muti*. Rome: Nottetempo, 2011.
8. Alderman, Naomi. *Senza toccare il fondo*. Rome: Nottetempo, 2011.

Franco Buffoni, 1948–

1. Barthelme, Donald. *Snow White*. Co-translated by Giancarlo Bonacina. Milan: Bompiani, 1972.

2. Graubard, Stephen. *Kissinger: ritratto di una mente*. Milan: Garzanti, 1974.
3. Keats, John. *Sonno e poesia*. Milan: Guanda, 1981.
4. Byron, George Gordon. *Manfred*. Milan: Guanda, 1984.
5. Coleridge, Samuel Taylor. *La ballata del vecchio marinaio*. Milan: Mondadori, 1987.
6. Kipling, Rudyard. *Ballate delle baracche e altre poesie*. Milan: Mondadori, 1989.
7. *Poeti romantici inglesi*. Milan: Bompiani, 1990.
8. Heaney, Seamus. *Scavando: poesie scelte (1966–1990)*. Rome: Fondazione Piazzolla, 1991.
9. Wilde, Oscar. *Ballata del carcere e altre poesie*. Milan: Mondadori, 1991.
10. *Songs of spring: quaderno di traduzione*. Milan: Marcos y Marcos, 1999.
11. *Una piccola tabaccheria*. Milan: Marcos y Marcos, 2012.
12. Byron, George Gordon. *I giullari del tempo*. Milan: Corriere della Sera, 2012.
13. Shelley, Percy Bysshe. *Con un fruscio d'ali*. Milan: Corriere della Sera, 2012.

Paolo Buzzi, 1874–1956

1. Baudelaire, Charles. *I fiori del male*. Milan: Istituto Editoriale Italiano, 1917.
2. Nadeau, Maurice. *Antologia del surrealismo*. Rome: Macchia, 1948.

Cristina Campo, 1923–1977

1. Törne, Bengt de. *Conversazioni con Sibelius*. Florence: Monsalvato, 1943.
2. Mansfield, Katherine. *Una tazza di tè e altri racconti*. Turin: Frassinelli, 1944.
3. Mörike, Eduard. *Poesie*. Milan: E. Cederna, 1948.
4. Williams, William Carlos. *Il fiore e il nostro segno*. Milan: All'insegna del pesce d'oro, 1958.
5. Weil, Simone. *Venezia salva: tragedia in tre atti*. Brescia: Morcelliana, 1963.
6. Donne, John. *Poesie amorose; Poesie teologiche*. Turin: Einaudi, 1971.
7. Weil, Simone. *La Grecia e le intuizioni precristiane*. Co-translated by Margherita Harwell Pieracci. Milan: Rusconi, 1974.
8. *Detti e fatti dei Padri del deserto*. Co-translated by Piero Draghi. Milan: Rusconi, 1975.
9. Koschel, Christine. *L' urgenza della luce: Cristina Campo traduce Christine Koschel*. Florence: Le lettere, 2004.

Giorgio Caproni, 1912–1990

1. Proust, Marcel. *Il tempo ritrovato*. Turin: Einaudi, 1951.
2. Baudelaire, Charles. *I fiori del male*. Rome: Curcio, 1962.
3. Char, René. *Poesie e prosa*. Milan: Feltrinelli, 1962.
4. Celine, Louis-Ferdinand, *Morte a credito*. Milan: Garzanti, 1964.
5. Maupassant, Guy de. *Bel-Ami*. Milan: Garzanti, 1965.

6. Cendrars, Blaise. *La mano mozza*. Milan: Garzanti, 1967.
7. Frénaud, André. *Il silenzio di Genova e altre poesie*. Turin: Einaudi, 1967.
8. Frénaud, André. *Non c'è paradiso*. Milan: Rizzoli, 1971.
9. Genet, Jean. *Tutto il teatro*. Milan: Il Saggiatore, 1971.
10. Busch, Wilhelm. *Max e Moritz ovvero Pippo e Peppo*. Milan: Rizzoli, 1974.
11. Genet, Jean. *Quattro romanzi e Diario del ladro*. Milan: Il Saggiatore, 1975.
12. Apollinaire, Guillaume. *Poesie*. Milan: Rizzoli, 1979.
13. Genet, Jean. *Querelle de Brest e Pompe funebre*. Milan: Mondadori, 1981.
14. *Quaderno di traduzioni*. Turin: Einaudi, 1998.

Vincenzo Cardarelli, 1887–1959

1. Diderot, Denis. *Ironie morali*. Milan: Facchi, 1919.

Roberto Carifi, 1948–

1. Rilke, Rainer Maria. *Poesie francesi*. Milan: Crocetti, 1989.
2. Michon, Pierre. *Padroni e servitori*. Parma: Guanda, 1990.
3. Prévert, Jacques. *Alberi*. Parma: Guanda, 1990.
4. Maunick, Edouard. *Poesie*. Milan: Jaca Book, 1992.
5. Trakl, Georg. *Canto del dipartito e altre poesie*. Florence: Le Lettere, 1992.
6. Racine, Jean. *Fedra*. Milan: Feltrinelli, 1993.
7. Weil, Simone. *Poesie*. Florence: Le Lettere, 1993.
8. Flaubert, Gustave. *Madame Bovary*. Milan: Feltrinelli, 1994.
9. Bataille, Georges. *L'arcangelico*. Florence: Le Lettere, 1995.
10. Saint-Pierre, Bernardin de. *Paul e Virginie*. Milan: Bompiani, 1995.
11. Prévert, Jacques. *Graffiti*. Parma: Guanda, 1995.
12. Prévert, Jacques. *Quand'ero bambino*. Parma: Guanda, 1995.
13. Rousseau, Jean-Jacques. *Il contratto sociale*. Milan: Mondadori, 1997.
14. Hesse, Herman. *La maturità rende giovani*. Co-translated by Silvia Bini. Parma: Guanda, 2001.
15. Adunis. *La preghiera e la spada: scritti sulla cultura araba*. Parma: Guanda, 2002.
16. Rilke, Rainer Maria. *L'angelo e altre poesie*. Pistoia: Via del vento, 2003.
17. Trakl, Georg. *La notte e altre poesie*. Co-translated by Massimo Baldi. Pistoia: Via del vento, 2008.

Raffaele Carrieri, 1905–1994

1. Cendrars, Blaise. *Blaise Cendrars*. Milan: All'insegna del pesce d'oro, 1958.

Patrizia Cavalli, 1947–

1. Molière. *Anfitrione*. Milan: Feltrinelli, 1982.
2. Shakespeare, William. *Sogno d'una notte d'estate*. Turin: Einaudi, 1996.

Alessandro Ceni, 1957–

1. Coleridge, Samuel Taylor. *La ballata del vecchio marinaio*. Milan: Marcos y Marcos, 1983.
2. Poe, Edgar Allan. *Eureka*. Bologna: Cappelli, 1983.
3. Milton, John. *Lycidas*. Milan: Marcos y Marcos, 1984.
4. Brown, Charles Brockden. *Wieland, o La trasfomazione*. Pordenone: Studio Tesi, 1988.
5. Emerson, Ralph Waldo. *Il trascendalista e altri saggi scelti*. Co-translated by Roberto Mussapi. Milan: Mondadori, 1989.
6. Stowe, Harriet Beecher. *La capanna dello zio Tom*. Florence: Bulgarini, 1989.
7. Christie, Agatha. *Viaggiare è il mio peccato*. Milan: Oscar Mondadori, 1990.
8. *Fiabe irlandesi*. Florence: Bulgarini, 1990.
9. *Fiabe africane*. Florence: Bulgarini, 1991.
10. Blatty, William Peter. *Gemini killer*. Milan: Mondadori, 1992.
11. Campbell, Joseph. *Il volo dell'anitra selvatica: esplorazioni nella dimensione del mito*. Milan: Mondadori, 1994.
12. Shelby, Philip. *Oasi di sogni*. Co-translated by Mariagrazia Bianchi Oddera. Milan: Mondadori, 1994.
13. Shelley, Mary. *Frankenstein*. Torriana: Orsa maggiore, 1995.
14. Vassi, Marco. *La soluzione salina*. Parma: Guanda, 1995.
15. Wilde, Oscar. *Il critico come artista; L'anima dell'uomo sotto il socialismo*. Milan: Feltrinelli, 1995.
16. Stevenson, R.L. *Il ragazzo rapito*. Milan: Bompiani, 1996.
17. *Storie di fantasmi inglesi*. Milan: Mondadori, 1996.
18. Pierson, Melissa Holbrook. *Il veicolo perfetto*. Milan: TEA, 2000.
19. Wharton, Edith. *Xingu*. Florence: Passigli, 2001.
20. Conrad, Joseph. *Lord Jim*. Milan: Feltrinelli, 2002.
21. Carroll, Lewis. *Le avventure di Alice nel paese delle meraviglie* e *Al di là dello specchio*. Turin: Einaudi, 2003.
22. Lawrence, D.H. *Biglietti, prego: cinque racconti di donne*. Florence: Passigli, 2003.
23. Lawrence, D.H. *Oscenità e pornografia*. Florence: Passigli, 2004.
24. Melville, Herman. *Il paradiso dei celibi: tre racconti doppi*. Florence: Passigli, 2005.
25. De Quincey, Thomas. *Il vendicatore*. Florence: Passigli, 2006.
26. Melville, Herman. *Moby Dick*. Milan: Feltrinelli, 2007.
27. Conrad, Joseph. *La linea d'ombra*. Milan: BUR, 2008.
28. Wharton, Edith. *L'età dell'innocenza*. Milan: BUR, 2008.
29. Melville, Herman. *Billy Budd*. Milan: Feltrinelli, 2009.
30. Whitman, Walt. *Foglie d'erba: la prima edizione del 1855*. Milan: Feltrinelli, 2012.

Giorgio Cesarano, 1928–1975

1. Langer, Walter C. *Psicanalisi di Hitler: rapporto segreto del tempo di guerra.* Milan: Garzanti, 1975.
2. Rousseau, Jean-Jacques. *Le confessioni.* Milan: Garzanti, 1994.

Gianfranco Ciabatti, 1936–1994

1. Dürrenmatt, Friedrich. *Lo scrittore nel tempo. Scritti su letteratura, teatro e cinema.* Co-translated by Brigitte Baumbusch. Turin: Einaudi, 1982.

Elena Clementelli, 1923–

1. *Antologia del canto flamenco.* Parma: Guanda, 1961.
2. Otero, Blas de. *Poesie.* Parma: Guanda, 1962.
3. *Antologia del blues.* Co-translated by Walter Mauro. Parma: Guanda, 1965.
4. Goytisolo, Juan. *Le terre di Nijar.* Milan: Feltrinelli, 1965.
5. Alberti, Rafael. *La tartaruga 427: poesie e disegni di Rafael Alberti.* Rome: Eutro, 1966.
6. *Negro spirituals.* Co-translated by Walter Mauro. Parma: Guanda, 1966.
7. Otero, Blas de. *Que trata de España.* Parma: Guanda, 1967.
8. Triana, Jose. *La notte degli assassini; La vita prestata.* Rome: Carte Segrete, 1967.
9. *Fados.* Parma: Guanda, 1969.
10. Allsop, Kenneth. *Ribelli vagabondi nell'America dell'ultima frontiera.* Bari: Laterza, 1969.
11. Franqui, Carlos. *Il cerchio di pietra.* Parma: Guanda, 1972.
12. Toynbee, Arthur. *La città aggressiva.* Bari: Laterza, 1972.
13. Carpentier, Alejo. *Il ricorso del metodo.* Rome: Editori rinuiti, 1976.
14. Bioy Casares, Adolfo. *L'avventura di un fotografo a La Plata.* Rome: Editori riuniti, 1987.
15. Ocampo, Silvia. *La penna magica e altri racconti.* Rome: Editori riuniti, 1989.
16. García Lorca, Federico. *Tutto il teatro.* Rome: Newton Compton, 1993.
17. Perez Galdos, Benito. *La donna di denari.* Milan: Frassinelli, 1993.
18. *Il fiore della libertà.* Co-translated by Walter Mauro. Rome: Newton Compton, 1993.
19. Ibáñez, Vicente Blasco. *Sangue e arena.* Rome: Newton Compton, 1995.
20. *Blues, spiritual, folk songs.* Rome: Newton Compton, 1996.
21. *Questa grande umanità.* Co-translated by Igor Bertello. Rome: Newton Compton, 1997.
22. Guevara, Ernesto. *Ideario.* Rome: Newton Compton, 2002.
23. Guevara, Ernesto. *Poesie e scritti sulla letteratura e arte.* Rome: Newton Compton, 1999.
24. García Lorca, Federico. *Tutte le poesie e tutto il teatro.* Co-translated by Claudio Rendina. Rome: Newton Compton, 2009.

Giuseppe Conte, 1945–

1. Lawrence, D.H. *La donna che fuggì a cavallo*. Milan: Feltrinelli, 1981.
2. Lawrence, D.H. *Poesie*. Milan: Mondadori, 1987.
3. Shelley, Percy Bysshe. *Poesie*. Milan: Rizzoli, 1989.
4. Rezvani, Serge. *L'ottavo flagello*. Milan: Rizzoli, 1991.
5. Whitman, Walt. *Foglie d'erba: scelta*. Milan: Mondadori, 1991.
6. Whitman, Walt. *O Capitano! Mio capitano!* Milan: Mondadori, 1995.

Rosita Copioli, 1948–

1. Yeats, W.B. *Il crepuscolo celtico*. Rome: Theoria, 1987.
2. Yeats, W.B. *Anima mundi*. Parma: Guanda, 1988.
3. Yeats, W.B. *La rosa segreta: i racconti*. Parma: Guanda, 1995.
4. Goethe, Johann Wolfgang von. *Gli anni di viaggio di Wilhelm Meister, o I Rinuncianti*. Milan: Medusa, 2005.
5. Sappho. *Più oro dell'oro*. Milan: Medusa, 2006.

Maurizio Cucchi, 1945–

1. Illich, Ivan. *La convivialità*. Milan: Mondadori, 1974.
2. Mallarmé, Stéphane. *Un colpo di dadi mai abolirà il caso*. Verona: Ampersand, 1976.
3. Prévert, Jacques. *Poesie*. Co-translated by Giovanni Raboni. Parma: Guanda, 1979.
4. Flaubert, Gustave. *Novembre*. Rome: Editori Riuniti, 1981.
5. Prévert, Jacques. *Le foglie morte*. Milan: Guanda, 1981.
6. Renoir, Jean. *Il delitto dell'Inglese*. Rome: Editori Riuniti, 1983.
7. Poe, Edgar Allan. *Il corvo e altre poesie*. Co-translated by Silvana Colonna. Milan: Mondadori, 1986.
8. Villiers de l'Isle-Adam, Auguste. *Racconti crudeli*. Rome: Editori Riuniti, 1987.
9. Lamartine, Alphonse de. *Meditazioni e altre poesie*. Milan: Mondadori, 1990.
10. Brassens, Georges. *Poesie e canzoni*. Parma: Guanda, 1994.
11. Stendhal. *Romanzi e racconti*, vol. 1. Milan: Mondadori, 1996.
12. Stendhal. *Romanzi e racconti*, vol. 2. Milan: Mondadori, 2002.
13. Balzac, Honoré de. *Papa Goriot*. Rome: Repubblica, 2004.
14. Stendhal. *Romanzi e racconti*, vol. 3. Milan: Mondadori, 2008.
15. Malherbe, François de. *Le lacrime di S. Pietro*. Milan: Lampi di stampa, 2009.

Beniamino Dal Fabbro, 1910–1989

1. Rodenbach, Georges. *Il regno del silenzio*. Milan: Industrie grafiche Pietro Vera, 1942.
2. Valéry, Paul. *Gli incanti*. Milan: Bompiani, 1942.

3. *La sera armoniosa*. Milan: Rosa e Ballo, 1944.
4. Flaubert, Gustave. *L'educazione sentimentale*. Turin: Einaudi, 1944.
5. Mallarmé, Stéphane. *Il demone dell'analogia*. Milan: Garotto, 1944.
6. Baudelaire, Charles. *Lettere alla madre*. Milan: Bompiani, 1945.
7. Breton, André. *Primo manifesto del surrealismo*. Venice: Edizioni del Cavallino, 1945.
8. Flaubert, Gustave. *Novembre*. Milan: A. Minuziano, 1945.
9. Proust, Marcel. *Malinconica villeggiatura*. Milan: A. Minuziano, 1945.
10. Rousseau, Jean-Jacques. *Le passeggiate solitarie*. Milan: Bompiani, 1945.
11. Alain. *Sistema delle arti*. Milan: Muggiani, 1947.
12. Rilke, Rainer Maria. *Le rose*. Milan: All'insegna del pesce d'oro, 1947.
13. Camus, Albert. *La peste*. Milan: Bompiani, 1948.
14. Supervielle, Jules. *Il ladro di ragazzi; Il sopravvissuto*. Co-translated by Vasco Pratolini. Milan: Bompiani, 1949.
15. Valéry, Paul. *Poesie*. Milan: Feltrinelli, 1960.
16. Peret, Benjamin. *Il disonore dei poeti*. Milan: Contra, 1965.
17. Valéry, Paul. *Degas danza disegno*. Milan: Feltrinelli, 1980.
18. Valéry, Paul. *Scritti su Leonardo*. Milan: Electa, 1984.

Milo de Angelis, 1951–

1. Blanchot, Maurice. *L'attesa l'oblio*. Milan: Guanda, 1978.
2. Baudelaire, Charles. *I paradisi artificiali*. Milan: Guanda, 1978.
3. Claudianus, Claudius. *Il rapimento di Proserpina*. Milan: Marcos y Marcos, 1984.
4. Maeterlinck, Maurice. *Serre calde; Quindici canzoni*. Milan: Mondadori, 1989.
5. Drieu La Rochelle, Pierre. *Diario di un delicato*. Milan: SE, 1998.
6. Lucretius Carus, Titus. *Passi scelti dal De Rerum Natura*. Milan: Satyros, 2001.
7. Lucretius Carus, Titus. *Sotto la scure silenziose: frammenti del De Rerum natura*. Milan: SE, 2005.
8. *L' amore, il vino, la morte: epigrammi dall' antologia palatina*. Milan: SE, 2005.

Gianni D'Elia, 1953–

1. Jabès, Edmond. *L'inferno di Dante*. Siena: Taccuini di Barbablù, 1987.
2. *Taccuino francese*. Siena: Edizioni di Barbablù, 1990.
3. Gide, André. *I nutrimenti terrestri*. Turin: Einaudi, 1994.
4. Baudelaire, Charles. *Lo spleen di Parigi*. Turin: Einaudi, 1997.

Libero de Libero, 1906–1981

1. Apollinaire, Guillaume. *Pittori cubisti. Meditazioni estetiche*. Rome: Edizioni del Secolo, 1944.

2. Huysman, J.K. *Qualcuno: Degas, Cezanne, Forain, Wisthler, Rops, Delacroix, Ingres*. Rome: Edizioni del Secolo, 1944.
3. Green, Julien. *Diario: 1928–1934*. Vol. 1. Milan: Mondadori, 1946.
4. Green, Julien. *Diario: 1935–1939*. Vol. 2. Milan: Mondadori, 1946.

Mario dell'Arco, 1905–1996

1. Martial. *Marziale per un mese*. Rome: M. Dell'Arco, 1963.
2. Catullus, Gaius Valerius, Horace, and Martial. *Il dolce far niente: Catullo Orazio Marziale arromanescati da Mario dell'Arco*. Rome: Il nuovo Cracas, 1964.
3. Martial. *Lasciatemi divertire, ovvero Marziale per un altro mese*. Rome: Laziografik, 1972.

Filippo De Pisis, 1896–1956

1. Barthelou, Maurice. *Il verbo di Bodhisattva*. Ferrara: A. Taddei, 1917.

Luciano Erba, 1922–2010

1. Laloup, Jean. *Uomini e macchine*. Milan: Massimo, 1956.
2. Bryen, Camille. *Poèmes et dessins. Jepeinsje*. Milan: All'insegna del pesce d'oro, 1959.
3. Cendrars, Blaise. *Antologia lirica*. Milan: Nuova Accademia, 1961.
4. Barth, John. *Giles ragazzo-capra*. Milan: Rizzoli, 1972.
5. Gunn, Thom. *Tatto*. Milan: Guanda, 1979.
6. *Dei cristalli naturali e altri versi tradotti: 1950–1990*. Milan: Guerini, 1991.

Luigi Fallacara, 1890–1963

1. Regnier, Henri de. *Racconti a sé stesso*. Florence: A. Quattrini, 1914.
2. Angela, da Foligno. *Il libro delle mirabili visioni e consolazioni*. Florence: Libreria Editrice Fiorentina, 1922.

Umberto Fiori, 1949–

1. Oakley, Giles. *La musica del diavolo: storia del blues*. Milan: Mazzotta, 1978.
2. Donovan. *Canzoni*. Rome: Lato side, 1980.
3. McCartney, Paul. *Blackbird Singing*. Milan: Mondadori, 2002.
4. Browning, Robert. *Il pifferaio magico di Hamelin*. Co-translated by Livia Brambilla. Milan: Topipittori, 2007.
5. Cohen, Leonard. *Il libro del desiderio*. Co-translated by Livia Brambilla. Milan: Mondadori, 2007.

Alessandro Fo, 1955–

1. Vernant, Jean Pierre. *Mito e tragedie due: da Edipo a Dioniso*. Co-translated by Clara Pavanello. Turin: Einaudi, 1991.

2. Rutilius Namatianus, Claudius. *Il ritorno*. Turin: Einaudi, 1992.
3. Apuleius. *Le metamorfosi, o L'asino d'oro*. Milan: Frassinelli, 2002.
4. Virgil. *Purché ci resti Mantova: le bucoliche 1 e 9*. Co-translated by Giorgio Bernardi Perini. Arezzo: Edizioni degli amici, 2002.

Franco Fortini, 1917–1994

1. Flaubert, Gustave. *Un cuore semplice*. Rome: Lettere d'Oggi, 1942.
2. Éluard, Paul. *Poesia ininterrotta*. Turin: Einaudi, 1947.
3. Ramuz, C.F. *Statura umana*. Milan: Edizioni di Comunità, 1947.
4. Doblin, Alfred. *Addio al Reno*. Co-translated by Ruth Leiser. Turin: Einaudi, 1949.
5. Gide, André. *Viaggio al Congo e ritorno dal Ciad*. Turin: Einaudi, 1950.
6. Brecht, Bertolt. *Madre coraggio e i suoi figli*. Turin: Einaudi, 1951.
7. Brecht, Bertolt. *Santa Giovanna dei Macelli*. Co-translated by Ruth Leiser. Turin: Einaudi, 1951.
8. Weil, Simone. *L'ombra e la Grazia*. Milan: Edizioni di Comunità, 1951.
9. Kierkegaard, Søren. *Timore e tremore*. Co-translated by Kirsten Montanari Gulbrandsen. Milan: Edizioni di Comunità, 1952.
10. Proust, Marcel. *Albertine scomparsa*. Turin: Einaud, 1952.
11. Weil, Simone. *La condizione operaia*. Milan: Edizioni di Comunità, 1952.
12. Proust, Marcel. *Jean Santeuil*. Turin: Einaudi, 1953.
13. Weil, Simone. *La prima radice*. Milan: Edizioni di Comunità, 1954.
14. Éluard, Paul. *Poesie*. Turin: Einaudi, 1955.
15. Einstein, Albert. *Idee e opinioni*. Milan: Schwarz, 1957.
16. Brecht, Bertolt. *Il romanzo da tre soldi*. Co-translated by Ruth Leiser. Turin: Einaudi, 1958.
17. Brecht, Bertolt. *Gli affari del signor Giulio Cesare e Storie da calendario*. Co-translated by Ruth Leiser. Turin: Einaudi, 1959.
18. Brecht, Bertolt. *Poesie e canzoni*. Co-translated by Ruth Leiser. Turin: Einaudi, 1959.
19. Queneau, Raymond. *Zazie nel metro*. Turin: Einaudi, 1960.
20. Goldmann, Lucien. *Pascal e Racine*. Co-translated by Luciano Amodio. Milan: Lerici, 1961.
21. Frénaud, André. *L'agonia del generale Krivitski*. Milan: Il Saggiatore, 1962.
22. Enzensberger, Hans Magnus. *Poesie per chi non legge poesie*. Milan: Feltrinelli, 1964.
23. Huchel, Peter. *Strade strade*. Co-translated by Ruth Leiser. Milan: Mondadori, 1970.
24. Goethe, Johann Wolfgang von. *Faust*. Milan: Mondadori, 1970.
25. Brecht, Bertolt. *Poesie di Svendborg*. Turin: Einaudi, 1976.

26. Döblin, Alfred. *Borghesi e soldati*. Co-translated by Ruth Leiser. Turin: Einaudi, 1982.
27. Fortini, Franco. *Il ladro di ciliegie e altre versioni di poesie*. Turin: Einaudi, 1982.
28. Proust, Marcel. *Poesie*. Turin: Einaudi, 1983.
29. Kafka, Franz. *Nella colonia penale e altri racconti*. Turin: Einaudi, 1986.

Biancamaria Frabotta, 1946–

1. Blandiana, Ana. *Un tempo gli alberi avevano occhi*. Co-translated by Bruno Mazzoni. Rome: Donzelli, 2004.

Gabriele Frasca, 1957–

1. Dick, Philip K. *Un oscuro scrutare*. Naples: Cronopio, 1993.
2. Beckett, Samuel. *Watt*. Turin: Einaudi, 1998.
3. Beckett, Samuel. *Le poesie*. Turin: Einaudi, 1999.
4. Beckett, Samuel. *Murphy*. Turin: Einaudi, 2003.
5. Beckett, Samuel. *In nessun modo ancora*. Turin: Einaudi, 2008.

Luciana Frezza, 1926–1992

1. Maurice, Martin. *William Shakespeare*. Milan: Rizzoli, 1955.
2. Magny, Claude Edmonde. *Romanzieri francesi del Novecento*. Milan: Feltrinelli, 1963.
3. Mallarmé, Stéphane. *Poesie*. Venice: Neri Pozza, 1963.
4. Laforgue, Jules. *Poesie*. Milan: Lerici, 1965.
5. Nouveau, Germain. *I baci e altre poesie*. Turin: Einaudi, 1972.
6. Verlaine, Paul. *Poesie*. Milan: Rizzoli, 1974.
7. Baudelaire, Charles. *I fiori del male*. Milan: Rizzoli, 1980.
8. Giraud, Albert. *Farfalle nere: rondo dal Pierre lunaire*. Rome: Edizioni dell'Elefante, 1980.
9. Fargue, Léon-Paul. *Poesie: 1886–1933*. Turin: Einaudi, 1981.
10. *Picasso e il Mediterraneo: Villa Medici, 27 novembre 1982 – 13 febbraio 1983*. Rome: Edizioni dell'Elefante, 1982.
11. Proust, Marcel. *Poesie*. Milan: Feltrinelli, 1993.

Marcello Frixione, 1960–

1. Smolensky, Paul. *Il Connessionismo: tra simboli e neuroni*. Genoa: Marietti, 1992.

Nicola Gardini, 1965–

1. Fletcher, Raffaella. *Caramelle pericolose*. Milan: Sperling and Kupfer, 1992.
2. Ovid. *Heroides*. Milan: Mondadori, 1994.
3. Ovid. *Tristia*. Milan: Mondadori, 1995.

4. Auden, W.H. *Un altro tempo*. Milan: Adelphi, 1997.
5. Hughes, Ted. *Fiori e insetti: qualche uccello e un paio di ragni*. Milan: Mondadori, 2000.
6. Dickinson, Emily. *Buongiorno notte*. Milan: Crocetti, 2001.
7. Marcus Aurelius. *Colloqui con sé stesso*. Milan: Medusa, 2005.
8. Woolf, Virginia. *Sulla malattia*. Turin: Bollati Boringhieri, 2006.
9. Hughes, Ted. *Poesie*. Co-translated by Anna Ravano. Milan: Mondadori, 2008.
10. Simic, Charles. *Club midnight*. Milan: Adelphi, 2008.

Alfonso Gatto, 1909–1976

1. Raspe, Rudolf Erich. *Avventure del Barone di Münchhausen*. Milan: Cooperativa Libro Popolare, 1950.

Amedeo Giacomini, 1939–2006

1. Paul, the Deacon. *Historia langobardorum*. Udine: Casamassima, 1967.
2. Le Clézio, J.M.G. *Terra amata*. Milan: Rizzoli, 1969.

Virgilio Giotti, 1885–1957

1. Esenin, Sergey. *Lettera alla madre*. Trieste: Arbor librorum, 2009.

Marco Giovenale, 1969–

1. Pirie, Madsen. *Come avere sempre ragione*. Milan: Ponte alle Grazie, 2011.

Giovanni Giudici, 1924–2011

1. Hitchcock, Henry Russell, and Arthur Drexler. *Architettura americana d'oggi*. Rome: De Luca, 1954.
2. Pound, Ezra. *Hugh Selwan Mauberley*. Milan: All'insegna del pesce d'oro, 1959.
3. Schlesinger Jr., Arthur. *Kennedy*. Milan: Edizioni di Comunità,1960.
4. Mansell, Gerard. *La tragedia d'Algeria*. Milan: Edizioni di Comunità, 1961.
5. Matthews, H.L. *La verità su Cuba*. Co-translated by Amerigo Guadagnin. Milan: Edizioni di Comunità, 1961.
6. Bronowski, Jacob, and Bruce Mazlish. *La tradizione intellettuale dell'Occidente da Leonardo a Hegel*. Milan: Edizioni di Comunità, 1962.
7. Chevalier, Haakon. *Cominciò ad Hiroshima*. Milan: Edizioni di Comunità, 1965.
8. Frost, Robert. *Conoscenza della notte e altre poesie*. Turin: Einaudi, 1965.
9. Crane, Hart. *Nei caraibi*. Milan: Scheiwiller, 1966.
10. Lidman, Sara. *Cinque diamanti*. Co-translated by Irene Tanzi. Milan: Rizzoli, 1966.

11. Wilson, Edmond. *Saggi letterari*. Co-translated by Giovanni Gualtieri. Milan: Garzanti, 1967.
12. Tynyanov, Yury. *Il problema del linguaggio poetico*. Co-translated by Ljudmila Kortikova. Milan: Il Saggiatore, 1968.
13. Orten, Jiří. *La cosa chiamata poesia*. Co-translated by Vladimír Mikeš. Turin: Einaudi, 1969.
14. Mao, Tse-tung. *Quattro poesie*. Co-translated by Margherita Guidacci. Milan: Scheiwiller, 1971.
15. Ransom, John Crowe. *Le donne e i cavalieri*. Milan: Mondadori, 1971.
16. Pushkin, Aleksandr. *Eugenio Onieghin*. Milan: Garzanti, 1975.
17. Plath, Sylvia. *Lady Lazarus e altre poesie*. Milan: Mondadori, 1976.
18. *Addio, proibito piangere*. Turin: Einaudi, 1982.
19. Ignatius, of Loyola. *Esercizi spirituali*. Milan: Mondadori, 1984.
20. Pushkin, Aleksandr. *Viaggio d'inverno e altre poesie*. Co-translated by Giovanna Spendel. Milan: Mondadori, 1985.
21. Coleridge, Samuel Taylor. *La rima del vecchio marinaio*. Milan: SE, 1987.
22. *A una casa non sua*. Milan: Mondadori, 1997.
23. Shakespeare, William. *14 X 14, dai sonetti di Shakespeare, tradotti da Giovanni Giudici*. Bocca di Magra: Edizioni Capannina, 2002.
24. *Vaga lingua strana*. Milan: Garzanti, 2003.

Alfredo Giuliani, 1924–2007

1. Eliot, T.S. *Sulla poesia e sui poeti*. Milan: Bompiani, 1960.
2. Robinson, Edwin Arlington. *Uomini e ombre*. Milan: Mondadori, 1965.
3. Mincu, Marin. *In agguato*. Co-translated by Marin Mincu. Milan: All'insegna del pesce d'oro, 1966.
4. *Poeti di Tel Quel*. Co-translated by Jacqueline Risset. Turin: Einaudi, 1968.
5. Michaux, Henri. *Un certo Piuma*. Milan: Bompiani, 1971.
6. Jonson, Ben. *Volpone*. Rome: Officina, 1977.
7. Shakespeare, William. *Pericle, principe di Tiro*. Genoa: Edizioni del Teatro di Genova, 1982.

Giuliano Gramigna, 1920–2006

1. Philippe, Charles-Louis. *Bubu de Montparnasse; Croquignole*. Milan: Garzanti, 1966.
2. Alain-Fournier. *Il grande Meaulnes*. Milan: Garzanti, 1981.

Adriano Grande, 1897–1972

1. Vigny, Alfred de. *Giornale di un poeta*. Rome: Ed. Della Bussola, 1944.
2. Sade, Marquis de. *La moglie pudica e altri racconti libertini*. Rome: Astrolabio, 1945.

3. Renard, Jules. *Romanzi e storie naturali.* Rome: Casini, 1952.
4. Bernanos, Georges. *Diario di un curato di campagna.* Verona: Mondadori, 1960.

Cesare Greppi, 1936–

1. Laforgue, Jules. *Il Concil féerique.* Varese: Magenta, 1965.
2. Bosquet, Alain. *Poesie.* Parma: Guanda, 1969.
3. Bourniquel, Camille. *Il lago.* Turin: Società editrice internazionale, 1970.
4. Góngora y Argote, Luis de. *Poesie.* Turin: Fogola, 1971.
5. Zumthor, Paul. *Il pozzo di Babele.* Turin: Società editrice internazionale, 1972.
6. Barthes, Roland. *Analisi strutturale ed esegesi biblica.* Turin: Società editrice internazionale, 1973.
7. Daix, Pierre. *La verità su Solzenitsyn.* Turin: Società editrice internazionale, 1974.
8. Castro, Josué de. *Uomini e granchi: romanzo verità.* Turin: Società editrice internazionale, 1974.
9. Salinas, Pedro. *Vigilia del piacere.* Turin: Einaudi, 1976.
10. Cortazar, Julio. *Tanto amore per Glenda.* Milan: Guanda, 1983.
11. Góngora y Argote, Luis de. *Solitudini.* Milan: Guanda, 1984.
12. Góngora y Argote, Luis de. *Sonetti.* Milan: Mondadori, 1985.
13. García Morales, Adelaida. *Il Sud e Bene.* Parma: Guanda, 1988.
14. Ronsard, Pierre de. *Amori.* Milan: Mondadori, 1990.
15. Bergamín, José. *L'arte del toreare e la sua musica silenziosa.* Milan: SE, 1992.
16. Bonnefoy, Yves. *Racconti in sogno.* Milan: EGEA, 1992.
17. Saint John of the Cross. *Fiamma d'amore viva.* Milan: SE, 1993.
18. Calderón de la Barca, Pedro. *Il veleno e l'antidoto.* Milan: SE, 1999.
19. Janes, Clara. *In un punto di quiete: fractales.* Milan: CUEM, 2000.
20. Ortega y Gasset, José. *La ribellione delle masse.* Milan: SE, 2001.
21. Lucretius Carus, Titus. *Domus: spazi di vita in antica Roma.* Milan: Medusa, 2007.
22. Fedier, François. *La voce dell'amico.* Milan: Marinotti, 2009.

Tonino Guerra, 1920–2012

1. *Lamento di una guardia di frontiera e altri lamenti.* Milan: Scheiwiller, 2000.

Adriano Guerrini, 1923–1985

1. Mallarmé, Stéphane. *Poesie e prose.* Co-translated by Valeria Ramacciotti. Milan: Garzanti, 1992.

Margherita Guidacci, 1921–1992

1. Beerbohm, Max. *L'ipocrita beato.* Florence: Vallecchi, 1946.
2. Donne, John. *Sermoni.* Florence: Libreria Editrice Fiorentina, 1946.

3. Dickinson, Emily. *Poesie*. Florence: Cya, 1947.
4. *Sacre rappresentazioni inglesi*. Florence: Libreria Editrice Fiorentina, 1950.
5. Mounier, Immanuel. *L'avventura cristiana*. Florence: Libreria Editrice Fiorentina, 1951.
6. Gissing, George. *Sulla riva dello Jonio*. Bologna: Cappelli, 1957.
7. Du, Fu. *Desiderio di pace*. Milan: Scheiwiller, 1957.
8. MacLeish, Archibald. *Quattro poesie*. Milan: Scheiwiller, 1958.
9. Pound, Ezra. *Patria mia*. Florence: Centro Internazionale del Libro, 1958.
10. Pound, Ezra. *Le Trachinie*. Florence: Centro Internazionale del Libro, 1958.
11. *Antichi racconti cinesi*. Bologna: Cappelli, 1959.
12. Guillén, Jorge. *Federico in persona: Carteggio*. Milan: Scheiwiller, 1960.
13. James, Henry. *Roderick Hudson*. Bologna: Cappelli, 1960.
14. Kluckhohn, Chuck. *Indiani Navajos*. Florence: Centro Internazionale del Libro, 1960.
15. Conrad, Joseph. *Destino*. Milan: Bompiani, 1961.
16. Dickinson, Emily. *Poesie e lettere*. Florence: Sansoni, 1961.
17. *Racconti popolari irlandesi*. Bologna: Cappelli, 1961.
18. Tao, Qian. *Poema per la bellezza della sua donna*. Milan: Scheiwiller, 1962.
19. Twain, Mark. *Vita sul Mississippi*. Rome: Opere Nuove, 1962.
20. Conrad, Joseph. *Racconti ascoltati; Ultimi saggi*. Milan: Bompiani, 1963.
21. Newman, John Henry. *Apologia pro vita sua*. Co-translated by Giovanni Veloci. Florence: Vallecchi, 1967.
22. Sitwell, Edith. *Autobiografia*. Milan: Rizzoli, 1968.
23. Mao, Tse-tung. *Quattro poesie*. Co-translated by Giovanni Giudici. Milan: Scheiwiller, 1971.
24. *Poeti estoni*. Co-translated by Vello Salo. Rome: ABETE, 1973.
25. Smart, Christopher. *Inno a David e altre poesie*. Turin: Einaudi, 1975.
26. John Paul II, Pope. *Pietra di luce*. Co-translated by Aleksandra Kurczab. Vatican City: Libreria Editrice Vaticana, 1979.
27. John Paul II, Pope. *Il sapore del pane: Poesie*. Co-translated by Aleksandra Kurczab. Vatican City: Libreria Editrice Vaticana, 1979.
28. *Due antichi poeti cinesi*. Milan: Scheiwiller, 1980.
29. Berenson, Bernard and Clotilde Marghieri. *Lo specchio doppio: carteggio 1927–1955*. Co-translated by Clotilde Marghieri. Milan: Rusconi, 1981.
30. Daly, Padraig J. *Dall'orlo marino del mondo*. Vatican City: Libreria Editrice Vaticana, 1981.
31. Milosz, Czeslaw. *Poesie del mondo illuminato*. Co-translated by Aleksandra Kurczab. Rome: Edizioni Prospettive del mondo, 1981.
32. Bishop, Elizabeth. *L'arte di perdere*. Milan: Rusconi, 1982.
33. Jewett, Sarah Orne. *Lady Ferry e altri racconti*. Milan: Donne, 1982.

34. John Paul II, Pope. *Giobbe e altri inediti: Un dramma e sei poesie.* Co-translated by Aleksandra Kurczab. Vatican City: Libreria Editrice Vaticana, 1982.
35. Powers, Jessica. *Luogo di splendore: Poesie.* Vatican City: Libreria Editrice Vaticana, 1982.
36. Feldman, Ruth. *Perdere la strada nel tempo: poesie scelte.* Venice: Edizioni del Leone, 1989.
37. Sitwell, Edith. *Una vita protetta.* Milan: SE, 1989.
38. Wilde, Oscar. *Il principe felice e altre bellissime fiabe.* Florence: Giunti-Nardini, 1989.
39. Guidacci, Margherita. *La voce dell'acqua: quaderno di traduzioni.* Edited by Giancarlo Battaglia and Ilaria Rabatti. Pistoia: C.R.T., 2002.

Armanda Guiducci, 1923–1992

1. Read, Herbert. *Il significato dell'arte.* Milan: Mondadori, 1962.
2. La Fayette, Madame de. *La principessa di Cleves.* Milan: Rizzoli, 1986.
3. Mansfield, Katherine. *Racconti.* Milan: Rizzoli, 1989.
4. Malinowski, Bronislaw. *Il padre nella psciologia primitiva.* Milan: Rizzoli, 1990.
5. Donne, John. *L'amore e il male.* Milan: Lanfranchi, 1996.

Riccardo Held, 1954–

1. Hugo, Victor. *Orientali.* Milan: Mondadori, 1985.
2. Rezvani, Serge. *Avevo un amico.* Naples: Cronopio, 1991.
3. Droogenbroodt, Germain. *Conosci il tuo paese?* Co-translated by Donatella Bisutti. Milan: Archivi del '900, 2001.

Andrea Inglese, 1967–

1. Vilton, Jean-Jacques. *Il commento definitivo: poesie 1884–2008.* Pesaro: Metauro, 2009.

Jolanda Insana, 1937–

1. Sappho. *Poesie.* Florence: Estro, 1985.
2. Shawqī, Aḥmad. *La passione di Cleopatra.* Co-translated by Francesca Corrao. Milan: Ubulibri, 1989.
3. Tvardovskiĭ, Aleksandr. *Per diritto di memoria.* Co-translated by Viviana Turova. Palermo: Acquario, 1989.
4. *Carmi priapei.* Milan: ES, 1991.
5. Le chapelain, André. *De amore.* Milan: ES, 1992.

Piero Jahier, 1884–1966

1. Halévy, Daniel. *Il castigo della democrazia.* Florence: Casa editrice italiana, 1911.

2. Calvin, John. *La religione individuale.* Lanciano: Carabba, 1912.
3. Claudel, Paul. *Partage de midi.* Florence: Libreria della Voce, 1912.
4. Claudel, Paul. *Arte poetica; Conoscenza del tempo; Trattato della conoscenza del mondo e di sé stesso.* Milan: Libreria editrice Milanese, 1913.
5. Proudhon, Pierre-Joseph. *La guerra e la pace.* Lanciano: Carabba, 1920.
6. Lin, Yutang. *Importanza di vivere.* Milan: Bompiani, 1939.
7. Lin, Yutang. *Il mio paese e il mio popolo.* Milan: Bompiani, 1940.
8. Lin, Yutang. *Momento a Pechino.* Milan: Bompiani, 1941.
9. Stevenson, R.L. *L'isola del tesoro.* Turin: Einaudi, 1943.
10. Shikibu, Murasaki. *La signora della barca e Il ponte dei sogni.* Milan: Bompiani, 1944.
11. Conrad, Joseph. *Racconti di mare e di costa.* Turin: Einaudi, 1946.
12. Conrad, Joseph. *Gioventù e altri racconti.* Milan: Bompiani, 1949.
13. Spender, Stephen. *Testimonianza europeai.* Milan: Bompiani, 1949.
14. Conrad, Joseph. *Appunti di vita e letteratura.* Co-translated by Maj-Lis Rissler Stoneman. Milan: Bompiani, 1950.
15. Collins, Wilkie. *La pietra lunare.* Co-translated by Maj-Lis Rissler Stoneman. Turin: Einaudi, 1953.
16. Greene, Graham. *La fine dell'avventura.* Co-translated by Maj-Lis Rissler Stoneman. Milan: Mondadori, 1953.
17. Molière. *Il borghese gentiluomo.* Turin: Einaudi, 1953.
18. Conrad, Joseph. *Lo specchio del mare.* Co-translated by Maj-Lis Rissler Stoneman. Turin: Einaudi, 1954.
19. Lin, Yutang. *La saggezza dell'America.* Milan: Bompiani, 1954.
20. Greene, Graham. *Le vie senza legge.* Co-translated by Maj-Lis Rissler Stoneman. Milan: Mondadori, 1955.
21. Hardy, Thomas. *Via dalla pazza folla.* Co-translated by Maj-Lis Rissler Stoneman. Milan: Garzanti, 1955.
22. Lin, Yutang. *Una vedova, Una monaca, Una corigiana e altre famose novelle cinesi.* Co-translated by Maj-Lis Rissler Stoneman. Milan: Bompiani, 1955.
23. *Chin P'ing Mei.* Co-translated by Maj-Lis Rissler Stoneman. Turin: Einaudi, 1955.
24. Greene, Graham. *Una pistola in vendita.* Milan: Mondadori, 1956.
25. Lin, Yutang. *Il cancello vermiglio.* Co-translated by Maj-Lis Rissler Stoneman. Milan: Bompiani, 1956.
26. Greene, Graham. *Il tranquillo americano.* Milan: Mondadori, 1957.
27. Lin, Yutang. *L'isola inaspettata.* Co-translated by Maj-Lis Rissler Stoneman Milan: Bompiani, 1957.
28. Greene, Graham. *Al di la del ponte e altri racconti.* Co-translated by Maj-Lis Rissler Stoneman. Milan: Mondadori, 1958.

29. Greene, Graham. *Saggi cattolici*. Co-translated by I.A. Chiusano. Milan: Mondadori, 1958.
30. Prescott, William H. *La Conquista del Messico*. Co-translated by Maria Vittoria Malvano. Turin: Einaudi, 1958.
31. Bibby, Geoffrey. *Le navi dei Vichinghi*. Turin: Einaudi, 1960.
32. Lin, Yutang. *Madama Wu*. Milan: Bompiani, 1963.
33. White, Patrick. *L'esploratore*. Turin: Einaudi, 1965.

Tomaso Kemeny, 1939–

1. Carroll, Lewis. *Le avventure di Alice nel paese delle Meraviglie e Dietro lo specchio*. Co-translated by Alfonso Galasso. Milan: Sugar, 1967.
2. Marlowe, Christopher. *Ero e Leandro*. Milan: Rizzoli, 1990.
3. *Notturno*. Milan: Rizzoli, 1992.
4. Byron, George Gordon. *Opere scelte*. Milan: Mondadori, 1993.
5. Jozsef, Attilio. *Poesie scelte*. Rome: Lithos, 2005.
6. Jozsef, Attilio. *Il mendicante di bellezza*. Milan: il Faggio, 2008.

Ermanno Krumm, 1942–2005

1. Sollers, Philippe. *H: romanzo*. Milan: Feltrinelli, 1975.

Vivian Lamarque, 1946-

1. Prévert, Jacques. *Sole di notte*. Milan: Guanda, 1983.
2. Valéry, Paul. *Scritti sull'arte*. Milan: Guanda, 1984.
3. Baudelaire, Charles. *Lo spleen di Parigi*. Milan: SE, 1987.
4. Grimm, Wilhelm. *L'intrepido sartino*. Novara: De Agostini, 1996.
5. Hanel, Wolfram. *Miu, gattino di mare*. Pordenone: Nord-Sud, 1997.
6. Pfister, Marcus. *Pit il piccolo pinguino*. Pordenone: Nord-Sud, 1997.
7. Scheffler, Ursel. *Tutti lo chiamavano Pomodoro*. Pordenone: Nord-Sud, 1997.
8. Celine, Louis-Ferdinand. *Storia del piccolo Mouck*. Milan: Rizzoli, 1998.
9. Pfister, Marcus. *Nuovi amici per Pit*. Pordenone: Nord-Sud, 1998.
10. Watts, Bernadette. *Il topo di campagna e il topo di città*. Pordenone: Nord-Sud, 1999.
11. Pfister, Marcus. *Ciao ciao, Pit!* Pordenone: Nord-Sud, 1999.
12. Pfister, Marcus. *Pit e Pat*. Pordenone: Nord-Sud, 1999.
13. Schikaneder, Emanuel, and Wolfgang Amadeus Mozart. *Il flauto magico*. Milan: Fabbri, 1999.
14. Hol, Coby. *Come è nata la luna*. Pordenone: Nord-Sud, 2000.
15. Schroeder, Binette. *Aurora*. Pordenone: Nord-Sud, 2000.
16. Wilde, Oscar. *Il principe felice*. Milan: Fabbri, 2000.
17. Pow, Tom. *Per chi è il mondo*. Pordenone: Nord-Sud, 2001.

18. Elschner, Geraldine. *La piccola indiana Foglia Danzante*. Pordenone: Nord-Sud, 2001.
19. Ball-Simon, Danièle. *Fratellino lupo*. Pordenone: Nord-Sud, 2002.
20. Moers, Hermann. *Fino ai confini del mare*. Pordenone: Nord-Sud, 2002.
21. Reider, Katja. *Sei malato, Berto?* Pordenone: Nord-Sud, 2002.
22. Tibo, Gilles. *Rosso timido*. Pordenone: Nord-Sud, 2002.
23. Hoffmann, E.T.A. *Schiaccianoci e il Re dei topi: Dalla fiaba di E.T.A. Hoffmann*. Milan: Fabbri, 2003.
24. Prokofiev, Sergey. *Pierino e il lupo*. Milan: Fabbri, 2003.
25. Andersen, H.C. *L'usignolo dell'imperatore: dalla fiaba di H.C.A.* Milan: Fabbri, 2004.

Gabriella Leto, 1930–

1. Ovid. *Le eroidi*. Turin: Einaudi, 1966.
2. Propertius, Sextus. *Elegie*. Turin: Einaudi, 1970.
3. Hugo, Victor. *Notre-Dame de Paris*. Milan: Mondadori, 1985.
4. Stendhal. *Cronache italiane*. Co-translated by Maria Bellonci. Milan: Mondadori, 1990.
5. Ovid. *Gli amori*. Turin: Einaudi, 1995.
6. Ovid. *Versi e precetti d'amore*. Turin: Einaudi, 1998.

Primo Levi, 1919–1987

1. Gilman, Henry. *Chimica organica superiore*. Co-translated by Giorgio Anglesio. Vol. 1. Turin: Einaudi, 1955.
2. Gilman, Henry. *Chimica organica superiore*. Co-translated by Giorgio Anglesio. Vol. 2. Turin: Einaudi, 1956.
3. Gilman, Henry. *Chimica organica superiore*. Co-translated by Giorgio Anglesio. Vol. 3. Turin: Einaudi, 1958.
4. Gilman, Henry. *Chimica organica superiore*. Co-translated by Giorgio Anglesio. Vol. 4. Turin: Bollati Boringhieri, 1960.
5. Presser, Jacob. *La notte dei girondini*. Milan: Adelphi, 1976.
6. Douglas, Mary. *I simboli naturali*. Turin: Einaudi, 1979.
7. Kafka, Franz. *Il processo*. Turin: Einaudi, 1983.
8. Levi-Strauss, Claude. *Lo sguardo da lontano*. Turin: Einaudi, 1984.
9. Levi-Strauss, Claude. *La via delle maschere*. Turin: Einaudi, 1985.

Rosaria Lo Russo, 1964–

1. Sexton, Anne. *Poesie d'amore*. Florence: Le Lettere, 1996.
2. Jong, Erica. *Miele and Sangue*. Milan: Bompiani, 2001.

Franco Loi, 1930–

1. Folengo, Teofilo. *Zanitonella sive innamoramentum Zaninae et Tonelli*. Milan: Mondadori, 1984.
2. Sue, Eugène. *I misteri di Parigi*. Vol. 1. Milan: Mondadori, 1996.
3. Sue, Eugène. *I misteri di Parigi*. Vol. 2. Milan: Mondadori, 1996.
4. Sue, Eugène. *I misteri di Parigi*. Vol. 3. Milan: Mondadori, 1996.
5. Toorn, Willem van. *Paesaggi*. Co-translated by William van Toorn. Venice: Edizioni del Leone, 2001.

Attilio Lolini, 1939–

1. Jabès, Edmond. *Canzoni per il pasto dell'orco*. Co-translated by Antonio Prete. Siena: Edizioni di Barbablù, 1985.
2. Jabès, Edmond. *Pages nouvelles*. Siena: Taccuini di Barbablù, 1990.
3. Lolini, Attilio. *Imitazioni*. Brescia: L'obliquo, 1989.

Angelo Lumelli, 1944–

1. Novalis. *Inni alla notte*. Milan: Guanda, 1979.
2. Rosei, Peter. *Chi era Edgar Allan?* Milan: Feltrinelli, 1980.

Mario Luzi, 1914–2005

1. Du Bos, Charles. *Vita e letteratura*. Padua: Cedam, 1943.
2. Coleridge, Samuel Taylor. *Poesie e prose*. Milan: Cederna, 1949.
3. Valéry, Paul. *Cantique des colonnes*. Rome: ERI, 1949.
4. Guillén, Jorge. *La fonte*. Milan: Scheiwiller, 1961.
5. Shakespeare, William. *Riccardo II*. Turin: Einaudi, 1966.
6. Coleridge, Samuel Taylor. *La ballata del vecchio marinaio*. Milan: Rizzoli, 1973.
7. *Francamente*. Florence: Vallecchi, 1980.
8. *La Cordigliera delle Ande*. Turin: Einaudi, 1983.
9. Elahi, Ostad. *Pensieri di luce*. Milan: Mondadori, 2000.

Valerio Magrelli, 1957–

1. Valéry, Paul. *L'idea fissa*. Napoli: Theoria, 1985.
2. Debussy, Claude. *Il signor Croche antidilettante*. Pordenone: Studio Tesi, 1986.
3. Verlaine, Paul. *La buona canzone*. Maser: Amadeus, 1986.
4. *Poeti francesi del Novecento*. Vol. 1. Rome: Lucarini, 1991.
5. *Poeti francesi del Novecento*. Vol. 2. Rome: Lucarini, 1991.
6. Koltes, B.M. *Lotta di negro e cani*. Genoa: Il Melangolo, 2003.

7. Beaumarchais, Pierre Augustin Caron de. *La folle giornata, o Il matrimonio di Figaro*. Turin: Edizione della Fondazione del Teatro Stabile di Torino, 2007.
8. Barthes, Roland. *Dove lei non è*. Turin: Einaudi, 2010.

Giorgio Manacorda, 1941–

1. Klee, Paul. *Poesie*. Milan: Guanda, 1978.
2. Wedekind, Frank. *Musica*. Cosenza: Lerici, 1979.
3. George, Stefan. *L'anno dell'anima*. Milan: SE, 1986.

Dacia Maraini, 1936–

1. Witkiewicz, Stanisław Ignacy. *Commedia ripugnante di una madre*. Rome: Bulzoni, 1970.
2. Conrad, Joseph. *Il compagno segreto*. Milan: Rizzoli, 1996.

Biagio Marin, 1891–1985

1. Fueter, Eduard. *Storia del sistema degli stati europei dal 1492–1559*. Florence: La Nuova Italia, 1932.

Filippo Tommaso Marinetti, 1876–1944

1. Mallarmé, Stéphane. *Versi e prosa*. Milan: Istituto Editoriale italiana, 1916.
2. Tacitus, Cornelius. *De origine et situ Germanorum*. Milan: Istituto Editoriale Italiano, 1928.

Fausto Maria Martini, 1886–1931

1. Rodenbach, Georges. *Bruges-la-mort*. Rome: E. Voghera, 1907.
2. Shelley, Percy Bysshe. *Una difesa della poesia*. Ortona a Mare: Tip. C. Visci, 1909.
3. Shelley, Percy Bysshe. *Le prose*. Rome: E. Voghera, 1911.
4. Hawthorne, Nathaniel. *La lettera scarlatta*. Milan: Mondadori, 1932.

Daria Menicanti, 1914–1995

1. Muirhead, John Henry. *Filosofi inglesi contemporanei*. Milan: Bompiani, 1939.
2. Nizan, Paul. *Aden Arabia*. Milan: Mondadori, 1961.
3. Nizan, Paul. *La cospirazione*. Milan: Mondadori, 1961.
4. Smith, Betty. *Al mattino viene la gioia*. Milan: Mondadori, 1965.
5. Paris, Jean. *James Joyce*. Milan: Il Saggiatore, 1966.
6. Plath, Sylvia. *La campana di vetro*. Milan: Mondadori, 1968.
7. Geraldy, Paul. *Toi et moi*. Milan: Mondadori, 1972.

Giuliano Mesa, 1957–2011

1. Rousseau, Jean-Jacques. *La nuova Eloisa*. Rome: Istituto della Enciclopedia Italiana, 1992.
2. Arevalo, Antonio. *Domus Aurea 1–2*. Rome: Il bulino, 1996.

Eugenio Montale, 1896–1981

1. Steinbeck, John. *La battaglia*. Milan: Bompiani, 1940.
2. Parker, Dorothy. *Il mio mondo è qui*. Milan: Bompiani, 1941.
3. Melville, Herman. *La storia di Billy Budd*. Milan: Bompiani, 1942.
4. O'Neill, Eugene. *Strano interludio*. Rome: Teatro dell'Università, 1943.
5. Steinbeck, John. *Al dio sconosciuto*. Milan: Mondadori, 1946.
6. Hawthorne, Nathaniel. *Il volto di Pietra*. Milan: Bompiani, 1947.
7. *Quaderno di traduzioni*. Milan: Meridiana, 1948.
8. Cervantes Saavedra, Miguel de. *Il cordovano*. Milan: Edizioni Suvini-Zerboni, 1949.
9. Shakespeare, William. *Amleto, principe di Danimarca*. Milan: Cederna, 1949.
10. Carlo, Omar del. *Proserpina e lo straniero*. Milan: Ricordi, 1952.
11. Wilson, Angus. *La cicuta e dopo*. Milan: Garzanti, 1956.
12. Eliot, T.S. *T.S. Eliot tradotto da Eugenio Montale*. Milan: All'insegna del pesce d'oro, 1958.
13. Guillén, Jorge. *Jorge Guillén tradotto da Eugenio Montale*. Milan: All'insegna del pesce d'oro, 1958.
14. Falla, Manuel de, and Jacinto Verdaguer. *Atlantida*. Milan: Ricordi, 1962.
15. Hudson, W.H. *La vita della foresta*. Turin: Einaudi, 1987.

Elsa Morante, 1912–1985

1. Mansfield, Katherine. *Il libro degli appunti*. Milan: Longanesi, 1972.

Marino Moretti, 1885–1979

1. Maupassant, Guy de. *Una vita*. Milan: Mondadori, 1931.
2. Marlowe, Christopher. *Ballata sulla vita e sulla morte del dottore Johannen Faust, grande mago*. Syracuse: TDS, 1970.

Gilda Musa, 1926–1999

1. *Incontri con T.S. Eliot, K. Mansfield, R. Bridges, R. Kipling, T. Hardy, W. Blunt, G. Hopkins, F. Thompson, M. Arnold, S. Coleridge, H. Longfellow: liriche scelte con un'appendice di poesie tratte da lirici greci*. Milan: Academia, 1950.
2. *Voci della Germania d'oggi: 12 poeti contemporanei*. Milan: Ed. Cremaschi, 1955.
3. *Poesia tedesca del dopoguerra*. Milan: Schwarz, 1958.

4. Weichert, Ernest. *Le mie poesie*. Vicenza: La locusta, 1959.
5. Krolow, Karl. *Karl Krolow: traduzione e scelta*. Milan: Centro di Attività e Documentazione di Poesia Contemporanea, 1962.
6. Drawe, Hans-Joachim. *Wolodja, Alexej e io*. Milan: Todariana, 1971.

Roberto Mussapi, 1952–

1. Andersen, Hans Christian. *La Forbice e l'Angelo di Hans Christian Andersen*. Bologna: Cappelli, 1979.
2. Shaw, Irwin. *La guerra di Archer*. Milan: Club degli editori, 1980.
3. Beckett, Samuel. *Compagnia*. Florence: Arte e pensiero, 1982.
4. Emerson, Ralph Waldo. *Cerchi*. Bologna: Cappelli, 1983.
5. Shakespeare, William. *Dodici sonetti*. Milan: Marcos y Marcos, 1983.
6. Thomas, Dylan. *Visione e preghiera*. Milan: Marcos y Marcos, 1984.
7. Melville, Herman. *Poesie di guerre e di mare*. Milan: Mondadori, 1984.
8. Coleridge, Samuel Taylor. *Gli smarrimenti di Caino*. Co-translated by Teresa Sorace Maresca. Florence: F. Cesati, 1985.
9. Whitman, Walt. *Dalla culla che oscilla eternamente*. Milan: Polena, 1985.
10. Beckett, Samuel. *Compagnia e Worstward ho*. Milan: Jaca Book, 1986.
11. Stevenson, Robert Lewis. *Poesie*. Co-translated by Teresa Sorace Maresca. Pordenone: Studio Tesi, 1986.
12. Beckett, Samuel. *Quello che è strano, via*. Milan: SE, 1989.
13. Emerson, Ralph Waldo. *Il trascendalista e altri saggi scelti*. Co-translated by Alessandro Ceni. Milan: Mondadori, 1989.
14. Highsmith, Patricia. *Il sepolto vivo*. Milan: Bompiani, 1990.
15. Melville, Herman. *Benito Cereno*. Milan: Feltrinelli, 1992.
16. Achebe, Chinua. *Attento, soul brother!* Co-translated by Teresa Sorace Maresca. Milan: Jaca Book, 1995.
17. Villon, François. *Ballate*. Milan: Nuages, 1995.
18. Heaney, Seamus. *Una porta sul buio*. Parma: Guanda, 1996.
19. La Fontaine, Jean de. *Favole*. Milan: Nuages, 1996.
20. Shelley, Percy Bysshe, John Keats and George Gordon Byron. *I ragazzi che amavano il vento*. Milan: Feltrinelli, 1996.
21. Bonnefoy, Yves. *L'uva di Zeusi*. Milan: Jaca Book, 1997.
22. Ovid. *Metamorfosi*. Milan: Nuages, 1997.
23. Stevenson, Robert Lewis. *Il mio letto è una nave: poesie per grandi incanti e piccoli lettori*. Milan: Feltrinelli, 1997.
24. Heaney, Seamus. *North*. Milan: Mondadori, 1998.
25. Heaney, Seamus. *The spirit level*. Milan: Mondadori, 2000.
26. Stevenson, Robert Louis. *Ticonderoga*. Milan: Nuages, 2002.

27. *Tanti baci ci vogliono a baciare: l'amore classico*. Milan: Salani, 2004.
28. Rouault, Georges. *Passione*. Milan: Jaca Book, 2005.
29. *E tacque attorno a te il silenzio: poesie del romanticismo per giovani innamorati*. Milan: Salani, 2005.
30. Shakespeare, William. *La tempesta di William Shakespeare: raccontato da Roberto Mussapi e illustrato da Giorgio Bacchin*. Milan: Jaca Book, 2008.
31. Goethe, Johann Wolfgang von. *Faust di Wolfgang Goethe: raccontato da Roberto Mussapi e illustrato da Giorgio Bacchin*. Milan: Jaca Book, 2009.
32. Molière. *L'avaro di Molière raccontato da Roberto Mussapi e illustrato da Giorgio bacchin*. Milan: Jaca Book, 2009.
33. Byron, George Gordon. *Beppo: una storia veneziana*. Milan: Feltrinelli, 2009.
34. Baudelaire, Charles. *Tu metteresti l'universo intero: poesie per giovani innamorati da "I fiori del male."* Milan: Salani, 2012.

Giovanni Nadiani, 1954–

1. Roggeman, Willem M. *L'invenzione della tenerezza*. Faenza: Mobydick, 1995.
2. *Poesia fiamminga contemporanea*. Faenza: Mobydick, 1998.
3. Hoste, Pol. *High key*. Faenza: Mobydick, 1998.
4. Augustin, Michael. *Prendo le sigarette e torno*. Faenza: Mobydick, 1999.
5. Andrade, Oswald de. *Amanda*. Faenza: Mobydick, 2000.
6. Lampe, Friedo. *Ai margini della notte*. Faenza: Mobydick, 2000.
7. Thies, Klaus. Johannes. *Tacchi a spillo sulla tastiera di Monk*. Faenza: Mobydick, 2000.
8. Wolf, Ror. *Tentativi di mantenere la calma*. Faenza: Mobydick, 2001.
9. Lampe, Friedo. *Temporale a settembre*. Faenza: Mobydick, 2002.
10. Haid, Hans. *Cosi parlo la montagna*. Faenza: Mobydick, 2003.
11. Jung, Markus Manfred. *Parole come l'erba: poesie in alemannico*. Faenza: Mobydick, 2004.
12. Kopland, Rutger. *Prima della scomparsa e dopo*. Venice: Edizioni del Leone, 2005.
13. Castillo, David. *Un presente abbandonato*. Faenza: Mobydick, 2006.
14. Politycki, Matthias. *La verita sui bevitori di Whiskey*. Faenza: Mobydick, 2009.
15. Kunert, Gunther. *L'omo in mare*. Faenza: Mobydick, 2010.

Ada Negri, 1870–1945

1. Prévost, Abbé. *Storia di Manon Lescaut e del cavaliere di Grieux*. Milan: Mondadori, 1931.

Giulia Niccolai, 1934–

1. Clinton-Baddeley, V.C. *L'amabile professore Davie*. Milan: Longanesi, 1972.
2. Sobin, Gustaf. *Il triangolo giallo*. Milan: Emme, 1972.
3. Gill, Bob. *I Su & i Giù*. Milan: Emme, 1973.
4. Vangelisti, Paul. *Il tenero continente*. Turin: Geiger, 1975.
5. MacNamara, Ellen. *Gli etruschi*. Co-translated by Adriano Spatola. Milan: LM, 1975.
6. La Fontaine, Jean de. *Favole*. Co-translated by Adriano Spatola. Milan: Emme, 1975.
7. Rowling, Marjorie. *Nel Medioevo*. Co-translated by Adriano Spatola. Milan: LM, 1975.
8. Edwardes, Michael. *Nell'India antica*. Co-translated by Adriano Spatola. Milan: LM, 1975.
9. Mérimée, Prosper. *La notte di San Bartolomeo*. Co-translated by Adriano Spatola. Milan: Emme, 1975.
10. Vangelisti, Paul. *La stanza stravagante*. Co-translated by Paul Vangelisti. Rivalba: Geiger, 1976.
11. Bisinger, Gerald. *Frammenti sull'io*. Turin: Geiger, 1977.
12. Spatola, Adriano. *Zeroglyphics*. Co-translated by Paul Vangelisti. Los Angeles: Red hill press, 1977.
13. Ruskin, John. *Il re del fiume d'oro*. Milan: Emme, 1978.
14. Leman, Martin. *Gatti gaudenti and gravi*. Milan: Emme, 1980.
15. Stein, Gertrude. *La storia geografica dell'America o Il rapporto della natura umana con la mente umana*. Milan: La Tartaruga, 1980.
16. Leman, Martin. *Bestie buone e beffarde*. Milan: Emme, 1981.
17. Thomas, Dylan. *Il mio Natale nel Galles*. Milan: Emme, 1981.
18. Neill, Alexander S. *La nuvola verde*. Milan: Emme, 1981.
19. Beisner, Monika. *Centouno indovinelli*. Milan: Emme, 1984.
20. Woolf, Virginia. *La vedova e il papapagallo*. Milan: Emme, 1984.
21. Heilbrun, Carolyn. *Un delitto per James Joyce*. Milan: Interno giallo, 1992.
22. Carter, Angela. *Gatto Marino e re Drago*. Milan: Mondadori, 2000.
23. Whalen, Philip. *Further notice*. Co-translated by Anna Ruchat. Riva San Vitale: Fondazione Franco Beltrametti, 2004.
24. Highsmith, Patricia. *Dei gatti e degli uomini*. Milan: Archinto, 2007.

Mario Novaro, 1868–1944

1. Malebranche, Nicolas de. *Pensieri metafisici*. Lanciano: Carabba, 1910.
2. Zhuangzi. *Acque d'autunno*. Lanciano: Carabba, 1922.

Aldo Nove, 1967–

1. Young, Murray Lachlan. *Casual sex e altri versi*. Milan: Bompiani, 1998.
2. Voltaire. *Candido: soap opera musical*. Co-translated by A. Liberovici. Genoa: Il Melangolo, 2004.

Arturo Onofri, 1885–1928

1. Gide, André. *Viaggio sull'Oceano patetico*. Florence: Casa L. Baldoni, 1912.
2. Wagner, Richard. *Tristano e Isotta*. Milan: Bottega di Poesia, 1924.
3. *Luna di Giada: poesie cinesi*. Edited by Carlo Alessio. Rome: Salerno, 1994.

Piera Oppezzo, 1934–

1. Gibran, Kahlil. *Il profeta*. Milan: Mondadori, 1985.
2. Renard, Jules. *Pel di carota*. Milan: Guanda, 1985.
3. Freud, Gisèle. *Il mondo e il mio obiettivo*. Milan: Abscondita, 2011.

Giorgio Orelli, 1921–

1. Goethe, Johann Wolfgang von. *Poesie scelte*. Milan: Mondadori, 1957.
2. Peer, Andri. *L'alba: poesie ladine*. Lugano: Pantarei, 1975.
3. Lucretius Carus, Titus. *Quale coloure*. Milan: All'insegna del pesce d'oro, 1996.

Nico Orengo, 1944–2009

1. Burton, Tim. *Morte malinconica del bambino Ostrica e altre storie*. Turin: Einaudi, 1998.
2. Wilde, Oscar. *Il principe felice*. Rivarolo Canavese: Schialvino, 2000.
3. Burton, Tim. *La sposa cadavere*. Turin: Einaudi, 2006.

Cosimo Ortesta, 1939–

1. Mallarmé, Stéphane. *Sonetti*. Milan: Guanda, 1980.
2. Mallarmé, Stéphane. *Poesia e prosa*. Milan: Guanda, 1982.
3. Baudelaire, Charles. *Lettera alla madre*. Milan: SE, 1985.
4. Rimbaud, Arthur. *Poesie*. Parma: Guanda: 1986.
5. Char, René. *Le vicinanze di Van Gogh*. Milan: SE, 1987.
6. Balzac, Honoré de. *La pelle di zigrino*. Milan: Garzanti, 1995.
7. Baudelaire, Charles. *I fiori del male*. Florence: Giunti, 1996.
8. Cheng, François. *Le parole di Tianyi*. Milan: Garzanti, 2000.
9. Carrière, Jean Claude. *Il circolo dei contastorie*. Milan: Garzanti, 2001.

Ottiero Ottieri, 1924–2002

1. Aeschylus. *Agamennone*. Rome: F. Capriotti, 1946.
2. Cooper, James Fenimore. *L'ultimo dei Mohicani*. Florence: Giunti-Marzocco, 1981.
3. Twain, Mark. *Il principe e il povero*. Florence: Giunti, 1994.

Elio Pagliarani, 1927–2012

1. Tracy, Don. *I congiurati dell'odio*. Rome: Il Liocorno, 1965.
2. Olson, Charles. *Le Lontananze*. Co-translated by William McCormick. Milan: Rizzoli, 1967.

Aldo Palazzeschi, 1885–1974

1. Daudet, Alphonse. *Tartarino*. Milan: Mondadori, 1931.

Giovanni Papini, 1881–1956

1. Shakespeare, William. *Re Lear: tre atti di Giovanni Papini dalla tragedia di Shakespeare*. Milan: Ricordi, 1939.

Renzo Paris, 1944–

1. Apollinaire, Guillaume. *Poesie*. Rome: Newton Compton, 1971.
2. Corbière, Tristan. *Gli amori gialli*. Rome: Addenda, 1972.
3. Prévert, Jacques. *Amori*. Milan: Tea, 1995.

Alessandro Parronchi, 1914–2007

1. Mallarmé, Stéphane. *L'après-Midi d'un Faune*. Florence: Il Fiore, 1945.
2. Nouveau, Germaine. *Poesie di humilis*. Florence: Libreria editrice Fiorentina, 1945.
3. Nerval, Gerard de. *Le Chimere*. Florence: Fussi, 1946.
4. Rimbaud, Arthur. *Una stagione all'inferno*. Florence: Fussi, 1949.
5. Guerin, Maurice de. *Il Centauro e altri poemi*. Florence: Fussi, 1951.
6. Mallarmé, Stéphane. *Il monologo, l'Improvviso e il Pomeriggio d'un Fauno*. Florence: Fussi, 1951.
7. Vitellius, Aulus, Emperor of Rome. *Teorema della bellezza*. Milan: Scheiwiller, 1957.
8. *Quaderno francese*. Florence: Vallecchi, 1989.
9. Romanus, Melodus, Saint. *Il natale*. Florence: Pananti, 1991.

Giovanni Pascoli, 1855–1912

1. *Traduzioni e riduzioni*. Bologna: Zanichelli, 1912.
2. *Antologia omerica*. Milan: Mondadori, 1934.

Pier Paolo Pasolini, 1922–1975

1. Aeschylus. *Orestaide*. Turin: Einaudi, 1960.
2. Plautus, Titus Maccius. *Il Vantone*. Milan: Garzanti, 1963.

Cesare Pavese, 1908–1950

1. Lewis, Sinclair. *Il nostro signor Wrenn*. Florence: Bemporad, 1931.
2. Anderson, Sherwood. *Riso nero*. Turin: Frassinelli, 1932.
3. Melville, Herman. *Moby Dick*. Turin: Frassinelli, 1932.
4. Joyce, James. *Dedalus*. Turin: Frassinelli, 1933.
5. Dos Passos, John. *Il 42 & parallelo…* Milan: Mondadori, 1934.
6. Dos Passos, John. *Un mucchio di quattrini*. Milan: Mondadori, 1937.
7. Defoe, Daniel. *Fortune e sfortune della famosa Moll Flanders*. Turin: Einaudi, 1938.
8. Stein, Gertrude. *Autobiografia di Alice B. Toklas*. Turin: Einaudi, 1938.
9. Steinbeck, John. *Uomini e topi*. Milan: Bompiani, 1938.
10. Dickens, Charles. *David Copperfield*. Turin: Einaudi, 1939.
11. Dawson, Christopher. *La formazione dell'unità europea dal secolo V al XI*. Turin: Einaudi, 1939.
12. Melville, Herman. *Benito Cereno*. Turin: Einaudi, 1940.
13. Stein, Gertrude. *Tre esistenze*. Turin: Einaudi, 1940.
14. Trevelyan, G.M. *La rivoluzione inglese del 1688–89*. Turin: Einaudi, 1940.
15. Morley, Christopher. *Il cavallo di Troia*. Milan: Bompiani, 1941.
16. Faulkner, William. *Il borgo*. Milan: Mondadori, 1942.
17. Henriques, Robert. *Capitano Smith*. Turin: Einaudi, 1947.
18. Toynbee, Arnold J. *La civiltà nella storia*. Co-translated by Charis de Bosis. Turin: Einaudi, 1950.
19. *Teognia e 3 inni omerici*. Turin: Einaudi, 1981.
20. Shelley, Percy Bysshe. *Promoteo slegato*. Turin: Einaudi, 1997.

Corrado Pavolini, 1898–1980

1. Stendhal. *Il rosso e il bianco*. Milan: Treves, 1930.
2. Conrad, Joseph. *Lord Jim*. Milan: Bompiani, 1949.
3. Tallemant Des Réaux. *Storie galanti*. Milan: Longanesi, 1955.
4. Forster, E.M. *Aspetti del romanzo*. Milan: Il Saggiatore, 1963.
5. Brecher, Michael. *Vita di Nehru*. Milan: Il Saggiatore, 1965.
6. Simenon, Georges. *Un natale di Maigret*. Milan: Mondadori, 1965.
7. Golding, William. *La piramide*. Milan: Rizzoli, 1968.
8. Malraux, André. *La via dei re*. Milan: Mondadori, 1971.
9. Sartre, Jean-Paul. *Santo Genet, commediante e martire*. Milan: Il Saggiatore, 1972.

10. Racine, Jean. *Andromaca*. Milan: Mondadori, 1975.
11. Sartre, Jean-Paul. *L'idiota della famiglia: Gustave Flaubert dal 1821 al 1857*. Vol. 1. Milan: Il Saggiatore, 1977.
12. Sartre, Jean-Paul. *L'idiota della famiglia: Gustave Flaubert dal 1821 al 1857*. Vol. 2. Milan: Il Saggiatore, 1977.
13. Gide, André. *Teatro*. Milan: Mondadori, 1980.
14. Cooper, James Fenimore. *Romanzi*. Florence: Casini, 1988.
15. Marlowe, Christopher. *La tragica storia del dottor Faust*. Milan: BUR, 2002.

Elio Pecora, 1936–

1. Theophilo, Marcia. *Catuete Curupira*. Rome: La Linea, 1983.
2. Portante, Jean. *Voglio dire*. Milan: La vita felice, 2012.

Sandro Penna, 1906–1977

1. Claudel, Paul. *Presenza e profezia*. Rome: Comunità, 1947.
2. Mérimée, Prosper. *Carmen e altri racconti*. Turin: Einaudi, 1977.

Camillo Pennati, 1931–

1. Gunn, Thom. *I miei tristi capitani e altre poesie*. Milan: Mondadori, 1968.
2. Larkin, Philip. *Le nozze di Pentecoste e altre poesie*. Co-translated by Renato Oliva. Turin: Einaudi, 1969.
3. Laing, R.D. *Nodi*. Turin: Einaudi, 1970.
4. Szasz, Thomas S. *I manipolatori della pazzia*. Milan: Feltrinelli, 1972.
5. Gutteridge, Lindsay. *Guerra fredda in giardino*. Milan: Bompiani, 1973.
6. Hughes, Ted. *Pensiero-volpe e altre poesie*. Milan: Mondadori, 1973.
7. Hawkes, John. *Arazzo d'amore*. Turin: Einaudi, 1974.
8. Tolkien, J.R.R. *Il cacciatore di draghi ovverossia Giles l'Agricoltore di Ham*. Turin: Einaudi, 1975.
9. White, Patrick. *I passeggeri del carro*. Turin: Einaudi, 1976.
10. Coward, Noel. *Commedie*. Turin: Einaudi, 1978.
11. Laing, R.D. *I fatti della vita*. Turin: Einaudi, 1978.
12. Compton-Burnett, Ivy. *Il presente e il passato*. Turin: Einaudi, 1980.
13. Pinter, Harold. *La donna del tenente francese; sceneggiatura del romanzo di John Fowles*. Turin: Einaudi, 1982.
14. Malamud, Bernard. *Dio mio, grazie*. Turin: Einaudi, 1984.
15. Commissione indipendente sui diritti Internazionali. *Fame: un disastro creato dall'uomo*. Milan: Bompiani, 1985.
16. Woolf, Virginia. *Un riflesso dell'altro: lettere 1929–1931*. Turin: Einaudi, 1985.
17. Atwood, Margaret. *Il racconto dell'ancella*. Milan: Mondadori, 1988.

Giaime Pintor, 1919–1943

1. Kleist, Heinrich von. *Kathchen di Heilbronn*. Florence: Parenti, 1942.
2. Rilke, Rainer Maria. *Poesie*. Turin: Einaudi, 1942.
3. Beckford, William. *Vathek*. Turin: Einaudi, 1946.
4. Turgenev, Ivan Sergeevich. *L'orologio: racconto*. Milan: Bompiani, 1946.
5. Rilke, Rainer Maria. *Poesie e prose; con aggiunte versioni da H. Hesse e G. Trakl*. Turin: Einaudi, 1948.

Antonio Porta, 1935–1989

1. Sendak, Maurice. *Nel paese dei mostri selvaggi*. Milan: Emme, 1963.
2. Pieyre de Mandiargues, André. *Il margine*. Milan: Feltrinelli, 1968.
3. Mayakovsky, Vladimir. *Il cavallino di fuoco*. Co-translated by Gabriella Schiaffino. Milan: Emme, 1969.
4. *Poeti ispanoamericani contemporanei*. Co-translated by M. Ravoni. Milan: Feltrinelli, 1970.
5. Borges, Jorge Luis, and Adolfo Bioy Casares. *Cielo e inferno*. Parma: F.M. Ricci, 1972.
6. Reverdy, Pierre. *Il ladro di talento*. Turin: Einaudi, 1972.
7. Plautus, Titus Maccius. *La stangata persiana*. Milan: Corpo 10, 1985.
8. Masters, Edgar Lee. *Antologia di Spoon River*. Milan: Mondadori, 1987.
9. Rosselli, Amelia. *Sonno-sleep*. Rome: Rossi and Spera, 1989.

Fabio Pusterla, 1957–

1. Jaccotett, Philippe. *Il Barbagianni; L'ignorante*. Turin: Einaudi, 1992.
2. Judice, Nuno. *Adagio*. Ripatransone: Sestante, 1994.
3. Jaccottet, Philippe. *Edera e calce: materiali per una lettura publica*. Ancona: Comune, Centro studi Scatagliani, 1995.
4. Jaccottet, Philippe. *Libretto*. Milan: Scheiwiller, 1995.
5. Jaccottet, Philippe. *Paesaggi con figure assenti*. Locarno: A. Dado, 1996.
6. Jaccottet, Philippe. *Alla luce d'inverno; Pensieri sotto le nuvole*. Milan: Marcos y Marcos, 1997.
7. *Nel pieno giorno dell'oscurita: antologia della poesia francese contemporanea*. Milan: Marcos y Marcos, 2000.
8. Jaccottet, Philippe. *E, tuttavia*. Milan: Marcos y Marcos, 2006.
9. Jaccottet, Philippe. *La ciotola del pellegrino Morandi*. Bellinzona: Casagrande, 2007.
10. *Nuovi poeti francesi*. Co-translated by Fabio Scotto. Turin: Einaudi, 2011.

Salvatore Quasimodo, 1901–1968

1. *Lirici greci*. Milan: Corrente, 1940.

2. Virgil. *Il fiore delle Georgiche*. Milan: Edizioni della Conchiglia, 1942.
3. Catullus, Gaius Valerius. *Veronensis Carmina*. Milan: Edizioni di Uomo, 1945.
4. Homer. *Dall'Odissea*. Milan: Rosa and Ballo, 1945.
5. *Il Vangelo secondo Giovanni*. Milan: Gentile, 1945.
6. Ruskin, John. *La Bibbia di Amiens*. Milan: Bompiani, 1946.
7. Sophocles. *Edipo re*. Milan: Bompiani, 1947.
8. Aeschylus. *Le Coefore*. Milan: Bompiani, 1949.
9. Shakespeare, William. *Romeo e Giulietta*. Milan: Mondadori, 1949.
10. Shakespeare, William. *Riccardo III*. Milan: Piccolo Teatro, 1950.
11. Neruda, Pablo. *Poesie*. Turin: Einaudi, 1952.
12. Shakespeare, William. *Macbeth*. Turin: Einaudi, 1952.
13. Sophocles. *Elettra*. Milan: Mondadori, 1954.
14. Shakespeare, William. *La tempesta*. Turin: Einaudi, 1956.
15. *Fiore dell'antologia Palatina*. Bologna: Guanda, 1957.
16. Cummings, E. E. *Poesie scelte*. Milan: Scheiwiller, 1958.
17. Molière. *Tartufo*. Milan: Bompiani, 1958.
18. Shakespeare, William. *Otello*. Milan: Mondadori, 1958.
19. Ovid. *Dalle Metamorfosi*. Milan: Scheiwiller, 1959.
20. Euripides. *Ecuba*. Urbino: Argalia, 1962.
21. Aiken, Conrad. *Mutevoli pensieri*. Milan: Scheiweiller, 1963.
22. *Tragici greci*. Milan: Mondadori, 1963.
23. Euripides. *Eracle*. Urbino: Argalia, 1964.
24. Arghezi, Tudor. *Poesie*. Milan: Mondadori, 1966.
25. Shakespeare, William. *Antonio e Cleopatra*. Milan: Mondadori, 1966.
26. Homer. *Iliade-Episodi scelti*. Milan: Mondadori, 1968.
27. Lecomte, Yves. *Il gioco degli astragali*. Milan: Moneta, 1968.
28. Éluard, Paul. *Donner à voir*. Milan: Mondadori, 1970.
29. Teilhard de Chardin, Pierre. *La messa sul mondo*. Milan: Scheiwiller, 1999.

Giovanni Raboni, 1932–2004

1. Flaubert, Gustave. *L'educazione sentimentale*. Milan: Garzanti, 1966.
2. Labro, Philippe, and the group di "Edition Spéciale." *Bilancio di Maggio*. Milan: Mondadori, 1968.
3. Aragon, Louis. *Bianca o l'oblio*. Milan: Mondadori, 1969.
4. Simons, Frans. *Discorso sull'infallibilità*. Co-translated by R. Mainardi. Milan: Mondadori, 1969.
5. Mauriac, François. *Un adolescente d'altri tempi*. Milan: Mondadori, 1971.
6. Baudelaire, Charles. *Poesie e prose*. Milan: Mondadori, 1973.
7. Ellin, Stanley. *La specialità di casa e altre storie d'inquietudine*. Co-translated by A. Camerino. Milan: Mondadori, 1973.

8. Apollinaire, Guillaume. *Bestiario*. Milan: Guanda, 1977.
9. Prévert, Jacques. *Poesie*. Co-translated by Maurizio Cucchi. Parma: Guanda, 1979.
10. Apollinaire, Guillaume. *Da Alcools*. Co-translated by Vittorio Sereni. Milan: Il Saggiatore, 1981.
11. Céline, Louis-Ferdinand. *Mea culpa; La bella rogna*. Co-translated by D. Gorret. Milan: Guanda, 1982.
12. Proust, Marcel. *Alla ricerca del tempo perduto*. Vol. 1. Turin: Einaudi, 1983.
13. Apollinaire, Guillaume. *La chiamavano Lu e altre poesie*. Co-translated by Vittorio Sereni. Milan: Mondadori, 1984.
14. Racine, Jean. *Fedra*. Milan: Rizzoli, 1984.
15. Proust, Marcel. *Alla ricerca del tempo perduto*. Vol. 2. Turin: Einaudi, 1986.
16. Proust, Marcel. *Alla ricerca del tempo perduto*. Vol. 3. Turin: Einaudi, 1989.
17. Proust, Marcel. *Alla ricerca del tempo perduto*. Vol. 4. Turin: Einaudi, 1994.
18. Hugo, Victor. *Ruy Blas*. Turin: Einaudi, 1996.
19. *Ventagli e altre imitazioni*. Varese: Nuova Editrice Magenta, 1999.
20. Vegliante, Jean-Charles. *Nel lutto della luce*. Turin: Einaudi, 2004.
21. Flaubert, Gustave. *Tre racconti*. Rome: Gruppo editoriale 'Espresso,' 2011.

Michele Ranchetti, 1925–2008

1. *Ultime lettere da Stalingrado*. Turin: Einaudi, 1958.
2. Wittgenstein, Ludwig. *Lezioni e conversazioni sull'etica, l'estetica, la psicologia e la credenza religiosa*. Milan: Adelphi, 1967.
3. Mehta, Ved. *Teologi senza Dio*. Turin: Einaudi, 1968.
4. Newman, John Henry. *Gli ariani del quarto secolo*. Milan: Jaca Book, 1981.
5. Wittgenstein, Ludwig. *Pensieri diversi*. Milan: Adelphi, 1981.
6. Freud, Sigmund. *Casi clinici: 3*. Macerata: Quodlibet, 1995.
7. Pascal, Blaise. *Compendio della vita di Gesu Cristo*. Macerata: Quodlibet: 1995.
8. Benjamin, Walter. *Sul concetto della storia*. Co-translated by Gianfranco Bonola. Turin: Einaudi, 1997.
9. Celan, Paul. *Conseguito silenzio*. Co-translated by Jutta Leskien.Turin: Einaudi, 1998.
10. Wittgenstein, Ludwig. *Movimenti del pensiero. Diari 1930–1932/1936–1937*. Co-translated by Francesca Tognina. Macerata: Quodlibet, 1999.
11. Celan, Paul. *Sotto il tiro di presagi*. Co-translated by Jutta Leskien. Turin: Einaudi, 2001.
12. Shmueli, Ilana. *Di' che Gerusalemme e: su Paul Celan: ottobre 1969–aprile 1970*. Co-translated by Jutta Leskien. Macerata: Quodlibet, 2003.
13. Rilke, Rainer Maria. *Elegie duinesi*. Co-translated by Jutta Leskien. Milan: Feltrinelli, 2006.

Clemente Rebora, 1885–1957

1. Andreyev, Leonid. *Lazzaro e altre novelle*. Florence: Vallecchi, 1919.
2. Tolstoy, Leo. *La felicità domestica*. Florence: La Voce, 1920.
3. Anonymous. *Gianardana*. Milan: Bottega di Poesia, 1922.
4. Gogol, Nikolai. *Il cappotto*. Milan: Il Convegno Editoriale, 1922.

Agostino Richelmy, 1900–1991

1. Musset, Alfred de. *Commedie e provverbi*. Turin: Einaudi, 1952.
2. Virgil. *Le georgiche*. Turin: Einaudi, 1955.
3. Phaedrus. *Favole*. Turin: Einaudi, 1959.
4. Virgil. *Le bucoliche*. Turin: Einaudi, 1970.
5. Voltaire. *Zadig*. Turin: Einaudi, 1973.
6. Flaubert, Gustave. *La tentazione di S. Antonio*. Turin: Einaudi, 1990.

Angelo Maria Ripellino, 1923–1978

1. Aksakov, S.T. *Nuovo bagrovo e le sue donne: Cronaca di famiglia*. Rome: Capriotti, 1946.
2. *Poesia russa del Novecento*. Guanda: Parma, 1954.
3. Pasternak, Boris. *Poesie*. Turin: Einaudi, 1957.
4. Blok, Aleksandr. *Poesie*. Milan: Lerici, 1960.
5. Bely, Andrey. *Pietroburgo*. Turin: Einaudi, 1961.
6. *Nuovi poeti sovietici*. Turin: Einaudi, 1961.
7. Holan, Vladimír. *Una notte con Amleto e altre poesie*. Turin: Einaudi, 1966.
8. Mayakovsky, Vladimir. *Lenin*. Turin: Einaudi, 1967.
9. Khlebnikov, Velimir. *Poesie*. Turin: Einaudi, 1968.
10. Linhartová, Věra. *Interanalisi del fluito prossimo*. Co-translated by Ela Ripellino. Turin: Einaudi, 1969.
11. Cechov, Anton Pavlovich. *Il gabbiano*. Torin: Einaudi, 1970.
12. Cechov, Anton Pavlovich. *Zio Vanja*. Turin: Einaudi, 1970.
13. Halas, František. *Imagena*. Turin: Einaudi, 1971.

Nelo Risi, 1920–

1. Supervielle, Jules. *In Viaggio con Supervielle*. Milan: All'insegna del pesce d'oro, 1956.
2. Jouve, Pierre Jean. *Poesie*. Rome: Carocci, 1957.
3. Jouve, Pierre Jean. *Paradiso perduto*. Bologna: Edizioni della lanterna, 1961.
4. Illyés, Gyula. *Ket Kez*. Co-translated by Edith Bruck. Milan: All'insegna del pesce d'oro, 1966.
5. Cavafy, Constantine. *Cinquantacinque poesie*. Co-translated by Margherita Dalmati. Turin: Einaudi, 1968.

6. Laforgue, Jules. *Moralita leggendarie*. Rome: Addenda, 1972.
7. Sophocles. *Edipo Re*. Milan: SE, 1985.
8. *Compito di francese e d'altre lingue 1943–1993*. Milan: Guerini, 1994.

Ceccardo Roccatagliata Ceccardi, 1871–1919

1. *Annali genovesi di Caffaro e dei suoi continuatori: (1099–1293): Caffaro*. Co-translated by G. Monleone. Vol. 1. Genoa: Municipo di Genova, 1923.

Amelia Rosselli, 1930–1996

1. Plath, Sylvia. *Le muse inquietanti e altre poesie*. Co-translated by Gabriella Moresca. Milan: Mondadori, 1985.
2. Marciani, Marcello. *Body Movements: Poems*. Stony Brook: Gradiva, 1988.
3. Evans, Paul. *Dialogo fra il poeta e la musa*. Rome: Fondazione Piazzolla, 1991.

Paolo Ruffilli, 1949–

1. Gibran, Kahlil. *Il profeta*. Cinisello Balsamo: Paoline, 1989.
2. Tagore, Rabindranath. *Gitanjali, canti di offerta*. Cinisello Balsamo: Paoline, 1993.
3. Laozi. *Il libro della saggezza*. Milan: Baldini Castoldi Dalai, 2004.
4. Confucius. *Il libro delle massime*. Milan: Baldini Castoldi Dalai, 2006.

Edoardo Sanguineti, 1930–2010

1. Euripides. *Le baccanti*. Milan: Feltrinelli, 1968.
2. Petronius Arbiter. *Il Satyricon*. Rome: Aldo Palazzi, 1969.
3. Seneca, Lucius Annaeus. *Fedra*. Turin: Einaudi, 1969.
4. Euripides. *Le Troiane*. Turin: Einaudi, 1974.
5. Aeschylus. *Le Coefore*. Milan: Il Saggiatore, 1978.
6. Sophocles. *Edipo tiranno*. Bologna: Cappelli, 1980.
7. Goethe, Johann Wolfgang von. *Faust: un travestimento*. Genoa: Costa and Nolan, 1985.
8. Aeschylus. *I sette contro Tebe*. Milan: Sipario, 1992.
9. Molière. *Don Giovanni*. Genoa: Il melangolo, 2000.
10. Aristophanes. *La festa della donna*. Genoa: Il Melangolo, 2001.
11. Brecht, Bertolt. *Il cerchio di gesso del Caucaso*. Genoa: Il Melangolo, 2003.
12. Goethe, Johann Wolfgang von. *Omaggio a Goethe*. Bellinzona: Edizioni Sottoscala, 2003.
13. Shakespeare, William. *Omaggio a Shakespeare. Nove sonetti*. Lecce: Manni, 2004.
14. Corneille, Pierre. *L'illusione comica*. Genoa: Il Melangolo, 2005.
15. *Quaderno di traduzioni*. Turin: Einaudi, 2006.

16. *Teatro antico. Traduzioni e ricordi*. Edited by Federico Condello and Claudio Longhi. Milan: Rizzoli, 2006.
17. Shakespeare, William. *Re Lear*. Genoa: Il Melangolo, 2008.
18. Euripides. *Ifigenia in Aulide*. Bologna: Bononia University Press, 2012.

Massimo Sannelli, 1973–

1. Boethius. *Sui sogni*. Genoa: Il Melangolo, 1997.
2. *Sulla gelosia*. Genoa: Il Melangolo, 1998.
3. Abelard, Peter. *Planctus*. Trento: La Finestra, 2002.
4. De Insulis, Alanus. *Anticlaudianus*. Trento: La Finestra, 2004.

Mario Santagostini, 1951–

1. Ambrose, Saint. *Inni*. Milan: Mondadori, 1992.
2. *Innario cistercense*. Milan: Mondadori, 1994.
3. *I simbolisti tedeschi*. Rome: Fazi, 1996.
4. Chamisso, Adalbert von. *Storia straordinaria di Peter Schlemihl; Poesie*. Rome: La Repubblica, 2004.
5. Goethe, Johann Wolfgang von. *Le affinita elettive*. Rome: L'espresso, 2004.
6. Kleist, Heinrich von. *La marchesa di O … e altri racconti*. Rome: La Repubblica, 2005.

Flavio Santi, 1973–

1. Rexroth, Kenneth. *Su quale pianeta*. Milan: Marcos y Marcos, 1999.
2. Gifford, Barry. *I vecchi tempi e altre storie*. Pavia: Sartorio, 2005.
3. Kelman, James. *Troppo tardi, Sammy*. Pavia: Sartorio, 2006.
4. O'Reilly, Sean. *Il ritmo delle cose*. Pavia: Sartorio, 2006.
5. Franklin, Tom. *Alabama blues*. Pavia: Sartorio, 2007.
6. Stone, Robert. *Baia delle anime*. Pavia: Sartorio, 2007.
7. James, Marlon. *Il diavolo di John Crow*. Milan: Baldini Castoldi Dalai, 2008.
8. Kilmer-Purcell, Josh. *In questi giorni sono fuori di me*. Milan: Baldini Castoldi Dalai, 2008.
9. Maturin, Charles Robert. *Melmoth l'errante*. Turin: UTET, 2008.
10. Mandanipour, Shahriar. *Censura: una storia d'amore iraniana*. Milan: Rizzoli, 2009.
11. Blackwood, Algernon. *John Silence e altri incubi*. Turin: UTET, 2010.
12. Catton, Eleanor. *La prova*. Rome: Fandango, 2010.
13. Stead, Rebecca. *Quando mi troverai*. Milan: Feltrinelli, 2010.
14. Wagner, Bruce. *Ti sto perdendo*. Milan: Baldini Castoldi Dalai, 2010.

Camillo Sbarbaro, 1888–1967

1. Flaubert, Gustave. *Salambo*. Turin: Einaudi, 1943.

2. Sophocles. *Antigone*. Milan: Bompiani, 1943.
3. Huysman, Joris-Karl. *Controcorrente*. Milan: Gentile, 1944.
4. Stendhal. *La certosa di Parma*. Turin: Einaudi, 1944.
5. Barbey d'Aurevilly, Jules. *Le diaboliche*. Milan: Bompiani, 1945.
6. Euripides. *Il Ciclope*. Genoa: Genovese Lettere e Arti, 1945.
7. Flaubert, Gustave. *Tre racconti*. Milan: Bompiani, 1945.
8. Villiers de L'Isle-Adam, Auguste. *Storie insolite e racconti crudeli*. Milan: Bompiani, 1945.
9. Maupassant, Guy de. *Il porto ed altri racconti*. Milan: Bompiani, 1945.
10. Supervielle, Jules. *La figlia del mare aperto*. Milan: Gentile, 1945.
11. Balzac, Honoré de. *La pelle di zigrino*. Turin: Einaudi, 1947.
12. Aeschylus. *Prometeo incatenato*. Milan: Bompiani, 1949.
13. Poulaille, Henri. *Il pane quotidiano*. Milan: Mondadori, 1949.
14. Martin du Gard, Roger. *I Thibault*. Vol. 1. Milan: Mondadori, 1951.
15. Martin du Gard, Roger. *I Thibault*. Vol. 2. Milan: Mondadori, 1951.
16. Zola, Emile. *Germinale*. Turin: Einaudi, 1951.
17. Montherlant, Henri de. *Il gran maestro di Santiago; La regina morta; Malatesta*. Co-translated by Massimo Bontempelli. Milan: Bompiani, 1952.
18. Euripides. *Alcesti; Il Ciclope*. Milan: Bompiani, 1952.
19. Green, Julien. *Veruna*. Milan: Mondadori, 1953.
20. Pythagoras. *I versi d'Oro*. Milan: Scheiwiller, 1958.
21. Montherlant, Henri de. *Il cardinale di Spagna, Port Royal*. Co-translated by Giuseppina Gozzini. Milan: Bompiani, 1961.
22. Flaubert, Gustave. *Bouvard e Pécuchet*. Turin: Einaudi, 1964.

Francesco Scarabicchi, 1951–

1. García Lorca, Federico. *Ninna nanna*. Ancona: La riva, 1992.
2. Machado, Antonio. *Canzoni a Guiomar*. Brescia: L'obliquo, 1993.
3. Machado, Antonio. *Il seminatore di stelle*. Ripatransone: Sestante, 1993.
4. García Lorca, Federico. *Taccuino da García Lorca*. Brescia: L'obliquo, 1998.
5. García Lorca, Federico. *Gli istanti feriti: poesie di Federico García Lorca*. Falconara: Errebi, 2000.
6. *Taccuino spagnolo*. Brescia: L'obliquo, 2000.

Franco Scataglini, 1930–1994

1. *La rosa*. Turin: Einaudi, 1992.

Vittorio Sereni, 1913–1983

1. Green, Julien. *Leviatan*. Milan: Mondadori, 1946.
2. Valéry, Paul. *Eupalinos; L'anima e la danza: Dialogo*. Milan: Mondadori, 1947.

3. Williams, William Carlos. *Poesie*. Milan: Triangolo, 1957.
4. Firbank, Ronald. *Il cardinal Pirelli, La principessa artificiale e Fuoco nero*. Co-translated by D. Bonacossa. Milan: Feltrinelli, 1964.
5. Char, René. *Fogli d'Ipnos*. Turin: Einaudi, 1968.
6. Char, René. *Ritorno sopramonte*. Milan: Mondadori, 1974.
7. Corneille, Pierre. *Illusione teatrale*. Milan: Guanda, 1979.
8. Apollinaire, Guillaume. *Eravamo da poco intanto nati*. Milan: Scheiwiller, 1980.
9. Apollinaire, Guillaume. *Da 'Alcools.'* Co-translated by Giovanni Raboni. Milan: Il Saggiatore, 1981.
10. *Il Musicante di Saint-Merry*. Turin: Einaudi, 1981.
11. Apollinaire, Guillaume. *La chiamavano Lu: e altre poesie*. Co-translated by Giovanni Raboni. Milan: Mondadori, 1984.
12. Char, René. *Due rive ci vogliono: quarantasette traduzioni inedite*. Rome: Donzelli, 2010.

Leonardo Sinisgalli, 1908–1981

1. Baudelaire, Charles. *Il riso, il comico, la caricatura*. Rome: Edizioni del Secolo, 1945.
2. Gautier, Théophile. *Baudelaire*. Rome: Edizioni del Secolo, 1947.
3. Green, Julien. *Passeggero sulla terra*. Milan: Il Saggiatore, 1959.
4. *Imitazioni dall'antologia palatina*. Rome: Cometa, 1980.

Ardengo Soffici, 1879–1964

1. Chekhov, Anton Pavlovich. *Racconti*. Co-translated by S. Jastrebzof. Florence: Casa editrice italiana, 1910.
2. Chekhov, Anton Pavlovich. *Le tre sorelle: dramma*. Co-translated by S. Jastrebzof. Lanciano: R. Carabba, 1913.
3. Georges, Karl Ernst. *Profitti e perdite dell'arte contemporanea*. Florence: Vallecchi, 1933.
4. Vollard, Ambroise. *Papa Ubu all'aviazione*. Reggio Emilia: Libreria antiquaria Prandi, 1975.

Sergio Solmi, 1899–1981

1. Ortega y Gasset, José. *Il tema del nostro tempo*. Milan: Rosa and Ballo, 1947.
2. Alain. *Cento e un ragionamenti*. Turin: Einaudi, 1960.
3. *Versioni poetiche da contemporanei*. Milan: All'insegna del pesce d'oro, 1963.
4. Laforgue, Jules. *Poesie*. Rome: Ateneo, 1966.
5. Jarry, Alfred. *Essere e vivere; Guignol; Ubu re; Scritti sul teatro*. Milan: Adelphi, 1969.

6. Jarry, Alfred. *I giorni e le notti; L'altra Alceste; L'amore assoluto*. Milan: Adelphi, 1969.
7. Jarry, Alfred. *La candela verde; Gesta e opinioni del dottor Faustroll; Ubu incatenato; La dragona*. Milan: Adelphi, 1969.
8. *Quaderno di traduzioni*. Turin: Einaudi, 1969.
9. Benn, Gottfried. *Cinque poesie di Gottfried Benn*. Milan: Scheiwiller, 1972.
10. *Quaderno di traduzioni*. Vol. 2. Turin: Einaudi, 1977.
11. Stefan, Jude. *Poesie*. Co-translated by Perla Cacciaguerra. Milan: Guanda, 1979.
12. Queneau, Raymond. *Piccola cosmogonia portatile*. Turin: Einaudi, 1982.

Adriano Spatola, 1941–1988

1. Sade, Marquis de. *Le disgrazie della virtù*. Bologna: Sampietro, 1967.
2. Berg, Jean de. *L'immagine*. Turin: Della Valle, 1968.
3. Kaganovich, A.L. *L'arte russa dal 17. al 18. secolo*. Bologna: Cappelli, 1968.
4. Kornilovich, Kira. *L'arte russa: dalle origini alla fine del 16 secolo*. Bologna: Cappelli, 1968.
5. Routisie, Albert de. *Irene*. Turin: Della Valle, 1968.
6. Sade, Marquis de. *Considerazioni sul romanzo; Juliette e Raunai; Le due prove*. Bologna: Sampietro, 1968.
7. Dubuffet, Jean. *Asfissiante cultura*. Milan: Feltrinelli, 1969.
8. Leduc, Violette. *Teresa e Isabella e La donna col renard*. Co-translated by Ginetta Vittorini. Milan: Feltrinelli, 1969.
9. Pieyre de Mandiargues, André. *Il castello dell'inglese*. Turin: Della Valle, 1969.
10. Vilmont, Anne. *Le carnivore*. Turin: Della Valle, 1969.
11. Metraux, Alfred. *Il vodu haitiano*. Turin: Einaudi, 1971.
12. Edwards, Michael. *Nell'India antica*. Co-translated by Giulia Niccolai. Milan: LM, 1975.
13. La Fontaine, Jean de. *Favole*. Co-translated by Giulia Niccolai. Milan: LM, 1975.
14. MacNamara, Ellen. *Gli Etruschi*. Co-translated by Giulia Niccolai. Milan: LM, 1975.
15. Mérimée, Prosper. *La notte di San Bartolomeo*. Co-translated by Giulia Niccolai. Milan: Emme 1975.
16. Rowling, Marjorie. *Nel Medioevo*. Co-translated by Giulia Niccolai. Milan: LM, 1975.
17. Lambert, Jean-Clarence. *L' orologica*. Co-translated by Jean-Clarence Lambert. Rivalba: Geiger, 1976.
18. Blaine, Julien. *Elefanti e primi testi*. Co-translated by Julien Blaine. Turin: Geiger, 1977.

19. Aragon, Louis. *Le con d'Irene*. Milan: ES, 1994.
20. Singer, Isaac Bashevis. *Una notte di Hanukkah*. Co-translated by Bianca Maria Bonazzi. Turin: Einaudi, 1994.

Maria Luisa Spaziani, 1924–

1. Clewes, Winston. *Amicizie violente*. Milan: Mondadori, 1951.
2. Gombrich, E.H. *Il mondo dell'arte*. Milan: Mondadori, 1952.
3. Audiberti, Jacques. *Il padrone di Milano*. Milan: Bompiani, 1956.
4. Moffet, Langston. *Il diavolo e la sua coda*. Milan: Club degli Editori, 1962.
5. Yourcenar, Marguerite. *Il colpo di grazia; Alexis*. Milan: Feltrinelli, 1962.
6. Sand, George. *Francesco il trovatello*. Turin: ERI, 1963.
7. Prudhomme, Sully. *Premio Nobel per la letteratura 1901*. Co-translated by Pietro Lazzaro. Milan: Fabbri, 1965.
8. Gobineau, Arthur. *Sull'ineguaglianza delle razze*. Milan: Longanesi, 1965.
9. Bellow, Saul. *La vittima*. Milan: Feltrinelli, 1966.
10. Toulet, Paul-Jean. *Poesie*. Turin: Einaudi, 1966.
11. *Due poeti: Charles d'Orléans e Sully Prudhomme*. Rome: Faro/Nuova Biblioteca Univaristaria, 1970.
12. *Ronsard: fra gli astri delle Pleaidi*. Turin: ERI, 1972.
13. Racine, Jean. *Bajazet*. Rome: Faro/Nuova Biblioteca Universitaria, 1973.
14. Tournier, Michel. *Le Meteore*. Milan: Mondadori, 1979.
15. Gide, André. *Oscar Wilde*. Co-translated by Elena Tognini Bonelli. Florence: Giusti, 1979.
16. Yourcenar, Marguerite. *Novelle orientali*. Milan: Rizzoli, 1983.
17. Tournier, Michel. *Gaspare Melchiorre e Baldassarre*. Milan: Garzanti, 1984.
18. Racine, Jean. *Britannico; Bajazet; Atalia*. Milan: Garzanti, 1986.
19. Gide, André. *Cosi sia ovvero Il gioco e fatto*. Milan: SE, 1987.
20. Tournier, Michel. *Il gallo cedrone*. Milan: Garzanti, 1988.
21. Yourcenar, Marguerite. *Fuochi*. Milan: Bompiani, 1988.
22. Yourcenar, Marguerite. *Il colpo di grazia*. Milan: Feltrinelli, 1990.
23. Flaubert, Gustave. *Madame Bovary*. Milan: Mondadori, 1997.
24. Desbordes-Valmore, Marceline. *Liriche d'amore*. Milan: Galliano, 2004.
25. Jammes, Francis. *Clairières dans le ciel*. Palermo: RueBallau, 2008.

Enrico Testa, 1956–

1. Larkin, Philip. *Finestre alte*. Turin: Einaudi, 2002.

Giovanni Testori, 1923–1993

1. Paul, the Apostle. *Traduzione della prima lettera ai Corinti*. Milan: Longanesi, 1991.

Pietro Tripodo, 1948–1999

1. Trakl, Georg. *Liriche scelte*. Rome: Salerno, 1991.
2. Callimachus, and Gaius Valerius Catullus. *La chioma di Berenice*. Rome: Salerno, 1995.
3. Georg, Stefan. *I canti del sogno e della morte; Ludwig Klages, Stefan George*. Co-translated by Giampiero Moretti. Rome: Fazi, 1995.
4. Arnaut Daniel. *Canti di schermo e d'amore*. Rome: Fazi, 1997.

Giuseppe Ungaretti, 1888–1970

1. *Traduzioni: St. J. Perse, William Blake, Gongora, Essenin, Jean Paulhan, Affrica*. Rome: Novissima, 1936.
2. Shakespeare, William. *XXII sonetti di Shakespeare scelti e tradotti da Giuseppe Ungaretti*. Rome: Documento Editore Libraio, 1944.
3. Shakespeare, William. *Vita d'un uomo: 40 sonetti di Shakespeare*. Milan: Mondadori, 1946.
4. Mallarmé, Stéphane. *L'après-midi et le Monologue d'un Faune tradotti da Giuseppe Ungaretti*. Milan: Balcone, 1947.
5. Góngora y Argote, Luis de, and Stéphane Mallarmé. *Vita di un uomo: Da Góngora e da Mallarmé*. Milan: Mondadori, 1948.
6. Racine, Jean. *Vita di un uomo: Fedra di Jean Racine*. Milan: Mondadori, 1950.
7. Mendes, Murilo. *Finestra del caos*. Milan: Scheiwiller, 1961.
8. Blake, William *Vita di un uomo: Visioni di William Blake*. Milan: Mondadori, 1965.
9. Moraes, Vinícius de. *Cinque poesie di Vinícius de Moraes*. Rome: Grafica Romero, 1969.
10. Racine, Jean. *Andromaca*. Co-translated by Corrado Pavolini. Milan: Mondadori, 1975.
11. Poe, Edgar Allan. *Silenzio*. Alpignano: Tallone, 2009.
12. *Vita d'un uomo: traduzioni poetiche*. Edited by Carlo Ossola and Giulia Radin. Milan: Mondadori, 2010.

Patrizia Valduga, 1953–

1. Donne, John. *Canzoni e sonetti*. Milan: Studio Editoriale, 1985.
2. Kantor, Tadeusz. *Stille Nach*. Milan: Ubulibri, 1991.
3. Mallarmé, Stéphane. *Poesie*. Milan: Mondadori, 1991.
4. Molière. *Il Misantropo*. Florence: Giunti, 1995.
5. Molière. *Il malato immaginario*. Florence: Giunti, 1995.
6. Valéry, Paul. *Il Cimitero marino*. Milan: Mondadori, 1995.
7. Shakespeare, William. *Riccardo III*. Turin: Einaudi, 1998.
8. Ronsard, Pierre de. *Respice et crede*. Milan: Il Faggio, 2005.

Diego Valeri, 1887–1976

1. Mistral, Federic. *Da 'Lis isclo d'or' e dal 'Calendau'*. Castiglione delle Stiviere: Pignotti, 1912.
2. Mistral, Federic. *Piccola antologia*. Milan: Istituto Editoriale Italiano, 1917.
3. *Alcassino e Nicoletta*. Milan: L'eroica, 1920.
4. Mistral, Federic. *Mirella*. Turin: UTET, 1930.
5. Flaubert, Gustave. *La Signora Bovary*. Milan: Mondadori, 1936.
6. Maupassant, Guy de. *Maupassant: scelta e traduzione*. Milan: Garzanti, 1942.
7. *Liriche tedesche*. Milan: All'insegna del pesce d'oro, 1942.
8. *Romanzi e racconti d'amore del Medio Evo francese*. Milan: Garzanti, 1943.
9. Focillon, Henri. *Vita delle forme*. Padova: Le Tre Venezie, 1945.
10. Journet, Charles. *Conoscenza e inconoscenza di Dio*. Milan: Edizioni di Comunità, 1947.
11. Stendhal. *Il rosso e il nero*. Turin: Einaudi, 1949.
12. La Fontaine, Jean de. *Quaranta favole*. Florence: Sansoni, 1952.
13. Goethe, Johann Wolfgang von. *Cinquanta poesie*. Florence: Sansoni, 1954.
14. Goethe, Johann Wolfgang von. *Ifigenia in Tauride*. Venice: Neri Pozza, 1954.
15. *Antichi poeti provenzali*. Milan: All'insegna del pesce d'oro, 1954.
16. Heine, Heinrich. *Da 'Lyrisches Intermezzo' di Heinrich Heine*. Padua: Centro d'arte degli Studenti, 1956.
17. Stendhal. *Lucien Leuwen*. Turin: Einaudi, 1956.
18. Jacobi, Hugo. *Miraggi veneziani*. Milan: All'insegna del pesce d'oro, 1957.
19. *I lirici francesi*. Milan: Mondadori, 1960.
20. *Lirici tedeschi*. Milan: Mondadori, 1964.
21. Molière. *Il signor di Pourceaugnac*. Turin: Einaudi, 1965.
22. *Quaderno francese del secolo*. Turin: Einaudi, 1965.
23. Aubanel, Theodore. *O venerable Rome; L'Escalier des Géants; Une vénitienne; La Vénus d'Arles*. Avignon: Les presses universelles, 1974.

Carlo Vallini, 1885–1920

1. Wilde, Oscar. *La ballata del carcere di Reading*. Milan: Modernissima, 1920.

Sebastiano Vassalli, 1941–

1. Perrault, Charles. *La bella addormentata*. Novara: Istituto Geografico de Agostini, 1996.

Giorgio Vigolo, 1894–1983

1. Hoffmann, E.T.A. *Maestro Pulce*. Rome: Petrella, 1944.
2. Hölderlin, Friedrich. *Poesie*. Turin: Einaudi, 1958.

Dario Villa, 1953–1996

1. Isherwood, Christopher. *Un uomo solo*. Milan: Guanda, 1981.
2. Hugo, Victor. *Eroismo e rivoluzione*. Co-translated by Lodovico Terzi. Casale Monferrato: Marietti, 1989.
3. Rayner, Richard. *L'elefante*. Milan: Mondadori, 1992.
4. Sherwood, Frances. *Vindication*. Milan: Mondadori, 1994.
5. Bunting, Basil. *Sonatas*. Valmadrera: Flussi, 1998.

Emilio Villa, 1914–2003

1. Plato. *Fedone*. Verona: La Scagliera, 1938.
2. Plato. *Gorgia*. Verona: La Scagliera, 1940.
3. *Antico teatro ebraico*. Milan: Poligono, 1947.
4. Balzac, Honoré de. *La cugina Betta*. Co-translated by Maria Adalgisa Denti. Milan: Mondadori, 1952.
5. Homer. *Odissea*. Parma: Guanda, 1964.
6. Thomas, of Celano. *Dies irae*. Terma: Edigrafital, 1992.
7. *Proverbi e Cantico: traduzioni dalla Bibbia*. Naples: Bibliopolis, 2005.

Cesare Viviani, 1947–

1. Verlaine, Paul. *Feste galanti*. Milan: Guanda, 1978.
2. Verlaine, Paul. *Feste galanti; La buona canzone*. Milan: Mondadori, 1988.
3. Verlaine, Paul. *Il profilo lieve delle voci antiche*. Recanati: CNSL, 1998.
4. Verlaine, Paul. *Romanze senza parole*. Milan: Feltrinelli, 2007.

Andrea Zanzotto, 1921–2011

1. Haddad, Malek. *Una gazzella per te. Seguita da L'ultima impressione*. Milan: Mondadori, 1960.
2. Aĭtmatov, Chingiz. *Giamilja e altri racconti*. Co-translated by Alberto Pescetto. Milan: Mondadori, 1961.
3. Leiris, Michel. *Età d'uomo e Notti senza notte*. Milan: Mondadori, 1966.
4. Bataille, Georges. *Nietzsche, il culmine e il possibile*. Milan: Rizzoli, 1970.
5. Bataille, Georges. *La letteratura e il male*. Milan: Rizzoli, 1973.
6. Balzac, Honoré de. *La ricerca dell'assoluto*. Milan: Garzanti, 1975.
7. Francastel, Pierre. *Studi di sociologia dell'arte*. Milan: Rizzoli, 1976.
8. Balzac, Honoré de. *Il medico di campagna*. Milan: Garzanti, 1977.

Edoardo Zuccato, 1963-

1. Coleridge, Samuel Taylor. *Diari 1794–1819*. Bergamo: Lubrina, 1991.
2. Hartnett, Michael. *Seminando*. Milan: Crocetti, 1995.
3. Shelley, Percy Bysshe. *Mont Blanc*. Verbania: Tarara, 1996.

4. *Antologia della poesia svedese contemporanea*. Co-translated by H. Sanson. Milan: Crocetti, 1996.
5. *Sotto la pioggia e il gin: antologia della poesia inglese contemporanea*. Milan: Marcos y Marcos, 1997.
6. Villon, François. *Biss, lüsèrt e alter galantomm. Ballate di François Villon*. Co-translated by C. Recalcati. Milan: Effigie, 2005.
7. Virgil. *I Bücòligh*. Milan: Medusa, 2007.
8. *Il dragomanno errante: quaderno di traduzioni*. Brescia: Atì editore, 2012.

Notes

Introduction

1 Aurelio Roncaglia, "De Quibusdam Provincialibus translatis in lingua nostra," in *Letteratura e Critica: Studi in onore di Natalino Sapegno*, vol. 2 (Rome: Bulzoni, 1975), 1–36; and Gianfranco Folena, *Volgarizzare e tradurre* (Turin: Einaudi, 1991), 25–9.
2 Michelangelo Picone, *Percorsi della lirica duecentesca* (Fiesole: Cadmo, 2003), 31.
3 Pascale Casanova, *La république mondiale des lettres* (Paris: Editions du Seuil, 1999), 58.
4 Ilenia de Bernardis, *L'illuminata imitazione: le origini del romanzo moderno in Italia, dalle traduzioni all'emulazione* (Bari: Palomar, 2007).
5 Gianfranco Folena, *Volgarizzare e tradurre*, 25.
6 Pier Vincenzo Mengaldo, "Il 'Monselice' e i poeti-traduttori," http://www.provincia.padova.it/comuni/monselice/traduzione/mengaldo.htm.
7 Cited in Anna Dolfi, "Translation and the European tradition: The Italian 'Third Generation,'" in *Twentieth-Century Poetic Translation: Literary Cultures in Italian and English*, ed. Daniela Caselli and Daniela La Penna (London: Continuum, 2008), 50.
8 Mario Luzi, *Discorso naturale* (Milan: Garzanti, 1984), 71.
9 Cited in Dolfi, "Translation," 55; emphasis in original.
10 Gianfranco Folena, *Volgarizzare e tradurre* (Turin: Einaudi, 1991). A first version of this book was in a 1973 essay, "'Volgarizzare' e 'tradurre': idea e terminologia della traduzione dal Medioevo italiano e romanzo all'Umanesimo europeo," in *La traduzione, saggi e studi* (Trieste: Lint, 1973), 57–120.
11 Cf. Alison Cornish, *Vernacular Translation in Dante's Italy: Illiterate Literature* (Cambridge: Cambridge University Press, 2010).

12 Gérard Genette, *Introduction à l'architexte* (Paris: Seuil, 1979); Guido Mazzoni, *Sulla poesia moderna* (Bologna: Il Mulino, 2005). The prevalence and influence of Petrarch's model of lyric poetry nevertheless does not belie the fact that theoretically epic poetry was held superior to lyric poetry.

13 Genette, *Introduction à l'architexte*, 11.

14 Nicola Gardini overstates the mark when he writes, "One could go as far as state that translation studies are thriving among Italianists." Nicola Gardini, "An Ancient Soul in a New Body: Giovanni Pascoli's Homeric Translations," *Italian Studies* 66, no. 1 (2011): 59.

15 Gianni Pozzi, *La poesia italiana del Novecento da Gozzano agli ermetici* (Turin: Einaudi, 1989).

16 Silvio Ramat, *Storia della poesia del Novecento* (Milan: Mursia, 1976).

17 Frederic J. Jones, *The Modern Italian Lyric* (Cardiff: University of Wales Press, 1986).

18 *Storia della letteratura italiana*, ed. Enrico Malato, 14 vols. (Rome: Salerno, 1995–2005).

19 E.g., *Storia letteraria d'Italia: Il novecento*, ed. Giorgio Luti, 2 vols. (Milan: Vallardi-Piccin, 1993).

20 I searched for the following title words: *traduzione, traduzioni, traduttore, traduttori, versione*, and *versioni*, during the period 1883–1995.

21 E.g., *Poesia del Novecento*, ed. Edoardo Sanguineti (Turin: Einaudi, 1969).

22 Exceptions are Maria Stella, *Cesare Pavese traduttore* (Rome: Bulzoni, 1977); Anna Manfredi, *Fortini traduttore di Eluard* (Lucca: M. Pacini Fazzi, 1992); George Talbot, *Montale's mestiere vile* (Dublin: Irish Academic Press, 1995); Isabel Violante Picon, *Une oeuvre originale de poésie: Giuseppe Ungaretti traducteur* (Paris: Presses de l'Université de Paris-Sorbonne, 1998); and Laura Toppan, *Le chinois: Luzi critico e traduttore di Mallarmé* (Pesaro: Metauro, 2006). Two unpublished dissertations examine the translation activity of Giorgio Caproni and Andrea Zanzotto: Elisa Bricco, "Giorgio Caproni traduttore della poesia francese" (PhD diss., Università di Bari, 1995); Silvia Bassi, "Un 'giardiniere e botanico delle lingue': Andrea Zanzotto traduttore e autotraduttore" (PhD diss., Università di Venezia, 2011). Another unpublished dissertation analyzes third and fourth generation Italian poet-translators: Leonardo Manigrasso, "Capitoli autobiografici. Poeti traduttori a confronto tra terza e quarta generazione" (PhD diss., Università degli Studi di Padova, 2012).

23 Cf. "Anthologies of Translation," in *The Routledge Encyclopedia of Translation Studies*, ed. Mona Baker (London: Routledge, 1998), 13–16. This entry is inexplicably eliminated from the second edition of the *Encyclopedia*.

24 This is a representative sampling: Pier Vincenzo Mengaldo, "Aspetti delle versioni poetiche di Solmi," *Studi novecenteschi* 9, no. 23 (1982): 45–96; Pier Vincenzo Mengaldo, "La panchina e i morti (su una versione di Montale)," in *La poesia di Eugenio Montale* (Milan: Librex, 1983), 133–48; Pier Vincenzo Mengaldo, "Confronti fra traduttori-poeti contemporanei (Sereni, Caproni, Luzi)," in *Tradizione/Traduzione/Società. Saggi per Franco Fortini* (Rome: Editori Riuniti, 1989), 243–60; Pier Vincenzo Mengaldo, "Caproni e Sereni: due versioni," in *Premio Città di Monselice per la traduzione letteraria e scientifica*, ed. G. Peron (Monselice: Amministrazione Comunale, 1993), 210–21; Pier Vincenzo Mengaldo, "Premessa," in Giorgio Caproni, *Quaderno di traduzioni*, ed. Enrico Testa (Turin: Einaudi, 1998), v–xi; Pier Vincenzo Mengaldo, "Introduzione," in Vittorio Sereni, *Il musicante di Saint-Merry* (Turin: Einaudi, 2001), v–xxvii.

25 Antonio Prete, *All'ombra dell'altra lingua: per una poetica della traduzione* (Turin: Bollati Boringhieri, 2011). This book reprints many of his essays on translation, including "Dialoghi sul confine. La traduzione della poesia," first published in *Storia della letteratura italiana. Il Novecento. Scenari di fine secolo*, ed. Nino Borsellino and Lucio Felici (Milan: Garzanti, 2001).

26 E.g., Laura Barile, "Traduzione e imitazione da Char," in *Il passato che non passa: le 'poetiche provvisorie' di Vittorio Sereni* (Florence: Le Lettere, 2004), 129–54; Laura Barile, *Oltreconfine. Incursioni nelle letterature europee* (Ospedaletto: Pacini, 2008); Laura Barile, *Adorate mie larve. Montale e la poesia anglosassone* (Bologna: Il Mulino, 1990).

27 Daniela La Penna, "Traduzioni e traduttori," in *Gli anni '60 e '70 in Italia: due decenni di ricerca poetica*, ed. Stefano Giovannuzzi (Genoa: San Marco dei Giustiniani, 2003), 297–322.

28 Francesca Billiani, "Renewing a Literary Culture through Translation: Poetry in Post-war Italy," in *Translation as Intervention*, ed. Jeremy Munday (London: Continuum, 2007), 140–60.

29 Some of the most notable are the following: Franco Fortini, "Traduzione e rifacimento,"*Problemi* 33 (1972): 125–31; "Cinque paragrafi sul tradurre," in *Premio Città di Monselice*, 2 (1973): 60–5; "Da una versione di Góngora," in *Nuovi saggi italiani* (Milan: Garzanti, 1987), 351–64; "Dei 'compensi' nelle versioni di poesia," in *La traduzione del testo poetico*, ed. Franco Buffoni (Milan: Marcos y Marcos, 2004), 72–7; "Il Rilke di Giaime Pintor," in *Saggi ed epigrammi*, ed. Luca Lenzini (Milan: Mondadori, 2003), 1318–23; "La traduzione come straniamento," in *Un dialogo ininterrotto: Interviste 1952–1994*, ed. Velio Abati (Turin: Bollati Boringhieri, 2003), 407–10; "Montale traduttore di Guillén," in *Nuovi saggi italiani* (Milan: Garzanti, 1987), 142–9.

30 Franco Buffoni, *Con il testo a fronte: indagine sul tradurre e l'essere tradotti* (Novara: Interlinea, 2007).
31 Francesca Billiani, *Culture nazionali e narrazioni straniere: Italia, 1903–1943* (Florence: Le Lettere, 2007).
32 Christopher Rundle, *Publishing Translations in Fascist Italy* (Bern: Peter Lang, 2010).
33 Valerio Ferme, *Tradurre è tradire: la traduzione come sovversione culturale sotto il Fascismo* (Ravenna: Longo, 2002).
34 *CLIO: catalogo dei libri italiani dell'Ottocento (1801–1900)*, ed. Michele Costa, Giuliano Vigini, and Mauro Zerbini (Milan: Editrice Bibliografica, 1991), 19 vols.
35 Gardini, "An ancient soul," 60; italics in the original. Salvatore Quasimodo's *Lirici greci*, undoubtedly the most famous translation of foreign poetry in twentieth-century Italy, is definitely an exception to the rule.
36 Jacob Blakesley, "Poet-translators in Modern Italy: A Statistical Survey," *Testo a Fronte* 47, no. 1 (2013): 31–41.
37 Franco Fortini, *Lezioni sulla traduzione*, ed. Maria Vittoria Tirinato (Macerata: Quodlibet, 2011), 160.
38 Cf. Francesca Billiani, "Return to Order as Return to Realism in Two Italian Elite Literary Magazines of the 1920s and 1930s: La Ronda and Orpheus," *MLR* 107, no. 3 (2013): 839–62.
39 Franco Fortini, *Lezioni sulla traduzione*, ed. Maria Vittoria Tirinato (Macerata: Quodlibet, 2011), 133.
40 Mario Praz, *Poeti inglesi dell'Ottocento* (Florence: Bemporad, 1925).
41 Pier Vincenzo Mengaldo, "Introduzione," in *Poeti italiani del Novecento* (Milan: Mondadori, 1978), xxx.
42 Franco Fortini, *Lezioni sulla traduzione*, ed. Maria Vittoria Tirinato (Macerata: Quodlibet, 2011), 133.
43 Franco Fortini, *I poeti del Novecento* (Bari: Laterza, 1988), 105.
44 Mario Luzi, *Conversazione. Interviste 1953–1998*, ed. Anna Maria Murdocca (Fiesole: Cadmo, 1999), 85.
45 Cesare Pavese, *Saggi letterari* (Turin: Einaudi, 1968), 223.
46 Cf. Laura Toppan, *Le Chinois: Luzi critico e traduttore di Mallarmé* (Pesaro: Metauro, 2006).
47 Rainer Maria Rilke, *Elegie duinesi*, trans. Leone Traverso (Florence: Parenti, 1937).
48 Friedrich Hölderlin, *Alcune poesie di Hölderlin*, trans. Gianfranco Contini (Florence: Parenti, 1941).
49 Rainer Maria Rilke, *Poesie*, trans. Giaime Pintor (Turin: Einaudi, 1942).

50 E.g., *Poesia spagnola del Novecento*, ed. Oreste Macrì (Parma: Guanda, 1952).
51 E.g., *Lirici spagnoli*, ed. Carlo Bo (Milan: Corrente, 1941).
52 E.g., *I poeti surrealisti spagnoli: saggio introduttivo e antologia*, ed. Vittorio Bodini (Turin: Einaudi, 1962).
53 Dario Puccini, *Romancero della Resistenza spagnola: 1936–1959* (Milan: Feltrinelli, 1960).
54 *La violetta notturna: antologia di poeti russi del novecento*, trans. Renato Poggioli (Lanciano: Carabba, 1933), and *Il fiore del verso russo*, trans. Renato Poggioli (Turin: Einaudi, 1949).
55 Alexander Pushkin, *Poemi e liriche*, trans. Tommaso Landolfi (Turin: Einaudi, 1960); Fyodor Tyutchev, *Poesie*, trans. Tommaso Landolfi (Turin: Einaudi, 1964).
56 E.g., *Poesia russa del Novecento*, trans. Angelo Maria Ripellino (Parma: Guanda, 1954).
57 *Lirici Nuovi: antologia di poesia contemporanea*, ed. Luciano Anceschi (Milan: Hoepli, 1942).
58 *Poeti antichi e moderni tradotti dai lirici nuovi*, ed. Luciano Anceschi and Domenico Porzio (Milan: Il Balcone, 1945).
59 Luciano Anceschi, *Chi importa chi parla? Dialoghi con Luciano Anceschi*, ed. Michele Gulinucci (Reggio Emilia: Edizioni Diabasis, 1992), 54.
60 Luciano Anceschi, *Chi importa chi parla? Dialoghi con Luciano Anceschi*, ed. Michele Gulinucci (Reggio Emilia: Edizioni Diabasis, 1992), 55.
61 Cf. Daniela La Penna, "Traduzioni e traduttori," in *Gli anni '60 e '70 in Italia: due decenni di ricerca poetica*, ed. Stefano Giovannuzzi (Genoa: San Marco dei Giustiniani, 2003), 300.
62 Leonardo Manigrasso, "Capitoli autobiografici. Poeti traduttori a confronto tra terza e quarta generazione" (PhD diss., Università degli Studi di Padova, 2012), 25.
63 Francesca Billiani, "Renewing a Literary Culture through Translation: Poetry in Post-war Italy," in *Translation as Intervention*, ed. Jeremy Munday (London: Continuum, 2007), 153.
64 Cf. Mila Milani, "Publishing Contemporary Foreign Poetry in Post-War Italy: A Bourdieusian Perspective on Mondadori and Scheiwiller," *New Voices in Translation Studies* 8 (2012): 99–114.
65 Sergio Solmi, *Versioni poetiche da contemporanei* (Milan: All'insegna del pesce d'oro, 1963).
66 See, for example, Carla Gubert, "Le belle infedeli: omaggio a Frénaud de 'L'Europa Letteraria,'" in *Frammenti di Europa: riviste e traduttori del Novecento*, ed. Carla Gubert (Pesaro: Metauro, 2003), 81–100.

67 Beatrice Sica, "Luzi e Fortini tra simbolismo e surrealismo," in *Antologie e poesia nel Novecento italiano*, ed. Giancarlo Quiriconi (Rome: Bulzoni, 2011), 120.
68 Riccardo Capoferro, "Antologie e Canone Letterario. Poesia inglese in Italia dagli anni Trenta agli anni Sessanta," in *Poesia e traduzione nell'Europa del Novecento*, ed. Anna Dolfi (Rome: Bulzoni, 2004), 321.
69 *Poeti italiani del Novecento*, ed. Pier Vincenzo Mengaldo (Milan: Mondadori, 1978).
70 *Antologia della poesia italiana: Novecento*, ed. Cesare Segre and Carlo Ossola, 2 vols. (Turin: Einaudi, 2003).
71 Vincenzo Monti, *Versioni poetiche di Vincenzo Monti: Persio, Voltaire, Omero, Pyrker, Lemercier, ec*, ed. Giosuè Carducci (Florence: Barbera, 1869).
72 Giosuè Carducci, *Versioni da antichi e da moderni* (Bologna: Zanichelli, 1940).
73 Giovanni Pascoli, *Traduzioni e Riduzioni* (Bologna: Zanichelli, 1913).
74 Almost nothing is known about him. No other publications are associated with his name.
75 Anna Dolfi, "Translation," 45.
76 Giuseppe Ungaretti, *Traduzioni: St.-J. Perse, William Blake, Gongora, Essenin, Jean Paulhan, Affrica* (Rome: Novissima, 1936).
77 Cf. notes by Giulia Radin.
78 Leone Traverso, *Poesia moderna straniera* (Rome: Edizioni di Prospettive, 1942).
79 Hölderlin, Rilke, Trakl, Benn, Éluard, and Yeats are among the most translated in this volume, and Traverso does include two Spanish poets.
80 Antonio Prete, *All'ombra dell'altra lingua: per una poetica della traduzione* (Turin: Bollati Boringhieri, 2011), 125.
81 The title is in contrast with the modest opening lines of his introduction: "Raccolgo qui alcune delle versioni da poeti stranieri che mi sono venute fatte via via in questi anni." Leone Traverso, *Poesia moderna straniera*, xiii.
82 Cf. Christopher Rundle; Francesca Billiani.
83 Beniamino Dal Fabbro, "Poesia e traduzione di poesia," in *La sera armoniosa* (Milan: Rizzoli, 1966), 11.
84 Teresa Spignoli, "'Un quaderno da squadernare.'" Le antologie europee della generazione ermetica," in *Antologie e poesie nel Novecento italiano*, ed. Giancarlo Quiriconi (Rome: Bulzoni, 2011), 97.
85 Some innovative mixtures of translations and original work are Franco Buffoni's *Del Maestro in bottega* (Rome: Empiria, 2002) and Antonella Anedda's *Nomi distanti* (Rome: Empiria, 1998).
86 He published another edition of French poetry, *Quaderno francese del secolo* (Turin: Einaudi, 1965).

87 Luzi, *La cordigliera delle Ande*, viii.
88 Sergio Solmi, *Quaderno di traduzioni* (Turin: Einaudi, 1969), 105.
89 Billiani, "Renewing a Literary Culture," 151.
90 Nelo Risi, *Compito di francese e d'altre lingue, 1943–1993* (Milan: Guerini, 1994).
91 Luciano Erba, *Il tranviere metafisico, seguito da Quadernetto di traduzioni* (Milan: Scheiwiller, 1987).
92 In a letter to Contini, he refers to it as a *Cahier di Traduzioni*. Cf. Eugenio Montale and Gianfranco Contini, *Eusebio e Trabucco*, ed. Dante Isella (Milan: Adelphi, 1997), 179.
93 Ippolito Nievo, *Quaderno di traduzioni*, ed. Iginio de Luca (Turin: Einaudi, 1964); Beppe Fenoglio, *Quaderno di traduzioni*, ed. Mark Pietralunga (Turin: Einaudi, 2000); and Margherita Guidacci, *La voce dell'acqua: quaderno di traduzioni*, ed. Giancarlo Battaglia and Ilaria Rabatti (Pistoia: C.R.T., 2002).
94 Pier Vincenzo Mengaldo, letter to author, 4 November 2009.
95 Pier Vincenzo Mengaldo, "Premessa," in Giorgio Caproni, *Quaderno di traduzioni*, ed. Enrico Testa (Turin: Einaudi, 1998), vi.
96 The *quaderni* of Sereni, Fortini, Giudici, and Luzi were published in the *Supercoralli* series, while the *quaderni* of Caproni and Sanguineti were published in the series *Collezione di poesia*.
97 Franco Fortini, "*Il Musicante di Saint Merry*," in *Nuovi saggi italiani* (Milan: Garzanti, 1987), 166.
98 I thank Daniela La Penna for this indication: Daniela La Penna, email message to author, 10 December 2012.
99 Giulio Einaudi to Giorgio Caproni, 14 January 1981. Fondo Caproni, L'Archivio Contemporaneo Bonsanti del Gabinetto G. P. Vieusseux di Firenze.
100 Zanzotto revealed the internal conflict about publishing his *quaderno di traduzioni*, in two interviews with Silvia Bassi, in her interesting dissertation on Zanzotto as translator. In the first interview, on 29 October 2008, the poet said, "Io volevo anche pubblicare un quaderno di traduzioni, che è qui da qualche parte. Ma le traduzioni di poesia mi sembrano proprio un nonsense. Si fanno, è bene anche farle, ma … " Cited in Silvia Bassi, "Un 'giardiniere e botanico delle lingue': Andrea Zanzotto traduttore e autotraduttore" (PhD diss., Università di Venezia, 2011), 279. In the second interview, on 27 March 2009, Zanzotto returned to the issue: "Avrei anche, completamente inedito, un quaderno di traduzioni, ma quando penso di pubblicarlo cominciano i dubbi." Cited in Silvia Bassi, "Un 'giardiniere e botanico delle lingue': Andrea Zanzotto traduttore e autotraduttore." Ibid., 287.

101 Sergio Solmi, *Quaderno di traduzioni* (Turin: Einaudi, 1969); and Sergio Solmi, *Quaderno di traduzioni: 2* (Turin: Einaudi, 1977).
102 The eventual absence of Zanzotto is definitely felt.
103 Vittorio Sereni, *Il musicante di Saint-Merry* (Turin: Einaudi, 1981).
104 Franco Fortini, *Il ladro di ciliege: e altre versioni di poesia* (Turin: Einaudi, 1982).
105 Giovanni Giudici, *Addio, proibito piangere e altri versi tradotti (1955–1980)* (Turin: Einaudi, 1982).
106 Mario Luzi, *La cordigliera delle Ande e altri versi tradotti* (Turin: Einaudi, 1983).
107 Giorgio Caproni, *Quaderno di traduzioni*, ed. Enrico Testa (Turin: Einaudi, 1998).
108 Edoardo Sanguineti, *Quaderno di traduzioni* (Turin: Einaudi, 2006). Also Fenoglio.
109 Cf. Daniela La Penna, "Poetic canons in translation," in *Twentieth-Century Poetic Translation: Literary Cultures in Italian and English*, ed. Daniela Caselli and Daniela La Penna (London: Continuum, 2008), 19.
110 Tolmino Baldassari, *Quaderno di traduzioni* (Forlì: Nuova compagnia editrice, 1990).
111 The novelist Giovanni Bonalumi is an exception, along with Fenoglio, to the rule that generally only poets compose *quaderni di traduzioni*.
112 Gianni D'Elia, *Taccuino francese* (Siena: Edizioni di Barbablù, 1990).
113 Luciano Erba, *Dei cristalli naturali e altri versi tradotti (1950–1990)* (Milan: Guerini, 1991).
114 Luciano Erba, *Il tranviere metafisico, seguito da Quadernetto di traduzioni* (Milan: Scheiwiller, 1987).
115 Tomaso Kemeny, *Notturno* (Milan: Rizzoli, 1992).
116 Attilio Lolini, *Imitazioni* (Brescia: L'obliquo, 1989).
117 Gilda Musa, *Incontri con T.S. Eliot, K. Mansfield, R. Bridges, R. Kipling, T. Hardy, W. Blunt, G. Hopkins, F. Thompson, M. Arnold, S. Coleridge, H. Longfellow: liriche scelte con un'appendice di poesie tratte da lirici greci* (Milan: Accademia, 1950).
118 Alessandro Parronchi, *Quaderno francese: poesie tradotte con alcuni commenti* (Florence: Vallecchi, 1989).
119 Attilio Bertolucci, *Imitazioni* (Milan: Libri Scheiwiller, 1994).
120 Gerard Genette, *Paratexts: Thresholds of Interpretation*, trans. Jane E. Lewin (Cambridge: Cambridge University Press, 1997), 55–104.
121 Giudici, *Addio, proibito piangere*, vii.
122 Silvia Zoico, "Come è fatto *Il musicante di Saint-Merry* di Vittorio Sereni," in *Stilistica, metrica e storia della lingua. Studi offerti dagli allievi a Pier*

Vincenzo Mengaldo, ed. Tina Matarrese, Marco Praloran, and Paolo Trovato (Padua: Antenore, 1997), 379.

123 Pier Vincenzo Mengaldo, "Introduzione," in *Poeti italiani del Novecento* (Milan: Mondadori, 1978), xxix.

1. A Brief Tour of Western Translation Theory

1 I.A. Richards, "Towards a Theory of Translation," in *Studies in Chinese Thought*, ed. Arthur F. Wright (Chicago: University of Chicago Press, 1953), 250.

2 Andrew Chesterman, *Memes of Translation* (Amsterdam: John Benjamins, 1997), 10.

3 Richard Dawkins, *The Selfish Gene: 30th Anniversary Edition* (Oxford: Oxford University Press, 2006), 192.

4 Cicero, "De optimo genere oratorum," in *De inventione. De optimo genere oratorum. Topica*, ed. and trans. H.M. Hubbell (Cambridge, MA: Harvard University Press, 1949), 16.

5 St. Jerome, "Letter to Pammachius," trans. Kathleen Davis, in *The Translation Studies Reader*, ed. Lawrence Venuti, 3rd ed. (London: Routledge, 2012), 23.

6 John Dryden, "From the Preface to *Ovid's Epistles*," in *The Translation Studies Reader*, ed. Lawrence Venuti, 3rd ed. (London: Routledge, 2012), 38–43.

7 Roger Bacon, "On the Usefulness of Grammar," in *Western Translation Theory: from Herodotus to Nietzsche*, ed. Douglas Robinson (Manchester: St. Jerome Publications, 2001), 45.

8 Joachim du Bellay, *La deffence, et illustration de la langue françoyse*, ed. Jean-Charles Monferran (Geneva: Droz, 2001), 88.

9 Theo Hermans, *Translation in Systems* (Manchester: St. Jerome, 1999), 96.

10 Ibid.

11 Cited in Wolfram Wilss, *The Science of Translation: Problems and Methods* (Tübingen: Gunter Narr, 1982), 35.

12 Wilhelm von Humboldt, "A Theory of Translation," in *Translating Literature: The German Tradition*, ed. and trans. André Lefevere (Assen: Van Gorcum and Co., 1977), 40.

13 Peter Newmark, *Approaches to Translation* (New York: Prentice Hall, 1988), 40.

14 Daniel Paull, et al., "Nuclear Genome Transfer in Human Oocytes Eliminates Mitochondrial DNA Variants," *Nature*, vol. 493 (2013): 632–7.

15 von Humboldt, "A Theory of Translation," 41.

16 Émile Benveniste, "Catégories de pensée et catégories de langue," in *Problèmes de linguistique générale* (Paris: Gallimard, 1966), 73.

17 Ibid., 72–3.

18 Ishtla Singh, "Language, Thought, and Representation," in *Language, Society and Power: An introduction*, ed. Linda Thomas and Shan Wareing (London: Routledge, 2013), 24.

19 Ibid., 25.

20 Roman Jakobson, "On Linguistic Aspects of Translation," in *The Translation Studies Reader*, ed. Lawrence Venuti, 3rd ed. (London: Routledge, 2012), 128.

21 David Bellos, *Is That a Fish in Your Ear? Translation and the Meaning of Everything* (New York: Faber and Faber, 2011), 153.

22 Ibid.

23 Douglas Robinson, "The Limits of Translation," in *The Oxford English Guide in English Translation*, ed. Peter France (Oxford: Oxford University Press, 2001), 19.

24 While I have problems with the highly domesticated translation of *mole* as "curry," Robinson's explanation of the different translation possibilities nevertheless retains its validity.

25 Robinson, "The Limits of Translation," 19.

26 Lawrence Venuti, "The Poet's Version; Or, an Ethics of Translation," in *Translation Changes Everything* (London: Routledge, 2013), 174.

27 Ibid.

28 Ibid.

29 Cited in Sarah van Gelder, "Poet Laureate W.S. Merwin: Doing the Impossible," *YES! Magazine* 59 (Fall 2011), http://www.yesmagazine.org/issues/new-livelihoods/w.s.-merwin-doing-the-impossible. This of course recalls von Humboldt's earlier assertion.

30 Notable exceptions remain George Steiner and translation scholar linguists like Kirsten Malmkjaer.

31 Cf. Kirsten Malmkjaer, "Analytic Philosophy and Translation," in *Routledge Encyclopedia of Translation Studies*, ed. Mona Baker (London: Routledge, 1998), 9.

32 William Arrowsmith and Roger Shattuck, "Forward," in *The Craft and Context of Translation: A Symposium* (New York: Anchor Books, 1964).

33 W.H. Quine, *Word and Object* (Cambridge, MA: MIT Press, 1960), 52.

34 Ibid., 27.

35 Davidson reaches the conclusion that "when all the evidence is in, there will remain, as Quine has emphasized, the trade-offs between the beliefs we attribute to a speaker and the interpretations we give his words. But the resulting indeterminacy cannot be so great but that any theory that passes the tests will serve to yield interpretations." Donald Davidson, *Inquiries into Truth and Interpretation* (Oxford: Clarendon Press, 1984), 139.

36 P. Hacker, "Wittgenstein and Quine: Proximity at Great Distance," in *Ludwig Wittgenstein and W.H. Quine*, ed. R. Arrington and H.J. Glock (New York: Routledge, 1996), 15–16.
37 Adapted from Anthony Pym, *Exploring Translation Theories*, 104, which in turn adapted these statements from Simon S.C. Chau's article "Hermeneutics and the Translator: The Ontological Dimension of Translating," *Multilingua* 3, no. 2 (1984): 71–7.
38 George Steiner, *After Babel* (Oxford: Oxford University Press, 1975), 263.
39 Ibid.
40 Jean-René Ladmiral, *Traduire: théorèmes pour la traduction* (Paris: Payot, 1979), 85.
41 This capsule history obviously leaves out other important trends in translation theory, such as functional and communicative models like Skopos Theory and Translatorial Action, which are less relevant for our purposes.
42 Jeremy Munday, *Introducing Translation Studies*, 3rd ed. (London: Routledge, 2012), 188–9.
43 Siobhan Brownlie, "Descriptive vs. Committed Approaches," in *Routledge Encyclopedia of Translation Studies*, ed. Mona Baker (London: Routledge, 1998), 77.
44 Ibid.
45 Theo Hermans, *Translation in Systems* (Manchester: St. Jerome, 1999), 7. Hermans's incisive book doesn't spare criticisms of DTS.
46 Jakobson, "On Linguistic Aspects of Translation," 131.
47 Ibid.
48 Dante Alighieri, *Convivio*, ed. Giorgio Inglese (Milan: Rizzoli, 1993), 62.
49 Federico M. Federici, *Translation as Stylistic Evolution: Italo Calvino, Creative Translator of Raymond Queneau* (Amsterdam: Rodopi, 2009), 64.
50 Cf. Vittorio Stella, "La traduzione dell'opera poetica nel pensiero di Croce," *Itinerari*, new series 16 (1977): 33.
51 Benedetto Croce, *Tesi fondamentali di un'estetica come scienza dell'espressione e linguistica generale: memoria letta all'Accademia pontaniana nelle tornate del 18 febbraio, 18 marzo e 6 maggio 1900* (Naples: Tessitore, 1900).
52 Benedetto Croce, *Estetica come scienza dell'espressione e linguistica generale* (Milan: Sandron, 1902). We will cite from the later edition: Benedetto Croce, *Estetica come scienza dell'espressione e linguistica generale*, ed. Giuseppe Galasso (Milan: Adelphi, 1990).
53 Benedetto Croce, *La poesia* (Bari: Laterza, 1936). We will cite from the later edition: Benedetto Croce, *La poesia: introduzione alla critica e storia della poesia e della letteratura*, ed. Giuseppe Galasso (Milan: Adelphi, 1994).

54 Benedetto Croce, *La poesia: introduzione alla critica e storia della poesia e della letteratura*, ed. Giuseppe Galasso (Milan: Adelphi, 1994), 86.
55 Croce, *La poesia*, 106.
56 Croce, *Estetica*, 87.
57 Norbert Matyus, "Il dibattito di Croce e Gentile sul problema della traduzione," accessed 6 May 2010, http://sedi.esteri.it/budapest/crocepdf/Matyus_it.PDF.
58 Croce, *Estetica*, 87.
59 Ibid., 94.
60 Croce, *La poesia*, 109.
61 Despite the contrary view of Giacomo Rinaldi, in "Italian Idealism and After," which attempts to minimize Croce's undeniable influence. Cf. Giacomo Rinaldi, "Italian Idealism and After," in *Routledge History of Philosophy: Twentieth-Century Continental Philosophy*, ed. Richard Kearney (London: Routledge, 1994), 350–89.
62 Giulio Lepschy, "Traduzione," in *Encyclopedia Einaudi*, vol. 14, ed. Ruggiero Romano (Turin: Einaudi, 1981), 446. It is strange that Lepschy finds no contradiction or possible issue in Croce's theory, proclaiming it "molto articolato e sfumato … [una] posizione, temperata di buon senso."
63 Galvano della Volpe, "Critica del gusto," in *Opere*, vol. 6, ed. Ignazio Ambrogio (Rome: Editori Riuniti, 1973), 124.
64 Cf. Kate Briggs, "Translation and the Question of Poetry," in *Twentieth-Century Poetic Translation*, ed. Daniela Caselli and Daniela La Penna (London: Continuum, 2008), 154–5.
65 della Volpe, "Critica del gusto," 117.
66 Ibid., 123.
67 Ibid., 124.
68 Ibid., 137.
69 Ibid., 135.
70 Luciano Anceschi, *Che importa chi parla? Dialoghi con Luciano Anceschi*, ed. Michele Gulinucci (Reggio Emilia: Diabasis, 1992), 52.
71 Cited in Anceschi, *Che importa chi parla?* 112.
72 Emilio Mattioli, "Introduzione al problema del tradurre," *Il verri* 19 (1965): 128.
73 John Dryden, "From the Preface to *Ovid's* Epistles," in *The Translation Studies Reader,* ed. Lawrence Venuti, 3rd ed. (London: Routledge, 2012), 40.
74 John Dryden, "Preface to *Sylvae*," in *John Dryden: The Major Works*, ed. Keith Walker (Oxford: Oxford University Press, 1993), 248.
75 Giacomo Leopardi, "Traduzione del libro secondo della Eneide," in *Tutte le opere*, vol. 1, ed. Francesco Flora (Milan: Mondadori, 1973), 617.
76 Maria Luisa Spaziani, a poet-translator herself, also cites Carlo Bo as one of the *illustrissimi esempi* of non-poets who successful translate poetry. Cf. Maria

Luisa Spaziani, "La traduzione di poesia come osmosi," in *La traduzione del testo poetico*, ed. Franco Buffoni (Milan: Marcos y Marcos, 2004), 110.

77 Anceschi, *Che importa chi parla?* 52.

78 Emilio Mattioli, *Contributi alla teoria della traduzione letteraria* (Palermo: Centro internazionale studi di estetica, 1993), 25–6.

79 Franco Fortini, *Il ladro di ciliege* (Turin: Einaudi, 1982), viii.

80 Jirí Levý's volume on literary translation, *The Art of Translation*, trans. Patrick Corness (Amsterdam: Benjamin, 2011), is very rewarding but it's not entirely devoted to poetic translation, and this is why I do not deal with it here.

81 Robert de Beaugrande, *Factors in a Theory of Poetic Translating* (Assen: Van Gorcum, 1978).

82 Cees Koster, *From World to World: An Armamentarium for the Study of Poetic Discourse in Translation* (Amsterdam: Rodopi, 2000).

83 Robert-Alain de Beaugrande and Wolfgang Ulrich Dressler, *Introduction to Text Linguistics* (London: Longman, 1981).

84 As he states in the foreword, "In developing this draft of a theory I have drawn largely on text linguistics (as opposed to descriptive structural linguistics or transformational grammar) and on reader-oriented theories of literature." Robert de Beaugrande, *Factors in a Theory of Poetic Translating* (Assen: Van Gorcum, 1978), 1.

85 She was one of his initial dissertation advisers.

86 Cees Koster, *From World to World*, 234.

87 Dirk Delabastita, Review of "From World to World. An 'Armamentarium' for the Study of Poetic Discourse in Translation (Approaches to Translation Studies, Volume 16)," *The Translator* 7, no. 1 (2000): 109.

88 Ibid.

89 Ibid., 105.

90 Cf. Lawrence Venuti: "Instrumentalism [the approach based on analyzing shifts] is, in a word, a falsehood that cannot offer an incisive and comprehensive understanding of translation." *Translation Changes Everything*, 3.

91 Francis Jones, *Poetry Translation as Expert Action* (Amsterdam: Benjamins, 2011), 11.

92 Ibid., 13.

93 I think in particular when she justifiably criticizes a poor translation of Louise Labé. Cf. Folkart, *Second Finding*, 325–31.

94 Friedrich Schleiermacher, "On the Different Methods of Translating," trans. Susan Bernofsky, in *The Translation Studies Reader*, ed. Lawrence Venuti, 3rd ed. (London: Routledge, 2012), 49.

95 Philip E. Lewis, "The Measure of Translation Effects," in *The Translation Studies Reader*, ed. Lawrence Venuti (London: Routledge, 2012), 235.

96 Ibid., 226.

97 Ibid., 227.

98 Dirk Delabastita, "Histories and Utopias: On Venuti's *The Translator's Invisibility*," *The Translator* 16, no. 1 (2010): 125.

99 See Antoine Berman, *L'épreuve de l'étranger: culture et traduction dans l'Allemagne romantique* (Paris: Gallimard, 1984).

100 Gentzler, *Contemporary Translation Theories*, 41.

101 Venuti, *The Translator's Invisibility*, 310.

102 Likewise, Maria Tymoczko and Anthony Pym have criticized it. See Maria Tymoczko, "Translation and Political Engagement: Activism, Social Change and the Role of Translation in Geopolitical Shifts," *The Translator* 6, no. 1 (2000): 23–47, and Anthony Pym, "Venuti's Visibility," *Target* 8, no. 2 (1996): 165–77.

103 Raymond Williams, *Marxism and Literature* (Oxford: Oxford University Press, 1977), 55.

104 Ibid.

105 Cited in Terry Eagleton, *Ideology* (London: Longman: 1994), 111.

106 Cited in ibid., 184.

107 Peter Fawcett and Jeremy Munday, "Ideology," in *Routledge Encyclopedia of Translation Studies*, ed. Mona Baker and Gabriela Saldanha, 2nd ed. (London: Routledge, 2009), 137. See also Jeremy Munday, *Style and Ideology in Translation: Latin American Writing in English* (London: Routledge, 2008).

108 Christina Schäffner, "Third Ways and New Centres: Ideological Unity or Difference?" in *Apropos of Ideology*, ed. María Calzada-Pérez (Manchester: St. Jerome, 2003), 23.

109 Keith Harvey, "A Descriptive Framework for Compensation," *The Translator* 1, no. 1 (1995): 67.

110 Jean-Paul Vinay and Jean Darbelnet, *Stylistique comparée du français et de l'anglais: méthode de traduction* (Paris: Didier, 1958).

111 Jean-Paul Vinay and Jean Darbelnet, *Comparative Stylistics of French and English: A Methodology for Translation*, trans. Juan C. Sager and M.J. Hamel (Amsterdam: John Benjamins, 1995), 169.

112 Eugene Nida and Charles Taber, *The Theory and Practice of Translation* (Leiden: Brill, 1969), 106.

113 Steiner, *After Babel*, 417.

114 Peter Newmark refers to Steiner unhelpfully as "a specialist in Gruselgeschichten, or giving you the creeps." Peter Newmark, *More Paragraphs on Translation* (Philadelphia: Multilingual Matters, 1998), 182.

115 Peter Newmark, *About Translation* (Bristol: Multilingual Matters, 1991), 144.

116 Sándor Hervey and Ian Higgins, *Thinking Translation: A Course in Translation Method: French to English* (London: Routledge, 1992).
117 Ibid., 35–9.
118 Harvey, "A Descriptive Framework," 65.
119 Franco Fortini, "Dei 'compensi' nelle versioni di poesia," in *La traduzione del testo poetico*, ed. Franco Buffoni (Milan: Marcos y Marcos, 2004), 74; first in *La traduzione del testo poetico*, ed. Franco Buffoni (Milan: Guerini, 1989), 115–20.
120 Lefevere outlined seven strategies: "phonemic translation," "literal translation," "metrical translation," "poetry into prose," "rhymed translation," "blank verse translation," and "interpretation."
121 Holmes defined four strategies: "mimetic form," "analogical form," "organic form," and "deviant form" or "extraneous form." I will not consider the last form, poorly theorized, which in any case is also described by Holmes as often "an older collateral of the organic form."
122 I am not discussing here Robert Bly's *The Eight Stages of Poetry Translation: With a Selection of Poems and Translations* (Boston: Rowan Tree Press, 1983), which is interesting, but ultimately more descriptive than theoretical.
123 This is Holmes's terminology; Lefevere uses the term "metrical translation," which is less indicative of the process at work.
124 Lefevere doesn't consider this translation properly called.
125 André Lefevere, *Translating Poetry: Seven Strategies and a Blueprint* (Assen: Von Gorcum, 1975), 37.
126 In Croce's words, they provide a Homer "alquanto rimbambinito." Benedetto Croce, *La letteratura della nuova italia: saggi critici*, vol. 4 (Bari: Laterza, 1956), 130.
127 Levý, *The Art of Translation*, 205–16.
128 Lefevere, *Translating Poetry*, 61.
129 James Holmes, *Translated! Papers on Literary Translation and Translation Studies*, ed. Raymond van den Broeck (Amsterdam: Rodopi, 1994), 27.
130 Alexander Tytler, *Essay on the Principles of Translation*, 3rd rev. ed. (Amsterdam: John Benjamins, 1978), 207.
131 Lefevere, *Translating Poetry*, 49.
132 Cited in Steiner, *After Babel*, 329.
133 Lefevere, *Translating Poetry*, 26.
134 Venuti, *The Translator's Invisibility*, 219.
135 In a translation of Horace, "Orazio al bordello basco," in *Composita solvantur* (Turin: Einaudi, 1994), 77. Fortini himself remarks of Zukofsky's translation that this method works only if the Latin text is read "con forte pronuncia yankee." Cf. Fortini, *Lezioni sulla traduzione*, 118.

136 Nicolas Perrot D'Ablancourt, "From Preface to French Translation of Thucydides," in *Western Translation Theory: From Herodotus to Nietzsche*, ed. Douglas Robinson (Manchester: St. Jerome, 1997), 158–9
137 Lefevere, *Translating Poetry*, 76.
138 Giacomo Leopardi, "Imitazione," in Giacomo Leopardi, *Canti*, ed. Niccolò Gallo and Cesare Garboli (Turin: Einaudi, 1962), 287.
139 Attilio Bertolucci, *Imitazioni* (Milan: Libri Scheiwiller, 1994).
140 As Buffoni says in his introduction to *Una piccola tabaccheria*, "Dieci anni dopo mi trovo qui a raccogliere una nuova messe di traduzioni e imitazioni."
141 Giorgio Caproni, "Imitazioni," in *Seme del piangere* (Milan: Garzanti, 1959), 107–10.
142 Franco Fortini, "Appendice di light verses e imitazioni," in *Composita solvantur* (Turin: Einaudi, 1994).
143 Giovanni Raboni, *Ventagli e altre imitazioni* (Varese: NEM, 1999).
144 Edoardo Sanguineti, *Omaggio a Goethe: viaggi in Italia, XXIX imitazioni* (Bellinzona: Edizioni Sottoscala, 2003).
145 E.g., Eugenio Montale's "adattamento" of Djuna Barnes's "Transfiguration" in his *Quaderno di traduzioni*.
146 Pier Vincenzo Mengaldo, "Diego Valeri traduttore di lirici francesi e tedeschi," in *Diego Valeri e il Novecento*, ed. Gloria Manghetti (Padua: Esedra, 2007), 89.
147 Lefevere, *Translating Poetry*, 42.
148 Valerio Magrelli, "La regola del 'Menouno,'" in *Traduzione e poesia nell'Europa del Novecento*, ed. Anna Dolfi (Rome: Bulzoni, 2004), 616.
149 Pier Vincenzo Mengaldo, "Fortini e *I poeti del Novecento*,'" in *Nuovi argomenti* 61 (1979): 176.
150 As noted, for instance, by Maria Vittoria Tirinato, "Larvatus prodeo. Franco Fortini e la traduzione poetica," in Franco Fortini, *Lezioni sulla traduzione* (Macerata: Quodlibet, 2011), 17.
151 Leopoldo Manigrasso, "Capitoli autobiografici. Poeti traduttori a confronto tra terza e quarta generazione" (PhD diss., Università degli Studi di Padova, 2012), 12–13.
152 Luciano Erba, *Dei cristalli naturali e altri versi tradotti: 1950–1990* (Milan: Guerini, 1991), 7.
153 Vittorio Sereni, *Il musicante di Saint-Merry e altri versi tradotti* (Turin: Einaudi, 1981), xxxiii.
154 Alessandro Parronchi, *Quaderno francese* (Florence: Vallecchi, 1989), 6.
155 Anna Dolfi, "Variazioni sui maestri di canto: su Montale, la traduzione, la poesia," *Semicerchio*, nos. 16–17 (1997): 17.
156 Giuseppe Ungaretti, "Poeta e uomini," in *Vita d'un uomo: Saggi e interventi*, ed. Mario Diacono and Luciano Rebay (Milan: Mondadori, 1974), 739.

157 Eugenio Montale, *Il secondo mestiere: prose 1920–1979*, ed. Giorgio Zampa (Milan: Mondadori, 2006), 1:1712 and 2:1805.
158 Giorgio Caproni, "I poeti e la tromba (o della traducibilità)," *Il lavoro nuovo*, 24 August 1949.
159 Edoardo Sanguineti, "Tradurre il teatro antico," *Prometeo rivista*, unpaginated. http://www.indafondazione.org/prometeus-rivista-online/tradurre-il-teatro-antico.
160 Andrea Zanzotto, "Europa, melograno di lingue," in *Le poesie e le prose scelte*, ed. Stefano Dal Bianco and Gian Maria Villalta (Milan: Mondadori, 2000), 1362.
161 Diego Valeri, *Lirici tedeschi* (Milan: Mondadori, 1959), 275.
162 Margherita Guidacci, "Traducendo due poetesse americane: Jessica Powers ed Elizabeth Bishop," in *La traduzione del testo poetico*, ed. Franco Buffoni (Milan: Marcos y Marcos, 2004), 157.
163 Cited in Mario Picchi, "Del tradurre," *La Fiera Letteraria*, 3 June 1956.
164 Fortini translated from German with the help of his wife, Ruth Leiser; Montale translated abundantly from English, often with the help of Lucia Rodocanachi and Maria Luisa Spaziani.
165 Venuti, *The Translator's Invisibility*, 273–307.
166 Sergio Solmi, "Chiarimento al primo *quaderno*," in *Opere di Sergio Solmi: Poesie, meditazioni e ricordi*, ed. Giovanni Pacchiano, vol. 1 (Milan: Adelphi, 1983), 227.
167 Vittorio Sereni, *Il musicante di Saint-Merry e altri versi tradotti* (Turin: Einaudi, 1981), vi.
168 Giorgio Caproni, "L'arte del tradurre," *La traduzione del testo poetico*, ed. Franco Buffoni (Milan: Marcos and Marcos, 2004), 33.
169 Sereni, *Il musicante*, vi.
170 Yet none takes this to the extreme of Nabokov's labours with *Eugene Onegin* – 1,000 pages of commentary accompanying a comparatively small text.

2. Eugenio Montale

1 Franco Contorbia, "Montale critico nello specchio delle lettere: una approssimazione," in *Montale, Genova, il modernismo e altri saggi montaliani* (Bologna: Pendragon, 1999), 73–87.
2 Eugenio Montale, *L'opera in versi*, ed. Rosanna Bettarini and Gianfranco Contini (Turin: Einaudi, 1980).
3 Eugenio Montale, *Ossi di seppia* (Turin: Gobetti, 1925).
4 Eugenio Montale, *Le occasioni* (Turin: Einaudi, 1939).
5 Eugenio Montale, *La bufera e altro* (Venice: Neri Pozza, 1956).

6 Eugenio Montale, *Satura* (Milan: Mondadori, 1971).
7 Eugenio Montale, *Diario del '71 e '72* (Milan: Mondadori, 1973).
8 Eugenio Montale, *Quaderno di quattro anni* (Milan: Mondadori, 1977).
9 Eugenio Montale, *Altri versi e poesie disperse* (Milan: Mondadori, 1981). I have obviously not included the dubious volume *Diario postumo* (Milan: Mondadori, 1996), written with Annalisa Cima.
10 Eugenio Montale, *Il secondo mestiere: arte, musica, società,* ed. Giorgio Zampa (Milan: Mondadori, 1996), 1622.
11 Ibid., 1480.
12 Cf. Piero Gadda Conti, *Concerto d'autunno* (Milan: Pan Editrice, 1976), 18.
13 Laura Barile, *Montale, Londra e la luna* (Florence: Le Lettere, 1998), 9.
14 Giorgio Zampa, "Introduzione," in *Tutte le poesie,* xxxvi–xxxvii.
15 Montale, *Secondo mestiere,* 1496.
16 Ibid., 1482.
17 Ibid.
18 Ibid., 1496.
19 Montale, *L'opera,* 138.
20 Ibid.
21 Ibid., 909.
22 Ibid.
23 Montale, *Secondo mestiere,* 1483.
24 Giovanni Macchia, "La Bufera o il romanzo di Clizia," in *Saggi italiani* (Milan: Mondadori, 1983).
25 Montale, *Secondo mestiere,* 1498.
26 Glauco Cambon, *Eugenio Montale: A Dream in Reason's Presence* (Princeton: Princeton, 1982), 34–5.
27 Montale, *Secondo mestiere,* 1516.
28 Montale, *L'opera,* 248.
29 Cited in Giulio Nascimbeni, *Montale: biografia di un poeta* (Milan: Longanesi, 1986), 122.
30 Montale, *L'opera,* 264.
31 Gianfranco Contini notes this in his *Una lunga fedeltà: Scritti su Eugenio Montale* (Turin: Einaudi, 1974), 97.
32 Marco Forti, *Eugenio Montale* (Milan: Mursia, 1974), 352.
33 Barile, *Montale, Londra e la luna,* 9.
34 Montale, *L'opera,* 696.
35 *Americana: raccolta di narratori dalle origini ai nostri giorni,* ed. Elio Vittorini (Milan: Bompiani, 1941).
36 This was first conclusively stated by Giuseppe Marcenaro in his *Una amica di Montale: vita di Lucia Rodocanachi* (Milan: Camunia, 1991).

37 Cf. Giovanni Cecchetti, "Sull'altro Montale," in *Essays in Honor of Dante della Terza*, ed. Franco Fido (Florence: Cadmo, 1998), 357.

38 Cf. Jacob Blakesley, "Montale, Second-hand Translator," forthcoming in *Moderna* 14, no. 2 (2013).

39 As the abstract of a letter to Spaziani reads, "[Montale] chiede un malloppo di pagine con interlinea maggiore e il lavoro finito in dieci giorni." Cf. *Catalogo delle lettere da Eugenio Montale a Maria Luisa Spaziani*, ed. Giuseppe Polimeni (Pavia: Università degli studi di Pavia, 1999), 53. The editor of the volume is thus wrong, when he states that "la traduzione di *La Cicuta e dopo* di Angus Wilson fu rivista dalla Spaziani" (118). The revision was in the opposite direction: Montale revised her translation.

40 Interview with Maria Luisa Spaziani, 15 April 2010.

41 Proof lies in the letters published by Marcello Staglieno in 1989, which contain, for example, the following lines: "Vorrebbero da me articoli (e molti) su recenti libri italiani francesi e inglesi. Per farlo bisognerebbe chiudersi in casa e non aver alcun obbligo di redazione; inoltre occorrebbe avere una casa, che io non ho. Non so nemmeno dove tenerli, i libri, all'albergo non ho spazio, in redazione me li rubano. E quando rincaso (per modo di dire) debbo fare l'infermiere, non il lettore. È una vita impossibile; tuttavia non oso lasciare il giornale perché non saprei come potrei vivere. Non potresti farmi tu un articolo al mese su libri inglesi o americani? Io ti darei poco, ma tutte le 9.000 lire che mi vengono date per articolo. Articoli brevi (due cartelle e mezzo al massimo), non farciti di erudizioni e tali che si possa pensare scritti da me. Io non farei che firmarli col mio nome e modificare qua e là il testo per renderlo più riconoscibilmente mio. S'intende che *nessuno* dovrebbe sapere la cosa, altrimenti perderei il posto." Cf. "Enrico aiutami: è una vita impossibile: lettere inedite di Eugenio Montale a Henry Furst," ed. Marcello Staglieno, *Il Giornale*, 24 October 1989.

42 Interview with Maria Luisa Spaziani, 15 April 2010. As for the prefaces, they are in the following editions: Giovanni Bocaccio, *Decamerone. VII Giornata*, ed. Mario Fubini, prefazione di Eugenio Montale (Milan: Feltrinelli, 1952), and Daniel Defoe, *Vita e avventure di Robinson Crusoe*, prefazione di Eugenio Montale (Milan: Feltrinelli, 1951). Cf. *Catalogo delle lettere di Eugenio Montale a Maria Luisa Spaziani*, 72 and 86.

43 Cited in Mario Picchi, "Del tradurre," *La Fiera Letteraria*, 3 June 1956.

44 Ibid.

45 Cf. Mario Sansone, "Croce e Montale," in *La poesia di Eugenio Montale: Atti del Convegno Internazionale tenuto a Genova dal 25 al 28 novembre 1982*, ed. Sergio Campailla and Cesare Federico Goffis (Florence: Le Monnier, 1984), 286–98.

46 Rocco Montano, "Note per un'interpretazione di Montale," *Studi Novecenteschi* 2 (1973): 246.
47 Franco Contorbia, "Eusebio, Trabucco e l'ombra di Croce," in *Riuscire postcrociani senza essere anticrociani. Gianfranco Contini e gli studi letterari del secondo Novecento*, ed. Angelo R. Pupino (Florence: Edizioni del Galluzzo per la Fondazione Ezio Franceschini, 2004), 50.
48 Eugenio Montale, *Secondo mestiere: prose*, 2999.
49 Ibid., 1180.
50 Gianfranco Contini, *La parte di Benedetto Croce nella cultura italiana* (Turin: Einaudi, 1989), 3.
51 Montale, *Secondo mestiere: prose*, 3000.
52 Ibid., 3001.
53 Montale, *Secondo mestiere: arte*, 1479.
54 Contorbia, "Montale critico," 56.
55 Sansone, "Croce e Montale," 288.
56 Croce, *Breviario*, 73.
57 Benedetto Croce, *Goethe: con una scelta di liriche nuovamente tradotte* (Bari: Laterza, 1946), 161.
58 Montale, *L'opera*, 1035.
59 Dolfi, "Variazioni," 17.
60 Montale, *Secondo mestiere: prose*, 2:2726.
61 Ibid.
62 Ibid., 3257.
63 Ibid., 1627–8.
64 "Yeats è un maestro del verso, un genio della grande tradizione europea che passa attraverso Baudelaire, un poeta del tutto intraducibile." Montale, *Secondo mestiere: prose*, 1805.
65 Ibid., 2302.
66 Ibid., 1712.
67 Ibid., 888.
68 Ibid., 991.
69 Ibid., 2190.
70 Ibid., 2724.
71 Montale, *Secondo mestiere: arte*, 1606.
72 Montale, *Secondo mestiere: prose*, 1208.
73 Ibid., 707.
74 Ibid., 71.
75 Ibid., 2777.
76 Ibid., 2030.
77 Ibid., 1155.
78 Ibid., 2597.

79 Croce, *Poesia*, 108.
80 Montale, *Lettere e poesie a Bianca e a Francesco Messina*, 149; Tiziana Arvigo, *Guida a Ossi di seppia* (Rome: Carocci, 2001), 93.
81 I do not consider demonstrative or possessive adjectives in this count.
82 Or four, if we consider *palme*, and not *palmier*.
83 Eugenio Montale and Valéry Larbaud, *Caro maestro e amico: carteggio con Valéry Larbaud*, ed. by Marco Sonzogni (Milan: Arcinto, 2003), 91.
84 Eugenio Montale, "Lettere a Nino Frank," in *Almanacco dello Specchio* 12 (Milan: Mondadori, 1986), 17–64.
85 Montale, *L'opera*, 1035.
86 Ibid., 1032.
87 Ibid., 931.
88 Cited in Isella, "Il giovane poeta," 232.
89 Eugenio Montale, "Prefazione," in Giorgia Valensin, *Liriche cinesi: 1753 a.c.–1278 d.c.* (Turin: Einaudi, 1943).
90 Montale, *Eusebio e Trabucco*, 176.
91 Ibid., 179.
92 Ibid., 194.
93 Montale, *Quaderno di traduzioni* (Rome: Meridiana, 1948), 203.
94 Montale, *L'opera*, 511.
95 Glauco Cambon, "Montale sull'ultima spiaggia," in *La poesia di Eugenio Montale: atti del convegno internazionale tenuto a Genova dal 25 al 28 novembre 1982*, 336. "Io volevo intitolarlo [il libro] *Giornale di 4 anni*, ma hanno preferito *Quaderno*."
96 Montale, *L'opera*, 1154. I will cite the *Quaderno di traduzioni* from the Contini-Bettarini edition of Montale's complete poems. Only when I need to cite the original languages will I cite from the third edition of Montale's *Quaderno di traduzioni*.
97 Romano Luperini, *Montale o l'identità negata* (Naples: Liguori, 1984), 175.
98 Laura Barile, *Adorate mie larve* (Bologna: Il mulino, 1990), 7.
99 Pier Vincenzo Mengaldo, *La tradizione del novecento: quarta serie* (Turin: Bollati Boringhieri, 2000), 89.
100 Montale significantly dated them "anteriori al '38," the year when Montale and Brandeis broke off communication.
101 Montale, *Quaderno di traduzioni*, 16.
102 Glauco Cambon, "Montale sull'ultima spiaggia. Pagine di diario," in *La poesia di Eugenio Montale: Atti del Convegno internazionale tenuto a Genova dal 25 al 28 novembre 1982*, ed. Sergio Campailla and Cesare Federico Goffis (Florence: Le Monnier, 1984), 342.
103 Montale, *L'opera*, 720.
104 Montale, *Quaderno*, 62.

105 Montale, *L'opera*, 720.
106 Ibid., 723.
107 Ibid., 738.
108 Eugenio Montale, "Poesie di Eugenio Montale," in *Secondo mestiere: arte*, 1494.
109 Roberto Ruberto, "Conversation with Eugenio Montale," *Italian quarterly* 17:68 (1974), 55.
110 Mario Praz, "T.S. Eliot e Eugenio Montale," in *Cronache letterarie anglosassoni*, vol. 1 (Rome: Edizioni di Storia e Letteratura, 1950), 189–92.
111 Ibid., 190.
112 Ibid., 189.
113 Stefano Maria Casella, "'By the Arena … Il Decaduto': T.S. Eliot & / in Italy," in *The International Reception of T.S. Eliot*, ed. Elisabeth Daumer and Shyamal Bagchee (London: Continuum, 2007), 126.
114 Luperini, *Montale*, 167–74.
115 Barile, *Adorate mie larve*, 61.
116 Talbot, *Montale's 'Mestiere vile,'* 59.
117 Cf. Ernesto Livorni, "Montale traduttore di Eliot: una questione di 'Belief,'" in *Traduzione e poesia nell'Europa del Novecento*, ed. Anna Dolfi (Rome: Bulzoni, 2004), 471–85.
118 Montale, *Quaderno*, 110.
119 Montale, *L'opera*, 740.
120 Ibid.
121 Ibid., 741.
122 Montale, *Quaderno*, 110.
123 Montale, *L'opera*, 740.
124 Montale, *Quaderno*, 110.
125 Montale, *L'opera*, 740.
126 Livorni, "Montale traduttore," 478.
127 Croce, *Estetica*, 87.
128 Roberto Gigliucci, *Realismo metafisico e Montale* (Rome: Nuova cultura, 2006), 87.
129 Montale, *L'opera*, 1163.
130 Ibid.
131 Ibid., 1163–4.
132 Ibid., 749.
133 Montale, *Quaderno*, 135.
134 Mario Puppo, "Montale e la letteratura spagnola," in *La poesia di Eugenio Montale: Atti del Convegno internazionale tenuto a Genova dal 25 al 28 novembre 1982*, ed. Sergio Campailla and Cesare Federico Goffis (Florence: Felice Le Monnier, 1984), 427.

135 Cited in Gigliucci, *Realismo metafisico*, 88.
136 Piero Bigongiari, *Poesia italiana del Novecento* (Florence: Vallecchi, 1960), 191.
137 Ibid.
138 Leonardo Sciascia, "La grande domanda," in *Letture montaliane in occasione del 80esimo compleanno del poeta*, ed. Sylvia Luzzatto (Genoa: Bozzi, 1977), 390.
139 Montale, *L'opera*, 413.
140 Ibid., 1156–7. It is worth noting that in an early poem from *Ossi di seppia*, we can see the image of the "suono scoppiettante di pigna verde buttata nel fuoco" first appear

Il fuoco che scoppietta
Nel caminetto verdeggia …
Un ramo aggiungi alla fiamma
Del focolare e una pigna
Matura alla cesta gettata
Nel canto …

There, too, we see the connection between the pigna and the fire and poetry (canto).
141 Loreto Busquets, *Montale y la cultura hispánica* (Rome: Bulzoni, 1986), 142.
142 Assumpta Camps, "Il 'Cant espiritual' di Montale," *Galleria* 47, no. 1 (1996): 92.
143 The first version, published in *Mondo europeo*, had "cose lungi o prossime."
144 Puppo, "Montale e la letteratura spagnola," 424.
145 Ibid.
146 Montale, *L'opera*, 40.
147 Ibid.
148 Croce, *Estetica*, 94.
149 In the new 1975 edition of his *Quaderno*, Montale added not only the translation of Barnes, but also three poems by Yeats ("Quando tu sarai vecchia," "Dopo un lungo silenzio," and "Verso Bisanzio"); Cavafy's "I barbari"; and Fernando Bandini's Latin version of Montale's "Bufera," namely, "Nimbus." In the *Quaderno* published in December of the same year Montale included an excerpt from Pound's *Mauberley*. In his *L'opera in versi*, the editors (Gianfranco Contini and Rosanna Bettarini) chose to omit Bandini's translation of Montale's poem.
150 Montale, *Secondo mestiere: prose*, 2887.
151 A.L. Johnson, "Interview with Eugenio Montale," *Littack* 3, no. 3 (1975): 225.
152 Rebecca West, *Eugenio Montale: Poet on the Edge* (Cambridge, MA: Harvard University Press, 1981).

153 Montale, *Secondo mestiere: prose*, 1805.
154 Eugenio Montale, "Il cammino della nuova poesia," in *Secondo mestiere: prose*, 1155.
155 Cf. Éanna Ó Ceallacháin, "Montale's late versions of Yeats," *Italian Studies*, no. 50 (1995): 72–85.
156 Emilio Guariglia, "Quando tu sarai vecchia," in *Quaderno montaliano*, ed. Pier Vincenzo Mengaldo (Padua: Liviana Editrice, 1989), 131–64.
157 Guariglia, "Quando tu sarai vecchia," 159.
158 E.g., Angelo Marchese, *Interpretazione semiologica della poesia di Montale* (Turin: SEI, 1977).
159 Cf. Eugenio Montale, *Quaderno genovese*, ed. Laura Barile (Milan: Mondadori, 1983), 90.
160 Fiorenzo Fantaccini, *W.B. Yeats e la cultura italiana* (Florence: Firenze University Press, 2009), 120.
161 Montale, *Quaderno di traduzioni*, 159 and 161.
162 Ibid., 160.
163 Montale, *L'opera*, 701.
164 Giuseppe Ungaretti, "Poeta e uomini," in *Vita d'un uomo: Saggi e interventi*, ed. Mario Diacono and Luciano Rebay (Milan: Mondadori, 1974), 739.
165 Ungaretti, "Poeta e uomini," 739.
166 Ibid.
167 Cf. Giuseppe Ungaretti, "Significato dei sonetti di Shakespeare," in *Vita d'un uomo: Saggi e interventi*, ed. by Mario Diacono and Luciano Rebay (Milan: Mondadori, 1974), 551. "È un lavoro al quale pensavo sino dal '31 ... Non sospettavo allora che sarebbe stata un'improba fatica, almeno per lungo tempo e, nel periodo del mio soggiorno in Brasile, tornai durante mesi, senza progredire d'un passo, a tormentare la pagina."
168 Ibid.
169 Ungaretti, *40 sonetti di Shakespeare* (Milan: Mondadori, 1956), 37.
170 Ibid., 11–12.
171 Ibid., 11.
172 Giuseppe Ungaretti, "Della metrica e del tradurre," in *Vita d'un uomo: Saggi e interventi*, ed. Mario Diacono and Luciano Rebay (Milan: Mondadori, 1974), 573.
173 Ungaretti, *40 Sonetti*, 12.
174 Agostino Lombardo, "Ungaretti e i sonetti di Shakespeare," in *Atti del Convegno internazionale su Giuseppe Ungaretti: Urbino, 3–6 Ottobre 1979*, ed. Carlo Bo, vol. 1. (Urbino: 4 Venti, 1981), 483–96.
175 Rosita Tordi, *Ungaretti e i suoi maîtres à penser* (Rome: Bulzoni, 1997), 140.

176 Tordi, *Ungaretti e i suoi*, 135.
177 Ungaretti, *40 sonetti*, 12.
178 Roberto Orlando, *Applicazioni montaliane* (Lucca: M. Pacini Fazzi, 2001), 7.
179 Ibid., 12.
180 Rachel Meoli Toulmin, "Shakespeare ed Eliot nelle versioni di Eugenio Montale," *Belfagor* 26 (1971): 459.
181 Gilberto Lonardi, "Fuori e dentro il tradurre montaliano," in *Il vecchio e il giovane e altri studi su Montale* (Bologna: Zanichelli, 1980), 153.
182 Barile, *Adorate mie larve*, 24–5.
183 Montale, *Secondo Mestiere: arte*, 1482.
184 Mengaldo, "La panchina e i morti," 133–48.
185 Montale, *L'opera*, 726.
186 Minne Gerben de Boer, "Leggere una poesia tradotta," in *"Innumerevoli contrasti d'innesti": La poesia del Novecento (e altro)*, ed. Bart Van den Bossche et alii, vol. 1 (Florence: Franco Cesati, 2007), 275.
187 Cf. Sergio Bozzola, "Le traduzioni montaliane di Steinbeck," in *Seminario Montaliano* (Rome: Bonacci, 2006), 117–47.
188 Lonardi, "Fuori e dentro," 152.
189 Cited in Picchi, "Del tradurre," 6.
190 Maria Pia Musatti, "Montale traduttore: la mediazione della poesia," *Strumenti critici* 41 (1980): 123.
191 Bigongiari, *Poesia italiana*, 229.
192 Cited in "Appendice: Lettere a Guglielmo Petroni," in *La narrativa di Guglielmo Petroni: atti della giornata di studio della Fondazione Camillo Caetani, Roma, 27 ottobre 2006*, ed. Massimiliano Tortora (Rome: L'Erma di Bretschneider, 2007), 184.

3. Giorgio Caproni

1 Parts of this chapter have been previously published in *Journal of Italian Translation* and *Semicerchio*, and I would like to acknowledge the kind permission given by Luigi Bonaffini and Francesco Stella to include them here.
2 P.V. Mengaldo, "Confronti fra traduttori-poeti contemporanei (Sereni, Caproni, Luzi)," in *Tradizione/Traduzione/Società. Saggi per Franco Fortini* (Rome: Editori Riuniti, 1989), 243–60; Sergio Marroni, *La lingua delle traduzioni di "Bel-Ami"* (Rome: Bulzoni, 1989); P.V. Mengaldo, "Caproni e Sereni: due versioni," in *Premio Città di Monselice per la traduzione letteraria e scientifica*, ed. G. Peron (Monselice: Amministrazione Comunale, 1993),

210–21; P.V. Mengaldo, "Prefazione," in Giorgio Caproni, *Quaderno di traduzioni*, ed. Enrico Testa (Turin: Einaudi, 1998); Enrico Testa, "Introduzione," in Giorgio Caproni, *Quaderno di traduzioni*, ed. Enrico Testa (Turin: Einaudi, 1998), xiii–xxii; Elisa Bricco, *André Frénaud e l'Italia: una scrittura poetica* (Fasano: Schena, 1999); Judith Lindenberg, "Le Quaderno di traduzioni de Giorgio Caproni," *Chroniques Italiennes*, no. 71–2 (2003): 43–56; Lorenzo Flabbi, *Dettar versi a Socrate: il traduttore di poesia come imitatore* (Florence: Le Lettere, 2008), 203–29; and Luca Pietromarchi, "Nota alla traduzione," in Charles Baudelaire, *I fiori del male*, trans. Giorgio Caproni (Venice: Marsilio, 2008), 53–9.

3 I have drawn on research conducted at Caproni's archives located at the Gabinetto Vieusseux, the Biblioteca Nazionale in Florence, and the Biblioteca Marconi in Rome, as well as Einaudi's archives in Turin. I have also profited from the generous help of Attilio Mauro Caproni and Enrico Testa.

4 Gian Luigi Beccaria, "Untitled," in *Giorgio Caproni: Poesie, 1932–1986* (Milan: Garzanti, 1986), 811.

5 Giuseppe Leonelli, "La poesia del pieno e del secondo Novecento," in *Storia della letteratura italiana*, ed. Enrico Malato, vol. 9 (Rome: Salerno, 1995), 1182.

6 Cited in Adele Dei, *Giorgio Caproni* (Milan: Mursia, 1992), 12.

7 Ibid.

8 Caproni, *L'opera*, 13.

9 Giorgio Caproni, *Stanze della funicolare* (Rome: De Luca, 1952).

10 Pier Vincenzo Mengaldo, "Per la poesia di Giorgio Caproni," in *Giorgio Caproni: L'opera in versi*, ed. Luca Zuliani (Milan: Mondadori, 1998), ix.

11 Leonelli, "La poesia," 1182.

12 Geno Pampaloni, "Nota," in *Giorgio Caproni: Poesie 1932–1986* (Milan: Garzanti, 1989), 815.

13 Caproni, *L'opera*, 126.

14 Ibid., 191.

15 Giovanni Raboni, [untitled], in *Giorgio Caproni: Poesie 1932–1986* (Milan: Garzanti, 1989), 798.

16 Caproni, *L'opera*, 243.

17 Ibid., 245.

18 Ibid., 331.

19 Ibid., 325.

20 Giovanni Testori, cited in *Giorgio Caproni: Poesie 1932–1986* (Milan: Garzanti, 1989), 799, note 1.

21 In truth, Pier Vincenzo Mengaldo was speaking specifically of *Il franco cacciatore*, but I think his description could equally be applied to *Il Conte di Kevenhüller*. Cf. Mengaldo, "Per la poesia," xxxiv.
22 Caproni, *L'opera*, 541.
23 Ibid., 1628.
24 Ibid., 1686.
25 Ibid., 765.
26 Giulio Ferroni, *Storia della letteratura italiana: Il Novecento*, vol. 4 (Turin: Einaudi, 2001), 495.
27 Marcel Proust, *Il tempo ritrovato*, trans. Giorgio Caproni (Turin: Einaudi, 1951).
28 Giorgio Caproni, *Come un'allegoria (1932–1935): versi* (Genoa: E. degli Orfini, 1936).
29 Giorgio Caproni, *Ballo a Fontanigorda* (Genoa: E. degli Orfini, 1938).
30 Giorgio Caproni, *Finzioni* (Rome: Istituto grafico tiberino, 1941).
31 Giorgio Caproni, *Cronistoria* (Florence: Vallecchi, 1943).
32 Many single poems were translated by Caproni during the 1950s and 1960s for anthologies and the radio, which lie unpublished in archives, along with his commentaries on modern poetry.
33 René Char, *Poesia e prosa*, trans. Giorgio Caproni and Vittorio Sereni (Milan: Feltrinelli, 1962).
34 Charles Baudelaire, *I fiori del male*, trans. Giorgio Caproni (Naples: Curcio, 1962). Caproni then renounced this version because of severe editorial changes by the publisher.
35 Louis-Ferdinand Céline, *Morte a credito*, trans. Giorgio Caproni (Milan: Garzanti, 1964).
36 Guy de Maupassant, *Bel-Ami*, trans. Giorgio Caproni (Milan: Garzanti, 1965).
37 Blaise Cendrars, *La mano mozza*, trans. Giorgio Caproni (Milan: Garzanti, 1967).
38 André Frénaud, *Il silenzio di Genova*, trans. Giorgio Caproni (Turin: Einaudi, 1967); André Frénaud, *Non c'è paradiso*, trans. Giorgio Caproni (Milan: Rizzoli, 1971).
39 Jean Genet, *Tutto il teatro*, trans. Giorgio Caproni and J. Rodolfo Wilcock (Milan: Il Saggiatore, 1971); Jean Genet, *Quattro romanzi e Diario del ladro*, trans. Giorgio Caproni (Milan: Il Saggiatore, 1975).
40 Federico García Lorca, *Il maleficio della farfalla*, trans. Giorgio Caproni (Turin: ERI, 1972).
41 Wilhelm Busch, *Max e Moritz ovvero Pippo e Peppo*, trans. Giorgio Caproni (Milan: Rizzoli, 1974).

42 Guillaume Apollinaire, *Poesie*, trans. Giorgio Caproni (Milan: Rizzoli, 1979).
43 Dei, *Giorgio Caproni*, 142.
44 Giorgio Caproni and Carlo Betocchi, *Una poesia indimenticabile: lettere 1936–1986*, ed. Daniele Santero (Lucca: M. Pacini Fazzi, 2007), 207.
45 Ibid., 236.
46 Giorgio Caproni to André Frénaud, 17 April 1969, Fondo Caproni, Biblioteca Nazionale di Firenze.
47 Caproni's translation of *Mort à crédit* was the first translation of this work. Céline's *Un viaggio al termine della notte* had been translated in the 1930s.
48 Fortini's translation of *L'agonia di generale Krivitski* was published by Einaudi in 1962 (André Frénaud, *L'agonia di generale Krivitski*, trans. Franco Fortini [Milan: Il saggiatore, 1962]), and Caproni's two volumes of Frénaud translations came out in 1967 and 1971.
49 The 1971 *Tutto il teatro* included five plays, three of which had never been translated. The 1959 Mondadori edition of Genet's prose, *Diario di un ladro e pagine scelte*, incorporated passages from Notre-dame-des-fleurs and from Mirâcle de la rose. Caproni published integral translations of not only *Diario di un ladro* but the other novels: *Querelle di Brest*, *Pompe funebri*, *Nostra Signora dei Fiori*, and *Miracolo della rosa*. So Caproni translated four plays, four novels, and *Diario di un ladro*.
50 The first edition of Char in Italian, as mentioned, is Caproni and Sereni's *Poesia e prosa*.
51 Caproni was one of the translators of the first complete edition of *À la recherche du temps perdu*, and his was the first translation of the final volume published in Italian.
52 Giorgio Caproni, "L'arte del tradurre," in *La traduzione del testo poetico*, ed. Franco Buffoni (Milan: Marcos and Marcos, 2004), 31.
53 Caproni, "Divagazioni sul tradurre," in *La scatola nera*, ed. Giovanni Raboni (Milan: Garzanti, 1996), 60.
54 Caproni, "L'arte del tradurre," 32; cited in Eugenio Manca, "Giorgio Caproni," in *I ferri del mestiere: Dieci interviste di Eugenio Manca* (Rome: L'unità, 1989), 60; cited in Giorgio Caproni, *Era così bello parlare: conversazioni radiofoniche con Giorgio Caproni* (Genoa: Il melangolo, 2004), 37.
55 The scholar Serge Karcevski first originated this metaphor, but it is unclear whether Caproni was familiar with his work. As Roman Jakobson wrote, "The Geneva linguist S. Karcevski used to compare such a gradual loss with a circular series of unfavorable currency transactions." Cf. Roman Jakobson, "On Linguistic Aspects," in *The Translation Studies Reader*, ed. Lawrence Venuti (London: Routledge, 2012), 126.

56 Giorgio Caproni, "Tre traduzioni," *La Fiera Letteraria*, 28 August 1947.
57 Giorgio Caproni, "I poeti e la tromba (o della traducibilità)," *Il lavoro nuovo*, 24 August 1949.
58 Cited in Georges Mounin, *Les belles infidèles* (Paris: Cahiers du Sud, 1955), 12.
59 Caproni, "L'arte del tradurre," 36.
60 Giorgio Caproni, "Il Valéry di Tutino," in *La scatola nera*, ed. Giovanni Raboni (Milan: Garzanti, 1996), 47.
61 Caproni, *Era così bello*, 144.
62 Caproni, "L'arte del tradurre," 34.
63 Ungaretti, "Poeta e uomini," 739.
64 Caproni, "Divagazioni sul tradurre," 60.
65 Ibid., 64.
66 Caproni, "Tre traduzioni."
67 Caproni, "Divagazioni sul tradurre," 65.
68 Caproni, *Una poesia indimenticabile*, 78.
69 Caproni, "Divagazioni sul tradurre," 65.
70 Friedrich Nietzsche, "Beyond Good and Evil," in *Basic writings of Nietzsche*, trans. Walter Kaufmann (New York: Random House, 2000), 230.
71 Fortini, "Dei 'compensi,'" 74.
72 Caproni, "Divagazioni sul tradurre," 65.
73 Caproni, "L'arte del tradurre," 31.
74 Ibid., 33.
75 Ibid.
76 Ibid., 33–4.
77 Sereni, *Il musicante*, xxxii.
78 Sereni's *quaderno* is in the Fondo Caproni at the Biblioteca Marconi in Rome.
79 Caproni, *Era così bello*, 145.
80 Flabbi, *Dettar versi*, 204.
81 Walter Benjamin, "Die Aufgabe des Übersetzers," in *Illuminationen: Ausgewählte Schriften*, ed. Siegfried Unseld (Frankfurt: Suhrkamp Verlag, 1961), 58.
82 Giorgio Caproni, "Diego Valeri ha tradotto Jacobi," *La Fiera Letteraria*, 31 March 1957.
83 Jakobson, "On Linguistic Aspects," 141.
84 Cited in Antonio Debenedetti, "Com'è difficile tradurre una musica," *Corriere della Sera*, 16 February 1980.
85 Ibid.
86 Ibid. Caproni, speaking of Mallarmé, notes: "ecco un'altra cosa che mi allontanava in certo senso, scandalizzava i fiorentini … l'enorme importanza di Mallarmé, che io stesso sfrutto [nelle poesie di Caproni],

no? coi bianchi, eccetera, però se avessi detto, non l'ho mai amato, l'ho ammirato, ma mai amato … e questo era grave per quei tempi, 'ma come? Era importante … ' Ancora oggi faccio fatica a leggerlo: in fondo, di fauni, delle ninfe, non me ne importa nulla, c'è poco da dire, m'importan di più le donne in ciabatte. E non è Neorealismo, intendiamoci." Caproni, *Era così bello*, 147–8.

87 Cited in Debenedetti, "Com'è difficile," 26.

88 Ibid.

89 Ibid.

90 Caproni, *Era così bello*, 149.

91 Caproni, "L'arte del tradurre," 37.

92 René Char, *Poèmes et prose choisis* (Paris: Gallimard, 1957), 246.

93 Giorgio Caproni, "Prefazione," in René Char, *Poesia e prosa*, trans. Giorgio Caproni and Vittorio Sereni (Milan: Feltrinelli, 1962), 7–8.

94 Bernard Simeone has left a fascinating account of their meeting: "… ce sont d'abord des regards: celui, frontal et taurin, de Char sous la casquette amarante, une flamme assurément, et celui, de côté, perdu en lui-même, de Caproni portant casquette grise. L'un massif dans le froid, l'autre frigorifié, mains jointes, avec au doigt un anneau en forme de serpent, mais dont la personne évoque, plus que la cendre, le noyau. De la sorte, ils sont profondément eux-mêmes, du moins tels qu'on les devine à la source, ou dans l'écho, de leurs livres. L'un traduit par l'autre qui, ce faisant, reste fidèle à son mystère, deux forces qui s'attirent et se compénètrent puis retournent séparément à l'énigme, deux 'alliés substantiels' qui, sur une photo, ne font que se côtoyer puisque la rencontre advint dans les textes." Bernard Simeone, "Ligure de Rome," in *Per Giorgio Caproni*, ed. Giorgio Devoto and Stefano Verdino (Genoa: San Marco dei Giustiniani, 1997), 470.

95 Giorgio Caproni to René Char, Fondo Caproni, Biblioteca Nazionale di Firenze.

96 Caproni, *Quaderno di traduzioni*, 112.

97 Ibid.

98 Ibid.

99 Ibid., 33.

100 Ibid., 113.

101 Ibid.

102 Ibid.

103 Ibid., 78–9.

104 René Char, *Fogli d'Ipnos, 1943–1944*, trans. Vittorio Sereni (Turin: Einaudi, 1968).

105 René Char, *Ritorno sopramonte e altre poesie*, trans. Vittorio Sereni (Milan: Mondadori, 1974).

106 The following translations have the same amount of verses: "Sette schegge del Luberon," "Annullarsi del pioppo," "Il colombo," "Fioritura successiva," "Uscita," "Tacito gioco," "Corso delle argille," "Il bacio," "Cerimonia di murmuri," "Rondine, massaia affaccendata," "Fame rossa," and "Senza eredi." The following versions have more verses in the translation, as indicated. "Tracciato sul baratro" (5 verses in the translation compared to 4 in the original), "Venasque" (6 v. 5), "I paraggi di Alsazia" (18 v. 16), "Ballo alle Baronie" (12 v. 10), "Yvonne" (7 v. 6), "Settetrione" (15 v. 12), "Lied del fico" (11 v. 9),"Il villaggio verticale" (18 v. 17), "Il giudizio di ottobre" (15 v. 14), "Ultima marcia" (13 v. 12), and "Di uno stesso legame" (16 v. 15).

107 Giuseppe Scaglione, "Le Vicinanze di René Char. Giorgio Caproni e Vittorio Sereni traduttori di A***," in *Studi novecenteschi* 36, no. 77 (2009): 137–50.

108 Ibid., 147.

109 Caproni's version dates from 1962, while Sereni's is from the 1970s.

110 Sereni, *Il musicante*, xxxiv.

111 "Frénaud ... uno dei più forti poeti francesi oggi viventi. Forse il più forte." Giorgio Caproni to Giulio Einaudi, November 27, 1964, Fasciolo Caproni, Archivio storico della casa editrice Giulio Einaudi Editore, Archivio di Stato di Torino.

112 Caproni, *L'opera*, 347.

113 Caproni, "Divagazione sul tradurre," 62.

114 Ibid., 63.

115 Fabio Scotto, "André Frénaud traducteur de l'italien," in *André Frénaud: La negation exigeante: Colloque de Cerisy 15–21 août 2000*, ed. Marie-Claire Bancquart (Cognac: Le Temps qu'il fait, 2004), 111.

116 Bricco, *André Frénaud*, 57.

117 Caproni, *Quaderno di traduzioni*, xxxv.

118 Bricco, *André Frénaud*, 49.

119 Ungaretti, *40 Sonetti*, 22–3.

120 Ungaretti, "Poeta e uomini," 739.

121 Carla Gubert, "Le belle infedeli: omaggio a Frénaud de 'L'Europa Letteraria,'" in *Frammenti di Europa: Riviste e traduttori del Novecento*, ed. Carla Gubert (Pesaro: Metauro, 2003), 90.

122 Caproni, "Divagazioni sul tradurre," 66.

123 Ibid.

124 Caproni, *Una poesia indimenticabile*, 106.

125 Cited in Luca Pietromarchi, "Nota alla traduzione," 54.

126 Charles Baudelaire, *I fiori del male*, trans. Giorgio Caproni, ed. Luca Pietromarchi (Venice: Marsilio, 2008).

127 Cited in Pietromarchi, "Nota alla traduzione," 57.

128 A choice that Attilio Bertolucci would follow in his own prose translation of *Les Fleurs du mal.*

129 Pietromarchi, "Nota alla traduzione," 57.

130 Ibid., 58.

131 Ibid.

132 Ibid.

133 Ibid., 58–9.

134 Marcel Proust, *Alla ricerca del tempo perduto,* trans. Giovanni Raboni, 4 vols. (Turin: Einaudi, 1983–94).

135 Gustave Flaubert, *L'educazione sentimentale,* trans. Giovanni Raboni (Milan: Garzanti, 1966).

136 Charles Baudelaire, *I fiori del male e altre poesie,* trans. Giovanni Raboni (Turin: Einaudi, 1999).

137 Guillaume Apollinaire, *Bestiario o il carteggio di Orfeo,* trans. Giovanni Raboni (Parma: Guanda, 1977); Guillaume Apollinaire, *Da Alcools,* trans. Giovanni Raboni and Vittorio Sereni (Milan: Il Saggiatore, 1981); and Guillaume Apollinaire, *La chiamavano Lu e altre poesie,* trans. Giovanni Raboni and Vittorio Sereni (Milan: Mondadori, 1984).

138 His translations can be found in the following anthologies: Jacques Prévert, *Parole,* trans. Rino Cortiana, Maurizio Cucchi, and Giovanni Raboni (Parma: Guanda, 1989); Jacques Prévert, *La pioggia e il bel tempo,* trans. Francesco Bruno, Maurizio Cucchi, and Giovanni Raboni (Parma: Guanda, 1989); Jacques Prévert, *Poesie,* trans. Maurizio Cucchi, and Giovanni Raboni (Milan: Guanda, 1979); Jacques Prévert, *Poesie d'amore,* trans. Ivos Margoni, Franca Madonia, Maurizio Cucchi, and Giovanni Raboni (Milan: CDE, 1986); Jacques Prévert, *Prévert: le poesie,* trans. Maurizio Cucchi and Giovanni Raboni (Rome: Lato side, 1980).

139 Giovanni Raboni, "Ovvero tradurre per amore," in *Traduzione e poesia nell'Europa del Novecento,* ed. Anna Dolfi (Rome: Bulzoni, 2004), 625.

140 Raboni, "Ovvero tradurre," 628.

141 Ibid., 627.

142 Ibid., 627. This recalls Perrot d'Ablancourt's claim that "it is better to be unfaithful in the small in order to be faithful in the great." Nicolas Perrot d'Ablancourt, "Preface to French translation of Thucydides," in *Western Translation Theory,* ed. Douglas Robinson (Manchester: St. Jerome, 1997), 160.

143 He published five distinct editions: Charles Baudelaire, *Poesie e prose,* ed. Giovanni Macchia, trans. Giovanni Raboni (Milan: Mondadori, 1973);

Charles Baudelaire, *I fiori del male e altre poesie*, trans. Giovanni Raboni (Turin: Einaudi, 1987); Charles Baudelaire, *I fiori del male e altre poesie*, trans. Giovanni Raboni (Turin: Einaudi, 1992); Charles Baudelaire, *Opere*, ed. Giovanni Raboni and Giuseppe Marcenaro (Milan: Mondadori, 1996); and Charles Baudelaire, *I fiori del male e altre poesie*, trans. Giovanni Raboni (Turin: Einaudi, 1999).

144 Charles Baudelaire, *Tutte le opere*, ed. Giovanni Macchia, trans. Giovanni Raboni (Milan: Mondadori, 1973).

145 Baudelaire, *I fiori del male.*

146 Raboni, "Ovvero tradurre," 626.

147 Baudelaire, *I fiori del male*, 225.

148 Caproni, *Quaderno di traduzioni*, 295.

149 Baudelaire, *I fiori del male*, 225.

150 Caproni, *Quaderno di traduzioni*, 295.

151 Baudelaire, *I fiori del male*, 225.

152 Ibid.

153 Caproni, *Quaderno di traduzioni*, 295.

154 Raboni, "Ovvero tradurre," 627.

155 "Ruines! ma famille! ô cerveaux congénères! / Je vous fais chaque soir un solennel adieu! / Où serez-vous demain, Eves octogénaires, / Sur qui pèse la griffe effroyable de Dieu?" Caproni, *Quaderno di traduzioni*, 309.

156 Flabbi, *Dettar versi*, 209.

157 Enrico Testa, "Introduzione," in Giorgio Caproni, *Quaderno di traduzioni*, ed. Enrico Testa (Turin: Einaudi, 1998), xv.

158 Giorgio Agamben, *Categorie italiane: studi di poetica e di letteratura*, 2nd ed. (Bari: Laterza, 2010), 93.

159 Bricco, *André Frénaud*, 80.

160 Caproni, *Una poesia indimenticabile*, 93.

161 Ibid., 238.

162 Flabbi, *Dettar versi*, 219.

163 Mengaldo, "Caproni e Sereni: due versioni," 211.

164 Laura Dolfi, "Giorgio Caproni traduttore del 'Llanto' (con un'appendice sul 'Maleficio de la mariposa')," in *Traduzione e poesia nell'Europa del Novecento*, ed. Anna Dolfi (Rome: Bulzoni, 2004), 492–3.

165 Caproni, "Il Valéry," 47.

166 Mengaldo, "Confronti," 179.

167 Giorgio Caproni, "Sulla poesia," in *La scatola nera*, ed. Giovanni Raboni (Milan: Garzanti, 1996), 35–6.

168 Bricco, *André Frénaud*, 130.

169 Antoine Berman, "Translation and the Trials of the Foreign," in *The Translation Studies Reader*, Lawrence Venuti, 3rd ed. (London: Routledge, 2012), 246.

170 Caproni, *Quaderno di traduzioni*, 280–1.

171 The deleted words: "Assise" (verse 2 of the original French poem), "par la" and "voir" (verse 3), "quand nous en triomphons" (verse 4); "lui," "veux-tu," and "où l'on" (verse 7); "veux-tu" and "nous" (verse 8); "pour la seconde fois" and "belle" (verse 10); "grandes," "verts," "a moi," and "dans ses yeux" (verse 14).

172 Caproni, *Quaderno di traduzioni*, 280.

173 Ibid., 232–47.

174 Flabbi, *Dettar versi*, 211.

175 Benzoni, *Da Céline a Caproni*, 194.

176 Indeed, if there is one symptomatic new translation, it would be the translation of "Merde à Dieu," which in Caproni's first edition was "mondo maiale," while in the revised edition it became the more faithful "Dio merda." Cf. Benzoni, *Da Céline a Caproni*, 203.

177 Cited in Testa, "Introduzione," xxvii.

178 Caproni, *L'opera*, 826. The editor notes that Caproni dated the poem "dom. 24/7/88 h.2, 30" (Sun[day] 7/24/[19]88 hour 21.30).

4. Giovanni Giudici

1 Part of this chapter was previously published in *Lettere Italiane,* and I would like to acknowledge the kind permission given by Carlo Ossola to include it here.

2 Aleksandr Pushkin, *Eugenio Onieghin*, trans. Giovanni Giudici (Milan: Garzanti, 1975); Aleksandr Pushkin, *Viaggio d'inverno e altre poesie*, trans. Giovanni Giudici and Giovanna Spendel (Milan: Mondadori, 1985); Evgenij Vinokurov, Genrich Sapgir, Robert Rozdestvenskij, Evgenij Evtushenko, and Aleksej Chvostenko, trans. Giovanni Giudici and Joanna Spendel, in *Poesia sovietica degli anni '60*, ed. C.G. De Michelis (Milan: Mondadori, 1971), 59–200, 329–48.

3 "Piccola antologia di poeti cechi del Novecento," in *Omaggio a Praga* (Milan: All'insegna del pesce d'oro, 1968), 33–156; Jiří Orten, *La cosa chiamata poesia*, trans. Giovanni Giudici and Vladimír Mikeš (Turin: Einaudi, 1969); "Tre poeti cechi," in *Paragone* 19, no. 224 (1968): 76–81.

4 Giorgio Manacorda, "La poesia è un grande teatro," *La Repubblica*, 10 December 1996.

5 Giovanni Giudici, *Omaggio a Praga. Hold Praze. Cinque poesie e tre prose con una piccola antologia di poeti cèchi del '900* (Milan: All'insegna del pesce d'oro, 1968).
6 Robert Frost, *Conoscenza della notte e altre poesie*, trans. Giovanni Giudici (Turin: Einaudi, 1965).
7 Sylvia Plath, *Lady Lazarus e altre poesie*, trans. Giovanni Giudici (Milan: Mondadori, 1976).
8 John Crowe Ransom, *Le donne e i cavalieri*, trans. Giovanni Giudici (Milan: Mondadori, 1971).
9 Hart Crane, *Nei caraibi*, trans. Giovanni Giudici (Milan: Scheiwiller, 1966).
10 Eugenio Montale, *Quaderno di traduzioni* (Milan: Edizioni della Meridiana, 1948).
11 Edoardo Sanguineti, *Quaderno di traduzioni* (Turin: Einaudi, 2006). Two notable exceptions are Franco Buffoni and Sergio Solmi.
12 Giovanni Giudici, *Addio, proibito piangere e altri versi tradotti (1955–1980)* (Turin: Einaudi, 1982).
13 Giovanni Giudici, *A una casa non sua: nuovi versi tradotti (1955–1995)* (Milan: Mondadori, 1997).
14 Giovanni Giudici, *Vaga lingua strana: dai versi tradotti* (Milan: Garzanti, 2003).
15 Cf. Rodolfo Zucco, "Introduzione," in Giovanni Giudici, *Vaga lingua strana: dai versi tradotti* (Milan: Garzanti, 2003), vii–xxviii; Massimo Bacigalupo, "Postfazione," in Giovanni Giudici, *A una casa non sua: nuovi versi tradotti (1955–1995)* (Milan: Mondadori, 1997), 195–208; and Antonello Satta Centanin, "Mistero, distanza e sardine sott'olio: teoria e pratica della traduzione in Giovanni Giudici," *Hortus. Rivista di poesie e arte*, no. 18 (1995): 99–110.
16 Giudici, *I versi della vita*, 315.
17 Giovanni Tesio, "Nel golfo di Giudici," *La Stampa*, 25 March 1995.
18 Angela Brintlinger, *Writing a Usable Past: Russian Literary Culture, 1917–1937* (Evanston: Northwestern University Press, 2000), 22.
19 Theo Hermans, *Translation in Systems* (Manchester: St. Jerome, 1999), 104.
20 Giovanni Giudici, *Andare in Cina a piedi. Racconto sulla poesia* (Rome: Edizioni e/o, 1992), 25.
21 Giovanni Giudici, "Come una poesia si costruisce," in *La dama non cercata: poetica e letteratura, 1968–1984* (Milan: Mondadori, 1985), 58.
22 Giovanni Giudici, "La musa inquietante," in *La dama non cercata: poetica e letteratura, 1968–1984* (Milan: Mondadori, 1985), 50.
23 Giovanni Giudici, "*Viola e durlindana*: riflessioni sulla lingua," in *La dama non cercata: poetica e letteratura, 1968–1984* (Milan: Mondadori, 1985), 157.

24 Italics in original. Giudici, "Come una poesia si costruisce," 61.
25 Italics in original. Giudici, *Andare in Cina*, 46.
26 Italics in original. Giudici, "Destino e poesia di Jiří Orten," in *La dama non cercata: poetica e letteratura, 1968–1984* (Milan: Mondadori, 1985), 170.
27 Cited in Grazia Cherchi, *Scompartimento per i lettori e i taciturni*, ed. Roberto Rossi (Milan: Feltrinelli, 1997), 215.
28 Giovanni Giudici, "Sotto il cielo di Praga," in *Per forza e per amore: critica e letteratura, 1966–1995* (Milan: Garzanti, 1996), 177.
29 Giudici, *Andare in Cina*, 41.
30 Giovanni Giudici, *Autobiologia* (Milan: Mondadori, 1969).
31 Giudici, *I versi della vita*, 211.
32 Noted by Rodolfo Zucco, in Giudici, *I versi della vita*, 1455.
33 Giovanni Giudici, *O beatrice* (Milan: Mondadori, 1972).
34 Romano Luperini rightly calls it "il libro di svolta." Cf. Romano Luperini, *Il Novecento* (Turin: Loescher, 1981), 2:827.
35 Giudici, *I versi della vita*, 526.
36 Giovanni Giudici, *Il male dei creditori* (Milan: Mondadori, 1977).
37 Giovanni Giudici, *Il ristorante dei morti* (Milan: Mondadori, 1981).
38 Giudici, *I versi della vita*, 390.
39 Ibid., 449.
40 Giovanni Giudici, *Poesie*, vol. 2 (Milan: Garzanti, 1990), 27.
41 Simona Morando, *Vita con le parole: la poesia di Giovanni Giudici* (Pasian di Prato: Campanotto, 2001), 88–9.
42 Giovanni Giudici, *Salutz: 1984–1986* (Turin: Einaudi, 1986).
43 Giudici, *I versi della vita*, 742.
44 Ibid., 737.
45 Giovanni Giudici, *Fortezza* (Milan: Mondadori, 1990).
46 Carlo di Alesio, cited in Morando, *Vita con le parole*, 115.
47 Giovanni Giudici, *Quanto spera di campare Giovanni* (Milan: Garzanti, 1993).
48 Giovanni Giudici, *Empie stelle: 1993–1996* (Milan: Garzanti, 1996).
49 Giovanni Giudici, *Eresia della sera* (Milan: Garzanti, 1999).
50 Giudici, *I versi della vita*, 969.
51 Giovanni Giudici, "La musa inquietante," in *La dama non cercata* (Milan: Mondadori, 1985), 48.
52 Ibid., 49.
53 Alfonso Bernardinelli, cited in Giulio Ferroni, *Letteratura italiana contemporanea: 1945–2007*, vol. 2 (Milan: Mondadori, 2007), 247.
54 His criticism of *il Gruppo* 63 is well known and is clearly seen in "Le neoavanguardie come opposizione di Sua Maestà": cf. Giovanni Giudici, *La letteratura dopo Hiroshima* (Rome: Editori riuniti, 1976), 199–206.

55 Giovanni Giudici, *La vita in versi* (Milan: Mondadori, 1965); Giovanni Giudici, *Autobiologia* (Milan: Mondadori, 1969); Giovanni Giudici, *O beatrice* (Milan: Mondadori, 1972); Giovanni Giudici, *Il male dei creditori* (Milan: Mondadori, 1977); Giovanni Giudici, *Il ristorante dei morti* (Milan: Mondadori, 1979); Giovanni Giudici, *Lume dei tuoi misteri* (Milan: Mondadori, 1984); Giovanni Giudici, *Fortezza* (Milan: Mondadori, 1990); Giovanni Giudici, *A una casa non sua* (Milan: Mondadori, 1997).

56 *Poeti italiani del Novecento*, ed. Pier Vincenzo Mengaldo (Milan: Mondadori, 1978).

57 *Antologia della poesia italiana: Novecento*, ed. Cesare Segre and Carlo Ossola, 2 vols. (Turin: Einaudi, 2003). Giudici is tied for ninth in number of allocated pages, which is no surprise given that Ossola is one of his strongest supporters.

58 Henry-Russell Hitchcock and Arthur Drexler, *Architettura americana d'oggi*, trans. Giovanni Giudici (Rome: De Luca, 1954); Arthur Schlesinger Jr., *Kennedy*, trans. Giovanni Giudici (Milan: Edizioni di Comunità, 1960); Gerard Mansell, *La tragedia d'Algeria*, trans. Giovanni Giudici (Milan: Edizioni di Comunità, 1961); Herbert L. Mathews, *La verità su Cuba*, trans. Giovanni Giudici and Amerigo Guadagnin (Milan: Edizioni di Comunità, 1961); Jacob Bronowski and Bruce Mazlish, *La tradizione intellettuale dell'Occidente da Leonardo a Hegel*, trans. Giovanni Giudici (Milan: Edizioni di Comunità, 1962); Haakon Chevalier, *Cominciò ad Hiroshima*, trans. Giovanni Giudici (Milan: Edizioni di Comunità, 1965); Robert Frost, *Conoscenza della notte* (Turin: Einaudi, 1965); Hart Crane, *Nei caraibi* (Milan: Scheiwiller, 1966); Sara Lidman, *Cinque diamanti*, trans. Giovanni Giudici and Irene Tanzi (Milan: Rizzoli, 1966); Stanislaus Joyce, *My Brother's Keeper, James Joyce's Early Years – Guardiano di mio fratello*, trans. Giovanni Giudici, in *Tutte le opere di James Joyce*, ed. Giacomo Debenedetti, vol. 1 (Milan: Mondadori, 1967); Edmund Wilson, *Saggi letterari*, trans. Giovanni Giudici and Giovanni Gualtieri (Milan: Garzanti, 1967); Yury Tynjanov, *Il problema del linguaggio poetico*, trans. Giovanni Giudici and Ljudmila Kortikova (Milan: Il Saggiatore, 1968); Giovanni Giudici, "Piccola antologia di poeti cechi del Novecento," in *Omaggio a Praga. Hold Praze* (Milan: Scheiwiller, 1968), 33–156; Jiří Orten, *La cosa chiamata poesia* (Turin: Einaudi, 1969); John Crowe Ransom, *Le donne e i cavalieri* (Milan: Mondadori, 1971); *Poesia sovietica degli anni sessanta*, ed. Cesare de Michelis, trans. Giovanni Giudici et al. (Milan: Mondadori, 1971); Mao Zedong, *Quattro poesie*, trans. Giovanni Giudici and Margherita Guidacci (Milan: Scheiwiller, 1971); Pushkin, *Eugenio Onieghin*, trans. Giudici; Sylvia Plath, *Lady Lazarus* (Milan: Mondadori, 1976); Giovanni Giudici, *Addio, proibito piangere* (Turin:

Einaudi, 1982); Ezra Pound, *Hugh Selwyn Mauberley*, trans. Giovanni Giudici (Milan: Il Saggiatore, 1982); Ignacio de Loyola, *Esercizi spirituali*, trans. Giovanni Giudici (Milan: SE, 1984); Aleksandr Pushkin, *Viaggio d'inverno e altre poesie*, trans. Giovanni Giudici and Joanna Spendel (Milan: Mondadori, 1985); Samuel Taylor Coleridge, *La rima del vecchio marinaio* (Milan: SE, 1987); Giovanni Giudici, *A una casa non sua* (Milan: Mondadori, 1997); William Shakespeare: *14 X 14, dai sonetti di Shakespeare tradotti da Giovanni Giudici* (Bocca di Magra: Edizioni Capannina, 2002); and Giovanni Giudici, *Vaga lingua strana: dai versi tradotti* (Milan: Garzanti, 2003).

59 Giovanni Giudici, *Fiorì d'improvviso* (Rome: Edizioni del Canzoniere, 1953).

60 Schlesinger Jr., *Kennedy*.

61 Gerard Mansell, *La tragedia d'Algeria*, trans. Giovanni Giudici (Milan: Edizioni di Comunità, 1961).

62 Herbert L. Mathews, *La verità su Cuba*, trans. Giovanni Giudici and Amerigo Guadagnin (Milan: Edizioni di Comunità, 1961).

63 Jacob Bronowski and Bruce Mazlish, *La tradizione intellettuale dell'Occidente da Leonardo a Hegel*, trans. Giovanni Giudici (Milan: Edizioni di Comunità, 1962).

64 Haakon Chevalier, *Cominciò ad Hiroshima*, trans. Giovanni Giudici (Milan: Edizioni di Comunità, 1965).

65 Sara Lidman, *Cinque diamanti*, trans. Giovanni Giudici and Irene Tanzi (Milan: Rizzoli, 1966).

66 Edmund Wilson, *Saggi letterari*, trans. Giovanni Giudici and Giovanni Gualtieri (Milan: Garzanti, 1967).

67 Joyce, *My Brother's Keeper, James Joyce's Early Years.*

68 Yury Tynjanov, *Il problema del linguaggio poetico*, trans. Giovanni Giudici and Ljudmila Kortikova (Milan: Il Saggiatore, 1968).

69 Giudici, *I versi della vita*, lxxx–lxxxiv.

70 Giudici, "Da un'officina di traduzioni," in *Per forza e per amore*, 22.

71 Ibid.

72 Giudici, *Andare in Cina*, 77–8.

73 Ibid., 77.

74 Ibid., 78.

75 Italics in the original. Ibid.

76 A term appropriately used by Bacigalupo to describe Giudici's translations in his afterword to *A una casa non sua*. Cf. Bacigalupo, "Postfazione," 195.

77 Italics in the original. Giudici, "Da un'officina di traduzioni," 29.

78 Lawrence Venuti, *The Translator's Invisibility: A History of Translation* (New York: Routledge, 1995), 20.

79 On various occasions he has co-translated with or asked for advice from informants or scholars in a specific language and literature, such as Russian, Czech, or English.

80 He still claimed a certain awkwardness at calling himself a poet: "La stessa parola 'poeta' mi fa sentire ancora oggi, a disagio." Giudici, *Andare in Cina*, 54.

81 Giudici, *Eugenio Onieghin*, 194.

82 A detailed comparison of the different editions of Giudici's translation of *Eugene Onegin* awaits study, after the preliminary analyses by Luca Lenzini and Nicola Gardini. Technically, there are four separate complete translations: the 1975, 1983, 1990, and 1999 editions. The greatest number of changes, as I have found, occur between the 1975 and the 1983 editions (260 of 364 stanzas, or 71 per cent, are changed in some way), while there are changes in 29 stanzas between the 1983 and 1990 editions, and only a few between the 1990 and 1999 editions.

83 Giudici, "Da un'officina di traduzioni," 30.

84 Ibid., 31.

85 Ibid., 31–2.

86 Giudici, "Come una poesia si costruisce," 62.

87 Giudici, "Da un'officina di traduzioni," 31.

88 Lo Gatto trained a generation or two of Italian Slavists and his importance for Italian scholarship dealing with Russian literature is immense. His history of Russian literature, whose most recent reprint is *Storia della letteratura russa* (Florence: Sansoni, 2000), is still well known and canonical.

89 The majority of Italian-Russian scholars, such as D. Cavaion and G.P. Samonà, preferred Lo Gatto's translation.

90 Aleksandr Pushkin, *Eugenio Onieghin di Aleksandr S. Puškin in versi italiani*, trans. Giovanni Giudici (Milan: Garzanti, 1999), 198.

91 Ibid., 199.

92 Sylvia Plath, *Lady Lazarus e altre poesie*, trans. Giovanni Giudici, 6th ed. (Milan: Mondadori, 1989), 12.

93 Giudici, *Eugenio Onieghin*, 196.

94 Giudici, "Da un'officina di traduzioni," 22.

95 Ibid., 34.

96 Giudici, *Eugenio Onieghin*, 198.

97 Nicola Gardini, "Il bicentenario di Aleksandr Puškin," *Poesia* 12, no. 132 (1999): 34.

98 Luca Lenzini, "L'Onieghin di Giovanni Giudici," in *Interazioni: tra poesia e romanzo* (Trento: Temi, 1998), 100.

99 Pier Vincenzo Mengaldo, *La tradizione del Novecento. Nuova serie* (Florence: Vallecchi, 1987), 42.
100 Giovanni Raboni, "Giudici e Puškin, un confronto in versi," *Corriere della Sera*, 6 June 1999.
101 Cited in Ludovica Ripa di Meane, *Diligenza e voluttà: Ludovica Ripa di Meane interroga Gianfranco Contini* (Milan: Mondadori, 1989), 208–9.
102 Cf. Danilo Cavaion, "Le traduzioni italiane in versi dell'*Eugenio Onegin* di Puškin," in *Premio città di Monselice per la traduzione letteraria e scientifica. Atti del nono convegno sui problemi della traduzione letteraria e scientifica* (Monselice: 1981), 71–91; G.P. Samonà, "L'*Onegin* tradotto da Giudici: riflessioni di metodo sulla traduzione di poesia," *Ricerche slavistiche*, vols. 24–6 (1977–9): 217–30; Michele Colucci, "Le traduzioni italiane poetiche dell'*Evgenij Onegin*," in *Puškin europeo*, ed. Sante Graciotti (Venice: Marsilio, 2001) 299–304; and Serena Vitale, "Disavventure di Puškin in Italia," *La Repubblica*, 15 October 1998.
103 Cited in Giuseppe Ghini, *Tradurre l'Onegin* (Urbino: Quattroventi, 2003), 53.
104 Ripa di Meane, *Diligenza e voluttà*, 209.
105 Gianfranco Folena, "Prefazione," in Giovanni Giudici, *Eugenio Onieghin di Aleksandr S. Puškin in versi italiani* (Milan: Garzanti, 1999), xv.
106 Pushkin, *Eugenio Onieghin di Aleksandr S. Puškin in versi italiani*, trans. Giovanni Giudici, 187.
107 Vladimir Nabokov, "Problems of Translation," *Partisan Review*, no. 22 (1955): 496–512.
108 Ibid., 496.
109 Aleksandr Pushkin, *Eugene Onegin*, trans. Vladimir Nabokov, vol. 1 (Princeton: Princeton University Press, 1975), 10.
110 Nabokov, "Problems of Translation," 503.
111 Vladimir Nabokov, "Nabokov's *Onegin*," *Encounter* 36, no. 5 (1966): 91–2.
112 Judson Rosengrant, "Nabokov, Onegin, and the Theory of Translation," *The Slavic and East European Journal* 38, no. 1 (1994): 20.
113 Edward J. Brown, "Round Two: Nabokov versus Pushkin," *Slavic Review* 36, no. 1 (1977): 104.
114 Alexander Gerschenkron, "A Manufactured Monument?" *Modern Philology* 63, no. 4 (1966): 340.
115 Giudici, "Da un'officina di traduzioni," 33.
116 Rodolfo Zucco, "Satura," in *Gli anni '60 e '70 in Italia*, ed. Stefano Giovannuzzi (Genoa: San Marco dei Giustiniani, 2003), 270.
117 Giudici, *Addio, proibito piangere*, xi.
118 Ibid.

119 Giudici, "Da un'officina di traduzioni," 30–1.

120 Giudici, *A una casa non sua*, 10. Cf. Giudici's remarks, quoted in Rodolfo Zucco, "Addizioni a *I versi della vita*," *Rassegna europea della letteratura italiana* 100, no. 31 (2008): 100: "Quel tentativo di riformare il comunismo, poi soffocato dall'Unione Sovietica, aveva aperto molte speranze nella sinstra europea, cioè che il socialismo fosse compatibile con la libertà, con la democrazia. Il tipo di governo che era stato creato in quell'anno in Cecoslovacchia, che restava socialista, senza compromissioni, è finito presto perché né le potenze occidentali, né quelle orientali avevano interesse a mantenere questa isola di socialismo."

121 Bacigalupo, "Postfazione," 206.

122 A perusal of the *Bibliografia degli studi italiani sulla cecoslovacchia (1918–1978)*, ed. A.W. Tosi (Rome: Bulzoni, 1980) confirms this.

123 Cf. *Bibliografia degli studi italiani sulla cecoslovacchia (1918–1978)*, ed. Tosi.

124 A.M. Ripellino had translated a poem about children by Orten in 1951: A.M. Ripellino, "Poeti cecoslovacchi parlano ai bambini," *La fiera letteraria* 6, no. 49 (1951): 3.

125 As well as three young Czech poets he translated for *Paragone* in 1968 but did not include in his anthology: Vladimír Mikeš, Vladimír Janovic, and Marie Leskovjanova. Cf. Giovanni Giudici, "Tre giovani poeti cechi," in *Paragone – Letteratura* 19, no. 224/44 (1968): 76–81.

126 Niccolò Scaffai, *Il poeta e il suo libro: Retorica e storia del libro di poesia nel Novecento* (Florence: Le Monnier, 2005), 134.

127 Giudici, *Addio, proibito piangere*, vii.

128 As it is, the order of the book is Donne (b. 1572), Crane (b. 1899), Dickinson (b. 1830), Pound (b. 1885), Frost (b. 1874), Ransom (b. 1888), Orten (b. 1919), Halas (b. 1901), Kolář (b. 1914), Pushkin (b. 1799), Yeats (b. 1865), and Coleridge (b. 1772).

129 Chronologically speaking, Giudici translated Halas before Orten and Kolář.

130 His complete translation of Coleridge would appear five years later.

131 Giudici, *Addio, proibito piangere*, vi.

132 Ibid.

133 Bacigalupo, "Postfazione," 195.

134 Giudici, *A una casa non sua*, 9.

135 Zucco, "Introduzione," xxvii.

136 Bacigalupo, "Postfazione," 193.

137 Giudici, *A una casa non sua*, 141.

138 Ibid., 178. The English gloss is mine.

139 Rodolfo Zucco chose to withdraw as editor of the volume, offended by Garzanti's poor editorial decisions that left him no freedom in organizing the volume.
140 Giacomo Leopardi, *Zibaldone*, ed. Rolando Damiani, vol. 1 (Milan: Mondadori, 1997), 1410.
141 Italics in the original. Giudici, "La poesia di Biagio Marin," in *La letteratura verso Hiroshima* (Rome: Editori Riuniti, 1976), 294.
142 Cadioli, "Al servizio della Lingua della Poesia," 103.
143 Giovanni Giudici, "Note di un traduttore del Mauberley," *Galleria* 36, nos. 3–6 (1986): 261–3.
144 Giudici, "Destino e poesia di Jiří Orten," 170.
145 Ibid., 176.
146 Margherita Guidacci, "Conoscenza delle lingue e l'importanza del tradurre," in *Le problematiche dell'espressione e della comunicazione in prospettiva duemila*, ed. Alberto Frattini (Rome: Studium, 1990), 31.
147 Maura del Serra, *Le foglie della Sibilla: scritti su Margherita Guidacci* (Rome: Studium, 2005), 77.
148 Margherita Guidacci, "Traducendo due poetesse americane: Jessica Powers ed Elizabeth Bishop," in *La traduzione del testo poetico*, ed. Franco Buffoni (Milan: Marcos and Marcos, 2004), 158: "Anche per il ritmo si devono evitare gli incespicamenti e quelli che io chiamo i 'ciabattamenti'; si dovranno fare, a volte, spostamenti, cambiamenti sintattici, ma l'importante è che il ritmo sia salvo nella lingua di arrivo così come era bello nella lingua di partenza. Se infatti per rispettare l'aspetto letterale ci si ostina a mantenere le parole nello stesso ordine, ne risulta spesso un ritmo assolutamente impoetico; in questo caso, non si è affatto fedeli al testo, bensì lo si tradisce."
149 Ibid.
150 Ibid.
151 "Sudai alcuni mesi sull'*Urna greca*, dopo di che conclusi che nemmeno se avessi avuto davanti a me quindici vite, tutte fresche e nuove, invece di averne una sola ed ormai alla fine, nemmeno allora avrei potuto tradurre Keats, perché le sue poesie non mi volevano." Cited in Franco Buffoni, "Gli incontri 'poietici' di Margherita Guidacci," in *Per Margherita Guidacci*, ed. Margherita Ghilardi (Florence: Le Lettere, 2001), 177. Buffoni, as we know, translated Keats's ode.
152 Emily Dickinson, *Poems*, ed. T.H. Johnson, 3 vols. (Cambridge: Harvard University Press, 1955).
153 Barbara Lanati rightly postulates one of the "varie edizioni, complete o ridotte, curate da Martha Dickinson Bianchi e pubblicate tra il 1914 e il

1937." Barbara Lanati, "Margherita traduce Emily," in *Per Margherita Guidacci*, ed. Margherita Ghilardi (Florence: Le lettere, 2001), 185.

154 "Resta il fatto … che nella raccolta da lei [Guidacci] curata nel '61 aggiunse poesie mai conosciute né tradotte prima dell'edizione Johnson, lavorando su quest'ultima ma conservando intatte tutte le poesie tradotte prima e risalenti all'edizione Bianchi. Così nell'edizione del '61, priva di testo a fronte, si alternano componimenti fedeli all'edizione Bianchi a componimenti fedeli a quella Johnson o Todd Bingham." Ibid., 187.

155 It is extremely unlikely that the text Guidacci used differed so much as to justify any of Guidacci's poetic inversions described below.

156 Bianca Tarozzi, "L'arte di perdere," in *Per Margherita Guidacci*, ed. Margherita Ghilardi (Florence: Le Lettere, 2001), 211.

157 Antonio Prete, "Margine leopardiano. Su Margherita Guidacci," in *Per Margherita Guidacci*, ed. Margherita Ghilardi (Florence: Le Lettere, 2001), 167.

158 Berman, "Translation and the Trials," 288.

159 Antonio Prete, "Dialoghi sul confine. La traduzione della poesia," in *Storia della letteratura italiana: Il novecento. Scenari di fine secolo*, vol. 1, ed. Nino Borsellino and Lucio Felice (Milan: Garzanti, 2001), 906.

160 Giovanni Giudici, "Premessa," in Robert Frost, *Conoscenza della notte* (Milan: Mondadori, 1988), 7.

161 Frost, *Conoscenza della notte*, 54–5.

162 Ibid., 51.

163 Giudici, *Vaga lingua strana*, 55.

164 Ibid.

165 Ibid., 61.

166 Ibid., 63.

167 Giudici, "Da un officina di traduzioni," 28.

168 Shoshana Blum-Kulka, "Shifts of Cohesion and Coherence in Translation," in *The Translation Studies Reader*, ed. Lawrence Venuti, 2nd ed. (London: Routledge, 2004), 290.

169 Giudici, *Vaga lingua strana*, 214–15.

170 Ghini, *Tradurre l'Onegin*, 70.

171 Giudici, *Vaga lingua strana*, 31.

172 Ibid., 263.

173 Ibid., 40–1.

174 Ibid., 80–1.

175 Ibid., 331.

176 Ibid., 97.

177 Ibid., 109.

178 Ibid., 323.
179 Franco Fortini, "Dei 'compensi' nelle versioni di poesia," in *La traduzione del testo poetico*, ed. Franco Buffoni (Padua: Marcos y Marcos, 2004), 72–7.
180 Giudici, *Vaga lingua strana*, 34–5.
181 Ibid., 285.
182 Ibid., 286.
183 Pushkin, *Eugenio Onieghin di Aleksandr S. Puškin in versi italiani*, trans. Giovanni Giudici, 8.
184 Ghini finds the following transliterated words: *chandrà, kvas, prisjadka, njanja, trojka, kibitka, banja, brička, ataman,* and *izbà*. Lo Gatto included only six such words. Cf. Ghini, *Tradurre l'Onegin*, 131.
185 Ibid., 132.
186 Giudici, *Vaga lingua strana*, 4–5.
187 Rodolfo Zucco, "Introduzione," xxiv.
188 Ibid., xviii–xx.
189 Ibid., xix.
190 Ibid.
191 Ibid., xviii.
192 Cited in Venuti, *The Translator's Invisibility*, 101.
193 Giudici, "Da un'officina di traduzioni," 28–9.
194 Morando, *Vita con le parole*, 119.
195 Giudici, "Kafka e dintorni," in *La dama non cercata: poetica e letteratura, 1968–1984* (Milan: Mondadori, 1985), 214.
196 Giudici, *I versi della vita*, 714.

5. Edoardo Sanguineti

1 A previously abridged version of this chapter was published in *Edoardo Sanguineti: Literature, Ideology and the Avant-Garde*, and I thank the editors John Picchione and Paolo Chirumbolo for permission to reprint it here in a much altered form.
2 Edoardo Sanguineti, "Introduzione," in *Teatro antico: traduzioni e ricordi*, ed. Federico Condello and Claudio Longhi (Milan: Rizzoli, 2006), 20.
3 Aeschylus, *Le Coefore*, trans. Edoardo Sanguineti (Milan: Il Saggiatore, 1978) and Aeschylus, *I sette contro Tebe*, trans. Edoardo Sanguineti (Milan: Sipario, 1992); Sophocles, *Edipo tiranno*, trans. Edoardo Sanguineti (Bologna: Cappelli, 1980) and Sophocles, *Antigone*, in Edoardo Sanguineti, *Per Musica* (Modena: Mucchi, 1993); Euripides, *Le Baccanti*, trans. Edoardo Sanguineti (Milan: Feltrinelli, 1968) and Euripides, *Le Troiane*, trans. Edoardo Sanguineti (Turin: Einaudi, 1974); Seneca, *Fedra*, trans. Edoardo Sanguineti (Turin: Einaudi, 1969); William Shakespeare, *La tragedia di Re*

Lear, trans. Edoardo Sanguineti (Genoa: Il Melangolo, 2008); Aristophanes, *La festa delle donne*, trans. Edoardo Sanguineti (Genoa: Il Melangolo, 2001); Pierre Corneille, *L'illusione comica*, trans. Edoardo Sanguineti (Genoa: Il Melangolo, 2005); Molière, *Don Giovanni*, trans. Edoardo Sanguineti (Genoa: Il Melangolo, 2000); and Bertolt Brecht, *Il cerchio di gesso del Caucaso*, trans. Edoardo Sanguineti (Genoa: Il Melangolo, 2003). *Macbeth remix*, Shakespeare's *Measure for Measure*, Brecht's *La resistibile ascesa di Arturo Ui*, and Ionesco's *Il re muore* remain unpublished.

4 Petronius, *Il Satyricon*, trans. Edoardo Sanguineti (Rome: Aldo Palazzi Editore, 1969).

5 Edoardo Sanguineti, *Faust. Un travestimento* (Genoa: Costa and Nolan, 1985).

6 E.g., James Joyce, *Poesie*, trans. Alfredo Giuliani, Alberto Rossi, Edoardo Sanguineti, and J. Rodolfo Wilcock (Milan: Mondadori, 1961); Edoardo Sanguineti, *Omaggio a Shakespeare: nove sonetti* (Lecce: Manni, 2004); and Edoardo Sanguineti, *Omaggio a Goethe* (Bellinzona: Edizioni di Sottoscala, 2003).

7 Edoardo Sanguineti, *Laborintus* (Varese: Magenta, 1956).

8 Nanni Balestrini, Alfredo Giuliani, Elio Pagliarani, Antonio Porta, and Edoardo Sanguineti, *I novissimi: poesie per gli anni '60*, ed. Alfredo Giuliani (Milan: Rusconi and Paolazzi, 1961).

9 Cited in Fausto Curi, *Gli stati d'animo del corpo: studi sulla letteratura italiana del Otto e Novecento* (Bologna: Pendragon, 2005), 262.

10 Edoardo Sanguineti, *Reisebilder*, in *Wirrwarr* (Milan: Feltrinelli, 1972).

11 Edoardo Sanguineti, *Scartabello 1980* (Macerata: Cristoforo Colombo Libraio, 1981).

12 Sanguineti, *Reisebilder*, 5.

13 Edoardo Sanguineti, *Postkarten 1972–1977* (Milan: Feltrinelli, 1978), 49.

14 Edoardo Sanguineti, *Commedia dell'inferno: un travestimento dantesco* (Genoa: Costa and Nolan, 1989).

15 Edoardo Sanguineti, *Il gatto lupesco: poesie (1982–2001)* (Milan: Feltrinelli, 2002), 81.

16 Edoardo Sanguineti, "I santi anarchici: la mia poesia," in *Edoardo Sanguineti e Gaetano delli Santi: due generazioni d'Avanguardia a confronto*, ed. Marisa Napoli (Milan: Fabio d'Ambrosio, 2006), 80.

17 Sanguineti, "I santi anarchici," 80.

18 Sanguineti was a representative in Italian Parliament (1979–83), as well as a city councilor in Genoa (1976–9).

19 Edoardo Sanguineti, *L'amore delle tre melarance: un travestimento fiabesco dal canovaccio di Carlo Gozzi* (Genoa: Il Melangolo, 2001).

20 Euripides, *Ifigenia in Aulide di Euripide*, trans. Edoardo Sanguineti, ed. Federico Condello (Bologna: Bononia University Press, 2012).

21 Edoardo Sanguineti, "Il traduttore, nostro contemporaneo," in *La Missione del critico* (Genoa: Marietti, 1987), 182–8.
22 Jan Kott, *Shakespeare Our Contemporary*, trans. Boleslaw Taborski (Garden City: Doubleday, 1964).
23 Edoardo Sanguineti, "Tradurre il teatro antico," *Prometeo rivista*, unpaginated, accessed 6 May 2013, http://www.indafondazione.org/prometeus-rivista-online/tradurre-il-teatro-antico/
24 Sanguineti, "Il traduttore, nostro contemporaneo," 186.
25 Ibid., 185.
26 Ibid., 187.
27 Gerard Genette, *Palimpsests: Literature in the Second Degree*, trans. Channa Newman and Claude Doubinsky (Lincoln: University of Nebraska Press), 58.
28 Sanguineti, *La tragedia di Re Lear*, 191.
29 Edoardo Sanguineti and Marco Sciaccaluga, "Il palcoscenico e il mondo: conversazione tra Edoardo Sanguineti e Marco Sciaccaluga," ed. Aldo Viganò, in William Shakespeare, *La tragedia di Re Lear*, trans. Edoardo Sanguineti (Genoa: Il Melangolo, 2008), 191.
30 Cited in Peter Brooker, "Key Words in Brecht's Theory and Practice of Theatre," in *The Cambridge Companion to Brecht*, ed. Peter Thomson and Glendyr Sacks, 2nd ed. (Cambridge: Cambridge University Press, 2006), 215.
31 Cited in Brooker, "Key Words," 215.
32 Edoardo Sanguineti, *Sanguineti/Novecento: conversazioni sulla cultura del ventesimo secolo*, ed. Giuliano Galletta (Genoa: Il Nuovo Melangolo, 2005), 53. Sanguineti didn't approve of the way Brecht's plays were staged, finding them too rigid and mechanical.
33 Edoardo Sanguineti, "Il grande teatro è solo hard: Dialoghetto sulla drammaturgia tra Edoardo Sanguineti e Eugenio Buonaccorsi," in *Sei personaggi.com: un travestimento pirandelliano* (Genoa: Il Melangolo, 2001), 8.
34 Benjamin, "Die Aufgabe des Übersetzers," 66.
35 Ibid., 69.
36 Sanguineti, "Introduzione," 18.
37 Sanguineti, "Tradurre il teatro antico," unpaginated..
38 Federico Condello, "Appunti su Sanguineti," *Poetiche* 8, no. 3 (2006): 565.
39 cf. Lawrence Venuti, *The Translator's Invisibility: A History of Translation* (New York: Routledge, 1995), 1–42.
40 Roman Jakobson, "On Linguistic Aspects of Translation," in *The Translation Studies Reader*, ed. Lawrence Venuti, 3rd ed. (London: Routledge, 2012), 139.
41 Carlo Gozzi, "L'amore delle tre melarance," in *Opere: teatro e polemiche teatrali*, ed. Giuseppe Petronio (Milan: Rizzoli, 1962), 57.
42 Sanguineti, *L'amore delle tre melarance*, 30.

43 Ibid., 58.
44 Paolo Chirumbolo, *Tra coscienza e autocoscienza: saggi sulla narrativa degli anni sessanta* (Soveria Mannelli: Rubbettino, 2009), 178.
45 Sanguineti, "Il mio Catullo," 200.
46 Petronius Arbiter, *Satyricon Reliquiae*, ed. Konrad Muller (Stutgardia: Teubner, 1995), 1.
47 Petronius Arbiter, *Satyricon di Petronio nella traduzione di Edoardo Sanguineti*, trans. Edoardo Sanguineti (Turin: Einaudi, 1993), 3.
48 Arbiter, *Satyricon Reliquiae*, 8.
49 Petronius, *Satyricon di Petronio nella traduzione di Edoardo Sanguineti*, 12.
50 Sanguineti, "Il mio Catullo," 200.
51 Ibid.
52 Ibid., 201.
53 Sanguineti, "Introduzione," 9.
54 Sophocles, *Tragoediae: 1*, ed. R.D. Dawe (Leipzig: B.G. Teubner Verlagsgesellschaft, 1984), 115.
55 Friedrich Hölderlin, *Sämtliche Werke und Briefe*, ed. Jochen Schmidt, vol. 2 (Frankfurt am Main: Deutscher Klassiker Verlag, 1994), 804.
56 Sanguineti, *Teatro antico*, 240.
57 Sophocles, *Edipo re*, in *Tragici greci tradotti da Salvatore Quasimodo* (Milan: Mondadori, 1963), 403.
58 Sanguineti, "Il traduttore, nostro contemporaneo," 188.
59 Edoardo Sanguineti, letter to author, 31 July 2009.
60 A decision shared by both Sanguineti and Einaudi.
61 Edoardo Sanguineti, letter to author, 31 July 2009. And in a 2001 interview, he revealingly states "I classici da rileggere: Lucrezio, Shakespeare, Goethe." Cf. Gian Luigi Paracchini, "Sanguineti: nel labirinto delle parole," *Corriere della Sera*, 21 July 2001.
62 Edoardo Sanguineti, letter to author, 31 July 2009.
63 Ibid.
64 Sanguineti, *Quaderno di traduzioni*, 15.
65 It should be noted that Sanguineti's work on Lucretius was also collaborative: before his death, he was preparing an expanded version to be staged by Luca Ronconi.
66 *Macbeth Remix*. Unpublished.
67 "Una traduzione affiatami per il teatro di Genova da Marco Sciaccaluga." Cf. Bruno Quaranta, "Sullo yacht con Re Lear," *La Stampa*, 2 August 2008.
68 "Misura per misura." Unfinished and unpublished.
69 Sanguineti and Liberovici, *Il mio amore è come una febbre*, 54–5.
70 Sanguineti, *Quaderno di traduzioni*, 35.
71 Ibid., 34.

72 Ibid., 40.
73 Ibid., 41.
74 Curi, *Gli stati d'animo*, 301.
75 Pieter de Meijer, "Appendice. Goethe, Faust e Sanguineti," in Edoardo Sanguineti, *Faust. Un travestimento*, ed. Niva Lorenzini (Rome: Carocci, 2005), 127.
76 Niva Lorenzini, "Il Faust di Sanguineti: la parola all'inferno," in Edoardo Sanguineti, *Faust. Un Travestimento*, ed. Niva Lorenzini (Rome: Carocci, 2005), 12.
77 Cited in Mariafrancesca Venturo, *Parole e travestimento nella poetica teatrale di Edoardo Sanguineti* (Rome: Fermenti, 2007), 141–2.
78 Lorenzini, "Il Faust di Sanguineti," 12.
79 Curi, *Gli stati*, 280.
80 Ibid.
81 Sanguineti, *Faust*, 123–4.
82 Johann Wolfgang Goethe, *Faust. Sämtliche Werke. Briefe, Tagebücher und Gespräche*, vol. 40, ed. Albrecht Schöne (Frankfurt am Main: Deutscher Klassiker Verlag, 1994), 109.
83 Sanguineti, *Faust*, 85.
84 Ibid., 68.
85 Sanguineti, *Quaderno di traduzioni*, 102.
86 Ibid., 103.
87 *Sanguineti's Song: conversazioni immorali*, ed. Antonio Gnoli (Milan: Feltrinelli, 2006), 94.
88 Sanguineti, *Quaderno di traduzioni*, 17.
89 Ibid., 40.
90 Ibid., 49.
91 He has noted on occasion how page number counts in anthologies are highly significant.
92 Edoardo Sanguineti, letter to author, 31 July 2009.
93 For example, his use of punctuation. For Sanguineti, only two types of punctuation exist: the comma and the colon. The colon signifies a temporary end of the phrase or sentence, being by its nature open-ended, and takes the place of semicolons and periods (which are always replaced in his translations by colons). Finality is not given in full stops. Commas are used over-abundantly both in his own verse and in his translations. For instance, in the nine sonnets by Shakespeare, Sanguineti uses eighty-three commas.
94 Sanguineti, "Tradurre il teatro antico," unpaginated.
95 Ibid.
96 Ibid.

97 *Grande dizionario della lingua italiana: Supplemento 2004*, ed. Edoardo Sanguineti (Turin: UTET, 2004), xvi.

98 Gianfranco Folena writes, "È noto che all'inizio di nuove tradizioni di lingua scritta e letteraria, fin dove possiamo spingere lo sguardo, sta molto spesso la traduzione: sicché al vulgato superbo motto idealistico *in principio fuit poëta* vien fatto di contrapporre oggi l'umile realtà che *in principio fuit interpres*." Gianfranco Folena, *Volgarizzare e tradurre* (Turin: Einaudi, 1992), 3.

99 Cit. in "Il palcoscenico e il mondo: conversazione tra Edoardo Sanguineti e Marco Sciaccaluga," ed. Aldo Viganò, in William Shakespeare, *La tragedia di Re Lear* (Genoa: Il Melangolo, 2008), 191.

100 Ferdinand de Saussure, *Cours de linguistique générale*, ed. Charles Bally, Albert Sechehaye, and Albert Reidlinger (Paris: Payot, 1949), 30–1.

6. Franco Buffoni

1 Franco Buffoni, *I tre desideri* (Genoa: San Marco dei Giustiniani, 1984); Franco Buffoni, *Quaranta a quindici* (Milan: Crocetti, 1987); Franco Buffoni, *Scuola di Atene* (Turin: Arzana, 1991); Franco Buffoni, *Adidas: poesie scelte 1975–1990* (Rome: Pieraldo, 1993); Franco Buffoni, *Nella casa riaperta* (Udine: Campanotto, 1994); Franco Buffoni, *Suora carmelitana e altri racconti in versi* (Parma: Guanda, 1997); Franco Buffoni, *Il profilo del Rosa* (Milan: Mondadori, 2000); Franco Buffoni, *Theios* (Novara: Interlinea, 2001); Franco Buffoni, *Del maestro in bottega* (Rome: Empiria, 2002); Franco Buffoni, *Guerra* (Milan: Mondadori, 2005); Franco Buffoni, *Noi e loro* (Rome: Donzelli, 2008); Franco Buffoni, *Roma* (Parma: Guanda, 2009); Franco Buffoni, *Poesie: 1975–2012* (Milan: Mondadori, 2012).

2 Franco Buffoni, *Reperto 74 e altri racconti* (Civitella in Val di Chiana: Zona, 2008); Franco Buffoni, *Zamel* (Milan: Marcos y Marcos, 2009); Franco Buffoni, *Il servo di Byron* (Rome: Fazi, 2012).

3 Franco Buffoni, *Chaucer, testone medievale* (Udine: Nuova Del Bianco industrie grafiche, 1981); Franco Buffoni, *I Racconti di Canterbury: un'opera unitaria* (Milan: Guerini, 1991); Franco Buffoni, *Perché era nato lord: studi sul romanticismo inglese* (Rome: Pieraldo, 1992); Franco Buffoni, *Ramsay e Fergusson precursori di Burns: poesia pastorale e poesia vernacolare nel Settecento scozzese* (Milan: Guerini, 1992); Franco Buffoni, *L'ipotesi di Malin: studio su Auden-poeta* (Milan: Marcos y Marcos, 1997); Franco Buffoni, *Carmide a Reading: establishment, generi letterari e ipocrisia al tramonto dell'eta vittoriana* (Rome: Empiria, 2002); Franco Buffoni, *Mid Atlantic: teatro e poesia nel novecento angloamericano* (Milan: Effigie, 2007); Franco Buffoni, *Con il testo a fronte: indagine sul tradurre e l'essere tradotti* (Novara: Interlinea, 2007).

4 Franco Buffoni, ed., *La traduzione del testo poetico* (Milan: Guerini, 1989).
5 Franco Buffoni, ed., *Ritmologia: atti del Convegno Il ritmo del linguaggio: poesia e traduzione* (Milan: Marcos y Marcos, 2002).
6 Franco Buffoni, ed., *Traduttologia: la teoria della traduzione letteraria*, 2 vols. (Rome: Ministero per i beni e le attività culturali, 2005).
7 Franco Buffoni, ed., *Un'altra voce: antologia della poesia italiana contemporanea con traduzione in arabo*, trans. Ezzedine Anaya (Milan: Marcos y Marcos, 2002).
8 Franco Buffoni, ed., *Un'altra voce: antologia della poesia italiana contemporanea con traduzione in cinese*, trans. Tongbing Zhang (Milan: Marcos y Marcos, 2005).
9 Franco Buffoni, ed., *Un'altra voce: antologia della poesia italiana contemporanea con traduzione in ebraico*, trans. Alon Altaras (Milan: Marcos y Marcos, 2003).
10 Franco Buffoni, ed., *Un'altra voce: antologia della poesia italiana contemporanea con traduzione in portoghese*, trans. Giulia Lanciani (Milan: Marcos y Marcos, 2003).
11 Franco Buffoni, ed., *Un'altra voce: antologia della poesia italiana contemporanea con traduzione in russo*, trans. Natalie Malinin (Milan: Marcos y Marcos, 2007).
12 Franco Buffoni, ed., *Un'altra voce: antologia della poesia italiana contemporanea con traduzione in spagnolo*, trans. Juan Carlos Reche (Milan: Marcos y Marcos, 2008).
13 Cf. Tommaso Lisa, "Cartografie dell'oggettualità," *L'apostrofo* 6, no. 18 (2002): 12.
14 Franco Brevini, "Nota introduttiva," in Franco Buffoni, *Adidas: poesie scelte 1975–1990* (Rome: Pieraldo, 1993), 8.
15 Ibid., 7.
16 Buffoni, *I tre desideri*, 41.
17 Buffoni, *Quaranta a quindici*, 11.
18 Buffoni, *Scuola di Atene*, 48.
19 E.g., Franco Buffoni, *Più luce, Padre: dialogo su Dio, la guerra e l'omosessualità* (Rome: L. Sossella, 2006), as well as Franco Buffoni, *Roma* (Parma: Guanda, 2009).
20 Buffoni, *Il profilo del Rosa*, 13.
21 Buffoni, *Theios*, 72.
22 Franco Buffoni, *Del maestro in bottega* (Rome: Empiria, 2002).
23 Andrea Cortellessa, "Motivazione del premio Maria Marino 2009," accessed 1 June 2011, http://www.francobuffoni.it/motivazione_cortellese.aspx.
24 Buffoni, *Guerra*, 54.
25 Buffoni, *Noi e loro*, 121.

26 Buffoni, *Roma*, 79.
27 Franco Buffoni, "Poesia e ragionevolezza," *Il rosso e il nero* 2, no. 5 (1993): 3.
28 Franco Buffoni, "Riflessioni sul fare poetico," *Nuovi argomenti* 36 (2006): 210.
29 Ibid.
30 Buffoni inserted two of these poems in his second *quaderno di traduzioni, Una piccola tabaccheria*, 124–33.
31 Stephen R. Graubard, *Kissinger: un ritratto di una mente*, trans. Franco Buffoni (Milan: Garzanti, 1974).
32 John Keats, *Sonno e poesia*, trans. Franco Buffoni (Milan: Guanda, 1981).
33 George Gordon Byron, *Manfred*, trans. Franco Buffoni (Milan: Guanda, 1984).
34 Samuel Taylor Coleridge, *La ballata del vecchio marinaio e altre poesie*, trans. Franco Buffoni (Turin: Einaudi, 1987).
35 Rudyard Kipling, *Ballate delle baracche e altre poesie*, trans. Franco Buffoni (Milan: Mondadori, 1989).
36 *Poeti romantici inglesi*, trans. Franco Buffoni, 2 vols. (Milan: Bompiani, 1990).
37 Seamus Heaney, *Scavando: poesie scelte (1966–1990)*, trans. Franco Buffoni (Rome: Fondazione Piazzolla, 1991).
38 Franco Buffoni, ed., *Songs of Spring: quaderno di traduzioni* (Milan: Marcos y Marcos, 1999).
39 Percy Bysshe Shelley, *Come un fruscio d'ali: Percy B. Shelley*, ed. and trans. Franco Buffoni (Milan: Corriere della Sera, 2012). This collection includes translations by Giuseppe Conte.
40 George Gordon Byron, *I giullari del tempo: George Gordon Byron*, ed. and trans. Franco Buffoni (Milan: Corriere della Sera, 2012).
41 Alfonso Maria Petrosino, "Intervista a Franco Buffoni," 1, accessed 1 June 2011, http://www.criticaletteraria.org/2010/08/intervista-franco-buffoni.html.
42 Luciano Anceschi, "Presentazione," in *Poeti antichi e moderni tradotti dai lirici nuovi*, ed. Luciano Anceschi and Domenico Porzio (Milan: Il Balcone, 1945), 16.
43 M. Cangiano, L. Nuzzo, and E. Santangelo, "Tabard intervista Franco Buffoni," *Tabard* 3, no. 7 (2008): 17.
44 Cf. Franco Buffoni, "Perché si parla di traduttologia," in *Con il testo a fronte*, 11.
45 Buffoni, "Premessa," in *Una piccola tabaccheria*, 6.
46 Buffoni, "Prefazione," in *Un'altra voce: Antologia di poesia italiana contemporanea con traduzione in portoghese*, 10.
47 Buffoni, "Prefazione," in *L'Imbuto bianco: Antologia di poesia italiana contemporanea con traduzione in arabo*, 6.

48 Franco Buffoni, email message to author, 4 July 2011.
49 Buffoni, "Premessa," 6.
50 Buffoni, "Da traduttologia a ritmologia," *Testo a Fronte* 38 (2008): 37.
51 Tiziana Migliaccio, "Intervista a Franco Buffoni," *Sincronie* nos. 21/22 (2007): 65.
52 Buffoni, ed., *Ritmologia*.
53 Jean Bellemin-Noël, "Psychoanalytic Reading and the Avant-texte," in *Genetic Criticism: Texts and Avant-Texts*, ed. and trans. Jed Deppman, Daniel Ferrer, and Michael Groden (Philadelphia: University of Pennsylvania Press, 2004), 28.
54 Tommaso Lisa, "Intervista a Franco Buffoni (ovvero traduzione e movimento)," in *Traduzione e poesia nell'Europa del Novecento*, ed. Anna Dolfi (Rome: Bulzoni, 2004), 595.
55 Franco Buffoni, email message to author, 4 July 2011.
56 Friedmar Apel, *Il movimento del linguaggio: una ricerca sul problema del tradurre*, ed. Emilio Mattioli and Riccarda Novello (Milan: Marcos and Marcos, 1997).
57 Franco Buffoni, email message to author, 4 July 2011.
58 Buffoni, "Da traduttologia a ritmologia," 31.
59 Buffoni's judgment on Eco's book is summed up in the following lines: "È volgare intellettualmente (il concetto di 'negoziazione' è invero di infimo rango) e si basa su una lunga serie di luoghi comuni, molto duri a morire, evidentemente." Cf. Marco Simonelli's interview with Franco Buffoni, accessed 11 September, 2012, http://www.francobuffoni.it/intervista_simonelli.aspx.
60 Buffoni, *Songs of Spring*, 16.
61 Buffoni, "Perché si parla di traduttologia," in *Con il testo a fronte*, 15.
62 Ibid., 16.
63 Cangiano, Nuzzo, and Santangelo, "Tabard," 17.
64 Franco Buffoni, "Gli incontri 'poietici' di Margherita Guidacci," in *Per Margherita Guidacci. Atti delle giornate di studio*, ed. Margherita Ghilardi (Florence: Le Lettere, 2001), 171.
65 Buffoni, *Una piccola tabaccheria*, 12.
66 Franco Buffoni, email message to author, 4 July 2011.
67 Buffoni, "Gli incontri 'poietici,'" 171.
68 Fabrizio Lombardo, "L'avventura di *Testo a fronte*. Intervista a Franco Buffoni di Fabrizio Lombardo," *VersoDove*, nos. 6–7 (1997): 4.
69 Petrosino, "Intervista," 1.
70 Buffoni, *Songs of Spring*, 152–3.
71 The three Jewish-Italian poets are more or less in the correct order.

72 Buffoni, *Songs of Spring*, 363.
73 Ibid.
74 Ibid., 352.
75 Ibid., 353.
76 In truth, there are two Italian versions. Buffoni literally translates Fergusson into Italian, and also translates his own Milanese version into Italian. I will only treat the Milanese translation into Italian here.
77 In Antonella Anedda's collection of translations and original poems, *Nomi distanti*, she does translate several dialect poems.
78 Buffoni, *Songs of Spring*, 54.
79 Ibid., 55.
80 Ibid.
81 Buffoni, *Del maestro in bottega*, 161.
82 Ibid., 162.
83 Buffoni, *Songs of Spring*, 57.
84 Ibid.
85 Ibid., 59.
86 Ibid.
87 Ibid., 57.
88 Ibid.
89 Ibid., 61.
90 Ibid.
91 Cf. Buffoni's explanation in Franco Buffoni, "Ritraducendo Seamus Heaney," in *Con il testo a fronte*, 147–62.
92 Buffoni, *Songs of Spring*, 326 and 328.
93 Ibid., 327 and 329.
94 This and all further references to the English original come from Buffoni, *Songs of Spring*, 326–9.
95 Ibid., 326.
96 Ibid., 327.
97 Ibid., 328.
98 Ibid.
99 Ibid., 329.
100 Ibid., 327.
101 Ibid., 326.
102 Ibid., 327.
103 Ibid.
104 Ibid., 326.
105 Ibid., 327.
106 Ibid., 328.

107 Ibid.
108 Ibid., 329.
109 Ibid., 327.
110 Ibid., 327.
111 Ibid., 108.
112 Ibid., 109.
113 Franco Buffoni, email message to author, 4 July 2011.
114 Buffoni, *Songs of Spring*, 356.
115 Buffoni, *Una piccola tabaccheria*, 31–2.
116 Franco Buffoni, email message to author, 4 July 2011.
117 Ibid.
118 Migliaccio, "Intervista," 66.
119 Buffoni, *Una piccola tabaccheria*, 148–52.
120 Buffoni, *Songs of Spring*, 364.
121 Kathleen Raine, Stephen Spender, David Gascoyne, Elaine Feinstein, Tomas Tranströmer, Marie-Claire Bancquart, Jim Burns, J. H. Prynne, Johann Hjalmarsson, Eddy van Vliet, Dave Smith, Jaime Siles, and Bernard Simeone.
122 Elaine Feinstein and Eddy van Vliet.
123 Charles Du Bos, *Vita e letteratura*, trans. Mario Luzi (Padua: Cedam, 1943); Samuel Taylor Coleridge, *Poesie e prose* (Milan: Cederna, 1949); Paul Valéry, *Cantique des colonnes* (Rome: ERI, 1949); Charles-Louis de Montesquieu, *Il tempio di Cnido*, in *Romanzi francesi dei secoli XVII e* XVIII, ed. M. Rago (Bompiani: Milan, 1951); Jean Racine, *Andromaca*, in *Il teatro franese del grand siecle* (Rome: ERI, 1960); Jorge Guillén, *La fonte* (Milan: Scheiwiller, 1961); William Shakespeare, *Riccardo II* (Turin: Einaudi, 1966); Mario Luzi, *Francamente* (Florence: Vallecchi, 1980); Mario Luzi, *La Cordigliera delle Ande* (Turin: Einaudi, 1983); Tirso de Molina, *Dannato per disperazione*, in *Teatro*, ed. Maria Grazia Profeti (Milan: Garzanti, 1991); and Ostad Elahi, *Pensieri di luce* (Milan: Mondadori, 2000).
124 Antonio Prete, *All'ombra dell'altra lingua*, 113.
125 Luzi, *Cordigliera*, vi.
126 Mario Luzi, *Colloquio: un dialogo con Mario Specchio* (Milan: Garzanti, 1999), 70.
127 Ibid.
128 Ibid., 71.
129 Ibid.
130 Luzi, *Cordigliera*, vi.
131 Luzi, *Colloquio*, 70.
132 Ibid.

133 Ibid.
134 Mario Luzi, "Riflessioni sulla traduzione," in *La traduzione del testo poetico*, ed. Franco Buffoni (Milan: Marcos y Marcos, 2004), 116.
135 Luzi, *Cordigliera*, vi.
136 Ibid.
137 Ibid.
138 Edoardo Zuccato, "The Translation of Coleridge's Poetry and His Influence on Twentieth-Century Italian Poetry," in *The Reception of S.T. Coleridge in Europe*, ed. Elinor Shaffer and Edoardo Zuccato (London: Continuum, 2007), 209.
139 Mario Praz, *Poeti inglesi dell'Ottocento* (Florence: Bemporad, 1925), 139.
140 Franco Nasi has pointed to (most probably) another misreading by Luzi: Franco Nasi, *Istituzioni poetiche e traduzioni: le Lyrical Ballads in Italia* (Milan: Medusa, 2004), 109.
141 Franco Buffoni, email message to author, 4 July 2011.
142 Zuccato, "The Translation of Coleridge's Poetry," 202.
143 Samuel Taylor Coleridge, *La ballata del vecchio marinaio e altre poesie*, ed. and trans. Franco Buffoni (Milan: Mondadori, 1987), 29.
144 Buffoni, *Songs of Spring*, 242.
145 Ibid., 243.
146 Ibid., 245.
147 Ibid., 103.
148 Ibid., 192.
149 Ibid., 193.
150 Ibid., 180.
151 Ibid., 181.
152 Ibid., 180.
153 Ibid., 181.
154 Ibid., 180.
155 Ibid., 181.
156 Ibid., 190.
157 Ibid., 191.
158 Ibid., 119.
159 Ibid., 84.
160 Ibid., 85.
161 Simone Giusti, "Ragioni di un traduttore astronomo," *L'apostrofo* 6, no. 18 (2001): 30.
162 Tommaso Lisa, "Intervista a Franco Buffoni (ovvero traduzione e movimento)," in *Traduzione e poesia nell'Europa del Novecento*, ed. Anna Dolfi (Rome: Bulzoni, 2004), 595.

Bibliography

Accame, Vincenzo, ed. *Poesia francese del Novecento*. 2 vols. Milan: Bompiani, 1985.

Aeschylus. *Le Coefore*. Trans. Edoardo Sanguineti. Milan: Il Saggiatore, 1978.

Aeschylus. *I sette contro Tebe*. Trans. Edoardo Sanguineti. Milan: Sipario, 1992.

Agamben, Giorgio. *Categorie italiane: studi di poetica e di letteratura*. 2nd ed. Bari: Laterza, 2010.

Alighieri, Dante. *La commedia secondo l'antica vulgata*. Ed. Giorgio Petrocchi. Turin: Einaudi, 1975.

Alighieri, Dante. *Convivio*. Ed. Giorgio Inglese. Milan: Rizzoli, 1993.

Alighieri, Dante. *Dante's Il Convivio: The Banquet*. Trans. Richard Lansing. London: Garland, 1990.

Anceschi, Luciano. *Che importa chi parla? Dialoghi con Luciano Anceschi*. Ed. Michele Gulinucci. Reggio Emilia: Diabasis, 1992.

Anceschi, Luciano. "Presentazione." In *Poeti antichi e moderni tradotti dai lirici nuovi*, ed. Luciano Anceschi and Domenico Porzio. Milan: Il Balcone, 1945.

Anceschi, Luciano, ed. *Lirici Nuovi: antologia di poesia contemporanea*. Milan: Hoepli, 1943.

Anceschi, Luciano, and Domenico Porzio, eds. *Poeti antichi e moderni tradotti dai lirici nuovi*. Milan: Il Balcone, 1945.

André Frénaud tradotto da 15 poeti italiani e da Elio Vittorini. Milan: All'insegna del pesce d'oro, 1964.

Anedda, Antonella. *Nomi distanti*. Rome: Empiria, 1998.

Antonello, Massimo. "Tre versioni montaliane da Shakespeare." *Annali della Scuola Normale di Pisa* 20 (1990): 983–1014.

Apel, Friedmar. *Il movimento del linguaggio: una ricerca sul problema del tradurre*. Ed. and trans. Emilio Mattioli, and Riccarda Novello. Milan: Marcos y Marcos, 1997.

Apollinaire, Guillaume. *Bestiario o il carteggio di Orfeo*. Trans. Giovanni Raboni. Parma: Guanda, 1977.

Apollinaire, Guillaume. *Da Alcools*. Trans. Giovanni Raboni and Vittorio Sereni. Milan: Il Saggiatore, 1981.

Apollinaire, Guillaume. *La chiamavano Lu e altre poesie*. Trans. Giovanni Raboni and Vittorio Sereni. Milan: Mondadori, 1984.

Apollinaire, Guillaume. *Poesie*. Trans. Giorgio Caproni. Milan: Rizzoli, 1979.

Ariosto, Lodovico. *Orlando Furioso: riduzione di Edoardo Sanguineti*. Ed. Giuseppe Bartolucci. Rome: Bulzoni, 1970.

Aristophanes. *La festa delle donne*. Trans. Edoardo Sanguineti. Genoa: Il Melangolo, 2001.

Arrowsmith, William, and Roger Shattuck, eds. *The Craft and Context of Translation: A Symposium*. Garden City: Anchor Books, 1964.

Arvigo, Tiziana. *Guida alla lettura di Montale: Ossi di seppia*. Rome: Carocci, 2001.

Asor Rosa, Alberto. *Storia europea della letteratura italiana*. 3 vols. Turin: Einaudi, 2009.

Aveto, Andrea. "Traduzioni d'autore e no. Elio Vittorini e la 'segreta' collaborazione con Lucia Rodocanachi." In *Lucia Rodocanachi: le carte, la vita*, ed. Franco Contorbia, 153–92. Florence: Società editrice fiorentina, 2006.

Bacigalupo, Massimo. "Postfazione." In Giovanni Giudici, *A una casa non sua*, 195–208. Milan: Mondadori, 1997.

Bacon, Roger. "On the Usefulness of Grammar." In *Western Translation Theory: From Herodotus to Nietszche*, ed. Douglas Robinson, 45–6. Manchester: St. Jerome, 2001.

Baldassari, Tolmino. *Quaderno di traduzioni*. Forlì: Nuova compagnia editrice, 1990.

Balestrini, Nanni, Alfredo Giuliani, Antonio Porta, and Edoardo Sanguineti. *I novissimi: poesie per gli anni '60*. Ed. Alfredo Giuliani. Milan: Rusconi and Paolazzi, 1961.

Barile, Laura. *Adorate mie larve*. Bologna: Il mulino, 1990.

Barile, Laura. *Bibliografia montaliana*. Milan: Mondadori, 1977.

Barile, Laura. *Montale, Londra e la luna*. Florence: Le Lettere, 1998.

Barile, Laura. *Oltreconfine. Incursioni nelle letterature europee*. Ospedaletto: Pacini, 2008.

Barile, Laura. "Traduzione e imitazione da Char." In *Il passato che non passa: le 'poetiche provissorie' di Vittorio Sereni*, 129–54. Florence: Le Lettere, 2004.

Bassi, Silvia. "Un 'giardiniere e botanico delle lingue': Andrea Zanzotto traduttore e autotraduttore." PhD diss., Università di Venezia, 2011.

Baudelaire, Charles. *I fiori del male*. Trans. Giorgio Caproni. Rome: Curcio, 1962.

Baudelaire, Charles. *I fiori del male*. Trans. Giorgio Caproni. Ed. Luca Pietromarchi. Venice: Marsilio, 2008.

Baudelaire, Charles. *I fiori del male e altre poesie*. Trans. Giovanni Raboni. Turin: Einaudi, 1987.

Baudelaire, Charles. *I fiori del male e altre poesie*. Trans. Giovanni Raboni. Turin: Einaudi, 1992.

Baudelaire, Charles. *I fiori del male e altre poesie*. Trans. Giovanni Raboni. Turin: Einaudi, 1999.

Baudelaire, Charles. *Opere*. Trans. Giovanni Raboni, and Giuseppe Marcenaro. Milan: Mondadori, 1996.

Baudelaire, Charles. *Tutte le opere*. Ed. Giovanni Macchia. Trans. Giovanni Raboni. Milan: Mondadori, 1973.

Beccaria, Gian Luigi. "[Untitled]." In *Giorgio Caproni: Poesie 1932–1986*, 809–12. Milan: Garzanti, 1989.

Bellemin-Noël, Jean. "Psychoanalytic Reading and the Avant-Texte." In *Genetic Criticism: Texts and Avant-Texts*, ed. and trans. Jed Deppman, Daniel Ferrer, and Michael Groden, 28–35. Philadelphia: University of Pennsylvania Press, 2004.

Bellos, David. *Is That a Fish in Your Ear? Translation and the Meaning of Everything*. London: Faber and Faber, 2011.

Benjamin, Walter. "Die Aufgabe des Übersetzers." In *Illuminationen: Ausgewählte Schriften*, ed. Siegfried Unseld, 56–69. Frankfurt: Suhrkamp Verlag, 1961.

Benveniste, Émile. "Catégories de pensée et catégories de langue." In *Problèmes de linguistique générale*, 63–74. Paris: Gallimard, 1966.

Benzoni, Pietro. *Da Céline a Caproni: la versione italiana di Mort à credit*. Venice: Istituto veneto di scienze, lettere ed arti, 2000.

Berman, Antoine. *L'épreuve de l'étranger: Culture et traduction dans l'Allemagne romantique*. Paris: Gallimard, 1984.

Berman, Antoine. "Translation and the Trials of the Foreign." In *The Translation Studies Reader*, 3rd ed., ed. Lawrence Venuti, 240–53. London: Routledge, 2012.

Bertolucci, Attilio. *Imitazioni*. Milan: Scheiwiller, 1994.

Bigongiari, Piero. *Nel mutismo dell'universo*. Ed. Anna Dolfi. Rome: Bulzoni, 2001.

Bigongiari, Piero. *Poesia italiana del Novecento*. Florence: Vallecchi, 1960.

Bigongiari, Piero, ed. *Il vento d'ottobre: da Alcmane a Dylan Thomas*. Trans. Piero Bigongiari. Milan: Mondadori, 1961.

Billiani, Francesca. *Culture nazionali e narrazioni straniere: Italia, 1903–1943*. Florence: Le Lettere, 2007.

Billiani, Francesca. "Renewing a Literary Culture through Translation: Poetry in Post-War Italy." In *Translation as Intervention*, ed. Jeremy Munday, 140–60. London: Continuum, 2007.

Billiani, Francesca. "Return to Order as Return to Realism in Two Italian Elite Literary Magazines of the 1920s and 1930s: La Ronda and Orpheus." *MLR* 107, no. 3 (2013): 839–62.

Blakesley, Jacob. "Edoardo Sanguineti: A Unique Translator." In *Edoardo Sanguineti: Literature, Ideology and the Avant-Garde*, ed. John Picchione and Paolo Chirumbolo, 143–57. London: Maney, 2013.

Blakesley, Jacob. "Franco Buffoni: The *poietic* encounter." *Journal of Italian Translation* 6, no. 1/2 (2012): 266–293.

Blakesley, Jacob. "Franco Buffoni: The Poietic Encounter." *Semicerchio* XLVI, no. 1 (2012): 35–50.

Blakesley, Jacob. "Giovanni Giudici: una lingua strana." *Lettere Italiane* 63, no. 4 (2011): 204–39.

Blakesley, Jacob. "Montale: Second-Hand Translator." *Moderna* 15, no. 1 (forthcoming).

Blakesley, Jacob. "Poet-Translators in Modern Italy: A Statistical Survey." *Testo a Fronte* 47, no. 1 (2013): 31–41.

Blum-Kulka, Shoshana. "Shifts of Cohesion and Coherence in Translation." In *The Translation Studies Reader*, 2nd ed., ed. Lawrence Venuti, 290–306. London: Routledge, 2004.

Bo, Carlo, ed. *Lirici spagnoli*. Trans. Carlo Bo. Milan: Corrente, 1941.

Bodini, Vittorio, ed. *I poeti surrealisti spagnoli: saggio introduttivo e antologia*. Trans. Vittorio Bodini. Turin: Einaudi, 1962.

Bonalumi, Giovanni. *Album inglese: quaderno di traduzioni*. Bergamo: Moretti and Vitali, 2000.

Bonalumi, Giovanni.·*La traversata del Gottardo: quaderno di traduzioni (1948–1998)*. Locarno: A. Dado, 2000.

Bozzola, Sergio. "Le traduzioni montaliane di Steinbeck." In Sergio Bozzola, *Seminario Montaliano*, 117–47. Rome: Bonacci, 2006.

Brecht, Bertolt. *Il cerchio di gesso del Caucaso*. Trans. Edoardo Sanguineti. Genoa: Il Melangolo, 2003.

Brevini, Franco. "Nota introduttiva." In Franco Buffoni, *Adidas. Poesie scelte 1975–1990*, 7–8. Rome: Pieraldo, 1993.

Bricco, Elisa. *André Frénaud e l'Italia: una scrittura poetica*. Fasano: Schena, 1999.

Bricco, Elisa. "Caproni poeta-traduttore-poeta." In *Per Giorgio Caproni*, ed. Giorgio Devoto and Stefano Verdino, 41–6. Genoa: San Marco dei Giustiniani, 1997.

Bricco, Elisa. "Giorgio Caproni traduttore della poesia francese." PhD diss., Università di Bari, 1995.

Briggs, Kate. "Translation and the Question of Poetry." In *Twentieth-Century Poetic Translation*. London: Continuum, 2008.

Brintlinger, Angela. *Writing a Usable Past: Russian Literary Culture, 1917–1937*. Evanston: Northwestern University Press, 2000.

Brodsky, Joseph. "Beyond Consolation." *New York Review of Books*, February 7, 1974.

Bronowski, Jacob, and Bruce Mazlish. *La tradizione intellettuale dell'Occidente da Leonardo a Hegel*. Trans. Giovanni Giudici. Milan: Edizioni di Comunità, 1962.

Brooker, Peter. "Key Words in Brecht's Theory and Practice of Theatre." In *The Cambridge Companion to Brecht*, 2nd ed., ed. Peter Thomson and Glendyr Sacks, 209–24. Cambridge: Cambridge University Press, 2006. http://dx.doi.org/10.1017/CCOL0521857090.014.

Brown, Edward J. "Round Two: Nabokov Versus Pushkin." *Slavic Review* 36, no. 1 (1977): 101–5. http://dx.doi.org/10.2307/2494674.

Brownlie, Siobhan. "Descriptive Vs. Committed Approaches." In *In the Routledge Encyclopedia of Translation Studies*, 2nd ed., ed. Mona Baker and Gabriela Sandanha, 77–81. London: Routledge, 2009.

Buffoni, Franco. *Adidas: poesie scelte 1975–1990*. Rome: Pieraldo, 1993.

Buffoni, Franco. *Carmide a Reading: establishment, generi letterari e ipocrisia al tramonta dell'eta vittoriana*. Rome: Empiria, 2002.

Buffoni, Franco. *Chaucer, testone medievale*. Udine: Nuova Del Bianco industrie grafiche, 1981.

Buffoni, Franco. *Con il testo a fronte: indagine sul tradurre e l'essere tradotti*. Novara: Interlinea, 2007.

Buffoni, Franco. "Da traduttologia a ritmologia." *Testo a Fronte* 38 (2008).

Buffoni, Franco. *Del maestro in bottega*. Rome: Empiria, 2002.

Buffoni, Franco. *Guerra*. Milan: Mondadori, 2005.

Buffoni, Franco. "Gli incontri 'poietici' di Margherita Guidacci." In *Per Margherita Guidacci*, ed. Margherita Ghilardi, 171–8. Florence: Le lettere, 2001.

Buffoni, Franco. *L'ipotesi di Malin: studio su Auden-poeta*. Milan: Marcos y Marcos, 1997.

Buffoni, Franco. *Mid Atlantic: teatro e poesia nel novecento angloamericano*. Milan: Effigie, 2007.

Buffoni, Franco. *Nella casa riaperta*. Udine: Campanotto, 1994.

Buffoni, Franco. *Noi e loro*. Rome: Donzelli, 2008.

Buffoni, Franco. *Perché era nato lord: studi sul romanticism inglese*. Rome: Pieraldo, 1992.
Buffoni, Franco. "Perché si parla di traduttologia." In *Con il testo a fronte: indagine sul tradurre e l'essere tradotti*, 7–20. Novara: Interlinea, 2007.
Buffoni, Franco. *Una piccola tabaccheria: quaderno di traduzioni*. Milan: Marcos y Marcos, 2012.
Buffoni, Franco. *Più luce, Padre: dialogo su Dio, la guerra e l'omosessualità*. Rome: L. Sossella, 2006.
Buffoni, Franco. "Poesia e ragionevolezza." *Il rosso e il nero* 2, no. 5 (1993): 63–7.
Buffoni, Franco. *Poesie: 1975–2012*. Milan: Mondadori, 2012.
Buffoni, Franco. "Prefazione." In *Un'altra voce: Antologia di poesia italiana contemporanea con traduzione in portoghese*, ed. Franco Buffoni, trans. Giulia Lanciani. Milan: Marcos y Marcos, 2003.
Buffoni, Franco. *Il profilo del Rosa*. Milan: Mondadori, 2000.
Buffoni, Franco. *Quaranta a quindici*. Milan: Crocetti, 1987.
Buffoni, Franco. *I Racconti di Canterbury: un'opera unitaria*. Milan: Guerini, 1991.
Buffoni, Franco. *Ramsay e Fergusson precursori di Burns: poesia pastorale e poesia vernacolare nel Settecento scozzese*. Milan: Guerini, 1992.
Buffoni, Franco. *Reperto 74 e altri racconti*. Civitella in Val di Chiana: Zona, 2008.
Buffoni, Franco. "Riflessioni sul fare poetico." *Nuovi argomenti* 36 (2006): 292–301.
Buffoni, Franco. "Ritraducendo Seamus Heaney." In *Con il testo a Fronte: indagine sul tradurre e l'essere tradotti*, 147–62. Novara: Interlinea, 2007.
Buffoni, Franco. *Roma*. Parma: Guanda, 2009.
Buffoni, Franco. *Scuola di Atene*. Turin: Arzana, 1991.
Buffoni, Franco. *Il servo di Byron*. Rome: Fazi, 2012.
Buffoni, Franco. *Songs of Spring: quaderno di traduzioni*. Milan: Marcos y Marcos, 1999.
Buffoni, Franco. *Suora carmelitana e altri racconti in versi*. Parma: Guanda, 1997.
Buffoni, Franco. *Theios*. Novara: Interlinea, 2001.
Buffoni, Franco. *La traduzione del testo poetico*. Ed. Franco Buffoni. Milan: Guerini, 1989.
Buffoni, Franco. *La traduzione del testo poetico*. Ed. Franco Buffoni. Milan: Marcos y Marcos, 2004.
Buffoni, Franco. "Le traduzioni di Sanguineti." In *Edoardo Sanguineti: Opere e introduzione critica*, ed. Fausto Curi, 131–5. Verona: Anterem, 1993.
Buffoni, Franco. *I tre desideri*. Genoa: San Marco dei Giustiniani, 1984.

Buffoni, Franco. *Zamel*. Milan: Marcos y Marcos, 2009.
Buffoni, Franco, ed. *Un'altra voce: antologia della poesia italiana contemporanea con traduzione in arabo*. Trans. Ezzedine Anaya. Milan: Marcos y Marcos, 2002.
Buffoni, Franco, ed. *Un'altra voce: antologia della poesia italiana contemporanea con traduzione in cinese*. Trans. Tongbing Zhang. Milan: Marcos y Marcos, 2005.
Buffoni, Franco, ed. *Un'altra voce: antologia della poesia italiana contemporanea con traduzione in ebraico*. Trans. Alon Altaras. Milan: Marcos y Marcos, 2003.
Buffoni, Franco, ed. *Un'altra voce: antologia della poesia italiana contemporanea con traduzione in portoghese*. Trans. Giulia Lanciani. Milan: Marcos y Marcos, 2003.
Buffoni, Franco, ed. *Un'altra voce: antologia della poesia italiana contemporanea con traduzione in russo*. Trans. Natalie Malinin. Milan: Marcos y Marcos, 2007.
Buffoni, Franco, ed. *Un'altra voce: antologia della poesia italiana contemporanea con traduzione in spagnolo*. Trans. Juan Carlos Reche. Milan: Marcos y Marcos, 2008.
Buffoni, Franco, ed. *Poeti romantici inglesi*. 2 vols. Trans. Franco Buffoni. Milan: Bompiani, 1990.
Buffoni, Franco, ed. *Ritmologia: atti del Convegno Il ritmo del linguaggio: poesia e traduzione*. Milan: Marcos y Marcos, 2002.
Buffoni, Franco, ed. *Traduttologia: la teoria della traduzione letteraria*. Ed. Franco Buffoni. 2 vols. Rome: Ministero per i beni e le attività culturali, 2005.
Buffoni, Franco, ed. *La traduzione del testo poetico*. Milan: Guerini, 1989.
Bulgheroni, Marisa. "Dickinson/Montale: il passo sull'erba." In *Eugenio Montale: profilo di un autore*, ed. Annalisa Cima and Cesare Segre, 91–114. Milan: Rizzoli, 1977.
Busch, Wilhelm. *Max e Moritz ovvero Pippo e Peppo*. Trans. Giorgio Caproni. Milan: Rizzoli, 1974.
Busquets, Loreto. *Eugenio Montale y la cultura hispanica*. Rome: Bulzoni, 1986.
Byron, George Gordon. *I giullari del tempo*. Ed. and trans. Franco Buffoni. Milan: Corriere della Sera, 2012.
Byron, George Gordon. *Manfred*. Trans. Franco Buffoni. Milan: Guanda, 1984.
Cadioli, Alberto. "Al servizio della Lingua della Poesia." In *Il Silenzio della parola*, 95–110. Milan: Unicopli, 2002.
Cambon, Glauco. "Montale sull'ultima spiaggia." In *La poesia di Eugenio Montale: atti del convegno internazionale tenuto a Genova dal 25 al 28 novembre 1982*, ed. Sergio Campailla and Cesare Federico Goffis, 335–56. Florence: Le Monnier, 1984.

Camon, Ferdinando. *Il mestiere di poeta*. Milan: Garzanti, 1982.

Camps, Assumpta. "Il 'Cant espiritual' di Montale." *Galleria* 47, no. 1 (1996): 88–95.

Cangiano, M., L. Nuzzo, and E. Santangelo. "Tabard intervista Franco Buffoni." *Tabard* 3, no. 7 (2008): 14–19.

Caproni, Giorgio. "L'arte del tradurre." In *La traduzione del testo poetico*, ed. Franco Buffoni, 31–8. Milan: Marcos y Marcos, 2004.

Caproni, Giorgio. *Ballo a Fontanigorda*. Genoa: E. Degli Orfini, 1938.

Caproni, Giorgio. *Come un'allegoria (1932–1935): versi*. Genoa: E. Degli Orfini, 1936.

Caproni, Giorgio. *Cronistoria*. Florence: Vallecchi, 1943.

Caproni, Giorgio. "Diego Valeri ha tradotto Jacobi." *La Fiera Letteraria*, March 31, 1957.

Caproni, Giorgio. "Divagazioni sul tradurre." In *La Scatola nera*, 59–68. Ed. Giovanni Raboni. Milan: Garzanti, 1996.

Caproni, Giorgio. *Era così bello parlare: conversazioni radiofoniche*. Ed. Luigi Surdich. Genoa: Il Melangolo, 2004.

Caproni, Giorgio. *Finzioni*. Rome: Istituto grafico tiberino, 1941.

Caproni, Giorgio. "Imitazioni." In *Seme del piangere*, 107–10. Milan: Garzanti, 1959.

Caproni, Giorgio. *L'opera in versi*. Ed. Luca Zuliani. Milan: Mondadori, 1998.

Caproni, Giorgio. "I poeti e la tromba (o della traducibilità)." *Il lavoro nuovo*, August 24, 1949.

Caproni, Giorgio. "Prefazione." In *Poesia e prosa*, by René Char, 7–14. Trans. Giorgio Caproni and Vittorio Sereni. Milan: Feltrinelli, 1962.

Caproni, Giorgio. *La scatola nera*. Ed. Giovanni Raboni. Milan: Garzanti, 1996.

Caproni, Giorgio. *Stanze della funicolare*. Rome: De Luca, 1952.

Caproni, Giorgio. "Sulla poesia." In *La scatola nera*, 28–33. Ed. Giovanni Raboni. Milan: Garzanti, 1996.

Caproni, Giorgio. "Tre traduzioni." *La Fiera Letteraria*, August 28, 1947.

Caproni, Giorgio. "Il Valéry di Tutino." In *La scatola nera*, 47–50. Ed. Giovanni Raboni. Milan: Garzanti, 1996.

Caproni, Giorgio, and Carlo Betocchi. *Una poesia indimenticabile*. Ed. Daniela Santero. Pisa: M. Pacini Fazzi, 2007.

Carducci, Giosuè. *Versioni da antichi e da moderni*. Bologna: Zanichelli, 1940.

Casanova, Pascale. *La République mondiale des lettres*. Paris: Editions de Seuil, 1999.

Casella, Stefano Maria. "'By the Arena . . . Il Decaduto': T.S. Eliot and / in Italy." In *The International Reception of T.S. Eliot*, ed. Elisabeth Daumer and Shyamal Bagchee, 123–40. London: Continuum, 2007.

Cavaion, Danilo. "Le traduzioni italiane in versi dell'*Eugenio Onegin* di Puškin." In *Atti del decimo convegno sui Problemi della traduzione letteraria*, 71–91. Monselice: presso l'amministrazione comunale, 1983.

Cecchetti, Giovanni. "Sull'altro Montale." In *Essays in Honor of Dante della Terza*, ed. Franco Fido, 351–61. Florence: Cadmo, 1998.

Céline, Louis-Ferdinand. *Morte a credito*. Trans. Giorgio Caproni. Milan: Garzanti, 1964.

Cendrars, Blaise. *La mano mozza*. Trans. Giorgio Caproni. Milan: Garzanti, 1967.

Centanin, Antonello Satta. "Mistero, distanza e sardine sott'olio: teoria e pratica della traduzione in Giovanni Giudici." *Hortus. Rivista di poesie e arte*, no. 18 (1995): 99–110.

Cervantes, Miguel de. "Colloquio di Scipione e Berganza." Trans. Eugenio Montale. In *Narratori spagnoli*, ed. Carlo Bo, 249–311. Milan: Bompiani, 1941.

Cervantes, Miguel de. "Intermezzo della sentinella all'erta." Trans. Eugenio Montale. In *Teatro Spagnolo*, ed. Elio Vittorini, 94–109. Milan: Bompiani, 1941.

Char, René. *Fogli d'Ipnos, 1943–1944*. Trans. Vittorio Sereni. Turin: Einaudi, 1968.

Char, René. *Poèmes et prose choisis*. Paris: Gallimard, 1957.

Char, René. *Poesia e prosa*. Trans. Giorgio Caproni and Vittorio Sereni. Milan: Feltrinelli, 1962.

Char, René. *Ritorno sopramonte e altre poesie*. Trans. Vittorio Sereni. Milan: Mondadori, 1974.

Chau, Simon S.C. "Hermeneutics and the Translator: The Ontological Dimension of Translating." In *Multilingua* 3 (1984): 71–7. http://dx.doi.org/10.1515/mult.1984.3.2.71.

Cherchi, Grazia. *Scompartimento per i lettori e i taciturni*. Ed. Piergiorgio Bellocchio. Milan: Feltrinelli, 1997.

Chesterman, Andrew. *Memes of Translation*. Amsterdam: John Benjamins, 1997.

Chevalier, Haakon. *Cominciò ad Hiroshima*. Trans. Giovanni Giudici. Milan: Edizioni di Comunità, 1965.

Chirumbolo, Paolo. *Tra coscienza e autocoscienza: saggi sulla narrativa degli anni sessanta*. Soveria Mannelli: Rubbettino, 2009.

Cicero. *De inventione. De optimo genere oratorum. Topica*. Ed. and trans. H.M. Hubbell. Cambridge: Harvard University Press, 1949.

Citati, Pietro. "[Untitled]." In *Giorgio Caproni: Poesie 1932–1986*, 799–802. Milan: Garzanti, 1989.

Coleridge, Samuel Taylor. *La ballata del vecchio marinaio e altre poesie*. Trans. Franco Buffoni. Turin: Einaudi, 1987.

Coleridge, Samuel Taylor. *Poesie e prose*. Trans. Mario Luzi. Milan: Cederna, 1949.

Coleridge, Samuel Taylor. *La rima del vecchio marinaio*. Ed. Massimo Bacigalupo. Trans. Giovanni Giudici. Milan: SE, 1987.

Colucci, Michele. "Le traduzioni italiane poetiche dell'*Evgenij Onegin*." In *Puškin europeo*, ed. Sante Graciotti, 299–304. Venice: Marsilio, 2001.

Condello, Federico. "Appunti su Sanguineti traduttore dei tragici." *Poetiche* 8, no. 3 (2006): 565–94.

Conti, Piero Gadda. *Concerto d'autunno*. Milan: Pan Editrice, 1976.

Contini, Gianfranco. *Una lunga fedeltà: Scritti su Eugenio Montale*. Turin: Einaudi, 1974.

Contini, Gianfranco. *La parte di Benedetto Croce nella cultura italiana*. Turin: Einaudi, 1989.

Contorbia, Franco. "Montale critico nello specchio delle lettere: una approssimazione." In *Montale, Genova, il modernismo e altri saggi montaliani*, 73–87. Bologna: Pendragon, 1999.

Corneille, Pierre. *L'illusione comica*. Trans. Edoardo Sanguineti. Genoa: Il Melangolo, 2005.

Cornish, Alison. *Vernacular Translation in Dante's Italy: Illiterate Literature*. Cambridge: Cambridge University Press, 2010. http://dx.doi.org/10.1017/CBO9780511734762.

Cortellessa, Andrea. "Motivazione del premio Maria Marino 2009." http://www.francobuffoni.it/motivazione_cortellese.aspx.

Costa, Michele, Giuliano Vigini, and Mauro Zerbini, eds. *CLIO: catalogo dei libri italiani dell'Ottocento (1801–1900)*. 19 vols. Milan: Editrice Bibliografica, 1991.

Crane, Hart. *Nei caraibi*. Trans. Giovanni Giudici. Milan: Scheiwiller, 1966.

Croce, Benedetto. *Breviario di estetica*. Ed. Giuseppe Galasso. Milan: Adelphi, 2001.

Croce, Benedetto. *Estetica come scienza dell'espressione e linguistica generale*. Milan: Sandron, 1902.

Croce, Benedetto. *Estetica come scienza dell'espressione e linguistica generale*. Ed. Giuseppe Galasso. Milan: Adelphi, 1990.

Croce, Benedetto. *La poesia*. Bari: Laterza, 1936.

Croce, Benedetto. *La poesia: introduzione alla critica e storia della poesia e della letteratura*. Ed. Giuseppe Galasso. Milan: Adelphi, 1994.

Croce, Benedetto. *Tesi fondamentali di un'estetica come scienza dell'espressione e linguistica generale: memoria letta all'Accademia pontaniana nelle tornate del 18 febbraio, 18 marzo e 6 maggio 1900*. Naples: Tessitore, 1900.

Curi, Fausto. *Gli stati d'animo del corpo: studi sulla letteratura italiana dell'Otto e del Novecento*. Bologna: Pendragon, 2005.

D'Ablancourt, Nicolas Perrot. "From Preface to French Translation of Thucydides." In *Western Translation Theory: From Herodotus to Nietzsche*, ed. Douglas Robinson, 159–61. Manchester: St. Jerome, 1997.

Dal Fabbro, Beniamino. *La sera armoniosa*. Milan: Rosa e Ballo, 1944.

Dal Fabbro, Beniamino. *La sera armoniosa*. Milan: Rizzoli, 1966.

Davidson, Donald. *Inquiries into Truth and Interpretation*. Oxford: Clarendon Press, 1984.

Dawkins, Richard. *The Selfish Gene: 30th Anniversary Edition*. Oxford: Oxford University Press, 2006.

de Beaugrande, Robert. *Factors in a Theory of Poetic Translating*. Assen: Van Gorcum, 1978.

de Beaugrande, Robert, and Wolfgang Ulrich Dressler. *Introduction to Text Linguistics*. London: Longman, 1981.

Debenedetti, Antonio. "Com'è difficile tradurre una musica." *Corriere della Sera*, February 16, 1980.

de Bernardis, Ilenia. *L'illuminata imitazione: le origini del romanzo moderno in Italia, dalle traduzioni all'emulazione*. Bari: Palomar, 2007.

de Boer, Minne Gerben. "Leggere una poesia tradotta." In *Innumerevoli contrasti d'innesti': La poesia del Novecento (e altro)*, ed. Bart Van den Bossche et al., 273–98. Vol. 1. Florence: Franco Cesati, 2007.

Delabastita, Dirk. "Histories and Utopias: On Venuti's *The Translator's Invisibility*." *Translator* 16 (2010): 125–34.

Delabastita, Dirk. "Review of "From World to World. An 'Armamentarium' for the Study of Poetic Discourse in Translation (Approaches to Translation Studies, Volume 16)." *Translator* 7 (2000): 103–10.

de las Nieves Muñiz Muñiz, María. "Sul dittico Montale – Guillén." In *Strategie di Montale: poeta tradotto e traduttore*, ed. María de las Nieves Muñiz Muñiz and Francisco Amella Vela, 175–90. Florence: Franco Cesati, 1998.

D'Elia, Gianni. *Taccuino francese*. Siena: Edizioni di Barbablù, 1990.

de Maupassant, Guy. *Bel-Ami*. Trans. Giorgio Caproni. Milan: Garzanti, 1965.

de Meijer, Pieter. "Appendice. Goethe, Faust e Sanguineti." In *Edoardo Sanguineti, Faust. Un travestimento*, ed. Niva Lorenzini, 127–40. Rome: Carocci, 2005.

De Michelis, Cesare, ed. *Poesia sovietica degli anni sessanta*. Trans. Giovanni Giudici, Joanna Spendel, and Gigliola Venturi. Milan: Mondadori, 1971.

de Saussure, Ferdinand. *Cours de linguistique générale*. Ed. Charles Bally, Albert Sechehaye, and Albert Reidlinger. Paris: Payot, 1949.

Dei, Adele. *Giorgio Caproni*. Milan: Mursia, 1992.

della Volpe, Gaetano. "Critica del gusto." In *Opere*, ed. Ignazio Ambrogio, 9–264. Vol. 6. Rome: Editori Riuniti, 1973.

del Serra, Maura. *Le foglie della Sibilla: scritti su Margherita Guidacci*. Rome: Studium, 2005.

Devoto, Giorgio, and Stefano Verdino, eds. *Genova a Giorgio Caproni*. Genoa: San Marco dei Giustiniani, 1992.

Dickinson, Emily. *Poems*. 3 vols. Ed. T.H. Johnson. Cambridge: Harvard, 1955.
Dolfi, Anna. "Translation and the European Tradition: The Italian 'Third Generation." In *Twentieth-Century Poetic Translation: Literary Cultures in Italian and English*, ed. Daniela Caselli and Daniela La Penna, 44–54. London: Continuum, 2008.
Dolfi, Anna. "Variazioni sui maestri di canto: su Montale, la traduzione, la poesia." *Semicerchio*, no. 16–17 (1997): 17–24.
Dolfi, Anna, ed. *Traduzione e poesia nell'Europa del Novecento*. Rome: Bulzoni, 2004.
Dolfi, Laura. "Giorgio Caproni traduttore del 'Llanto' (con un'appendice sul 'Maleficio de la mariposa')." In *Traduzione e poesia nell'Europa del Novecento*, ed. Anna Dolfi, 485–525. Rome: Bulzoni, 2004.
Dryden, John. "From the Preface to Ovid's Epistles." In *The Translation Studies Reader*, 3rd ed., ed. Lawrence Venuti, 38–43. London: Routledge, 2012.
du Bellay, Joachim. *La deffence, et illustration de la langue françoyse*. Ed. Jean-Charles Monferran. Geneva: Droz, 2001.
Du Bos, Charles. *Vita e letteratura*. Trans. Mario Luzi. Padua: Cedam, 1943.
Eagleton, Terry. *Ideology*. London: Longman, 1994.
Eco, Umberto. *Dire quasi la stessa cosa: esperienze di traduzione*. Milan: Bompiani, 2003.
Elahi, Ostad. *Pensieri di luce*. Trans. Mario Luzi. Milan: Mondadori, 2000.
Erba, Luciano. *Dei cristalli naturali e altri versi tradotti: 1950–1990*. Milan: Guerini, 1991.
Erba, Luciano. *Il tranviere metafisico: seguito da Quadernetto di traduzioni*. Milan: Scheiwiller, 1987.
Euripides. *Le Baccanti*. Trans. Edoardo Sanguineti. Milan: Feltrinelli, 1968.
Euripides. *Ifigenia in Aulide di Euripides*. Trans. Edoardo Sanguineti. Ed. Federico Condello. Bologna: Bononia University Press, 2012.
Euripides. *Le Troiane*. Trans. Edoardo Sanguineti. Turin: Einaudi, 1974.
Fantaccini, Fiorenzo. *W.B. Yeats e la cultura italiana*. Florence: Firenze University Press, 2009.
Federici, Federico M. *Translation as Stylistic Evolution: Italo Calvino Creative Translator of Raymond Queneau*. Amsterdam: Rodopi, 2009.
Fenoglio, Beppe. *Quaderno di traduzioni*. Ed. Mark Pietralunga. Turin: Einaudi, 2000.
Ferme, Valerio. *Tradurre è tradire: la traduzione come sovversione culturale sotto il Fascismo*. Ravenna: Longo, 2002.
Ferroni, Giulio. *Letteratura Italiana Contemporanea: 1945–2007*. Vol. 2. Milan: Mondadori, 2007.
Ferroni, Giulio. *Storia della letteratura italiana: Il Novecento*. Vol. 4. Turin: Einaudi, 2001.

Flabbi, Lorenzo. *Dettar versi a Socrate: il traduttore di poesia come imitatore.* Florence: Le Lettere, 2008.

Flaubert, Gustave. *L'educazione sentimentale.* Trans. Giovanni Raboni. Milan: Garzanti, 1966.

Folena, Gianfranco. "Un cambio di cavalli." In *Eugenio Onieghin di Aleksandr S. Puškin in versi italiani,* by Aleksandr Pushkin, xvii–xv. Trans. Giovanni Giudici. Milan: Garzanti, 1999.

Folena, Gianfranco. "'Volgarizzare' e 'tradurre': idea e terminologia della traduzione dal Medioevo italiano e romanzo all'Umanesimo europeo." In AA.VV., *La traduzione, saggi e studi,* 57–120. Trieste: Lint, 1973.

Folena, Gianfranco. *Volgarizzare e tradurre.* Turin: Einaudi, 1991.

Forti, Marco. *Eugenio Montale.* Milan: Mursia, 1974.

Fortini, Franco. "Appendice di light verses e imitazioni." In *Composita solvantur,* 52–67. Turin: Einaudi, 1994.

Fortini, Franco. "Cinque paragrafi sul tradurre." *Premio Città di Monselice* 2 (1973): 60–5.

Fortini, Franco. *Composita solvantur.* Turin: Einaudi, 1994.

Fortini, Franco. "Dei 'compensi' nelle versioni di poesia." In *La Traduzione del testo poetico,* ed. Franco Buffoni, 72–7. Padua: Marcos y Marcos, 2004.

Fortini, Franco. *Il Ladro di Ciliege.* Turin: Einaudi, 1982.

Fortini, Franco. *Lezioni sulla traduzione.* Ed. Maria Vittoria Tirinato. Macerata: Quodlibet, 2011.

Fortini, Franco. "Montale traduttore di Guillén." In *Nuovi Saggi Italiani,* 142–9. Milan: Garzanti, 1987.

Fortini, Franco. "*Il Musicante di Saint-Merry.*" In *Nuovi Saggi Italiani,* 164–9. Milan: Garzanti, 1987.

Fortini, Franco. *I poeti del novecento.* Bari: Laterza, 1981.

Fortini, Franco. *Saggi ed epigrammi.* Ed. Luca Lenzini. Milan: Mondadori, 2003.

Fortini, Franco. "La traduzione come straniamento." In *Un dialogo ininterrotto: Interviste 1952–1994,* ed. Velio Abati, 407–10. Turin: Bollati Boringhieri, 2003.

Fortini, Franco. "Traduzione e rifacimento." *Problemi* 33 (1972): 125–31.

Frank, Armin Paul. "Anthologies of Translation." In *In the Routledge Encyclopedia of Translation Studies,* ed. Mona Baker, 13–16. London: Routledge, 1998.

Frattini, Alberto, ed. *Le problematiche dell'espressione e della comunicazione in prospettiva duemila.* Rome: Studium, 1990.

Frénaud, André. *L'agonia di generale Krivitski.* Trans. Franco Fortini. Turin: Einaudi, 1962.

Frénaud, André. *Non c'è paradiso.* Trans. Giorgio Caproni. Milan: Rizzoli, 1971.

Frénaud, André. *Non c'è paradiso.* Trans. Giorgio Caproni. Milan: Mondadori, 1998.

Frénaud, André. *Il silenzio di Genova*. Trans. Giorgio Caproni. Turin: Einaudi, 1967.

Frost, Robert. *Conoscenza della notte*. Trans. Giovanni Giudici. Turin: Einaudi, 1965.

Frost, Robert. *Conoscenza della notte*. Trans. Giovanni Giudici. Milan: Mondadori, 1988.

Gambaro, Fabio, ed. *Colloquio con Edoardo Sanguineti: Quarant'anni di cultura italiana attraverso i ricordi di un poeta intellettuale*. Milan: Anabasi, 1993.

García Lorca, Federico. *Il maleficio della farfalla*. Trans. Giorgio Caproni. Turin: ERI, 1972.

Gardini, Nicola. "An Ancient Soul in a New Body: Giovanni Pascoli's Homeric Translations." *Italian Studies* 66, no. 1 (2011): 59–75. http://dx.doi.org/10.1179/007516311X12918079775622.

Gardini, Nicola. "Il bicentenario di Aleksandr Puškin." *Poesia* 12, no. 132 (1999): 32–8.

Gardini, Nicola. "Mallarmé nel Novecento." In *L'antico, il nuovo, lo straniero*, 36–40. Milan: Mondadori, 2000.

Genet, Jean. *Quattro romanzi e Diario del ladro*. Trans. Giorgio Caproni. Milan: Il Saggiatore, 1975.

Genet, Jean. *Tutto il teatro*. Trans. Giorgio Caproni, and J. Rodolfo Wilcock. Milan: Il Saggiatore, 1971.

Genette, Gérard. *Introduction à l'architexte*. Paris: Seuil, 1979.

Genette, Gérard. *Palimpsests: Literature in the Second Degree*. Trans. Channa Newman and Claude Doubinsky. Lincoln: University of Nebraska Press, 1997.

Genette, Gérard. *Paratexts: Thresholds of Interpretation*. Trans. Jane E. Lewin. Cambridge: Cambridge University Press, 1997. http://dx.doi.org/10.1017/CBO9780511549373.

Gentile, Giovanni. "Sul torto e diretto della traduzione." In *Frammenti di Estetica e Letteratura*, 369–75. Lanciano: Carabba, 1920.

Gentzler, Edwin. *Contemporary Translation Theories*. 2nd ed. Clevedon: Multilingual Matters, 2001.

Gerschenkron, Alexander. "A Manufactured Monument?" *Modern Philology* 63, no. 4 (1966): 336–47. http://dx.doi.org/10.1086/389793.

Ghini, Giuseppe. *Tradurre l'Onegin*. Urbino: Quattroventi, 2003.

Ghilardi, Margherita, ed. *Per Margherita Guidacci*. Florence: Le Lettere, 2001.

Gigliucci, Roberto. *Realismo metafisico e montale*. Rome: Nuova Cultura, 2005.

Giudici, Giovanni. *Addio, proibito piangere e altri versi tradotti (1955–1980)*. Turin: Einaudi, 1982.

Giudici, Giovanni. *Andare in Cina a piedi. Racconto sulla poesia*. Rome: Edizioni e/o, 1992.

Giudici, Giovanni. *A una casa non sua: nuovi versi tradotti (1955–1995)*. Milan: Mondadori, 1997.

Giudici, Giovanni. *Autobiologia*. Milan: Mondadori, 1969.

Giudici, Giovanni. "Come una poesia si costruisce." In *La dama non cercata: poetica e letteratura, 1968–1984*, 56–75. Milan: Mondadori, 1985.

Giudici, Giovanni. "Da un'officina di traduzioni." In *Per forza e per amore: critica e letteratura, 1966–1995*, 20–33. Milan: Garzanti, 1996.

Giudici, Giovanni. "Il design della poesia." In *Per forza e per amore: critica e letteratura, 1966–1995*, 13–21. Milan: Garzanti, 1996.

Giudici, Giovanni. "Destino e poesia di Jiří Orten." In *La dama non cercata: poetica e letteratura, 1968–1984*, 169–79. Milan: Mondadori, 1985.

Giudici, Giovanni. *Fiorì d'improvviso*. Rome: Edizioni del Canzoniere, 1953.

Giudici, Giovanni. *Fortezza*. Milan: Mondadori, 1990.

Giudici, Giovanni. "Kafka e dintorni." In *La dama non cercata: poetica e letteratura, 1968–1984*, 211–227. Milan: Mondadori, 1985.

Giudici, Giovanni. *Il male dei creditori*. Milan: Mondadori, 1977.

Giudici, Giovanni. "La musa inquietante." In *La dama non cercata: poetica e letteratura, 1968–1984*, 46–56. Milan: Mondadori, 1985.

Giudici, Giovanni. "Le neoavanguardie come opposizione di Sua Maestra." In *La letteratura dopo Hiroshima: e altri scritti 1959–1975*, 199–206. Rome: Editori Riuniti, 1976.

Giudici, Giovanni. "Note di un traduttore del Mauberley." *Galleria* 36, no. 3–6 (1986): 261–3.

Giudici, Giovanni. *O beatrice*. Milan: Mondadori, 1972.

Giudici, Giovanni. *Omaggio a Praga. Hold Praze. Cinque poesie e tre prose con una piccola antologia di poeti cèchi del '900*. Milan: All'insegna del pesce d'oro, 1968.

Giudici, Giovanni. "Piccola antologia di poeti cechi del Novecento." In *Omaggio a Praga*, 33–156. Milan: All'insegna del pesce d'oro, 1968.

Giudici, Giovanni. "La poesia di Biagio Marin." In *La letteratura verso Hiroshima: e altri scritti 1959–1975*, 291–298. Rome: Editori Riuniti, 1976.

Giudici, Giovanni. *Poesie*. Milan: Garzanti, 1990.

Giudici, Giovanni. *Un poeta del golfo*. Ed. Carlo Di Alesio. Milan: Longanesi, 1995.

Giudici, Giovanni. "Premessa." In *Conoscenza della notte*, by Robert Frost, 7–9. Turin: Einaudi, 1965.

Giudici, Giovanni. *Quanto spera di campare Giovanni*. Milan: Garzanti, 1993.

Giudici, Giovanni. *Il ristorante dei morti*. Milan: Mondadori, 1981.

Giudici, Giovanni. *Salutz: 1984–1986*. Turin: Einaudi, 1986.

Giudici, Giovanni. "Sotto il cielo di Praga." In *Per forza e per amore: critica e letteratura, 1966–1995*, 177–82. Milan: Garzanti, 1996.

Giudici, Giovanni. "Tre giovani poeti cechi." *Paragone – Letteratura* 19, no. 224 (1968): 76–81.

Giudici, Giovanni. *Vaga lingua strana: dai versi tradotti.* Milan: Garzanti, 2003.

Giudici, Giovanni. "Viola e durlindana: riflessioni sulla lingua." In *La dama non cercata: poetica e letteratura, 1968–1984.* 155–61. Milan: Mondadori, 1985.

Giusti, Simone. "Ragioni di un traduttore astronomo." *L'apostrofo* 6, no. 18 (2001): 29–32.

Gnoli, Antonio, ed. *Sanguineti's Song: conversazioni immorali.* Milan: Feltrinelli, 2006.

Goethe, Johann Wolfgang von. *Faust. Sämtliche Werke. Briefe, Tagebücher und Gespräche.* Vol. 40. Ed. Albrecht Schöne. Frankfurt am Main: Deutscher Klassiker Verlag, 1994.

Gozzi, Carlo. *Opere: teatro e polemiche teatrali.* Ed. Giuseppe Petronio. Milan: Rizzoli, 1962.

Graubard, Stephen R. *Kissinger: un ritratto di una mente.* Trans. Franco Buffoni. Milan: Garzanti, 1974.

Guariglia, Emilio. "Quando tu sarai vecchia." In *Quaderno Montaliano,* ed. Pier Vincenzo Mengaldo, 131–64. Padua: Liviana Editrice, 1989.

Gubert, Carla. "Le belle infedeli: omaggio a Frénaud de 'L'Europa letteraria.'" In *Frammenti di Europa. Riviste e traduttori del Novecento,* ed. Carla Gubert, 81–100. Pesaro: Metauro, 2003.

Guidacci, Margherita. "Conoscenza delle lingue e l'importanza del tradurre." In *Le problematiche dell'espressione e della comunicazione in prospettiva duemila,* ed. Alberto Frattini, 25–35. Rome: Studium, 1990.

Guidacci, Margherita. "Traducendo due poetesse americane: Jessica Powers ed Elizabeth Bishop." In *La traduzione del testo poetico,* ed. Franco Buffoni, 157–63. Milan: Marcos y Marcos, 2004.

Guidacci, Margherita. *La voce dell'acqua: quaderno di traduzioni.* Ed. G. Battaglia. Pistoia: CRT, 2002.

Guillén, Jorge. *La fuente.* Trans. Mario Luzi. Milan: Scheiwiller, 1961.

Hacker, Peter. "Wittgenstein and Quine: Proximity at Great Distance." In *Ludwig Wittgenstein and W.H. Quine,* ed. R. Arrington and H.J. Glock, 1–38. New York: Routledge, 1996.

Harvey, Keith. "A Descriptive Framework for Compensation." *Translator* 1, no. 1 (1995): 65–86.

Heaney, Seamus. *Scavando: poesie scelte (1966–1990).* Trans. Franco Buffoni. Rome: Fondazione Piazzolla, 1991.

Hermans, Theo. *Translation in Systems.* Manchester: St. Jerome, 1999.

Hervey, Sándor, and Ian Higgins. *Thinking Translation: A Course in Translation Method: French to English.* London: Routledge, 1992.

Hitchcock, Henry Russell, and Arthur Drexler. *Architettura americana d'oggi*. Trans. Giovanni Giudici. Rome: De Luca, 1954.

Holan, Vladimír. *Una notte con Amleto e altre poesie*. Trans. Angelo Maria Ripellino. Turin: Einaudi, 1966.

Hölderlin, Friedrich. *Alcune poesie di Hölderlin*. Trans. Gianfranco Contini. Florence: Parenti, 1941.

Hölderlin, Friedrich. *Sämtliche Werke und Briefe*. Vol. 2. Ed. Jochen Schmidt. Frankfurt am Main: Deutscher Klassiker Verlag, 1994.

Holmes, James. *Translated! Papers on Literary Translation and Translation Studies*. Ed. Raymond van den Broeck. Amsterdam: Rodopi, 1994.

Ionesco, Eugène. "Il re muore." Trans. Edoardo Sanguineti. Unpublished.

Isella, Dante. "Il giovane poeta Guglielmo Crollalanza." In Dante Isella, *L'idillio di Meulan*, 229–43. Turin: Einaudi, 1994.

Jakobson, Roman. "On Linguistic Aspects of Translation." In *The Translation Studies Reader*, 3rd ed., ed. Lawrence Venuti, 126–32. London: Routledge, 2012.

Jakobson, Roman, and Yury Tynjanov. "Problems in the Study of Language and Literature." In *Roman Jakobson, Selected Writings*, vol. 3, ed. Stephen Rudy, 3–6. The Hague: Mouton, 1981. http://dx.doi.org/10.1515/9783110802122.3.

Johnson, A.L. "Interview with Eugenio Montale." *Littack* 3, no. 3 (1975): 220–6.

Jones, Francis. *Poetry Translation as Expert Action*. Amsterdam: Benjamins, 2011.

Joyce, James. *Poesie*. Trans. Alfredo Giuliani, Alberto Rossi, Edoardo Sanguineti, and J. Rodolfo Wilcock. Milan: Mondadori, 1969.

Joyce, Stanislaus. *My Brother's Keeper, James Joyce's Early Years – Guardiano di mio fratello*. Trans. Giovanni Giudici. In *Tutte le opere di James Joyce*, vol. 1, ed. Giacomo Debenedetti, 1–167. Milan: Mondadori, 1967.

Keats, John. *Sonno e poesia*. Trans. Franco Buffoni. Milan: Guanda, 1981.

Kemeny, Tomaso. *Notturno*. Milan: Rizzoli, 1992.

Kipling, Rudyard. *Ballate delle baracche e altre poesie*. Trans. Franco Buffoni. Milan: Mondadori, 1989.

Koster, Cees. *From World to World: An Armamentarium for the Study of Poetic Discourse in Translation*. Amsterdam: Rodopi, 2000.

Kott, Jan. *Shakespeare Our Contemporary*. Trans. Boleslaw Taborski. Garden City: Doubleday, 1964.

Ladmiral, Jean-René. *Traduire: Théorèmes pour la traduction*. Paris: Payot, 1979.

Lanati, Barbara. "Margherita traduce Emily." In *Per Margherita Guidacci*, ed. Margherita Ghilardi, 179–201. Florence: Le Lettere, 2001.

La Penna, Daniela. "Traduzioni e traduttori." In *Gli anni '60 e '70 in Italia: due decenni di ricerca poetica*, ed. Stefano Giovannuzzi, 297–322. Genoa: San Marco dei Giustiniani, 2003.

La Penna, Daniela. "Historicizing Value, Negotiating Visibility: English and Italian Poetic Canons in Translation." In *Twentieth-Century Poetic Translation: Literary Cultures in Italian and English*, ed. Daniela Caselli and Daniela La Penna, 1–22. London: Continuum, 2008.

Lefevere, André. *Translating Poetry: Seven Strategies and a Blueprint*. Assen: Von Gorcum, 1975.

Lenzini, Luca. "L'Onieghin di Giovanni Giudici." In *Interazioni: tra poesia e romanzo*, 85–103. Trento: Temi, 1998.

Lenzini, Luca. *Il poeta di nome Fortini*. Lecce: P. Manni, 1999.

Leonelli, Giuseppe. *Giorgio Caproni: storia d'una poesia tra musica e retorica*. Milan: Garzanti, 1997.

Leonelli, Giuseppe. "La poesia del pieno e del secondo Novecento." In *Storia della letteratura italiana*, ed. Enrico Malato, 1157–245. Vol. 9. Rome: Salerno, 1995.

Leopardi, Giacomo. *Canti*. Ed. Niccolò Gallo and Cesare Garboli. Turin: Einaudi, 1962.

Leopardi, Giacomo. *Tutte le opere*. Vol. 1. Ed. Francesco Flora. Milan: Mondadori, 1973.

Leopardi, Giacomo. *Zibaldone*. Vol. 1. Ed. Rolando Damiani. Milan: Mondadori, 1997.

Lepschy, Giulio. "Traduzione." In *Enciclopedia Einaudi*, 446–58. Vol. 14. Turin: Einaudi, 1981.

Levý, Jiří. *The Art of Translation*. Trans. Patrick Corness. Amsterdam: John Benjamins, 2011.

Lewis, Philip E. "The Measure of Translation Effects." In *The Translation Studies Reader*, 3rd ed., ed. Lawrence Venuti, 220–40. London: Routledge, 2012.

Lidman, Sara. *Cinque diamanti*. Trans. Giovanni Giudici and Irene Tanzi. Milan: Rizzoli, 1966.

Lindenberg, Judith. "Le *Quaderno di traduzioni* de Giorgio Caproni." Chroniques Italiennes, no. 71–2 (2003): 43–56.

Lisa, Tommaso. "Cartografie dell'oggettualità." *L'apostrofo* 6, no. 18 (2002): 11–15.

Lisa, Tommaso. "Intervista a Franco Buffoni (ovvero traduzione e movimento)." In *Traduzione e poesia nell'Europa del Novecento*, ed. Anna Dolfi, 593–600. Rome: Bulzoni, 2004.

Livorni, Ernesto. "Montale traduttore di Eliot: una questione di 'Belief." In *Traduzione e poesia nell'Europa del Novecento*, ed. Anna Dolfi, 471–85. Rome: Bulzoni, 2004.

Lo Gatto, Ettore. *Storia della letteratura russa*. Florence: Sansoni, 2000.

Lolini, Attilio. *Imitazioni*. Brescia: L'obliquo, 1989.

Lombardo, Agostino. "Ungaretti e i sonetti di Shakespeare." In *Atti del Convegno internazionale su Giuseppe Ungaretti: Urbino, 3–6 Ottobre 1979*, ed. Carlo Bo, 483–96. Vol. 1. Urbino: 4Venti, 1981.

Lombardo, Fabrizio. "L'avventura di *Testo a fronte*. Intervista a Franco Buffoni di Fabrizio Lombardo." *VersoDove*, no. 6–7 (1997): 1–5.

Lonardi, Gilberto. "Fuori e dentro il tradurre montaliano." In *Il vecchio e il giovane e altri studi su Montale*, 144–63. Bologna: Zanichelli, 1980.

Lorenzini, Niva. "Il Faust di Sanguineti: la parola all'inferno." In Edoardo Sanguineti, *Faust. Un travestimento*, 7–47. Rome: Carocci, 2003.

Lorenzini, Niva. "Uno Shakespeare praticabile." In Edoardo Sanguineti, *Omaggio a Shakespeare. Nove sonetti*, 59–67. Lecce: Manni, 2004.

Lowell, Robert. *Imitations*. New York: Farrar, Straus and Giroux, 1961.

Loyola, Ignacio de. *Esercizi spirituali*. Trans. Giovanni Giudici. Milan: SE, 1984.

Luperini. Romano. *Montale o l'identità negata*. Naples: Liguori, 1984.

Luperini, Romano. *Il Novecento*. 2 vols. Turin: Loescher, 1981.

Luperini, Romano. *Storia di Montale*. Rome: Laterza, 1999.

Luzi, Mario. *Colloquio: un dialogo con Mario Specchio*. Milan: Garzanti, 1999.

Luzi, Mario. *Conversazione: Interviste 1953–1998*. Ed. Anna Maria Murdocca. Fiesole: Cadmo, 1999.

Luzi, Mario. *La Cordigliera delle Ande*. Turin: Einaudi, 1983.

Luzi, Mario. *Discorso naturale*. Milan: Garzanti, 1984.

Luzi, Mario. *Francamente*. Florence: Vallecchi, 1980.

Luzi, Mario. "Riflessioni sulla traduzione." In *La traduzione del testo poetico*, 2nd ed., ed. Franco Buffoni, 145–49. Milan: Marcos y Marcos, 2004.

Macchia, Giovanni. "La Bufera o il romanzo di Clizia." In *Saggi Italiani*, 302–16. Milan: Mondadori, 1983.

Macrì, Oreste, ed. *Poesia spagnola del Novecento*. Trans. Oreste Macrì. Parma: Guanda, 1952.

Magrelli, Valerio. "La regola del 'Menouno." In *Traduzione di Poesia nell'Europa del Novecento*, ed. Anna Dolfi, 613–24. Rome: Bulzoni, 2004.

Malmkjaer, Kirsten. "Analytic Philosophy and Translation." In *In the Routledge Encyclopedia of Translation Studies*, ed. Mona Baker, 8–13. London: Routledge, 1998.

Manacorda, Giorgio. "La poesia è un grande teatro." *La Repubblica*, December 10, 1996.

Manca, Eugenio. "Giorgio Caproni." In *I ferri del mestiere: Dieci interviste di Eugenio Manca*, 52–63. Rome: L'unità, 1989.

Manfredi, Anna. *Fortini traduttore di Eluard*. Lucca: M.P. Fazzi, 1992.

Manfredini, Manuela. "Sondaggi sul lessico forestiero nella poesia contemporanea." Studi di lessicografia italiana, 17 (2000): 237–78.

Manigrasso, Leonardo. "Capitoli autobiografici. Poeti traduttori a confronto tra terza e quarta generazione." PhD diss., Università degli Studi di Padova, 2012.

Mansell, Gerard. *La tragedia d'Algeria*. Trans. Giovanni Giudici. Milan: Edizioni di Comunità, 1961.

Marcenaro, Giuseppe. *Una amica di Montale: Vita di Lucia Rodocanachi*. Milan: Camunia, 1991.

Marcenaro, Giuseppe. *Eugenio Montale*. Milan: Mondadori, 1999.

Marchese, Angelo. *Interpretazione semiologica della poesia di Montale*. Turin: SEI, 1977.

Marlowe, Christopher. "*La tragica storia del dottor Faust*." Trans. Eugenio Montale. In *Teatro elisabettiano*, 61–132. Ed. Alfredo Obertello. Milan: Bompiani, 1951.

Marroni, Sergio. *La lingua delle traduzioni di "Bel-Ami."* Rome: Bulzoni, 1989.

Mathews, Herbert L. *La verità su Cuba*. Trans. Giovanni Giudici and Amerigo Guadagnin. Milan: Edizioni di Comunità, 1961.

Mattioli, Emilio. *Contributi alla teoria della traduzione letteraria*. Palermo: Centro internazionale studi di estetica, 1993.

Mattioli, Emilio. "Introduzione al problema del tradurre." In *Il verri* 19 (1965): 107–28.

Matyus, Norbert. "Il dibattito di Croce e Gentile sul problema della traduzione." Accessed 6 May 2010, http://sedi.esteri.it/budapest/crocepdf/Matyus_it.PDF.

Mazzoni, Guido. *Sulla poesia moderna*. Bologna: Il Mulino, 2005.

Mengaldo, Pier Vincenzo. "Aspetti delle versioni poetiche di Solmi." In *La tradizione del Novecento. Nuova serie*, 307–56. Florence: Vallecchi, 1987.

Mengaldo, Pier Vincenzo. "Caproni e Sereni: due versioni." In *La tradizione del Novecento. Quarta Serie*, 208–19. Turin: Bollati Boringhieri, 2000.

Mengaldo, Pier Vincenzo. "Confronti fra traduttori-poeti contemporanei (Sereni, Caproni, Luzi)." In *La tradizione del Novecento. Terza serie*, 175–91. Turin: Einaudi, 1991.

Mengaldo, Pier Vincenzo. "Diego Valeri traduttore di lirici francesi e tedeschi." In *Diego Valeri e il Novecento*, ed. Gloria Manghetti, 87–94. Padua: Esedra, 2007.

Mengaldo, Pier Vincenzo. "Fortini e *I poeti del Novecento*." *Nuovi argomenti* 61 (1979): 159–77.

Mengaldo, Pier Vincenzo. "Introduzione." In Vittorio Sereni, *Il musicante di Saint-Merry*, v–xxvii. Turin: Einaudi, 2001.

Mengaldo, Pier Vincenzo. "Il 'Monselice' e i poeti-traduttori" Accessed 12 January 2013, http://www.provincia.padova.it/comuni/monselice/traduzione/mengaldo.htm.
Mengaldo, Pier Vincenzo. "La panchina e i morti (su una versione di Montale)." In *La poesia di Eugenio Montale*, 133–48. Milan: Librex, 1983.
Mengaldo, Pier Vincenzo. "Per la poesia di Giorgio Caproni." In Giorgio Caproni, *L'opera in versi*, ed. Luca Zuliani, xi–xxxiv. Milan: Mondadori, 1999.
Mengaldo, Pier Vincenzo. "Premessa." In Giorgio Caproni, *Quaderno di traduzioni*, ed. Enrico Testa, v–xi. Turin: Einaudi, 1998.
Mengaldo, Pier Vincenzo. *La tradizione del Novecento. Nuova serie*. Florence: Vallecchi, 1987.
Mengaldo, Pier Vincenzo. *La tradizione del Novecento: quarta serie*. Turin: Bollati Boringhieri, 2000.
Mengaldo, Pier Vincenzo, ed. *Poeti italiani del Novecento*. Milan: Mondadori, 1979.
Meoli Toulmin, Rachel. "Shakespeare ed Eliot nelle versioni di Eugenio Montale." *Belfagor* 26 (1971): 453–71.
Merlanti, Federica. "Da Firenze alla Liguria, 'passando per Trieste.' Eugenio Montale e Lucia Rodocanachi." In *Lucia Rodocanachi: le carte, la vita*, ed. Franco Contorbia, 37–100. Florence: Società editrice fiorentina, 2006.
Migliaccio, Tiziana. "Il caso Apollinaire." *Sincronie*, no. 16 (2004): 125–34.
Migliaccio, Tiziana. "Intervista a Franco Buffoni." *Sincronie* no. 21/22 (2007): 65–8.
Molière. *Don Giovanni*. Trans. Edoardo Sanguineti. Genoa: Il Melangolo, 2000.
de Molina, Tirso. "Dannato per disperazione." Trans. Mario Luzi. In *Teatro*, ed. Maria Grazia Profeti, 658–935. Milan: Garzanti, 1991.
Montale, Eugenio. "16 November, 1942." In *La narrativa di Guglielmo Petroni: atti della giornata di studio della Fondazione Camillo Caetani, Roma, 27 ottobre 2006*, ed. Massimiliano Tortora, 184–5. Rome: L'Erma di Bretschneider, 2007.
Montale, Eugenio. *Altri versi e poesie disperse*. Milan: Mondadori, 1981.
Montale, Eugenio. *Auto da fé*. Milan: Il Saggiatore, 1965.
Montale, Eugenio. *La bufera e altro*. Venice: Neri Pozza, 1956.
Montale, Eugenio. *Diario del '71 e '72*. Milan: Mondadori, 1973.
Montale, Eugenio. *Diario postumo*. Milan: Mondadori, 1996.
Montale, Eugenio. "Lettere a Nino Frank." *Almanacco dello Specchio* 12 (1986): 17–64.
Montale, Eugenio. *Lettere e poesie a Bianca e a Francesco Messina*. Ed. Laura Barile. Milan: Scheiwiller, 1995.
Montale, Eugenio. *Le occasioni*. Turin: Einaudi, 1939.

Montale, Eugenio. *Ossi di seppia*. Turin: Gobetti, 1925.

Montale, Eugenio. "[Poesie di Eugenio Montale]." In *Il secondo mestiere: Arte, musica, società*. Ed. Giorgio Zampa, 1494–6. Milan: Mondadori, 1996.

Montale. Eugenio. Preface to Giovanni Bocaccio, *Decamerone. VII Giornata*. Ed. Mario Fubini. Milan: Feltrinelli, 1952.

Montale, Eugenio. Preface to Daniel Defoe, *Vita e avventure di Robinson Crusoe*. Milan: Feltrinelli, 1951.

Montale, Eugenio. "Prefazione." In Giorgia Valensin, *Liriche cinesi: 1753 a.c. – 1278 d.c.* Turin: Einaudi, 1943.

Montale, Eugenio. *Quaderno di quattro anni*. Milan: Mondadori, 1977.

Montale, Eugenio. *Quaderno di traduzioni*. Milan: Edizioni della Meridiana, 1948.

Montale, Eugenio. *Quaderno di traduzioni*. Milan: Mondadori, 1975.

Montale, Eugenio. *Quaderno di traduzioni*. Milan: Mondadori, 1982.

Montale, Eugenio. *Quaderno genovese*. Ed. Laura Barile. Milan: Mondadori, 1983.

Montale, Eugenio. *Satura*. Milan: Mondadori, 1971.

Montale, Eugenio. *Il secondo mestiere: arte, musica, società*. Ed. Giorgio Zampa. Milan: Mondadori, 1996.

Montale, Eugenio. *Il secondo mestiere: prose 1920–1979*. 2 vols. Ed. Giorgio Zampa. Milan: Mondadori, 1996.

Montale, Eugenio. *Sulla poesia*. Ed. Giorgio Zampa. Milan: Mondadori, 1976.

Montale, Eugenio, and Gianfranco Contini. *Eusebio e Trabucco: carteggio di Eugenio Montale e Gianfranco Contini*. Ed. Dante Isella. Milan: Adelphi, 1997.

Montale, Eugenio, and Valéry Larbaud. *Caro maestro e amico: carteggio con Valéry Larbaud*. Ed. Marco Sonzogni. Milan: Arcinto, 2003.

Montano, Rocco. "Note per un'interpretazione di Montale." *Studi Novecenteschi* 2 (1973): 227–47.

Montesquieu, Charles-Louis de. "Il tempio di Cnido." Trans. Mario Luzi. In *Romanzi francesi dei secoli XVII e XVIII*, ed. Michele Rago, 551–81. Milan: Bompiani, 1951.

Monti, Vincenzo. *Versioni poetiche di Vincenzo Monti: Persio, Voltaire, Omero, Pyrker, Lemercier, ec.* Ed. Giosuè Carducci. Florence: Barbera, 1869.

Morando, Simona. *Vita con le parole: la poesia di Giovanni Giudici*. Pasian di Prato: Campanotto, 2001.

Mounin, Georges. *Les Belles Infidèles*. Paris: Cahiers du Sud, 1955.

Munday, Jeremy. *Introducing Translation Studies*. 3rd ed. London: Routledge, 2012.

Musa, Gilda. *Incontri con T.S. Eliot, K. Mansfield, R. Bridges, R. Kipling, T. Hardy, W. Blunt, G. Hopkins, F. Thompson, M. Arnold, S. Coleridge, H. Longfellow: liriche scelte con un'appendice di poesie tratte da lirici greci*. Milan: Accademia, 1950.

Musatti, Maria Pia. "Montale traduttore: la mediazione della poesia." *Strumenti critici*, no. 41 (1980): 122–48.

Nabokov, Vladimir. "Nabokov's *Onegin*." *Encounter* 36, no. 5 (1966): 91–2.

Nabokov, Vladimir. "Problems of Translation." *Partisan Review (New York, N.Y.)* no. 22 (1955): 496–512.

Nascimbeni, Giulio. *Montale: biografia di un poeta*. Milan: Longanesi, 1986.

Nasi, Franco. *Istituzioni poetiche e traduzioni: le Lyrical Ballads in Italia*. Milan: Medusa, 2004.

Newmark, Peter. *About Translation*. Bristol: Multilingual Matters, 1991.

Newmark, Peter. *Approaches to Translation*. New York: Prentice Hall, 1988.

Newmark, Peter. *More Paragraphs on Translation*. Philadelphia: Multilingual Matters, 1998.

Nida, Eugene, and Charles Taber. *The Theory and Practice of Translation*. Leiden: Brill, 1969.

Nietzsche, Friedrich. *Basic Writings of Nietzsche*. Trans. Walter Kaufmann. New York: Random House, 2000.

Nievo, Ippolito. *Quaderno di traduzioni*. Ed. Iginio de Luca. Turin: Einaudi, 1964.

Ó Ceallacháin, Éanna. "Montale's Late Versions of Yeats." *Italian Studies* 50 (1995): 72–85.

Orlando, Roberto. *Applicazioni montaliane*. Lucca: M. Pacini Fazzi, 2001.

Orten, Jiří. *La cosa chiamata poesia*. Trans. Giovanni Giudici and Vladimír Mikeš. Turin: Einaudi, 1969.

Ossola, Carlo. *Giuseppe Ungaretti*. Milan: Mursia, 1975.

Pampaloni, Geno. "Nota." In *Giorgio Caproni: Poesie 1932–1986*, 815–18. Milan: Garzanti, 1989.

Paracchini, Gian Luigi. "Sanguineti: nel labirinto delle parole." *Corriere della Sera*, 21 July 2001.

Parronchi, Alessandro. *Quaderno francese: poesie tradotte con alcuni commenti*. Florence: Vallecchi, 1989.

Pascoli, Giovanni. *Traduzioni e riduzioni*. Bologna: Zanichelli, 1913.

Passannante, Andrea. "'The Indian to His Love'-'L'indiano all'amata.'" In *Quaderno montaliano*, ed. Pier Vincenzo Mengaldo, 119–29. Padua: Liviana, 1989.

Paterlini, Caterina. "Sanguineti 2004–2006." *Poetiche* 8, no. 3 (2006): 623–43.

Paull, Daniel, Valentina Emmanuele, Keren A. Weiss, et al. "Nuclear Genome Transfer in Human Oocytes Eliminates Mitochondrial DNA Variants." *Nature* 493 (2013): 632–7. http://dx.doi.org/10.1038/nature11800 Medline:23254936.

Pavese, Cesare. *Saggi letterari*. Turin: Einaudi, 1968.

Pesce, Maria Dolores. *Edoardo Sanguineti e il teatro: la poetica del travestimento*. Alessandria: Edizioni dell'Orso, 2003.

Petronius Arbiter. *Il Satyricon*. Trans. Edoardo Sanguineti. Rome: Aldo Palazzi Editore, 1969.

Petronius Arbiter. *Satyricon di Petronio nella traduzione di Edoardo Sanguineti*. Trans. Edoardo Sanguineti. Turin: Einaudi, 1993.

Petronius Arbiter. *Satyricon Reliquiae*. 4th ed. Ed. Konrad Müller. Stuttgart: Teubner, 1995.

Petrosino, Alfonso Maria. "Intervista a Franco Buffoni." Accessed 5 November 2011, http://www.criticaletteraria.org/2010/08/intervista-franco-buffoni.html.

Picchi, Mario, ed. *Del tradurre*. La Fiera Letteraria, 3 June 1956.

Picon, Isabel V. *Une oeuvre originale de poesie: Giuseppe Ungaretti traducteur*. Paris: Presses de l'Université de Paris-Sorbonne, 1998.

Picone, Michelangelo. *Percorsi della lirica duecentesca*. Fiesole: Cadmo, 2003.

Pietromarchi, Luca. "Nota alla traduzione." In Charles Baudelaire, *I fiori del male*, trans. Giorgio Caproni. 53–9. Venice: Marsilio, 2008.

Pietropaoli, Antonio, ed. *Per Edoardo Sanguineti: Good Luck (and Look)*. Naples: Edizioni scientifiche italiane, 2002.

Pietropaoli, Antonio. *Unità e trinità di Edoardo Sanguineti*. Naples: Edizioni scientifiche italiane, 1991.

Plath, Sylvia. *Lady Lazarus e altre poesie*. Trans. Giovanni Giudici. Milan: Mondadori, 1976.

Plath, Sylvia. *Lady Lazarus e altre poesie*. 6th ed. Trans. Giovanni Giudici. Milan: Mondadori, 1989.

Poggioli, Renato, ed. *Il fiore del verso russo*. Trans. Renato Poggioli. Turin: Einaudi, 1949.

Poggioli, Renato, ed. *La violetta notturna: antologia di poeti russi del Novecento*. Trans. Renato Poggioli. Lanciano: Carabba, 1933.

Polimeni, Giuseppe, ed. *Catalogo delle lettere da Eugenio Montale a Maria Luisa Spaziani*. Pavia: Università di Pavia, 1999.

Pound, Ezra. *Hugh Selwyn Mauberley*. Trans. Giovanni Giudici. Milan: Il Saggiatore, 1982.

Pound, Ezra. *Translations*. New York: New Directions, 1963.

Pozzi, Gianni. *La poesia italiana del Novecento da Gozzano agli ermetici*. Turin: Einaudi, 1989.

Praz, Mario. *Poeti inglesi dell'Ottocento*. Florence: Bemporad, 1925.

Praz, Mario. "Prefazione." In *William Shakespeare, Teatro*. Vol. 1. Ed. Mario Praz. Florence: Sansoni, 1943.

Praz, Mario. "T.S. Eliot e Eugenio Montale." In *Cronache letterarie anglosassoni*, 189–92. Vol. 1. Rome: Edizioni di Storia e Letteratura, 1950.

Prete, Antonio. *All'ombra dell' altra lingua: per una poetica della traduzione*. Turin: Bollati Boringhieri, 2011.

Prete, Antonio. "Dialoghi sul confine. La traduzione della poesia." In *La Storia della Letteratura Italiana: Il Novecento*, ed. Nino Borsellino and Lucio Felici, vol. 3, 879–916. Milan: Garzanti, 2001.

Prete, Antonio. "Traduzione e imitazione." In *Finitudine e infinito*, 143–70. Milan: Feltrinelli, 1998.

Prévert, Jacques. *Parole*. Trans. Rino Cortiana, Maurizio Cucchi, and Giovanni Raboni. Parma: Guanda, 1989.

Prévert, Jacques. *La pioggia e il bel tempo*. Trans. Francesco Bruno, Maurizio Cucchi, and Giovanni Raboni. Parma: Guanda, 1989.

Prévert, Jacques. *Poesie*. Trans. Maurizio Cucchi, and Giovanni Raboni. Milan: Guanda, 1979.

Prévert, Jacques. *Poesie d'amore*. Trans. Ivos Margoni, Franca Madonia, Maurizio Cucchi, and Giovanni Raboni. Milan: CDE, 1986.

Prévert, Jacques. *Prevert: le poesie*. Trans. Maurizio Cucchi and Giovanni Raboni. Rome: Lato side, 1980.

Proust, Marcel. *Alla ricerca del tempo perduto*. Trans. Giovanni Raboni. Vols. 1–4. Turin: Einaudi, 1983–94.

Proust, Marcel. *Il tempo ritrovato*. Trans. Giorgio Caproni. Turin: Einaudi, 1951.

Puccini, Dario. *Romancero della Resistenza spagnola: 1936–1959*. Milan: Feltrinelli, 1960.

Puppo, Mario. "Montale e la letteratura spagnola." In *La poesia di Eugenio Montale: Atti del Convegno internazionale tenuto a Genova dal 25 al 28 novembre 1982*, ed. Sergio Campailla and Cesare Federico Goffis, 421–31. Florence: Felice Le Monnier, 1984.

Pushkin, Aleksandr. *Eugene Onegin*. Trans. Vladimir Nabokov. Vol. 1. Princeton: Princeton, 1975.

Pushkin, Aleksandr. *Eugenio Onieghin*. Trans. Giovanni Giudici. Milan: Garzanti, 1975.

Pushkin, Aleksandr. *Eugenio Onieghin*. Trans. Giovanni Giudici. Milan: Garzanti, 1980.

Pushkin, Aleksandr. *Eugenio Onieghin*. Trans. Giovanni Giudici. Milan: Garzanti, 1983.

Pushkin, Aleksandr. *Eugenio Onieghin*. Trans. Giovanni Giudici. Milan: Garzanti, 1984.

Pushkin, Aleksandr. *Eugenio Onieghin*. Trans. Giovanni Giudici. Turin: Fogola, 1990.

Pushkin, Aleksandr. *Eugenio Onieghin di Aleksandr S. Puškin in versi italiani*. Trans. Giovanni Giudici. Milan: Garzanti, 1999.

Pushkin, Aleksandr. "*Evgenij Onegin*, dedica e primo capitolo." Trans. Giovanni Giudici. In *Almancco dello specchio*, ed. Marco Forti, 14–45. Milan: Mondadori, 1972.

Pushkin, Aleksandr. "*Evgenij Onegin*. Second capitolo." Trans. Giovanni Giudici. *Resine* 3, no. 9 (1974): 80–95.

Pushkin, Aleksandr. *Poemi e liriche*. Trans. Tommaso Landolfi. Turin: Einaudi, 1960.

Pushkin, Aleksandr. *Viaggio d'inverno e altre poesie*. Trans. Giovanni Giudici and Giovanna Spendel. Milan: Mondadori, 1985.

Pym, Anthony. *Exploring Translation Theories*. London: Routledge, 2010.

Pym, Anthony. "Venuti's Visibility." *Target* 8, no. 1 (1996): 165–77. http://dx.doi.org/10.1075/target.8.1.12pym.

Quaranta, Bruno. "Sullo yacht con Re Lear." *La Stampa*, August 2, 2008.

Quasimodo, Salvatore, ed. *Lirici greci*. Trans. Salvatore Quasimodo. Milan: Corrente, 1940.

Quine, W.H. *Word and Object*. Cambridge: MIT Press, 1960.

Quiriconi, Giancarlo, ed. *Antologie e poesie nel Novecento italiano*. Rome: Bulzoni, 2011.

Raboni, Giovanni. "Giudici e Puškin, un confronto in versi." *Corriere della Sera*, June 6, 1999.

Raboni, Giovanni. "Introduzione." In Charles Baudelaire, *I Fiori del male*. Trans. Attilio Bertolucci. Milan: Garzanti, 1975.

Raboni, Giovanni. "Ovvero tradurre per amore." In *Traduzione e poesia nell'Europa del Novecento*, ed. Anna Dolfi, 625–9. Rome: Bulzoni, 2004.

Raboni, Giovanni. "[Untitled]." In *Giorgio Caproni: Poesie 1932–1986*, 793–8. Milan: Garzanti, 1989.

Raboni, Giovanni. *Ventagli e altre imitazioni*. Varese: NEM, 1999.

Racine, Jean. "Andromaca." Trans. Mario Luzi. In *Teatro francese del grande secolo*, ed. Giovanni Macchia, 465–513. Rome: ERI, 1960.

Ransom, John Crowe. *Le donne e i cavalieri*. Trans. Giovanni Giudici. Milan: Mondadori, 1971.

Richards, I.A. "Towards a Theory of Translation." In *Studies in Chinese Thought*, ed. Arthur F. Wright, 247–63. Chicago: University of Chicago Press, 1953.

Ripa di Meane, Ludovica, ed. *Diligenza e voluttà: Ludovica Ripa di Meane interroga Gianfranco Contini*. Milan: Mondadori, 1989.

Rilke, Rainer Maria. *Elegie duinesi*. Trans. Leone Traverso. Florence: Parenti, 1937.

Rilke, Rainer Maria. *Poesie*. Trans. Giaime Pintor. Turin: Einaudi, 1942.

Rinaldi, Giacomo. "Italian Idealism and After." In *The Routledge History of Philosophy: Twentieth-Century Continental Philosophy*, ed. Richard Kearney, 350–89. London: Routledge, 1994.

Ripellino, Angelo Maria, ed. *Poesia russa del Novecento*. Trans. Angelo Maria Ripellino. Parma: Guanda, 1954.

Risi, Nelo. *Compito di francese e altre lingue*. Milan: Guerini, 1994.

Robinson, Douglas. "The Limits of Translation." In *The Oxford Guide to Literature in English Translation*, ed. Peter France, 15–19. Oxford: Oxford University Press, 2001.

Roncaglia, Aurelio. "De Quibusdam Provincialibus translatis in lingua nostra." In *Letteratura e Critica: Studi in onore di Natalino Sapegno*, 1–36. Vol. 2. Rome: Bulzoni, 1975.

Rosengrant, Judson. "Nabokov, Onegin, and the Theory of Translation." *Slavic and East European Journal* 38, no. 1 (1994): 13–32. http://dx.doi.org/10.2307/308543.

Rossetti, Dante Gabriele. *Dante and His Circle*. Boston: Little Brown, 1899.

Ruberto, Roberto, ed. "Conversation with Eugenio Montale." *Italian Quarterly* 17, no. 68 (1974): 51–7.

Rundle, Christopher. *Publishing Translations in Fascist Italy*. Bern: Peter Lang, 2010.

Saint Jerome. "Letter to Pammachius." Trans. Kathleen Davis. In *The Translation Studies Reader*, 3rd ed., ed. Lawrence Venuti, 21–31. London: Routledge, 2012.

Samonà, G.P. "*L'Onegin* tradotto da Giudici: riflessioni di metodo sulla traduzione di poesia." *Ricerche slavistiche*, nos. 24–26 (1979): 217–30.

Sanguineti, Edoardo. *L'amore delle tre melarance: un travestimento fiabesco dal canovaccio di Carlo Gozzi*. Genoa: Il Melangolo, 2001.

Sanguineti, Edoardo. *Capriccio italiano*. Milan: Feltrinelli, 1963.

Sanguineti, Edoardo. *Catamerone*. Milan: Feltrinelli, 1974.

Sanguineti, Edoardo. *Commedia dell'Inferno. Un travestimento dantesco*. Genoa: Costa and Nolan, 1989.

Sanguineti, Edoardo. *Cultura e Realtà*. Ed. Erminio Risso. Milan: Feltrinelli, 2010.

Sanguineti, Edoardo. *Faust. Un travestimento*. Genoa: Costa & Nolan, 1985.

Sanguineti, Edoardo. *Faust. Un travestimento*. Ed. Niva Lorenzini. Rome: Carocci, 2005.

Sanguineti, Edoardo. *Il gatto lupesco*. Milan: Feltrinelli, 2002.
Sanguineti, Edoardo. *Il giuoco dell'Oca*. Milan: Feltrinelli, 1967.
Sanguineti, Edoardo. *Il giuoco del Satyricon: un'imitazione da Petronio*. Turin: Einaudi, 1970.
Sanguineti, Edoardo. "Introduzione." In *Teatro antico: traduzioni e ricordi*, ed. Federico Condello and Claudio Longhi, 5–20. Milan: Rizzoli, 2006.
Sanguineti, Edoardo. *Laborintus*. Varese: Magenta, 1956.
Sanguineti, Edoardo. *Macbeth Remix*. Unpublished.
Sanguineti, Edoardo. *Mikrokosmos*. Milan: Feltrinelli, 2004.
Sanguineti, Edoardo. "Il mio Catullo." In *Insula Sirmie. Società e cultura della 'Cisalpina' verso l'anno Mille*, ed. N. Criniti, 197–205. Brescia: Grafo, 1997.
Sanguineti, Edoardo. *Novissimum Testamentum*. Lecce: Manni, 1986.
Sanguineti, Edoardo. *Omaggio a Goethe: viaggi in Italia, XXIX imitazioni*. Bellinzona: Edizioni Sottoscala, 2003.
Sanguineti, Edoardo. *Omaggio a Shakespeare. Nove sonetti*. Lecce: Manni, 2004.
Sanguineti, Edoardo. *Opus metricum*. Milan: Rusconi e Paolazzi, 1960.
Sanguineti, Edoardo. *Per Musica*. Modena: Mucchi, 1993.
Sanguineti, Edoardo. *Postkarten*. Milan: Feltrinelli, 1978.
Sanguineti, Edoardo. *Quaderno di traduzioni*. Torino: Einaudi, 2006.
Sanguineti, Edoardo. "Reisebilder." In *Wirrwarr*. Milan: Feltrinelli, 1972.
Sanguineti, Edoardo. *Sanguineti/Novecento: conversazioni sulla cultura del ventesimo secolo*. Ed. Giuliano Galletta. Genoa: Il Nuovo melangolo, 2005.
Sanguineti, Edoardo. "I santi anarchici: la mia poesia." In *Edoardo Sanguineti e Gaetano delli Santi: due generazioni d'Avanguardia a confronto*, ed. Marisa Napoli, 78–80. Milan: Fabio d'Ambrosio, 2006.
Sanguineti, Edoardo. *Scartabello 1980*. Macerata: Cristoforo Colombo libraio, 1981.
Sanguineti, Edoardo. *Smorfie*. Milan: Feltrinelli, 2007.
Sanguineti, Edoardo. *Teatro antico. Traduzioni e ricordi*. Ed. Federico Condello and Claudio Longhi. Milan: BUR, 2006.
Sanguineti, Edoardo. "Tradurre il teatro antico." In *Prometeo rivista*. Accessed 6 May 2013, http://www.indafondazione.org/prometeus-rivista-online/tradurre-il-teatro-antico. Unpaginated.
Sanguineti, Edoardo. "Il traduttore, nostro contemporaneo." In *La Missione del critico*, 182–8. Genoa: Marietti, 1987.
Sanguineti, Edoardo. "Traumdeutung." *Il Menabo* 8 (1965): 37–49.
Sanguineti, Edoardo. *Varie ed eventuali: poesie 1995–2010*. Ed. Niva Lorenzini. Milan: Feltrinelli, 2010.
Sanguineti, Edoardo. *Wunderkammer*. Rome: Il Bulino, 1998.
Sanguineti, Edoardo. *Wirrwarr*. Milan: Feltrinelli, 1972.

Sanguineti, Edoardo, ed. *Grande Dizionario della lingua italiana: Supplemento 2004*. Turin: UTET, 2004.

Sanguineti, Edoardo, ed. *Poesia del Novecento*. 2 vols. Turin: Einaudi, 1969.

Sanguineti, Edoardo, and Andrea Liberovici. *Il mio amore è come una febbre e mi rovescio*. Milan: Bompiani, 1998.

Sanguineti, Edoardo, and Eugenio Buonaccorsi. "Il grande teatro è solo hard: Dialoghetto sulla drammaturgia tra Edoardo Sanguineti e Eugenio Buonaccorsi." In *Sei personaggi.com: un travestimento pirandelliano*, 7–21. Genoa: Il Melangolo, 2001.

Sanguineti, Edoardo, and Marco Sciaccaluga. "Il palcoscenico e il mondo: conversazione tra Edoardo Sanguineti e Marco Sciaccaluga." In William Shakespeare, *La tragedia di Re Lear*, trans. Edoardo Sanguineti, ed. Aldo Viganò, 191–9. Genoa: Il Melangolo, 2008.

Sansone, Mario. "Croce e Montale." In *La poesia di Eugenio Montale: Atti del Convegno Internazionale tenuto a Genova dal 25 al 28 novembre 1982*, ed. Sergio Campailla and Cesare Federico Goffis, 286–98. Florence: Le Monnier, 1984.

Scaffai, Niccolò. *Il poeta e il suo libro: Retorica e storia del libro di poesia nel Novecento*. Florence: Le Monnier, 2005.

Scaglione, Giuseppe. "Le Vicinanze di René Char: Giorgio Caproni e Vittorio Sereni traduttori di A***." *Studi Novecenteschi*, no. 77 (2009): 137–50.

Schäffner, Christina. "Third Ways and New Centres: Ideological Unity or Difference?" In *Apropos of ideology*, ed. María Calzada-Pérez, 23–41. Manchester: St. Jerome, 2003.

Schleiermacher, Friedrich. "On the Different Methods of Translation." Trans. Susan Bernofsky. In *The Translation Studies Reader*, 3rd ed., ed. Lawrence Venuti, 43–64. London: Routledge, 2004.

Schlesinger Jr., Arthur. *Kennedy*. Trans. Giovanni Giudici. Milan: Edizioni di Comunità, 1960.

Sciascia, Leonardo. "La grande domanda." In *Letture montaliane in occasione del 80esimo compleanno del poeta*, ed. Silvia Luzzatto, 387–93. Genoa: Bozzi, 1977.

Scotto, Fabio. "André Frénaud traducteur de l'italien." In André Frénaud, *La negation exigeante: Colloque de Cerisy 15–21 août 2000*, ed. Marie-Claire Bancquart, 101–18. Cognac: Le Temps qu'il fait, 2004.

Segre, Cesare, and Carlo Ossola, eds. *Antologia della poesia italiana: Novecento*. 2 vols. Turin: Einaudi, 2003.

Seneca. *Fedra*. Trans. Edoardo Sanguineti. Torino: Einaudi, 1969.

Sereni, Vittorio. *Il Musicante di Saint-Merry e altri versi tradotti*. Turin: Einaudi, 1981.

Shakespeare, William. *14 X 14, dai sonetti di Shakespeare tradotti da G. Giudici*. Trans. Giovanni Giudici. Bocca di Magra: Edizioni Capannina, 2002.

Shakespeare, William. *Misura per misura*. Trans. Edoardo Sanguineti. Unpublished.

Shakespeare, William. *Riccardo II*. Trans. Mario Luzi. Turin: Einaudi, 1966.

Shakespeare, William. *Sonnets*. Ed. Katherine Duncan-Jones. In *The Arden Shakespeare: Complete Works*. Revised edition. Ed. Richard Proudfoot, Ann Thompson, David Scott Kastan, and H.R. Woudhuysen, 18–44. London: Cengage, 2001.

Shakespeare, William. *La tragedia di Re Lear*. Trans. Edoardo Sanguineti. Genoa: Il Melangolo, 2008.

Shelley, Percy Bysshe. *Come un fruscio d'ali: Percy B. Shelley*. Ed. and trans. Franco Buffoni. Milan: Corriere della Sera, 2012.

Simeone, Bernard. "Ligure de Rome." In *Per Giorgio Caproni*, ed. Giorgio Devoto and Stefano Verdino, 467–72. Genoa: San Marco dei Giustiniani, 1997.

Simonelli, Marco. "Intervista Simonelli." Accessed 11 September 2012, http://www.francobuffoni.it/intervista_simonelli.aspx.

Solmi, Sergio. "Chiarimento al primo *quaderno*." In *Opere di Sergio Solmi: Poesie, meditazioni e ricordi*, vol. 1, ed. Giovanni Pacchiano, 91–8. Milan: Adelphi, 1983.

Solmi, Sergio. *Opere di Sergio Solmi: Poesie, meditazioni e ricordi*. Vol. 1. Ed. Giovanni Pacchiano. Milan: Adelphi, 1983.

Solmi, Sergio. *Quaderno di traduzioni*. Turin: Einaudi, 1969.

Solmi, Sergio. *Quaderno di traduzioni*. Vol. 2. Turin: Einaudi, 1977.

Solmi, Sergio. *Versioni poetiche da contemporanei*. Milan: All'insegna del pesce d'oro, 1963.

Sophocles. *Edipo re*. In *Tragici greci tradotti da Salvatore Quasimodo*, 353–545. Trans. Salvatore Quasimodo. Milan: Mondadori, 1963.

Sophocles. *Edipo tiranno*. Trans. Edoardo Sanguineti. Bologna: Cappelli, 1980.

Sophocles. *Tragoediae: 1*. Ed. R.D. Dawe. Leipzig: B.G. Teubner Verlagsgesellschaft, 1984.

Spaziani, Maria Luisa. "La traduzione di poesia come osmosi." In *La traduzione del testo poetico*, ed. Franco Buffoni, 110–19. Milan: Marcos y Marcos, 2004.

Spignoli, Teresa. "'Un quaderno da squadernare.' Le antologie europee della generazione ermetica." In *Antologie e poesie nel Novecento italiano*, ed. Giancarlo Quiriconi, 63–111. Rome: Bulzoni, 2011.

Staglieno, Marcello, ed. *'Enrico aiutami: è una vita impossibile': lettere inedite di Eugenio Montale a Henry Furst*. Il Giornale, 24 October 1989.

Steiner, George. *After Babel: Aspects of Language and Translation*. 3rd ed. Oxford: Oxford University Press, 1998.

Stella, Maria. *Cesare Pavese traduttore*. Rome: Bulzoni, 1977.

Stella, Vittorio. "La traduzione dell'opera poetica nel pensiero di Croce." *Itinerari*, nuova serie, no. 16 (1977): 33–57.

Talbot, George. *Montale's 'Mestiere vile.'* Dublin: Irish Academic Press, 1995.
Tarozzi, Bianca. "L'arte di perdere." In *Per Margherita Guidacci*, ed. Margherita Ghilardi, 201–14. Florence: Le Lettere, 2001.
Terracini, Benvenuto. *Conflitti di lingue e culture*. Venice: N. Pozza, 1957.
Tesio, Giovanni. "Nel golfo di Giudici." *La Stampa*, March 25, 1995.
Testa, Enrico. "Introduzione." In *Quaderno di traduzioni*, by Giorgio Caproni, xiii–xxii, ed. Enrico Testa. Turin: Einaudi, 1998.
Thomas, Linda, et al. *Language, Society and Power: An Introduction*. London: Routledge, 2004.
Toppan, Laura. *Le Chinois: Luzi critico e traduttore di Mallarmé*. Pesaro: Metauro, 2006.
Tordi, Rosita. *Ungaretti e i suoi maîtres à penser*. Rome: Bulzoni, 1997.
Tosi, A.W., ed. *Bibliografia degli studi italiani sulla cecoslovacchia (1918–1978)*. Rome: Bulzoni, 1980.
Traverso, Leone. *Poesia moderna straniera*. Rome: Prospettive, 1942.
di Treville, Luigi. *Saggio di traduzioni poetiche*. Turin: V. Bona, 1883.
Tymoczko, Maria. "Translation and Political Engagement. Activism, Social Change and the Role of Translation in Geopolitical Shifts." *Translator* 6, no. 1 (2000): 23–47.
Tynjanov, Yury. *Il problema del linguaggio poetico*. Trans. Giovanni Giudici and Ljudmila Kortikova. Milan: Il Saggiatore, 1968.
Tytler, Alexander. *Essay on the Principles of Translation*. 3rd rev. ed. Amsterdam: John Benjamins, 1978.
Tyutchev, Fyodor. *Poesie*. Trans. Tommaso Landolfi. Turin: Einaudi, 1964.
Ungaretti, Giuseppe. *40 Sonetti di Shakespeare*. Milan: Mondadori, 1946.
Ungaretti, Giuseppe. "Della metrica e del tradurre." In *Saggi e interventi*, 571–77. Ed. Mario Diacono and Luciano Rebay. Milan: Mondadori, 1974.
Ungaretti, Giuseppe. "Poeta e uomini." In *Saggi e interventi*, 737–41. Ed Mario Diacono and Luciano Rebay. Milan: Mondadori, 1974.
Ungaretti, Giuseppe. *Saggi e interventi*. Ed. Mario Diacono and Luciano Rebay. Milan: Mondadori, 1974.
Ungaretti, Giuseppe. "Significato dei sonetti di Shakespeare." In *Saggi e interventi*, 551–71. Ed. Mario Diacono and Luciano Rebay. Milan: Mondadori, 1974.
Ungaretti, Giuseppe. *Traduzioni*. Rome: Edizioni di Novissima, 1936.
Ungaretti, Giuseppe. *Vita d'un uomo: traduzioni poetiche*. Ed. Carlo Ossola and Giulia Radin. Milan: Mondadori, 2010.
Valeri, Diego, ed. *Lirici francesi*. Trans. Diego Valeri. Milan: Mondadori, 1960.
Valeri, Diego, ed. *Lirici tedeschi*. Trans. Diego Valeri. Milan: Mondadori, 1959.
Valeri, Diego, ed. *Quaderno francese del secolo*. Trans. Diego Valeri. Turin: Einaudi, 1965.
Valéry, Paul. *Cantique des colonnes*. Trans. Mario Luzi. Rome: ERI, 1949.

van Gelder, Sarah. "Poet Laureate W.S. Merwin: Doing the Impossible," *YES! Magazine* 59 (Fall 2011). Accessed 20 December 2012, http://www.yesmagazine.org/issues/new-livelihoods/w.s.-merwin-doing-the-impossible.

Vazzoler, Franco. *Il chierico e la scena: cinque capitoli su Sanguineti e il teatro*. Genoa: Il Melangolo, 2009.

Venturo, Mariafrancesca. *Parole e travestimento nella poetica teatrale di Edoardo Sanguineti*. Rome: Fermenti, 2007.

Venuti, Lawrence. *L'Invisibilità del traduttore: Una storia della traduzione*. Trans. Marina Guglielmi. Rome: Armando, 1999.

Venuti, Lawrence. "The Poet's Version; or, An Ethics of Translation." In *Translation Changes Everything*, 173–92. London: Routledge, 2013.

Venuti, Lawrence. *Scandals of Translation: Towards an Ethics of Difference*. London: Routledge, 1998. http://dx.doi.org/10.4324/9780203269701.

Venuti, Lawrence. *Translation Changes Everything*. London: Routledge, 2013.

Venuti, Lawrence. *The Translator's Invisibility: A History of Translation*. New York: Routledge, 1995. http://dx.doi.org/10.4324/9780203360064.

Venuti, Lawrence, ed. *Rethinking Translation: Discourse, Subjectivity, Ideology*. London: Routledge, 1992.

Venuti, Lawrence, ed. *The Translation Studies Reader*. 2nd ed. London: Routledge, 2004.

Venuti, Lawrence, ed. *The Translation Studies Reader*. 3rd ed. London: Routledge, 2012.

Vinay, Jean-Paul, and Jean Darbelnet. *Comparative Stylistics of French and English: A Methodology for Translation*. Trans. Juan C. Sagerand M.J. Hamel. Amsterdam: John Benjamins, 1995.

Vinay, Jean-Paul, and Jean Darbelnet. *Stylistique comparée du français et de l'anglais: méthode de traduction*. Paris: Didier, 1958.

Vitale, Serena. "Disavventure di Puškin in Italia." *La Repubblica*, 15 October 1998.

von Humboldt, Wilhelm. "A Theory of Translation." In *Translating Literature: The German Tradition*, ed. and trans. André Lefevere, 40–5. Assen: Van Gorcum and Co, 1977.

Weissbort, Daniel, ed. *Translation: Theory and Practice: A Historical Reader*. Oxford: Oxford, 2006.

West, Rebecca J. *Eugenio Montale: Poet on the Edge*. Cambridge: Harvard University Press, 1981.

Wilde, Oscar. *Ballata del carcere e altre poesie*. Trans. Franco Buffoni. Milan: Mondadori, 1991.

Williams, Raymond. *Marxism and Literature*. Oxford: Oxford University Press, 1977.

Wilson, Edmund. *Saggi letterari*. Trans. Giovanni Giudici and Giovanni Gualtieri. Milan: Garzanti, 1967.

Wilss, Wolfram. *The Science of Translation. Problems and Methods*. Tübingen: Gunter Narr, 1982.

Zaccaria, Giuseppe. "Il Lavoro del poeta. Dal carteggio fra Montale, Vittorini e Bompiani." *Sigma* 20, no. 3 (1995): 85–114.

Zampa, Giorgio. "Cronologia." In *Tutte le poesie*, by Eugenio Montale, lvii–lxxix, ed. Giorgio Zampa. Milan: Mondadori, 1990.

Zampa, Giorgio. "Introduzione." In *Tutte le poesie*, by Eugenio Montale, xi–liii, ed. Giorgio Zampa. Milan: Mondadori, 1990.

Zanella, Giacomo. *Versioni poetiche*. Florence: Successori Le Monnier, 1887.

Zanzotto, Andrea. "Europa, melograno di lingue." In *Le poesie e le prose scelte*, ed. Stefano Dal Bianco and Gian Maria Villalta, 1353–62. Milan: Mondadori, 2000.

Zanzotto, Andrea. *Le poesie e le prose scelte*. Ed. Stefano Dal Bianco and Gian Maria Villalta. Milan: Mondadori, 2000.

Zedong, Mao. *Quattro poesie*. Trans. Giovanni Giudici and Margherita Guidacci. Milan: Scheiwiller, 1971.

Zoboli, Paolo. *La rinascita della tragedia: le versioni dei tragici greci da D'Annunzio a Pasolini*. Lecce: Pensa Multimedia, 2004.

Zoico, Silvia. "Come è fatto il Musicante di Saint-Merry di Vittorio Sereni." In *Stilistica, metrica e storia della lingua: studi offerti dagli allievi a Pier Vincenzo Mengaldo*, edited by Tina Matarrese, Marco Praloran, and Paolo Trovato, 369–86. Padoa: Antenore, 1997.

Zuccato, Edoardo. "The Translation of Coleridge's Poetry and His Influence on Twentieth-Century Italian Poetry." In *The Reception of S.T. Coleridge in Europe*, ed. Elinor Shaffer and Edoardo Zuccato, 197–212. London: Continuum, 2007.

Zucco, Rodolfo. "Addizioni a *I versi della vita*." *Rassegna europea della letteratura italiana*, no. 31 (2008): 93–110.

Zucco, Rodolfo. "Introduzione." In Giovanni Giudici, *Vaga lingua strana: dai versi tradotti*, vii–xxviii. Milan: Garzanti, 2003.

Zucco, Rodolfo. "Satura." In *Gli anni '60 e '70 in Italia*, ed. Stefano Giovannuzzi, 261–81. Genoa: San Marco dei Giustiniani, 2003.

Index

www.ingramcontent.com/pod-product-compliance
Lightning Source LLC
LaVergne TN
LVHW040153080826
844660LV00014B/947/J

* 9 7 8 1 4 4 2 6 4 6 4 2 1 *